Practical Town Planning:
A Land and Housing Policy

Practical Town Planning:
A Land and Housing Policy

PRACTICAL TOWN PLANNING

BY J. S. NETTLEFOLD

Author of "Practical Housing"
Chairman of Harborne Tenants Ltd

LONDON: THE ST CATHERINE PRESS
34 NORFOLK ST · STRAND · W.C.
MCMXIV

TO MY WIFE

CHAPTERS

APPENDICES

1. Showing how to provide adequate access to cheap land.
2. Extract from Report of Royal Commission on Sewage Disposal (1908).
3. Report of Mr John D. Watson, M.I.C.E., Engineer to the Birmingham Tame and Rea District Drainage Board, July 10, 1912.
4. Epitome of the Local Government Board regulations governing the preparation of town planning schemes divided into stages and steps.
5. Model set of general provisions for town planning schemes.
6. Précis of Local Government Board report on intercepting traps.
7. Public Health (Sewers and Drains No. 2) Bill presented to the House of Commons by Mr Henry Vivian on July 7, 1908.
8. Housing and Town Planning, etc., Act, 1909.
9. Local Government Board regulations.
10. Speech by Chairman of Birmingham Corporation Housing Committee, July 3, 1906.
11. Housing of the Working Classes Bill presented by Sir Arthur Griffith Boscawen, February 19, 1912, and comments thereon.
12. Professor Marshall on the incidence of local taxation.
13. Miss Annie Hankinson, of Manchester, on Slum Reform.
14. Legal aspects of town planning by Mr John L. Jack, Town Clerk of the City and Royal Burgh of Dunfermline.
15. Notes on State-aided Housing in Ireland and Rural Housing in England.
16. Unionist Land Policy.

Contents
Practical Town Planning

INTRODUCTORY

Book itself explains general principles—Appendices give technical information needed—Necessary repetition—Gratitude to all who have helped—Vested interests and human interests—Town planning needed everywhere—Rating of land values essential to success—Subject matter of each chapter—Economic laws more powerful than rules and regulations.

CHAPTER I. ADEQUATE ACCESS TO CHEAP LAND.

Old method of town development—Need for foresight and economy—Empty slums into country—Artificial price of building land—Protect cheap land before providing facilities for development—If this is done ten houses per gross acre will become a sound business proposition; if not, little improvement will be effected—Adequate access is essential to quick development—Objections to the old way of improving means of communication—Economic and other advantages of cutting new main arteries through back land—It pays landowners to assist in the provision of adequate access—Risk of loss to the ratepayers far less than under the old method—Assessable value increased instead of diminished—Public expenditure need not be incurred until rate income is coming in to pay for it—More room for traffic—Better gradients—No awkward corners—Better roads.

CHAPTER II. SITE VALUES

Cost of land and development—Fewer houses per acre means lower land values, not higher house rents—Dear land not suitable for housing—The only sure way of stopping land sweating is to pass a general law prohibiting the erection of too many houses per acre—Rating of land values a danger, unless safeguarded by a general law to stop land sweating—Protect shortsighted local authorities against

CHAPTER III. PREPARATION OF TOWN PLANNING SCHEMES

CHAPTER IV. SAVINGS

CHAPTER V. EXAMPLES

CHAPTER VI. DELAY AND ITS CAUSES

Town Planning Act has up to the present made things worse instead of better—Obstructive regulations—Municipal house building a failure—Local Government Board—Town planning questionnaire—Garden city and suburb questionnaire—Analysis of information obtained—Causes of delay—Local Government Board—Local authorities—By-law rut—Dear land—Dear capital —Unjust and excessive rates—Abolish obligation to apply for permission to prepare—Encourage and assist reasonable landowners and builders—Simplify regulations—Birmingham's bad scheme and Birkenhead's good one—Town planning before trams—Betterment—Landjobbers support by-laws—Property—Light and air cheaper and better than kerbs and gutters—High price of land per yard causes inadequate air space per house—Artificial land values perpetuated by land sweating—Folly of waiting till price goes up before buying land—New and direct main arteries essential to quick development—Look ahead—Four Dwellings Farm, Quinton —Price not purpose should be the determining factor in purchase of land for public use—Allotments—Foresight and economy badly needed—Wholesale public land purchase very dangerous— Town planning dependent on rating of land values—Each one per cent interest on capital represents 8d. per week on 6s. 6d. house —Creation of ground rents—Bad housing must be made unprofitable—Landowners' offer of cheap land—Economic soundness of State loans on careful lines—Our unjust and irrational rating system.

CHAPTER VII. THE NEED FOR FURTHER LEGISLATION AND BETTER ADMINISTRATION

No one remedy sufficient by itself—Essentials to success—A new Government department—Educational propaganda—Information needed—Apply town planning to existing towns as well as undeveloped districts—Secure betterment for the ratepayers— Protect the public with regard to land purchase—Abolish obligation to apply for permission to prepare—Town planning competitions— Landowners' right of appeal—Conditions on which State loans might be wisely granted—Tenants to subscribe—Co-partnership housing—Criticisms and replies—Co-operation of all the arts and sciences—Mortmain — Entail — Acquisition of Land Bill—Gen-

CHAPTER VIII. TOWN PLANNING AND CITY EXTENSION

CHAPTER IX.

Let us aim to administer Justice before Charity.

The only way to ensure Better Housing is to make good housing reasonably profitable for the owner and to make bad housing bad business.

A strong economic incentive in the right direction is far more effective for reform than all the rules and regulations that were ever framed.

Practical Town Planning:
A Land and Housing Policy

INTRODUCTORY

THE subject dealt with in this book is so complicated and involves the consideration of so many contributory causes that it has not been quite easy to keep within a reasonable compass. In order to combine brevity with clearness purely technical matter has been put into an appendix. This arrangement makes the appendices almost as long as the book, but it has this advantage, that busy men will be able to get hold of the gist of my argument with the least possible expenditure of time and trouble, and at the same time those responsible for carrying out in a practical manner any of the work described, will find in the appendices full details of the necessary technical information.

An objection may rightly be raised that there is too much repetition, but a certain amount is unavoidable. Questions present themselves for consideration under different aspects and an author has little chance of convincing his public, unless he repeats his points as occasion arises, even at the risk of some weariness.

I have sought information from many and distant sources, I have spared no pains to verify my facts, and I have received much help from many different quarters. Whilst it is impossible to name all, individually, I feel my indebtedness to them is great and I can assure them my gratitude is sincere.

It stands to reason that when difficult problems have to be solved, there must from time to time be differences of opinion as to which is the best way to solve them, but provided there is a common object these difficulties can always be adjusted; what is impossible, and always will be impossible, is to bring the greed for excessive personal or class profit into harmony with the ideals of genuine reform.

It is almost a misfortune for town planning that it has become so suddenly and widely popular, and for this reason. Its assured popularity makes it a welcome subject for platform panegyrics. Any charlatan is ready to undertake it, and the less he has studied the subject, the more he thinks he knows about it. The result of this is that in many cases the methods adopted are, intentionally or otherwise, in direct opposition to the aims of land and housing reformers, and are merely an attempt to carry on the old methods of land and housing development under a new name. We should learn to differentiate between town planning schemes inspired by a desire for efficiency and economy, and those based merely on municipal expediency.

Vested interests have a right to be considered, and it would be economically unwise not to recognize this right. It is, on the other hand, quite unsound to allow vested interests to obscure the interests of the ratepayers, of the tenant, and the human interests of the community.

This book has been written with a view to explaining how to set about the preparation of a town planning scheme, what should be done and what should be avoided.

Several people are of opinion that although town planning may be advisable and possible in one locality, it is not possible in their district. This is a mistake. Town planning is possible, and urgently needed, all over England.

In the following pages various general principles are explained, which it will be seen are essential to success. It has been necessary to illustrate them by actual examples, and, perhaps, an undue share of these has been taken from Birmingham, but it is always best to describe those things with which one is most familiar, and most of my practical work has been done in Birmingham.

Facts and figures have been carefully verified, and on general questions, such as site values, etc., etc., two, three or more sources of information have been applied to, and the results compared, before any statement of fact has been ventured upon.

The rating and taxing of land on its value and not on its use is, in my opinion, the most important and most far-reaching reform suggested, and the most likely to achieve the ends in view, provided it is accompanied by the safeguard advocated in this book. Those even who disapprove of rating land values still see the importance of freeing the land, and have other methods for achieving this end.

Chapter I explains how to increase the supply of building land by opening up cheap land, and at the same time protecting it against land sweating.

Chapter II explains the site value now carried by a typical small house, that is the 6s. 6d. weekly house now being built in the suburbs of large towns. It then explains how to provide for small house property with reasonable amenities without exceeding this site value.

...tar are thrust out into the country in a solid phalanx
...nd very expensive roads constructed according to
...y-laws, driving in front of them allotments, play
... playing fields, which have to be provided elsewhere
...ense to the ratepayers and great inconvenience to those
...em. The worst feature of all is that the very great ex-
...incurred by the old methods makes it financially im-
...o provide anything like so many of these essentials to
...lth and rational enjoyment as are justly demanded by
...er classes.

...esight were exercised and economy practised in this import-
...tter of town and estate development much money could be
...for the ratepayers and far better results achieved for the
community. It is said that town planning is going to be very expensive, and so it would be under certain systems carried out
by men who do not understand the work, or who are not really
in...d b... in social and economic reform, but scientific methods
ho...ea... arried out should yield very different results.

L...a... authorities can use their town planning powers either in
a way which will ensure that land shall be dear, that methods of
building shall be costly, and consequently, rents high and dwellings
overcrowded, or in a way which will ensure that land shall not be
dear, that cheap but sound methods of construction shall be used,
and that, consequently, there shall be an abundant supply of
dwellings at moderate rents. There is unfortunately on many local
authorities a large proportion of members who have motives for
desiring that the rents of existing houses shall continue to be very
high. An abundant supply of cheap houses is exactly what these
...men do not want, but it is at the same time exactly what
...lanners should aim for. This can only be done by:

...hrowing plenty of cheap land into the market and protecting

...eeping down the cost of town and estate development.
...bolishing all by-laws that increase the cost of building
... increasing the efficiency of the house.

...arteries must be wide enough for present and future traffic,
... streets should not be more expensively constructed than
...utely necessary for the traffic that they have to carry
...he interest of owners of dear land and to the owners of
...ses th...t land in all other districts shall be dear, because
...ere b... a larger supply of cheap small houses provided
...land in ...ccessible positions the price of land and the rents

Chapter III explains the various stages and steps in the preparation of a town planning scheme. It also draws attention to
what should be done and what avoided at each stage.

Appendix V contains a model set of general provisions for
town planning schemes which are of too technical a nature to be
placed in the body of the book.

Chapter IV explains the savings to be effected for ratepayers,
landowners, builders and tenants, if economical town planning
methods are adopted.

Chapter V deals with various examples of town planning in
order to explain what should be done and what left undone.

Chapter VI compares the progress made by private enterprise
and public bodies in town planning and better housing. It also
explains the causes of delay in execution of the work.

Chapter VII suggests various amendments to existing legislation,
also the new legislation and improved administration required
to overcome the present very serious and unnecessary delay in
the solution of this pressing problem.

Chapter VIII deals with the relationship between town planning
and city extension and is respectfully submitted for the consideration of Parliamentary committees dealing with the rearrangement of administrative boundaries.

The last chapter presents the general conclusions and also has
notes on some subsidiary questions such as slum reform and rural
housing.

It is the fashion with some reformers to blame the landowners
and speculative builders for the evils from which Great Britain
is suffering, and no doubt there are black sheep in every flock,
but it is an undeniable fact that there are in this country at the
present time, many landowners willing and anxious to develop
their estates on modern lines, if only they were given half a chance
of doing so. It is acknowledged very generally that to-day land takes
an undue toll from industry, and that far too much public and
private money is spent on making it available for housing and other
purposes, but individuals are not to blame for this. It is the system
that is at fault, and that must be attacked and destroyed. Freedom
must take the place of monopoly and bureaucratic methods must be
ruled by reason. In the following pages, an attempt has been made
to show how this could be done. " IT MIGHT BE DONE AND
ENGLAND SHOULD DO IT."

There are great difficulties in the way. On the one hand, there
are those who think that our present system has worked very

well in the past. Their object is to do nothing that shall injure vested interests, and they advocate wholesale public land purchase and State or municipal house building in the hope that by this means friction with vested interests will be avoided. They ignore the fact that wrongs cannot be righted without interfering with those who have profited and are profiting from them, and they seem to forget that public bodies are often worse than any private landjobber. All monopolies are bad and public monopolies are often the worst of all. Our present system has worked very well so far as the richer classes are concerned, but no impartial man who has studied the question can possibly pretend that the poorer classes have been treated at all fairly in the matter of land and housing. Experience shows that in the long run what benefits the poorer classes also benefits the richer and national prosperity must have a surer foundation than the exploitation of one class by another.

Another great difficulty in the way of land and housing reform is the confiding faith of many men in rules and regulations. They will not wait for the problem to right itself by the working of economic laws. In their opinion, that would take too long and in their eagerness to live for the present as well as for the future, they pass Acts of Parliament and make regulations that contravene economic laws, thereby hindering progress instead of helping it. Rules and regulations are useful up to a point, but it is very easy to overdo this line of policy. The only safe plan is to make good housing pay and bad housing unprofitable. The object of this book is to show how this can be done.

Practical
A Land and

CHAPTER I. ADEQUA...
CHEAP LAN...

THE problem of town planning is one o... great problems which are engaging the atte... reformers, and it is coming to be recognized a... of most important, because it is concerned with the living conditio... the whole population. England is a small country geographically, it is all the more important that the best possible use shoul... of the land which is available. It is only in the last few y...s there has been any idea that the regulation of these living co...i for the benefit of the poor, as well as the rich, is one of the d... of a modern State, just as much as the provision of pure foo... water. It must necessarily be difficult to fit fresh regulatio... accordance with new ideals to the older manners and cus... but this is a difficulty which confronts all progress. So far... has been talked about but little has been accomplished for ...lanning. The present work is an attempt to state the proble... ...o show how it may be dealt with, and the conclusions a... ...at are the result of many years' study and much practical...

The main objective of town planning in this country is t... all classes of the community to live and work in decent... ings so that they may be fit for their work and able... in a rational manner. The first necessity is an a... of good, cheap houses with a sufficiency of ope... to each, and a free circulation of light a... possibility of enjoying air and exercise, we ca... a healthy people and the concrete form that th... exercise and healthy recreation takes is t...vi... side... play grounds, parks and playing fields f...

How do we at present deal with this... spaces for any purpose whatsoever a... in all our large towns are notorious... perpetuated in the suburban building t...

of the dear houses on dear land would, of course, be greatly reduced. All the great influence of landjobbers and their friends is, therefore, exercised to compel or induce local authorities to insist upon the most expensive regulations and not to provide adequate access to cheap land.

When town planning falls into the wrong hands, the cost of town and estate development is kept up in order that cheap land and housing shall not come into the market to compete with the old expensive methods, and to depreciate the value of insanitary property, which is exactly what all genuine town planners are aiming for, and what the landjobbers and their friends will prevent if they can.

In order to provide all classes of the community with the amenities they need, and have a right to, it is necessary to empty the slums into the country, and it must be real country, not a fresh slum. This implies that in the development of new districts plenty of room must be left for allotments, playgrounds, and playing fields, and in districts a little further out small holdings should be provided, from which it follows that there must not be too many houses per acre.

The great obstacle in the way of restricting building to a reasonable number of houses per acre, is the very high and quite artificial price of building land round large towns. The supply is strictly limited by the fact that proper roads, tramways, or motor-buses are not provided until there is a sufficient population to make these services pay. And under the old extravagant methods, it takes much longer for this to come about than it should do. Builders, on the other hand, will only put up houses where there are good means of communication, with the result that the monopoly in building land is accentuated and the price driven up to a purely artificial figure, and this price is still further raised by allowing too many houses per acre. The more intensively land is used the more valuable it becomes, and the more valuable it becomes the more houses must the builder put per acre in order to make his speculation pay.

There is also the fact, familiar to all observers, that whenever a tram or railway taps a new district, that neighbourhood is at once pounced upon by land and building speculators, whose so-called improvements very soon spoil it. We are, in fact, missing our opportunities. Quick and cheap means of communication are persuading the people back to the land, and we are by our old-fashioned methods of town and estate development, saying to them, " No, you shall not get back to the land, and even if you have the sense to leave the slums and move a little further out we will see to it that the new and unspoilt district into which you have moved shall be made into a fresh slum as quickly as possible." The cause, and at the same time the effect, of this ever-increasing congestion is the very high price of building land in small house property districts. Rich men live on land for which they pay at a rate that represents a capital value of about £500 per acre, sometimes more, but more often a great deal less. Poor men have to pay for the land on which they exist at a rate representing a capital value of at least five times as much. There would not be the slightest difficulty in giving actual cases where poor men pay ten times as much as the rich man. This would be laughable if it were not so serious to the national health and well-being. Town planning provides a remedy if the people's representatives on municipal bodies care to apply it.

The only way to break the land monopoly is for local authorities to put an end to their policy of drift. They must, as already explained, look ahead and provide for the future, instead of waiting till the mischief has been done. They must:

1. Open up cheap land by means of new main arteries and other facilities for development.

2. Protect this cheap land from an excessive rise in price by forbidding overcrowding.

3. Provide no facilities for development until the land has been protected.

If this policy is adopted and rigidly adhered to, there will be plenty of building land available at such a price that, with estate development on economical town planning lines, ten houses per gross acre will be a thoroughly sound business proposition. This is the greatest number that ought to be allowed. Experience shows that even with this density of building there is none too much room left for the amenities that ought to be provided on every building estate.

Land that has already gone up so much in value as to make ten houses per acre at the old, or lower, rents an economic impossibility must be used for other purposes than that of housing the poorer classes, if we really mean to provide the people of England with decent housing at rents that they can afford. Chapter II on site values will deal with the economics of ten houses per acre. This chapter must be confined to the problem of providing adequate access to cheap land.

The English Housing and Town Planning Act of 1909 only deals with land "in course of development or likely to be used for building purposes," except in cases where "land already built upon or not likely to be used for building purposes is so situated with respect to any land likely to be used for building purposes that it ought to be included in a town planning scheme." We are, therefore at present, principally concerned with the protection of new suburbs against the overcrowding of houses and the crowding out of allotments, play grounds and playing fields, but the exception referred to above is of vital importance to the success of town planning schemes, because it makes it possible to provide adequate access to the new area from the centre of the town or city to which it belongs, and in the preparation of town planning schemes there is nothing more important than the provision of adequate access to the area town planned. It is no use providing for good development unless quick development is also encouraged. This is one of the great inducements we have to offer landowners, in return for keeping within reasonable bounds the value of their land for building purposes, by severely restricting the number of houses allowed per acre. As they are not to get so much per acre for their land, at least they must be enabled to lease or sell more acres more quickly. The old way of improving communication is to widen existing roads. This method is so costly that it is seldom or never done as soon as it ought to be, and the results, as shall be shown presently, are much inferior to those that can be achieved by cutting new roads through back land under the 1909 Act and possibly with the assistance of the Road Board. The objections to widening old thoroughfares and the advantages of cutting new roads shall now be considered seriatim.

Objections to old method:

1. The great expense incurred by the ratepayers. The land required for widening is bought at very high prices owing to the buildings on it, and the accumulated values of the frontages; no account being taken of the fact that the landowner gets a new frontage, for which he pays nothing, and which is even more valuable than the one he has sold to the ratepayers at a very high price. The ratepayers also pay for the whole of the street works, which, as will be seen presently, are far more costly in the case of old streets than when new roads are cut through back land.

In short, the ratepayers find the capital on which they have to pay interest and sinking fund, they also take the risk, whereas the landowners take the profits. No wonder rates are rising in all our large towns, and no wonder it is so difficult to persuade the ratepayers to approve such schemes.*

If the widening of existing roads is carried out under the Town Planning Act instead of, as at present, under the Public Health Act of 1875, large savings can be effected for the ratepayers and the work done more expeditiously. Before the Housing and Town Planning Act, 1909, no local authority could make a yard of road against the will of the landowner. Under the Public Health Act, 1875, a landowner can block a street improvement for many years by refusing to sell at any price, or by demanding an exorbitant price. Procedure under the Lands Clauses Consolidation Act is, to say the least, lengthy and expensive and under local tramway or other Acts the compulsory purchase clauses always involve very heavy compensation, and quite unfair expenditure by the ratepayers. Under the Town Planning Act, on the other hand, Clause 58, subsection (3), entitles the ratepayers to one-half of the betterment due to the improvement. The 1909 Act makes it possible for local authorities to insist upon street widenings which up till then may have hung fire for many years. The Harborne and Quinton town planning scheme for instance included streets for the widening of which negotiations had been in hand for a very long time. In one street in particular, the negotiations had been hanging on for eight or nine years. Some of the owners would agree to a 42-ft. road, and others would not agree to anything. The town planning scheme brought them all into line at a very small cost to the ratepayers, and the road will now be 60 feet wide instead of the 42 feet originally asked for. The widening included among other things the buying of cottages which, except under the 1909 Act, could not have been carried through without a provisional order. The Town Planning Act and Scheme have made this and other questions at issue a comparatively simple and inexpensive matter. The widening of old thoroughfares under the 1909 Act is a great advance on old methods, but even with this assistance, the cost of widening old roads is nearly always greater than that of cutting new ones, especially when it is a question of providing adequate access to undeveloped districts.

2. The next objection to the old method is that assessable value is often decreased and every decrease in the assessable value of a district means higher rates on what remains. The reason for this

* See excerpt from Marshall's " Principles of Economics," Appendix 12.

decrease in assessable value is not far to seek. No rates are paid on land that has been thrown into a street, whereas land with buildings on it is charged in with the buildings.

3. It is hardly ever financially possible to obtain sufficient width for present and future traffic. The advent of motor-cars, motor-omnibuses and motor-vans added to tramways, has accentuated the urgent need for providing wider main roads at a reasonable cost to the ratepayers. Travelling has now become so quick and so cheap that a much larger proportion of the population uses the streets than was the case a few years ago. This tendency is far more likely to increase than to diminish, and, as a matter of fact, those of us who are genuinely desirous of doing everything possible to empty the slums into real country must insist on a method of town development that will not only make possible, but absolutely ensure the provision of main arteries wide enough to facilitate and, therefore, increase this tendency on the part of the people to live further out. That is to say, we must reject the extravagant and ineffective policy of widening old roads.

4. Another objection is that old roads often have in them very bad gradients. These roads were seldom designed beforehand. They generally grew out of an accommodation road to some farm, and only by degrees, and more or less by accident, became the means of communication between one part of a district and another. Those who go about with their eyes open may see signs (such as awkward corners and narrow necks) of the haphazard way in which our roads have grown into what they now are.

The pettifogging by-law method of dealing with roads has hopelessly broken down. The standard by-law widths are either too narrow or too wide. They are too narrow for main arteries, and too wide and too expensive for purely residential roads or drives; they also cause a great amount of insanitary dust, which could and should in future be avoided.

5. The objection to allowing roads to " grow like Topsy " instead of designing them beforehand and controlling their development is clearly seen in the route taken by roads that have been left to " grow " in the old haphazard way. How often these old roads turn and twist in order to avoid some property or other, sometimes almost doubling back upon themselves!

For these reasons it is wiser, as well as more economical, to provide new main arteries by cutting through back land, and impossible as this may seem at first sight, new ways can generally be found by those who wish to find them, even in districts that have already been developed. In Appendix 1 will be found examples of this policy. Its advantages are:

1. The landowner gains so much by getting his back land turned into front land, that it is well worth his while to give all the land needed for the road, and as a matter of fact, it costs him nothing to do so, because under town planning schemes in reckoning the number of houses to be allowed per acre the road is counted in the area to be covered. It is also well worth his while to contribute towards the cost of road-making. Under the old system, he would have borne the cost of an ordinary by-law road which he would have had to make himself in order to develop his property. Under the new system, it pays him better to contribute a like amount to the cost of the new main artery made by the local authority, because his contribution is not called for until his land comes into rating, that is, earning income for him. He ought, in fact to contribute rather more than this amount in return for getting his land opened up rather earlier than would otherwise have been the case, and if the local authority is wise enough to execute at first only so much of the street works as are necessary for the initial traffic this contribution from the landowner will at least cover the expenditure incurred by the ratepayers. Old-fashioned experts object to this proposal on the ground that the ratepayers are called upon to advance money for the development of other people's property without any assurance that they will get a return on their money. The answer is simple. Engage capable men to do your town planning, who can design and construct a new main artery on economical lines, that is, with a well-made but not too wide roadway, suitable for motor-buses, with wide grass margins and inexpensive footpaths on either side, then run a service of motor-buses to the new area, and this means of quick communication will soon produce the new assessable value needed to give the ratepayers a very satisfactory return on their investment, with this additional advantage, that the capital invested by the ratepayers will be repaid by the landowners as and when their land comes into rating, instead of the ratepayers being burdened with a loan that will not be paid off for many years. There is a risk that the money invested in this new road will not earn interest in the shape of increased assessable value for the next year or two, which is no worse (indeed it is better) than what happens in the case of a great deal of public expenditure under the old method. Against this, there is the certainty that the money will eventually be repaid by the landowner, and will not in the

long run have to be found by the ratepayers, as under the old method.

I have referred in an earlier part of this chapter to the difficulty of getting the ratepayers to approve of schemes for street widenings, owing to the very heavy cost. In practice, there is amongst a certain section of the ratepayers' representatives much greater opposition to the construction of new main arteries on the lines indicated above. Schemes for widening old roads are more attractive to those gentlemen than the construction of new ones, a year or two in advance of actual requirements, whereas in the interests of the ratepayers it ought to be just the other way about. The vested interests of owners of existing frontages play an important part in the consideration of these questions behind the scenes and the ratepayers do not understand this " inner working " as they should do, or they would soon insist upon an end being put to the expenditure of their money on widening old roads whenever it can possibly be avoided. In one of the districts visited by me in the course of my investigations into town planning in this country, I found that main arteries had been constructed on the lines I suggest. The landowners gave some of the land and sold the rest to the local authority at a profit of 300 per cent on what it was worth before the new road was projected, and when the new main artery was completed, the same landowners sold their frontages at a further profit of 400 per cent on the very comfortable price that they had obtained from the local authority for land required for the road. Is it really so unreasonable and risky, as some people say it is, to suggest that our municipal representatives should take time by the forelock and endeavour to secure for their ratepayers some part of the very handsome profits due to the growth of our towns? In the case that I have just described, it was not even necessary to run an experimental line of motor-buses. All that was done was to make a new road which, in eighteen months, produced a very considerable increase of assessable value, but owing to the old ideas that still prevail it was the landowners, and not the ratepayers, who secured by far the greater part of the profits that were due to the foresight and courage of municipal representatives and officials.

2. The next advantage is that the assessable value of the town, city, or district is increased instead of decreased. This has been explained in the last paragraph, and need not be further enlarged upon. Suffice it to say that increased assessable value is as effectual in producing income for civic needs as a rise in rates, and in these

days no opportunity should be missed of avoiding the necessity for raising the rates.

3. Another advantage is that sufficient width is available for dividing the various classes of traffic as soon as it is necessary to do so, and where tramways are considered necessary, these can be laid on an independent track, thereby saving £3,000 per mile in the cost of construction, and £300 per mile per annum in the cost of upkeep. By this means, tramways do not interfere with or obstruct the general traffic and the general traffic does not interfere with or obstruct them, and whereas the horrible screeching noise of the tramcar wheels on the rails is magnified by the sounding board provided where the rails are laid in wood or stone setts, this objectionable noise can be very much diminished, if the independent tramway track is finished off with a soft material. Last, but not least, the poles and wires can be masked by planting trees, which will add to the general appearance of the road, instead of detracting from it as ordinary tramways undoubtedly do. Crossings would, of course, have to be provided for the general traffic to get from one side to the other, but this would be a very small item of expense compared with the huge cost of laying tram lines down the middle of an ordinary street.

4. By cutting through back land instead of going along existing highways, the road designer is able to follow the lie of the land, thereby getting much better gradients than are possible where houses and other buildings have already been erected; and when a district is so hilly as not to admit of reasonable gradients without making cuttings and embankments, the frontages are not thrown out of building development, as they would be under the old cast-iron by-law methods, provided the cuttings and embankments are of a moderate depth or height, because with town planning methods of estate development the builder can accommodate himself to the land in a way that is quite impossible when he has to build long monotonous rows of houses, a definite distance from the centre of the road with no latitude either way. Hilly districts are of necessity more expensive to develop than flat ones, but by town planning methods this extra expense can be reduced to a minimum, and a hilly district well developed is certainly more attractive than a flat one, which means that the houses will command a higher rent, thereby repaying the builder for his extra outlay.

5. It is also generally possible to shorten the distance. With modern methods of transit, it does not make much difference in

the time required for the journey, but it is an advantage for the ratepayers to have less length of roadway to construct and maintain, and there is far less liability to traffic accidents on a road with easy curves and no awkward corners.

6. Another advantage of new roads over old is that a clean start can be made with full knowledge of what is required for modern traffic (see Chapters III, IV and V).

The requirements of modern traffic have necessitated a revolution in the science of road-making, and the construction of entirely new roads provides excellent opportunities for taking full advantage of the knowledge that has been obtained by those who have been carefully studying the new conditions for the last few years.

7. In the construction of these new main arteries, it is by no means necessary to carry out immediately all the street works that will eventually be required. It is much better not to do so. Wise town planners will, in the first instance, construct the minimum street works that will suffice for the traffic at the moment, thereby spending the least possible amount of money and no more. The greater part of the road should at first be laid down in grass, and if this grass is dealt with as on country roads, it will cost little or nothing in upkeep. As the new district develops and traffic increases the local authority will see what is needed and can provide it as and when it is needed, but not before. It may well be that experience will materially modify their original ideas and then it will be a great advantage for the ratepayers, if no money has been wasted on unnecessary street works. One thing must not be forgotten in the initial construction of these new main arteries, and that is, whatever width of roadway is constructed, it should be thoroughly well made. The surface must be waterproof, smooth and clean, it must be dustless in summer and mudless in winter, and the road bed must be solid and stable. Motor vehicles have come to stay, and they must be provided for; where the road is badly made, there is vibration with consequent annoyance to residents and damage to property, but where the road is properly made these losses and annoyances do not occur. Sixteen or twenty-four feet wide modern roadways properly constructed need no stone gutter, and require only quite a light kerb. This suggestion will be heresy to the old-fashioned borough surveyor to whom immaculate kerbs and gutters are the sign manual of proper town and estate development. I am not concerned with men of that type. My object is to show that wise town planning will save the pockets of the ratepayers as well as provide better roads and

better housing. When designing these new roads, careful consideration should be given as to which part of them will always be grass, even when the road is completed and all sorts of traffic have been provided for, and under this permanent grass the main sewer should be placed. By this means, we shall avoid the manholes in the roadway, which are so expensive to construct and so unpleasant to drive over, owing to the softer material round them wearing away faster than they do and therefore being constantly out of repair.

8. Quick development of town planned areas may be achieved by adopting the policy and methods advocated above, and, provided those responsible for the town planning scheme are endowed with average ability and honesty, large savings can be effected for the ratepayers in a very few years' time, and the adequate access essential to the quick development of new districts can be immediately provided without running nearly so much risk as heretofore. I will go further. Under the old method there is a certainty of very heavy expense with no adequate return. Under the new method very large sums can assuredly be saved to the community for the simple reason that there will be a fairer division of expenditure and profits between the general body of ratepayers and a few favoured individuals who happen to own land in or near centres of population.

In order to deal successfully with so complicated a subject as town planning, it is necessary to get the theory clear. The policy outlined above is designed to meet the great difficulties of dealing with an area that has long been built on and requires reconstruction of one sort or another—roads or buildings—for modern needs. Although this method of attacking the problem may be conceded in theory yet it is constantly held that it would be impossible to work it out practically. Appendix 1 gives four concrete examples which illustrate my meaning, and show how the theory could be carried out in practice.

CHAPTER II. SITE VALUES.

UNLESS building density is severely restricted in residential areas for the poorer classes, as well as for the rich, there cannot be sufficient room to live, and no answer to the problem before us can be acceptable which does not make reasonable building density at the usual rents, a sound business proposition. Nothing else can be permanently satisfactory or be regarded otherwise than as an amiable hobby.

The practical difficulty in the way of decent housing at reasonable rents is the excessive ground rents paid by tenants of small house property, in comparison with the amount of land they get for their money. Ground rents are the interest on the cost of the sites, and it is the cost of the site on which small house property is built which must therefore be analysed in the first place. The three main items that go to make up site values are:

1. Price paid for the land.
2. Cost of development.
3. Landjobbers' profits and professional fees.

1. PRICE PAID FOR THE LAND

So long as land is used for agricultural purposes, it is let or sold at so much per acre, but the moment it is brought within the building zone it is at once valued at so much per yard, before anything has been spent on it by the owner. This unreasonable and purely artificial rise in price prevents the builder from giving enough land to each house and makes it impossible for him to arrange his houses in such a way that each shall get a sufficiency of light and air, let alone provide the other amenities essential to good health and the rational enjoyment of life.

The only effective way of surmounting this difficulty is to protect cheap land that is going to be opened up in the way described in the last chapter, that is to say, before roads and tram or motor-bus services are provided in building areas, a town planning scheme must be adopted severely restricting building density. Wherever this policy is used, excessive rise in the price of agricultural land the moment it is brought into the building zone will become a thing of the past, and this is what must be accomplished, if the poorer classes are to have a fair chance of decent living conditions. The underlying fact is that the fewer houses allowed per acre, the lower will land values be. It is asserted on the contrary, that fewer houses per acre will result in higher house rents, but

this scarcely carries conviction, because it is known that people of
small means are already paying just as much as they can possibly
afford for house rent, and it is impossible to get any more out of
them. All intelligent land agents admit in private that fewer houses
per acre mean lower land values,* although, as they say themselves,
it is not reasonable to expect them to admit it in public; but that is
no reason why we should be misled by the bogey of higher house
rents into making town planning schemes that allow more houses
per acre than are consistent with reasonable housing and living
conditions for the poorer classes. Landowners and their agents
will not unnaturally make every effort to get the number of houses
allowed per acre as high as possible. It is the duty of those who
represent the community to see that private interests are not allowed to override the general welfare.

Mr J. F. Roxburgh, W.S., Edinburgh, in his pamphlet " Town
Planning in Scotland," puts the position very clearly:

" At the recent Town Planning Conference held in Glasgow it
was almost pathetic to hear speaker after speaker assert that
garden cities were impossible in Scotland on account of the high
price of land, and that for the housing at least of the artisan class
nothing but buildings of the present tenement type were possible.
This statement is a complete inversion of the facts of the case.
It is not the high price of land which makes tenements necessary.
It is the prevalence of the tenement type of building which inflates
the price of land.

" In Scotland sixty to eighty families are crowded on each acre,
and this it is that raises the price of ground. The feuing rate in
Edinburgh for land for tenements ranges from £100 to £250 per
acre per annum, which is equivalent to a capital value of £2,200
to £5,500 per acre. In England, where the tenement habit is rare,
the price of building land is much lower. In Germany, on
the other hand, where the same conditions exist as in Scotland,
we find the same phenomena in regard to the price of building
land.

" The economic fact which lies at the back of this difference
is that the ground rent which can be drawn from any piece of
ground is in proportion to the rent of the houses which can be
erected on it. In other words, the value of building land is the use

* One of the municipal leaders of town planning in Birmingham is of
opinion that limiting the number of houses per acre, thereby increasing the
size of each plot, must to that extent increase house rents. This expression
of opinion is a confession of ignorance of the science of town planning.

to which it can be put. If by crowding more houses upon it you can obtain a larger rent, the land will have a larger price. Unrestricted land in and around Edinburgh and other Scottish towns is valued on the basis that it can be used for the erection of four-storey tenements and for the purpose of housing some sixty to eighty families per acre. The large number of houses which can be put on a given acre inflates the price of land and that inflated price prevents rational housing, and so on in a vicious circle.

" It is difficult for the town planner in England to realize the difference which the tenement system makes. It has been argued by Mr Raymond Unwin and others that the ground landlord does not gain by crowding an undue number of houses upon his land, because if a smaller number is built the saving in the cost of the roads and drains will more than compensate for the loss of ground rent. While this contention may be sound when dealing with separate cottages it does not apply in the case of flatted buildings of the Scottish tenement type, for additional storeys added upwards do not increase the cost of the roads and drains."*

Where cheap agricultural land is opened up for building, it is quite possible to protect the public interest without really injuring the landowners. Except in a very few special cases, purely agricultural land without buildings is not worth more than £20 per acre; call it £40. Those who develop building estates at the rate of ten houses per gross acre can generally afford to pay £120† per acre for the land before anything has been spent on it. That leaves a very good profit for the landowner who, without doing anything himself or spending any money, has the good luck to own land that is required for town development, but where land that has already been forced up to an artificial price is included in a town planning area the problem is not so simple. The private owners whose interests are affected will, quite properly from their point of view, endeavour to get their land excluded from the scheme. This would be an apparently easy way out of the difficulty, but would be fatal to any real improvement; " Facilis descensus Averni." There are three classes of cases to be dealt with.

1. Where undeveloped building land has already risen to an

* The economic fact mentioned by Mr Roxburgh applies to all building land, no matter whether used for tenement buildings or separate cottages.

† Under the new system they may often get it for less. In March, 1911, the Birmingham City Council was informed in writing by the local Property Owners' Association that £200 per acre is not as much as ought to be obtained for undeveloped land on which only ten houses per acre will be allowed; but this ex parte statement was made in haste on insufficient data.

excessive price the way to deal with it is not to exclude it from the town planning area, but to make very careful inquiries as to whether it has changed hands at this price during the last few years. If it has not changed hands for many years, then the owner is not really injured. He is not deprived of anything he has already got. He is only disappointed at not getting something he was expecting to get, which the Housing and Town Planning Act of 1909 was expressly passed to prevent him from getting in order that the people of England should be better housed in the future than they have been in the past. In " Practical Housing " written before this Act was passed, I pointed out that town planning properly administered means smaller profits and quicker returns. The landowner will get less per acre, but he will lease or sell more acres more quickly. What we need is not to take away from anyone what they have already got, but to ensure that no more excessive profits shall be made out of housing the people to the detriment of the national health and well-being. This being so, no landowner can justly complain because his anticipations of future profits out of land for housing do not materialize. There is no public obligation to the landowner who is merely anticipating future profits.

2. Where land has changed hands within the last few years at prices paid in anticipation of being allowed to overcrowd it with houses, the position is different. In these cases some allowance might be made, but it is not possible to say exactly what form it should take. Each case must be dealt with on its merits, due allowance being made for the quicker rate and lower cost of development under wise town planning administration. What must be borne in mind is that nothing must be allowed to interfere with decent housing at reasonable rents.

3. The third class of cases is the most difficult of all, that is where money has been actually spent on contracts entered into on the old extravagant by-law basis. Where this has happened, it is possible that rather more than the standard number of houses per acre may have to be allowed.

The best way out of the difficulty in all these cases is to put dear land to some other use than that of housing the people. It is abundantly clear to all careful students of this problem that nothing approaching a sufficient supply of healthy houses with decent surroundings at low rents can be provided unless there is an abundant supply of cheap land for the purpose.

With regard to keeping down land values by restricting building density, it is regrettable to have to say that up to the present town planning schemes have not gone far enough in this direction. Too much is left to the discretion of local authorities, with the result that local interests get too much consideration, and national well-being too little. An illustration in point is the case of early closing; so long as the closing of shops depended upon local agreements nothing was done, and it was not until early closing was made the general law of the land, that shop assistants obtained the consideration and leisure they have a right to expect. The building restrictions now proposed are so inadequate as to call for a general law that on no housing estate shall there be more than ten houses per gross acre, except where the landowner can show special cause why he should be allowed to put a greater number. The onus should rest on him to prove his right to more than the standard number of houses per acre, not, as at present, on the local authority to prove the reasonableness of insisting that the people should be decently housed. This is the only effective way of keeping land values within reasonable bounds and ensuring better housing for the people at rents they can afford to pay. A general law such as that suggested above would be a drastic, but not unjust, measure, provided a little time were to elapse between its enactment and its coming into force. It would put a time limit on land sweating, which is the root-cause of bad housing, and bad housing is at the root of much of our social trouble. It is not reasonable that a few private individuals should be allowed to continue making huge profits which result in great avoidable suffering and very heavy expenditure by the rest of the community. The proposal to rate land values makes this enactment specially urgent. The effect of rating or taxing land values in other countries has been not only to throw more land into the market, and in that way reduce the price; it has also tended to force owners to put their land to the " best use," which in the case of towns and urban districts is, so far as money making is concerned, to put as much building on it as the regulations allow. Experience shows that by-laws and even town planning regulations drafted locally and approved by the central authority are by no means a reliable safeguard against land sweating. We are fortunate in being able to learn from the experience of other countries in this matter. For instance, the rating of land values in Wellington, New Zealand, undeniably hastened development, but, from the point of view of the town planner and the housing economist, that development was wasteful. Wellington has nominally 80,000 people and has

c

adopted unimproved rating. Auckland has a population well over 100,000, is the older city, and, with one or two minor exceptions, rates on the annual value less 20 per cent. In Auckland, the larger and older city, land values are considerably lower than in Wellington, rents on an average nearly 20 per cent less, whilst the average frontage per plot in suburban estates developed by land agents ranges from 40 to 50 feet as against 30 to 40 feet in Wellington. These figures were only arrived at after comparing a very large number of plans of ordinary estates in both cities, the statutory limitations as to widths of roads and air space for houses being the same in each case. Owing to a difference in configuration between the two cities, it was necessary to choose estates that in some degree corresponded in this respect as well as in others.

The rating of land values without proper town planning and the building restrictions provided thereunder has hastened congestion in areas already built on both in Australia and New Zealand. If land is anywhere near a business centre, it is not unusual to find that a row of shops is erected on the main road frontage and the ground at the back cut up and developed for residential purposes on the ordinary haphazard lines, congestion and overcrowding follow, land values and rents rise, and so the way for the slum is prepared.

Recent figures disclose that overcrowding in these colonies is rapidly increasing. It would be wrong to say that this is wholly due to rating of land values without adequate town planning and building regulations, but it must be clear that the rating of land values without any law restricting building density is a very dangerous policy; where open spaces are needed, the land should be protected by town planning regulations and valued for taxation according to the use to which it is put. If there were a general law forbidding more than ten houses per acre in residential districts, unimproved rating would not accentuate existing overcrowding or send up rents, but without this safeguard there is grave danger that these evils might result. It must not be forgotten that the town planning authority is also the rating authority. Greater building density means higher land values, that is higher assessments per acre, which would be a great temptation to short-sighted local authorities to allow too many houses per acre in order to get more rates from the land.

The rating of land values properly safeguarded would greatly assist town planning and housing reform, but without a general restriction of building density, experience shows that it would probably do more harm than good, and incidentally land permanently reserved for open spaces, public or private, or permanently protected against overcrowding, should not, no matter what position it may be in, be assessed so highly as that used for intensive building. This is the best and fairest way of ensuring better living and working conditions, and by no other means can we surmount what is at present a constantly recurring obstacle to decent housing at reasonable rents. Time after time housing reformers have come across landowners and builders in various parts of the country, who are willing and anxious to provide decent housing on their estate. At the preliminary interviews everything looks bright and promising; but when the time comes for going into details with trustees and other professional men, they explain that they have no right to let or sell the land in question below a certain figure, which always proves to be a figure that will make decent housing commercially impossible. Building land is, and has for a long time past been, valued at £400, £1,000 or £2,000 per acre, and they say, with a great deal of reason on their side, that they have no right to take less than the market price, that they would not be doing their duty to the beneficiaries of the estate if they were to do so. The accepted valuation is purely fictitious and artificial and is due to the old system of town and estate development, which it is now generally agreed must be stopped, but the only way to stop it is to break down the artificial land values that have arisen under the old discredited system, by passing a law to make land sweating illegal. We shall then return to a more natural state of things and trustees and others responsible will be within their rights in being satisfied with a reasonable profit on building land instead of being forced, as they consider themselves to be at present, to insist upon prices that must perpetuate the present unsatisfactory conditions.

The proposal to pass a general law such as that suggested above would raise a great outcry among the landjobbers. They are used to very large profits and will not give them up without a struggle. The bogey of higher house rents will be raised " ad nauseam." Let us examine it again. The more a man has to pay for any commodity the more he has to earn on it in order to get a return on his investment. In the case of land for housing, the only way to do this is to put a larger number of houses per acre so as to obtain a bigger lump sum for ground rent. For instance, the experts all agree that take the country over, a 6s. 6d. house carries an average ground rent of 1s. per week, no matter how many or how few houses there may be to the acre. This is the proportion of the total rent that goes in ground rent. The capital value of 1s. per week ground rent at 23 years' purchase comes to within a few shillings of £60. If there are fifty-five 6s. 6d. houses per acre (the maximum allowed by the by-laws) this works out at £3,300 per acre for fully-developed land. At forty houses per acre it is £2,400 and at ten it is £600.

The tenants of small houses are already paying as much ground rent per house as they can afford, or rather manage, to pay, from which it follows that fewer ground rents mean a smaller lump sum per annum per acre of land, and, therefore, lower land values. That is why the landjobbers always fight so hard for as many houses as possible per acre. In public they say, with their tongues in their cheeks, that fewer houses per acre will mean higher house rents. In private, they admit that it will mean lower land values. If fewer houses per acre meant higher house rents, then obviously more houses or tenements would mean lower house rents. What are the facts?

In Scotland, where tenements are very prevalent, house rent is higher than in England and the accommodation not so good; 7s. weekly tenements (corresponding to the English 6s. 6d. house) 80 to the acre, pay just as much feu-duty as self-contained houses of equal rent, fifty or less to the acre; the only difference being that the landowner gets more ground rent per acre for his land.

In Brussels, the price of land is such as not to preclude gardens to houses of moderate rental, and this in spite of the fine wide avenues in that city. In Paris, on the other hand, where the streets are also wide, building density is much greater than in Brussels, and therefore, according to the landjobbers' theory, house rents should be lower. House rents are very high in Paris, and the accommodation far from satisfactory. In Paris, only very rich people can afford a self-contained house with garden or backyard attached, whereas in Brussels self-contained houses with gardens are to be had at moderate rentals.

In the small town of Teltow, which forms part of Greater Berlin, when it seemed probable that only detached and semi-detached houses, of not more than two storeys in height, would be allowed, instead of the ordinary five-storey tenements, the prices of shares in companies owning land there fell at once 37 per cent.

German town planning practice in the past has been to allow very much greater building density than is allowed in this country, even under the by-laws. As against forty to fifty houses per acre under the by-laws in England, there are in Germany 100 or more houses, or rather tenements, and these are built five or more storeys high. Housing accommodation is worse than in this country, and house rents are higher. Land values, on the other hand, are £5,000 to £15,000 per acre in German working-class districts, as against £2,000 to £3,000 in this country. The landjobbers are well paid, but their tenants have been badly caught by these successful philanthropists, on whose land they are huddled together with the ostensible object of providing houses at lower rents, and the best German town planners are now taking measures to reduce building density in residential areas. In the words of Professor Eberstadt, of Berlin, " After 1870, the power of town planning passed from the State officials to the new municipal bodies, and these by degrees fell almost entirely into the hands of professional speculators. This may teach the English people a useful lesson as to the necessity—and the difficulty—of prohibiting private interest from barring national progress." The lesson for us to learn from Germany is two-fold.

1. Vital points like the restriction of building density and the consequent regulation of land values should be settled by general legislation and not left to be settled by administration.

2. Fewer houses per acre means lower land values and lower house rents.

There are plenty of landowners and builders in this country able and willing to provide better housing at the old or lower rents. All we have to do is to see that our housing and town planning legislation and administration are such as to enable and assist these reasonable men to carry out their wishes. With the land-jobbers, it is impossible to come to terms, because nothing will satisfy them but a continuance of their old exorbitant profits. They are not in the least degree interested in better housing. All they want is to get rich very quickly by means of speculation. Their energies must be diverted into other channels. They must not any longer be allowed to gamble with the lives of the people.

The landowning class as a whole will gain, not lose, by honest and sensible town planning methods. The decline in value of artificially high-priced building land will be more than counterbalanced by the rise in value of low-priced land which is at present more or less inaccessible, and even those who get a lower price per acre for their land than they might have got will by no means always lose under the new method. They will sell more acres more quickly. Under the old system building land often lies idle for twenty, thirty or more years, bringing no appreciable income to its owner with compound interest piling up all the time. Under the new system, properly administered, development of new districts will be greatly expedited, and, as we shall see presently, quicker development presents very substantial financial advantages to the landowner which should more than counterbalance the lower price that he gets for each acre.

2. COST OF DEVELOPMENT

It is no use keeping down land values unless the cost of estate development is also reduced, and the rate of development increased, nor would it be fair to the landowner to do so. It should be borne in mind as a business proposition that the more profitable we can make decent housing at reasonable rents, the more we shall get of it.

There are two ways of expediting estate development:

1. Provide immediate access to new districts.

2. Abolish our pettifogging by-law system, which not only hinders all improvement, but actually encourages bad housing, and substitute more practical and up-to-date methods of administration.

The first of these methods has been fully explained in Chapter I, and we can therefore pass straight on to the second. In '' Practical Housing,'' attention is drawn to the wicked waste of public and private money due to obsolete by-laws for roadways in purely residential districts, for drainage, and for the houses themselves.

ROADS. Under the old system there is too much length of roadway as well as too much width. In order to get as many houses per acre as the by-laws will allow a great number of cross roads are put, and at the corner of each of these a considerable amount of frontage is of necessity wasted. Small houses do not need to front on to two roads, but at these corners they are obliged to do so. If estates are developed with fewer houses per acre and the amenities located on back land as advocated in '' Practical Housing,'' this waste of frontage can be avoided, and, therefore, the length of roadway very much reduced. With regard to width of roadways, there must, of course, be plenty of room for traffic on main arteries, but on side streets and in purely residential districts 16 feet of macadam is ample for the longer roads. This allows two streams of traffic to pass each other at full speed. For roads or drives that only lead to groups of small houses eight feet of macadam will accommodate all the traffic there is ever likely to be, provided that there is a circle at the end in which to turn round. There must, of course, be sufficient distance between the fronts of the houses, and this is more pleasantly, as well as more cheaply, filled in with narrow roadways, tree-planted grass verges and gravel or asphalt footpaths, than with the dreary deserts of macadam and very expensive stone footpaths demanded by the by-laws. Another large item in the cost of roadmaking is the kerbs and gutters. These must be sufficient for carrying off the surface water and keeping traffic off the grass or footpaths, but for these narrow residential roads they can be of a much cheaper design than is considered necessary for the wider roadways. There will be so much less water to carry off a narrow roadway than a wide one.

DRAINAGE. In many places, it has been considered necessary to have two main sewers, one for surface water and the other for sewage. The Report of the Royal Commission on Sewage Disposal (1908) strongly recommends that there should be only one main sewer to take both surface water and sewage.

The following passages from this report are very striking:*

" In our opinion, the cases in which the provision of a separate system can properly be justified are rare, and it appears to us that the relative merits of the separate and combined systems have not always been sufficiently considered. . .

" The witnesses who have given evidence on this question have agreed that the first flush of water from a surface-water system during a storm is of such a foul nature that it ought to be purified if practicable, especially if the system brings water from paved open spaces, such as markets, squares, etc. . . .

" Experience also shows that with two sets of drains to each house there is danger of the sewage drain being connected with the surface-water sewer, and in densely populated areas slops and other filthy liquids are often emptied into street gullies and pass directly into the surface-water sewer. . . .

" We may also observe that the flushing of sewers by rain water, which occurs with the combined system, is in itself useful, and that there is some evidence to show that filters work better when storm sewage from which the solids have been settled has occasionally passed through them." . . .

" As regards the cases in which the adoption of a separate system for surface water may be allowed, we may refer to the evidence of Dr Fowler, Mr Watson and Mr Wilkinson. These

* A fuller extract will be found in Appendix 2.

gentlemen have had considerable experience and they expressed the view that in large towns the separate system is impracticable; that in urban districts the combined system is justified on sanitary and economical grounds and that only in villages, country districts and suburban areas where there is little traffic and where the surface water may not be very foul, may the separate system sometimes be adopted with advantage.''

It will be seen from these extracts that in the opinion of the highest authorities the combined system of sewers is from the purely sanitary point of view, far better than the separate system, and it will be obvious to every practical man that very large savings will be effected in the development of residential estates, where the recommendation of these leading authorities on sanitary questions is adopted.

Mr John D. Watson, Engineer to the Birmingham, Tame and Rea District Drainage Board, whose reputation on this question is not confined to the British Isles, let alone Birmingham, is also very emphatic on this point, and his opinion carries great weight with all the leading experts on sewage disposal. In a recent report to the Drainage Board, he says: '' The disadvantages of the separate system are:

'' 1. It costs the local authority about two-thirds more. There is additional cost for maintenance, and it entails greater expense in the erection of dwellings and other property drained on that system.

'' 2. There is some danger of a foul-water drain being connected to the rain-water drain, and in densely populated districts, of slops entering into the surface-water gullies.

'' 3. The system tends to engender a false security. For instance, when the system is first started, the surface water may contain nothing more harmful than road grit and sand, but as the population grows imperceptibly organic matter is added and foulness results.

'' The merits or demerits of the separate system chiefly concern the Constituent Authority, but the Drainage Board are interested to know that under the separate system there is no guarantee that only sewage will reach the sewage disposal works.

'' A Drainage Board must always have a vital interest in the volume of liquid sent to the sewage works, but in my opinion it should not be assumed that the Board favours what is called the separate system.''*

* For full report see Appendix 3.

The Birmingham Public Works Committee have decided to ignore these opinions on the ground that "nothing should be done to render it necessary to duplicate or enlarge the existing trunk sewers to meet a purpose for which they were not designed." It is only fair to mention that the sewage from all new areas must be conveyed through existing trunk sewers, and that some of the trunk sewers of Birmingham were designed to meet the conditions of the combined system in the old parts of the city and the separate system in suburban and rural areas. These sewers were designed when it was considered by drainage authorities to be a distinct advantage to limit the volume of sewage for the purification of which they were responsible. The development of the biological system of purification has completely altered the whole situation, and nowadays the best practice is to treat on sewage farms not less than six times the dry-weather flow. The work of eliminating solids from sewage—whether that sewage is augmented by storm water or not—is best done at the sewage works; the quantity must, of course, be limited by the capacity of the sewers. The difficulty raised by Birmingham can generally be surmounted by judiciously placed storm-water overflows, and these would serve the same purpose (namely, limiting the volume of sewage which is conveyed to a sewage works) as the separate system at far less cost to the community. There are, of course, cases where storm-water over-flows cannot be put in; for example, where sewers are laid at a lower level than the adjacent streams, when the result would probably be the delivery of a larger volume of sewage at the outfall works than is expedient, but if each case is considered on its own merits with a fixed determination to use, wherever possible, the more economical and efficient combined system assisted by storm-water overflows, it will be found that under intelligent and pains-taking authorities, the use of the separate system is in very few cases unavoidable. It is sometimes suggested that the separate system may be of distinct advantage in certain suburban districts, but the best authorities are of opinion that the disadvantages far outweigh the advantages where there is a prospect of that suburban district becoming an urban district in the comparatively near future.

It is disappointing to see Birmingham refusing to move with the times in this matter of economical and efficient sewerage, but it is to be hoped that other places will not hesitate to take advantage of the progress of science, not only in the interests of public health, but also in relief of the public, as well as many private, purses.

Another means of saving on drainage is to allow the drains of several small houses to be gathered up and connected by a common drain with the main sewer, instead of, as under the old system, insisting that each small house shall be directly connected with the main sewer. The reason for this extravagant method is the uncertainty of the law as to what is and what is not a public sewer repairable at the expense of the ratepayers. It has been held that the common drains suggested above are in this category, and, therefore, many places do not allow them. There are two ways of surmounting this difficulty:

1. Lay it down in town planning schemes that where the drainage of several houses is collected into a common drain, instead of each house being directly connected with the main sewer, these common drains shall be repairable by the owner and not by the inhabitants at large.

2. Pass a short Act of Parliament on the lines of the Bill introduced into the House of Commons by Mr Henry Vivian in 1908, and for some occult reason opposed by the Local Government Board.

This matter is of considerable importance to the builders and tenants of small house property and, therefore, in view of ancient prejudices in administrative circles, it would be well for Parliament to pass a special Act " to reduce the existing chaos into system and order."* (Mr Vivian's Bill will be found in Appendix 7.)

HOUSES. With regard to the houses themselves, there are many details where by-laws can be altered so as to reduce the cost of building, and at the same time improve the resulting house. There is, for instance, the question of materials. Where bricks are dear, builders should look about for something cheaper, and in town planning schemes they should be given full liberty to use any material that can be shown to reasonably answer the purpose. Cast-iron by-laws have in this respect been a great hindrance to better and cheaper housing and should be abrogated. Another defect in the by-laws is that they insist upon a certain height of bedroom without ensuring that the room shall get an adequate supply of light and air. For instance, a bedroom, 8 ft. 6 in. high, whose only window is completely shadowed by a neighbouring wall, is not nearly so healthy as a bedroom of less height but with more floor space and a good long window, the light and air to which is not obstructed or impeded. The lower bedroom will be cheaper to build, as well as healthier to sleep in, but such is the strength of

* See Lord Russell of Killowen's judgment in 1896.

habit and custom that it is very difficult to get by-law officials to move out of their by-law rut, and they are still, even under town planning schemes, doing their best, more or less unconsciously, to prevent healthier and cheaper housing, and to perpetuate the old extravagant method of housing the people at forty or more houses to the acre. There are in fact amongst town planners two schools of thought:

(a) The stupid school, who pin their faith to rigid regulations and think town development is a question of accurate kerbs and gutters.

(b) The practical men who recognize that light and air are far more important to public health, as well as much cheaper, than kerbs and gutters.

The general line of the kerb-and-gutter school is to force landowners and builders into doing what they think right by rigid regulations. The policy of the practical man is to make better housing a sound business proposition for landowners and builders, so that improvement shall come automatically and without the constant driving that under the old system has produced such very unsatisfactory results.

A city surveyor once showed the comparative importance he attached to allowing great density of population and providing the area with immaculate kerbs and gutters by explaining how he had enabled a friend of his to put 80 houses to the acre without breaking the by-laws of the district, while he praised his friend as a public-spirited benefactor because he " was as good as gold about the kerbs and gutters."

The details of estate development are too numerous for all of them to be gone into here. Suffice it to say, that very great savings can be effected in the cost of development and therefore in the cost of sites for small houses by:

1. Reducing length of roads.

2. Making roadways wide enough, and no more, for the traffic they have to carry.

3. Demanding only one main sewer for surface water and sewage, and allowing this and other public services to be located under the grass margins of roads.

4. Allowing several houses to be connected to the main sewer by one common drain.

5. Permitting greater elasticity in the materials used for building, and

6. Not insisting upon exact dimensions of rooms provided they are

well lighted, sufficiently ventilated, and have sufficient cubic contents in relation to the number of persons that will use them.

Since " Practical Housing " was written many experiments have been made in the direction of reducing the cost of estate development.

The best authorities reckon that under economical and efficient town planning methods the cost of estate development can be reduced to one-half or one-third of the expenditure incurred by the old method. In other words, under the new method any given amount of capital will develop two or three times as much land as could be dealt with under the old system. This means that in addition to reducing the cost of sites of small houses by economical town planning methods, we also encourage quicker development because, among other reasons, less capital will be required per acre for development, which is a great advantage to the landowner and will in many cases, if not indeed in every case, well repay him for taking less per acre for his land.

FINANCIAL ADVANTAGE OF QUICKER DEVELOPMENT.

Assume that the local authority has:

1. Provided adequate access.
2. Restricted building density to ten houses per acre.

At ten houses per acre four times as much land will be required to house any given population as would be needed if 40 per acre were allowed. That is to say, in any given period, four times as much land will be brought into a state of earning revenue. This accelerated rate of development will be still further hastened by the provision of adequate access as compared with land without proper means of communication. By adequate access is understood motor-bus or tram service on direct roads. An enlightened landowner working in co-operation with a progressive local authority will therefore develop his land far more quickly than the unenlightened owner, who prefers to wait until he can get a price for his land on the basis of 40 houses per acre. An average price for building land that has had nothing spent on it for roads or sewers, and which is marked out for development at 40 houses per acre, is £400. If the enlightened landowner only gets £100 per acre for his land before he has spent any money on it, he will yet realize a larger gross sum than the other because he will possibly, we may even say probably, develop twelve acres in the time it takes to develop one acre under the old system. That is to say, he gets the ground rents due to building development instead of only agricultural rents many years earlier than under the old method. Supposing the landowner we are speaking of has much land; having developed his first 100 acres much more quickly under the new method than he would have done under the old, he is now ready to start on the next 100 acres far sooner than would otherwise have been the case. Under the new method of town and estate development the price per acre realized for building land must be very much smaller than it used to be in order to make it commercially possible to give the people room to live decently, but the lump sum realized each year should be very much larger with a consequent advantage to the landowner. Large landowners will undoubtedly benefit financially from the new method, and it is they who are responsible for hemming in towns. Small landowners may not always benefit. In these cases some allowance may have to be made, and, as I said earlier in this chapter, each case must be dealt with on its merits. The chief and never-to-be-forgotten point is that the people must be given room to live decently.

LANDJOBBERS' PROFITS AND PROFESSIONAL FEES. THE OLD METHOD AND THE NEW.

By careful investigations in several different towns and districts, it has been ascertained that under the old system a house rented at 6s. 6d. per week, whether leasehold or freehold, carries a site value of about £60, and this does not vary with the size of its garden or yard. Ground rents do vary, but as low ground rents are better secured than high ground rents, they fetch a greater number of years' purchase, that is to say, the lower the ground rent, the more years' purchase, and the higher the ground rent the fewer years' purchase it will fetch, and therefore the capital value of the site always comes out at about the same figure. Under the old system there are 40 or more houses per acre. Take the lowest figure, 40, multiply it by £60 (the site value of a 6s. 6d. house) and we get £2,400 per acre, interest on which is paid by the tenants in their weekly rents. When this land was open fields, its value was £20 or less per acre, and when required for building, or rather land sweating, it was probably sold or leased on the basis of £200 to £400 per acre. In some cases, even more than £400 per acre is paid for undeveloped building land.

Say for Land	£400
Cost of by-law estate development, financing builders, etc., etc.	750
Profits and fees	1,250
	£2,400

These are fair average figures— £2,400 is by no means the highest ground rent per acre paid by tenants of small house property. The individual items given above will vary with differing circumstances, in which case one speculator will get more and another less, but the total result remains the same.

The item of £1,250 (profits and fees) plus the £380 increase in price of the land over agricultural value, does not all go to one man; it may be divided between two, three or more individuals. We are not concerned as to who gets the profits, we are concerned that the tenants of small house property get so little real value for the money they pay. Land whose original value is at the outside £20 per acre plus £750 for by-law estate development, financing builders, etc., making a total of £770, is sold or let to the tenants of small house property for £2,400. No wonder the poorer classes are so badly housed, and no wonder that those who share in this wholesale plunder strain every nerve to preserve the old system. No wonder they demand that town planning schemes shall contain as many houses as possible per acre, not, as they protest, in order to keep down house rents, but in order to keep up their profits. If decent housing is to be provided at reasonable rents on a sound commercial basis, these profits must be seriously reduced, but at the same time a good profit must be left for landowners and builders, or there will be no inducement to develop land, and a shortage in the supply of houses will result. Hence the necessity for quicker and more economical estate development, to compensate for the lower price of land.

If the methods advocated in this and the previous chapter are adopted, the cost of estate development should not exceed £180 per acre, even where contributions have to be made towards the cost of main arteries opening up cheap land. We can now arrive at the cost of sites for small houses under the new method, and compare it with the old. Land that was worth £20 per acre before a town planning scheme was proposed will show a good profit at £120.

	Per gross acre
Say for land	£120
Development	180
	——
Total	£300*

* Some so-called experts will say that it is ridiculous to suggest only £300 per acre for land and development. For Hereford garden suburb the actual cost of land and development was £242 per acre. See Chapter V, example 3.

Divide £300 by ten houses per acre and the cost of a site for a 6s. 6d. house is £30, which leaves a very handsome profit for the speculators, if these sites are sold at the present market price of £60 or thereabouts. There should be no difficulty in disposing of small house sites on these lines, because a house with a garden, producing the year round from one to two shillings' worth of vegetables per week, is more valuable than a house with nothing but a back yard. It is not merely on hygienic and æsthetic grounds that garden suburbs are more attractive than monotonous by-law suburbs; it is on strictly economic grounds that garden suburbs have come to stay and will eventually supersede the old-fashioned extravagant methods, just as railways superseded the old mail coaches and motor vehicles are displacing those drawn by horses. I will not pretend that town planning properly administered will leave as much profit for the landjobbers as they have got in the past, but I do say most emphatically that where local authorities are reasonable in their requirements as to estate development and will co-operate with those who are willing to restrict the number of houses to ten or less per acre with adequate open space for their tenants, there will be a very comfortable profit for reasonable landowners and builders, and the poorer classes will be housed like human beings at rents they can afford, instead of being huddled together in places little better than cattle pens, as is the case at present.

Better living conditions at reasonable rents can only be obtained by putting an end to the extravagant profits that have in the past been got by land and building speculation, but if land and building developers will work with local authorities for the object of producing a better article at a reasonable profit, and if local authorities will on their side meet private enterprise whenever they can do so without interfering with practical efficiency, there will still be very comfortable profits for private enterprise, as well as more satisfactory results for the community.

THE SMALL INVESTOR AND TRUSTEE SECURITIES

The next question we have to consider is whether those who hand over their cash to the land and building speculators are justified by the soundness of the securities they get in supporting a system that is admittedly most deleterious to national physique and ruinously expensive for the ratepayers. In order to ascertain the answer to this question, we must examine the securities received by the investing public. Land and building speculation depends upon:

1. Selling houses to the small investor.
2. Borrowing on mortgage.
3. Selling ground rents.

1. Small houses are often sold to the small investor for less than they cost to build. They are, however, subject to a ground rent, and if the small investor realized how grossly the ground rent or site value has been inflated, he would not be so pleased with his bargain. The purchase is made attractive to him by selling the house below cost, but the apparent loss on the house is recouped by the speculator many times over by the profit on the land. This arrangement entirely misleads people who have had little or no experience of financial operations large or small. They think because the house itself is sold to them below cost that they are getting a great bargain. They do not realize that the liability incurred by them for ground rent makes their bargain a very bad one. The speculator who sells to them, whilst posing as a philanthropist, makes a fortune out of the mistakes of his credulous customers. These fortunes do not often come to the builder who actually does the work; they generally go to men in the background who finance the builder. In every large town there are plenty of examples to be found of fortunes that have been made in this way out of the savings of the people. The small investor generally borrows two-thirds of the purchase money on mortgage at 4 per cent, thereby getting $7\frac{1}{2}$ per cent on his equity, that is his percentage on the actual cash that he has to find himself. This return will continue for a few years, but it is very uncertain how long it will last. Small investors would be wiser to put their money into something that will bring them a regular 4 per cent or 5 per cent, than to risk it in a $7\frac{1}{2}$ per cent investment where they are liable at any time to have the mortgage called in at six months' notice, without any certainty of their being able to borrow elsewhere, in which case they may have to sell at a heavy sacrifice—a by no means uncommon occurrence. As a matter of fact, they are bolstering up with their hard-earned savings a system of estate development that condemns them and their class to living conditions which are generally admitted to be very far from satisfactory.

2. Mortgages on real property are classed as trustee securities, and little or no regard is given as to whether the property is really fit for human habitation. A great deal of trust money has of late

years been lost in this class of investments and it is high time
that those responsible for saying what is and what is not a trustee
investment, should take careful stock of recent happenings to
money invested in mortgages on small house property with a view
to deciding whether this class of security should any longer be
accepted without question as a trustee investment. Much more
careful inquiry than is at present thought necessary ought to be
made into the condition and arrangement of small houses before
money is lent on mortgages upon them, and those responsible for
recommending such investments should be held liable for loss
incurred, unless it can be proved that every reasonable precaution
was taken. This will seem to many lawyers and land agents a most
revolutionary proposal. I contend that it is only reasonable to judge
investments by their results. Mortgages on real property have resulted in heavy losses to people of small means who were advised
by professional men of indisputable standing that their money
was quite safe in a trustee investment. This is due to a custom that
may have been right when it first started, but which now needs
severely revising to meet the spirit of modern times. A few years
ago, people were not interested in the sanitary conditions of a
house, and so long as it was a house, that was all that mattered.
Nowadays it is the duty of local authorities to close and, if necessary,
demolish houses unfit for human habitation, and it is every day
becoming more and more recognized that houses built at 40 or more
to the acre, are not such as the people have a right to expect for the
rent they pay. This being so, the question as to whether mortgages
on small houses in congested districts should be any longer classed
as trustee investments ought to be very carefully reconsidered.
If land and building speculators were no longer able to borrow
on mortgage, unless their estates were developed in accordance
with modern ideas, there would soon be an end to the creation of
any more of those dreary and unhealthy suburbs which are a
disgrace to a civilized community.

3. SELLING GROUND RENTS. We are told quite freely by
those in the know that "The price realized for these by no means
represents their economic value, they are only a means of raising
money." They are, as has been seen, grossly inflated, compared
with what it cost the land and building speculator to create them,
and, therefore, it is only fair to warn the general public to be more
careful in future concerning this class of investment. It is true that,
to-day, they may be all right because the ground rent is being paid
by the tenant in his weekly rent. But the question is, how long

will this last? Garden suburbs are rapidly growing in popularity, and as tenants on these estates get far better value for their money, it is not unreasonable to anticipate that as town planning develops, old-fashioned small house property will become more and more difficult to let, thereby reducing the security for the ground rent.

Enough has been said to make it clear that the security for investments in small house property on the old lines is at least questionable, no matter whether the money be invested in buying houses, lending on mortgage, or in the purchase of ground rents. It should be equally clear that if land and building speculation on the old lines were no longer financed by the investing public, it would very soon collapse. The general public are constantly reviling the old system of town and estate development; the remedy is in their own hands. They have only to cease to invest in small house property, unless it is arranged and erected on what are known as town planning or garden suburb lines, and the land and building speculators will very soon provide what their customers ask for. As a matter of fact, I know of several landowners and builders who would have adopted garden-suburb methods long ago, if the landjobbers had allowed them to do so. There is yet another class who provide housing accommodation for the working classes, and that is the numerous provident building societies, which have done a great work in the last fifty years in assisting working men to buy their own houses. Unfortunately, their work originated under the old by-law system, and, consequently, there is often much to be desired in the arrangement of the land and houses they can offer. Societies of this sort should be among the first to take advantage of improved opportunities for their clients.

In dealing with this question of land and housing speculation, consideration has been directed to districts where the leasehold system prevails. In those districts where the freehold system is in force the detail methods of procedure are different, but general principles remain the same, and the total result is identical. Tenants of small houses get very poor value for the rent they pay, investors buy a grossly inflated investment, and the speculators go off with the profits.

SHORTAGE IN THE SUPPLY OF 6s. TO 4s. 6d. HOUSES

It is constantly said, and with a great deal of truth, that garden suburbs have not as yet solved the problem of housing the poorest classes of urban communities. The garden suburbs in this country that are already developed or nearly so were started before the

passing of the Housing and Town Planning Act of 1909, which
enables local authorities to limit the number of houses per acre
without paying compensation to the landowners. It follows that
when the land for these garden suburbs was bought or leased there
was no law to prevent land sweating, and therefore a purely
artificial price had to be paid for the land. Thanks to the fact that
the promoters of garden suburbs are satisfied with reasonable
profits, they have been able to give their tenants very much better
value for their money; but thanks to the high price of building land
created by the old system, they have not, except in a few special
cases, provided houses at 4s. 6d. per week, including rates.

Ordinary builders, on the other hand, have not of recent years
in any urban district that I have come across erected any houses
at all at 4s. 6d. per week including rates. In a recently published
pamphlet entitled "Lower Rates and a Better Birmingham," I gave
figures based upon an actual experiment showing that with land
at £100 per acre and development at £120 per acre, which is all
that is necessary for these very small houses, there is a 6 per cent
equity for the landowner, and an 8·4 per cent equity for the builder,
on 4s. 6d. houses at ten to the acre, where bricks are cheap and houses
are being built quickly in large quantities. But there is no likelihood
of the ordinary builder, under present conditions, erecting this
class of house. The reason is not far to seek. Under the by-laws
or under town planning schemes up to the present, the builder
is allowed a certain number of houses per acre quite irrespective
of the weekly rents he is going to charge, and he can without
breaking the by-laws or contravening any town planning regulations that have as yet been proposed, arrange for the maximum
number of houses allowed per acre of a type that will let for 6s. 6d.
per week including rates. The ordinary 6s. 6d. house is built on the
narrowest frontage allowed by the by-laws, and even if the other
dimensions of the house were reduced in order to let houses at
lower rents the regulations would not admit a greater number of
houses per acre than are now built and let at 6s. 6d. per week.
A 6s. 6d. house carries, as we have seen, a ground rent of 1s. per
week; a 5s. 6d. or 4s. 6d. house could not possibly carry as much,
and, therefore, with the same number of houses per acre at lower
ground rents per house, the speculator would obviously get a worse
return on his land. This being so, there is no inducement for the
ordinary builder in large towns to build any houses to let at less
than 6s. 6d. per week, the inducement is all in a contrary direction.
The object of land and building speculators is quite naturally to get

D 2

the most possible out of their land, and as the present regulations do not allow the highest profit on houses let at less than 6s. 6d. per week, these regulations must be altered so as to make them fit in with economic laws instead of ignoring them.

A further question to be considered is the advantage to the community as a whole of building down to low wages. This is more than doubtful; the only result of doing that would be to keep wages down, whereas our axiom should be to level up, not down. At the same time, there is a large class of highly respectable people, widows and others, unable to afford more than 4s. 6d. per week, and with no prospects of doing so for many years to come, who will have to live wretchedly with other families in a house beyond their means, or else live in a slum house, unless they are provided for on modern lines in decent surroundings. If such people are provided for decently at rents they can afford, the result may well be that they or their children will be encouraged and assisted to rise in the world. These people have at least as much claim on town planners and housing reformers as any other class of the community. Surely we ought to give them a fair chance and not condemn them to slum surroundings which tend to produce such unprofitable citizens. The effect of slum conditions upon the rising generation is disastrous, and it does not need great imagination to see how much money would be saved locally as well as nationally (cure of consumption, upkeep of prisons and reformatories, inebriates' homes, police force, the Insurance Act, etc., etc.) if better living conditions were obtainable by those who can only afford very low rents.

It is not impossible to remedy the shortage in supply of decent 5s. 6d. and 4s. 6d. houses, if it is desired to do so. By-law builders have of recent years, for the reasons stated above, erected very few, if any, such houses in urban districts, but it has been done on Harborne Tenants' Moor Pool estate with most satisfactory results.

Modern methods can be made to yield a fair profit for land-owners and builders on 6s. 6d. houses at ten to the acre. A 6s. 6d. house carries an average ground rent of 1s. per week, and therefore a 5s. 6d. house can bear 10d. per week for ground rent and a 4s. 6d. house 8d. per week. Ground rents of 1s. per week at ten to the acre give a weekly ground rent of 10s. per acre. Ground rents of 10d. at twelve to the acre will also produce 10s. per acre, and at 8d. per week fifteen houses to the acre will produce the same return on the land as ten at 1s. The remedy for the shortage of cheap houses, therefore, is to allow the builder twelve houses per acre, instead of ten, where the houses are let at not more than 5s. 6d. per week, including rates, and fifteen houses to the acre where they are let at 4s. 6d. per week including rates. Experts will object that no builder will guarantee a rent including rates, because rates may rise and they are beyond his control. This is a valid objection. I have begun by speaking of gross rents because they are more easily understood by the general public. In an actual town planning scheme net rents, not gross rents, would have to be cited. That is to say the general provision would be ten houses per gross acre at a net rent of 5s. or more per week exclusive of rates; twelve houses per gross acre at a net rent of 4s. 3d.; fifteen houses per gross acre at a net rent of 3s. 6d.

This badly needed improvement in existing regulations is provided for in general provision 17, sub-section cv of the model set of general provisions given in Appendix 5.

It may be objected that a general provision of this nature could not be enforced and the fact may be stated that restrictions on freehold land are very often ignored by the purchaser, in which case there is no remedy against him, unless it can be proved that he knew of them. The 1909 Act provides a direct remedy for this state of affairs. No one can pretend that he does not know of the restrictions on land in a town planning area, or at any rate if he is ignorant on the point it will be his own affair, and not in any way nullify the restrictions on the land. Town planning schemes, when approved by the central authority and not objected to by Parliament, have the same force as an Act of Parliament, and it becomes the business of those affected now or hereafter to know what these schemes contain. Ignorance of the law does not absolve a man from punishment for breaking it. Ignorance of the contents of town planning schemes will not enable a man to contravene their conditions with impunity. By means of agreements between local authorities and landowners under clause 34 of the model set of general provisions (Appendix 5) it will be quite easy to ensure the observance of general provision 17, subsection cv. and thereby encourage the erection of 5s. 6d. and 4s. 6d. houses on terms that will pay land and building speculators, as well as, if not better than, the erection of 6s. 6d. houses, without running any risk of this privilege being abused or resulting in an artificial and unintended rise of land values.

CHAPTER III. THE PREPARATION OF TOWN PLANNING SCHEMES.

BEFORE explaining the procedure under the 1909 Act, and what business points must be watched at each stage, it will be advisable to examine the old procedure and notice the principal difficulties in the way of preparing properly co-ordinated and economical town planning schemes.

1. For the purposes of municipal administration local authorities divide themselves into committees which do most of their work independently of one another, regardless of the fact that it must of necessity often overlap; especially in the case of town development. Different local authorities divide their committee work in different ways, so that it is impossible to make a list that exactly applies to every place, but the following is a fair indication of those committees which are most closely concerned with town development.

(a) Public works, whose duty it is to maintain and improve old streets, and sometimes to construct new ones, to construct sewers and supervise estate development and building.

(b) Tramways, which should include motor-buses, and on whom depends the provision of quick, cheap communication between the centre of a town or district and its suburbs. These communications should be provided to new areas after, and not before, they have been protected by a town planning scheme.

(c) Housing, whose duty it is to see that old insanitary houses are mended or ended, and that there is a sufficiency of new houses provided on sound and economical lines.

(d) Health, whose curative and preventive work gives them a very special interest in better housing at reasonable rents. For instance, much public money is now being spent on the cure of consumption. There is no surer way of preventing consumption than by arranging in town planning schemes for plenty of light and air round the new houses that are built.

(e) Parks, playgrounds, playing fields, allotments and small holdings. These essentials to good health and rational enjoyment cannot be provided in sufficient quantities unless the committee responsible is in the closest possible touch with any town planning that is being done for the district.

(f) Estates, whose duty it is to manage all property acquired by the local authority that is not allocated to any other committee.

Several other committees will, as the area is developed, need sites for their buildings which will be obtained much more cheaply, as well as being more conveniently arranged, if there is cordial co-operation with the town development committee.

Under the old system of municipal management each independent committee of the council does its own work, regardless of all the others, and very often there is considerable jealousy between them, so that if even one committee approaches another with a view to co-operation in the work and economy for the ratepayers, the committee approached bitterly resents what it considers to be impertinent interference, and no useful result is attained. For instance, if a town planning committee approaches a tramway committee with a proposal for a new road wide enough for trams on an independent track, the tramway committee has been known to say that trams have nothing to do with town planning, and rather than have its work interfered with in any way by another committee, it promptly brings out a scheme for running trams along an old and most inconvenient road to a new area long before that area has been protected from overcrowding by a town planning scheme. In the same way, a parks committee proposes the purchase of a piece of land at an exorbitant figure, rather than, as it considers, demean itself by ascertaining from the town planning committee whether there is not a cheaper and more convenient site available. A public works committee that, up to the passing of the 1909 Act, was responsible for town and estate development on the old lines, often resents the advent of new and better methods. If it does take this line and insist upon by-law streets and bedrooms all hope of better town planning and decent housing must be abandoned. Any number of examples might be given of this petty, but disastrous, retail muddling. Enough has been said to explain the lack of co-ordination in committee work, which is so largely responsible for extravagant town development and administration. This state of affairs has been so long in existence that it is very difficult to break down, but that it must be broken down if we are to get comprehensive and economical town planning will be evident to all thinking people. There is only one way of breaking it down and that is to federate the committees chiefly concerned with town development and call them together at regular intervals to vote on all important points of policy affecting the work of any two or more committees, such as: whether the construction of tramways should precede or follow the approval of town planning schemes; whether old roads should be widened or new ones provided; whether land should or should not be bought in advance of immediate requirements, and before it has gone up to famine prices. By this means and not otherwise can a general policy for town development be formulated and properly co-ordinated town planning schemes produced. It should be the duty of this federated town development committee to direct general policy and prepare the scheme. Detail administrative work would be left to the individual committees.

The finance committee whose duty it is to protect the pockets of the ratepayers can, if they will, give valuable advice and assistance to this federated town development committee. For instance, they should support proposals for advance purchases of land before it has gone up to an excessive price. They should resist any proposal to construct sewers or project tramways into a town planning area before the town planning scheme has been prepared, and they should see to it that the right of the ratepayers under the 1909 Act to one-half of the betterment due to town planning schemes is not thrown away by careless and thoughtless municipal administration. The avowed object of every finance committee is to keep down the rates, and therefore reasonable finance committees will support every proposal for the more equitable division of the cost of town development between ratepayers and landowners, than which there is no surer way of keeping down the rates. To put it shortly: sincere finance committees can greatly assist town development and help to effect many municipal economies if only they will take a long-headed view of the problems submitted to them.

The first business of a properly federated grand committee for town development on up-to-date lines would be to consider the procedure under the Housing and Town Planning Act, 1909, and the regulations laid down by the Local Government Board.

In chapter VII will be found various proposals for amending the Act and simplifying the regulations, but in this chapter we must deal with things as they are to-day and, in order to make clearer a very complicated business, I have divided the procedure into four main stages, and these four main stages have, where necessary, been sub-divided into steps. The Local Government Board regulations are most confusing and therefore in Appendix 4 is given an epitome of these regulations divided in the same manner.

The four main stages are:

1. Consideration as to advisability of preparing a scheme.
2. Application for permission to prepare a scheme.
3. Preparation of scheme.
4. Approval of scheme.

Much of the advice that follows as to what should be done and what pitfalls avoided at each successive step will, it is hoped, prove permanently useful even when the 1909 Act has been amended, and the regulations made more reasonable and workable.

FIRST STAGE
CONSIDERATION AS TO ADVISABILITY OF PREPARING A SCHEME

The first business is to appoint a committee. In several instances, local authorities have constituted the whole council, members of the town planning committee, and in small places especially this has its advantages. Where this is, owing to the size of the council, considered to be an unwieldy method, then a federated town development committee should be appointed to settle general policy, details being left to smaller committees. It will probably be convenient to at once appoint a sub-committee to prepare a report for the grand committee. This sub-committee should examine a correct map of the whole district, and study what developments are already taking place and to what extent these developments can be more adequately encouraged and controlled. They should also consider what new areas could be developed on modern lines, if they were opened up by the provision of adequate access from the centre of the town or district. They must also consider how far town planning provisions as to the number of houses to be allowed per acre, the open spaces and other amenities to be arranged for, will hinder development in one area and drive it into some other area, either in the district controlled by their own local authority or outside it. This information carefully collected and collated will enable the sub-committee to decide what areas within and without their district need the protection and encouragement that can be provided by a town planning scheme. This sub-committee will probably find that the only safe method is to include in their town planning area, all the undeveloped land in their district and possibly also some of the land outside it. Some of this land may appear to be too far out and not " likely to be used for building purposes " for the next fifty years, and it might on that score under the 1909 Act be ruled out by the Local Government Board, but in this connexion there are two points to be remembered, which make it impossible for anyone to be dogmatic as to what is going to happen on the outskirts of towns and even villages during the next fifty years:

1. The restriction of building density, if sufficiently drastic, will drive people further out to cheaper land, which is just what all

genuine reformers want, but they do not want this cheaper land ruined because there is no town planning scheme to protect it, and therefore, they will extend their schemes into the country as far as they can. It is not fair to the owner to restrict one piece of land and leave some other land, almost equally convenient for building, unrestricted. The owners of restricted land may be seriously injured by their unrestricted neighbours. To prevent this is one of the objects of the Act.

2. The policy of bringing the country to the town and the town to the country, which is the underlying idea of town planning, will soon result in small holdings being recognized (as indeed they ought to have been long ago) as an important constituent of all reasonable towns. Good cheap food is vital to the health of a community, and, by making small holdings part of a town, producer and consumer would be brought nearer together, greatly to the benefit of both parties, with this additional advantage, that these small holdings would help to ventilate the suburbs and keep them healthy.

In view of these and other considerations, it is safer to err on the side of including too much land than too little.

With regard to land that has been plotted and a few plots sold with houses already erected, it is certainly better to include it in the area. A little negotiation may produce very good results, especially remembering that although there is no money compensation in respect of the limitation of the number of houses to the acre, the local authority can, if it will, make considerable concessions in the cost of estate development and help the landowner in other ways in return for amenities provided by him. If the local authority meets owners in a reasonable way and negotiates with them on common-sense, business-like, give-and-take lines, results satisfactory to both parties will generally be arrived at. There will at first be the usual opposition to what is called new-fangled legislation, but gradually all reasonable owners (and most of them are reasonable if they are treated reasonably) will realize the benefits they can obtain under the 1909 Act as well as the concessions that are expected from them.

Having decided upon the area or areas, the development of which they wish to protect and encourage, the next business of the sub-committee must be to ascertain exactly what access exists already and what further access is needed in order to expedite development. It is obviously useless to arrange for good development of new areas unless steps are taken to speed it up. This will involve another careful study of the map and the contours of the whole district, as it is highly probable that adequate access to the new areas cannot be provided at a reasonable cost to the ratepayers without cutting one or more new main arteries through land that is already fully or partially developed. This can be done under section 54, sub-section (3) of the 1909 Act, which permits the inclusion in a town planning scheme of land needed for providing adequate access to the area. The Local Government Board has laid it down that their first inquiry (see stage 2) settles the boundaries of town planning schemes, and that this question cannot afterwards be reopened. It is, therefore, absolutely necessary at this early stage in the proceedings to consider the question of adequate access before deciding upon the boundaries of the area to be town planned.

To put it shortly, the sub-committee will have to consider how far it is wise to include:

1. All the undeveloped land in the local authority's area.

2. Land alleged not to be likely to be used for building purposes.

3. Land which needs including in order to protect the amenity of neighbouring land, which may or may not be in the area of the proposed scheme.

4. Land already built upon, through which access to the undeveloped district or districts will have to be provided.

5. Land divided into plots, some of which have been sold or in respect of which contracts have been entered into.

6. Land under the jurisdiction of neighbouring local authorities.

Having settled the boundaries of the town planning area or areas, the next thing to do is to contour the land, or—as it is more correctly described—make an altitude survey of the area. This survey may be made most accurately and expeditiously by means of a field instrument known as a tacheometer.* The contour lines should be plotted to show differences of five feet in level. This is the only method by which can be ensured the best possible gradients for main arteries. Town plans should be made to fit the site, and not, as sometimes happens, the natural lie of the land ignored when roads and even drainage schemes are being designed. "Don't do as the Romans did, cut straight roads across hills and valleys. Adjust your roads to the lie of the land; make your gradients as easy as practicable."†

* A map with accurate contour lines is much more useful than a model, as well as being far less expensive to prepare. It is impossible to make a model sufficiently exact, whereas a properly qualified surveyor can read contour lines quite easily and plan his roads in accord with them.

† Sir George Gibb at the International Road Congress, 1913.

Before finally deciding upon the line of main arteries and sewers, a special map should be prepared showing the various ownerships of the land. It may well happen, indeed it often does happen, that so far as the lie of the land and other existing conditions are concerned, there is not much to choose between one, two or three different routes for main arteries and sewers. In these cases, it will be wise, before deciding upon a route, to ascertain which landowner is the most reasonable in his ideas as to what profit he ought to make out of the scheme. Under the Local Government Board regulations, this ownership map is required as map No. 7, article XX, a very late stage in the procedure. It cannot be too strongly impressed upon town planners that there is great economy to be effected for the ratepayers by ascertaining ownerships at this first stage in the preparation of a town planning scheme. It will then be possible to arrange main arteries and other facilities where the best bargains can be made for the ratepayers, instead of leaving them at the mercy of an individual with a monopoly, as so often happens under the old system. It will also be useful, in negotiation with landowners, to know what income is being obtained from the land affected.

Even at this early stage there will often be cases where it is without question a great saving to the ratepayers to purchase provisionally one or more odd pieces of land at once. For instance, local authorities often pay for easements for sewers as much as the land is worth. It would obviously be much better to buy the land outright and give the ratepayers something for their money, instead of paying a landowner for the right to run a sewer across his land, thereby, at the public expense, improving privately owned land and at the same time paying full value for it, but not getting it. No private individual would think of doing such a thing; why should public bodies fritter away other people's money in this way? These purchases will have to be made subject to the approval of the council and the Local Government Board. That is no reason for not making them. A striking example of this is mentioned in the second illustration given in Appendix 1. Sewers, water pipes, etc. improve the value of land, and if local authorities are allowed to buy the land at its original price before it has been improved by public expenditure, the result will be a profit instead of a loss to the ratepayers. Other examples of the advantage to the ratepayers of taking time by the forelock, instead of putting up the price against themselves by improving other people's land before they buy it, will be given later on.

In most town planning areas the moment map No. 1 is published, it will be perfectly obvious that certain lands must be used for some special purpose, and when anyone is obliged to buy something the price always goes up to a fancy figure. By making a provisional bargain before their intentions are public property, the town development grand committee or sub-committee will secure what they must have at its natural price, instead of having to pay a fancy figure later on. Municipal land purchase, carried out with care and discretion, is a useful check on private land speculation, which has in the past done so much harm to this and other countries. The landjobbers' party, whose policy is to wait until the price goes up before buying land for the ratepayers, will denounce the policy recommended above and all sorts of wild talk will be indulged in. Town planners must not be deterred by this from doing their duty to the community whose interests they are elected to protect. It may make them unpopular at the moment, but sooner or later, it will be recognized that they were right.

In connexion with some town planning schemes there may be other steps that must be taken before anything is made public. It is not possible here to go into every detail, but emphatic attention should be drawn to the necessity for absolute secrecy until the ratepayers have been protected as far as it is possible to protect them under the Act and regulations as they stand. If this policy is not adopted the landjobbers will be on the war path to make as much as they can for themselves, which is exactly what has happened in the past, and which should, by means of town planning, be put a stop to in the future. Town planning in itself is no royal road to better and more economical town development. It all depends upon the spirit in which the Act is administered. As a matter of fact, town planning has often proved by no means beneficial to the community, although it has been very profitable to private speculators. The success or failure of this great movement depends upon the application of the power that has been given to public authorities, which by its own weight is apt to slide into the hands of professional and private interests. That is what we ought to try and prevent, and it is only by keeping our proposals strictly private as long as we possibly can, that this object will be attained. Successful town planning in this or any other country will not be achieved without the greatest foresight and discretion. Another essential to success is absolute loyalty to the ratepayers on the part of those responsible for administering the law. These conditions demand that before asking the council to pass a resolution that it

is advisable to make a scheme, and before making public even the
boundaries of the area to be dealt with, a great deal more shall be
done than is called for by the Local Government Board Regulations.
The council having passed a resolution deeming it advisable that a
town planning scheme should be prepared, we reach the second
stage.

SECOND STAGE
APPLICATION FOR PERMISSION TO PREPARE A SCHEME

The three important steps at this stage are:

(a) Public meeting of property owners interested in the area.

(b) Town development committee's report to the council and
debate thereon.

(c) Local Government Board inquiry into the application for
permission to prepare a scheme.

SECOND STAGE—FIRST STEP
(a) PUBLIC MEETING OF OWNERS

At this meeting an explanation should be given of the boundaries
of the area and why they have been chosen. It will also help the
owners, if the lines of main arteries are indicated approximately.
A general description of what town planning really means would
not be out of place. At the same time, it must be made quite clear
that the local authority is at this stage in no way bound by any of
its proposals, as to main arteries or other details of the scheme that
may be indicated. All that is to be definitely settled at this and the
two following stages is the boundaries of the area. The Local
Government Board regulations do not say that any information shall
be given to property owners at this stage, beyond the question of
boundaries. At the same time, they do not forbid it, and town
planners will find it very helpful if at this public meeting they
publish as much information as they safely can, especially with regard to main arteries. They can then invite landowners to submit
plans for the development of their estates on economical town
planning lines. This is a point of first-rate importance. Up to the
present there has been very great reluctance on the part of some
officials to give up their old extravagant notions, as to what is
needed in the way of roads and drains for purely residential estates.
Every one who has given the slightest attention to the subject is
aware that garden suburb development at ordinary rents cannot
be made a sound business proposition for the builder, unless local

authorities will allow economies on their present development practice. This means, among other things, less expenditure on such costly items as kerbs and gutters. They must recognize the great general principle that light and air are cheaper, as well as more essential to health, than immaculate kerbs and gutters, but the builder cannot afford more of the former, unless he is released from some of the costly obligations with regard to the latter. It is perfectly feasible to provide an efficient and serviceable by-road much more cheaply than is done at present. If this fact is recognized and acted upon by the local authority, and if landowners are invited and encouraged to submit development plans of their estates on these lines, we shall begin to get improved suburbs.

Each estate is different from its neighbour and must be treated differently, if the best is to be made of it. Building land varies greatly in its quality and suitability; it is up and down and in and out. A development plan suitable for one estate will be ridiculous for another. We need a variety of ideas, not a stock scheme, regardless of hills, valleys and other natural characteristics. In town planning there must be variety and also elasticity, and, therefore, owners and agents should be encouraged to submit plans of their individual estates. It is only by preparing plans that owners can ascertain with any degree of certainty how the development of their estates on economical town planning lines will work out per acre, and without that information they cannot wisely agree to the number of houses per acre or any other conditions in the scheme. It will, therefore, expedite matters if these individual estate plans are got out in the rough and discussed with the local authority as soon as possible, and owners who have only worked on the old-fashioned lines will be surprised at the economies to be effected by rational town planning.

Out of these separate estate plans is pretty sure to arise one or more cases where an exchange of land between adjoining owners would be most beneficial to both parties. This is one of the many benefits conferred on landowners by the 1909 Act in return for restricting the number of houses per acre and every pains should be taken by the local authority to bring owners together in these cases and see fair play between them for the mutual benefit of all concerned.

Another means of making town planning and garden suburb development an attractive business proposition for landowners and builders is to provide the essentials to quick building development, such as adequate access to the area town planned, which implies:

1. Direct main arteries with the easiest possible gradients, on which should be run, in the first instance, at any rate, a service of motor-buses—not trams.

2. Proper drainage facilities;

3. And, of course, an adequate supply of water, gas and electricity.

The new method of development, if carried out on genuine lines, means a smaller percentage of profit for land and building speculators than was obtained under the old method, and, therefore, we must as a "quid pro quo" do everything possible to expedite development of the new area so that speculators may get a quicker return on their outlay. This principle of smaller profits and quicker returns is, as I pointed out in "Practical Housing," one of the main principles of genuine town planning. Here again, there is the difficulty, familiar to all reformers, of persuading the old school to forsake their old methods. They are constantly spending very large sums upon improving communications according to by-law regulations, without getting any return on their expenditure of public money. On the contrary, the ratepayers generally lose heavily by the transaction; but when it comes to a proposal for encouraging quick development on good lines, they object to spending public money a few years in advance of the return, which, in this case, is bound to come very soon. These old stagers do not understand that in public life as in business, THE TRUE ECONOMISTS ARE THOSE WHO KNOW WHEN TO SPEND AS WELL AS WHEN TO SAVE. They say they are in favour of town planning, but they miss the whole essence of it, which is to look ahead, and, thereby, save large sums for the future while spending the least possible in the present. It costs very little to design in advance, and the immediate expenditure is very small compared with similar work on the old lines, whereas the return to the public on their expenditure in a very few years' time will be most satisfactory.

Adequate access must be provided in order to secure quick development, so as to make decent housing pay. But neither this nor any other concession must be made by the local authority until agreements have been signed by the landowners, and the ratepayers' interests fully protected. Consult owners and others on every conceivable point, but do not give away the ratepayers' position by making concessions without getting a "quid pro quo." On the question of adequate access, it will be wise to consult practical men outside the council house. No reasonable being will contend that all the brains of a community are concentrated in its municipal buildings. Some even dare to think that the greater freedom of general practice in surveying and architecture produces more originality and initiative than daily attention to the restrictions of red tape. It must be an advantage to the community to get as many brains as possible to work on town planning, and, furthermore, if the local authority shows a genuine desire to co-operate as far as it can with private enterprise, negotiations as to the number of houses per acre, and many other vital points, will be much easier, and the results more satisfactory, than if town planning is administered in the narrow spirit of our discredited by-law system. By inviting the co-operation of private enterprise at this, the earliest possible moment, a greater variety of ideas will be obtained and there will also be many opportunities of hearing from practical men what concessions are necessary in the cost of road-making, drainage, etc., in order to make decent housing at reasonable rents a sound business proposition for landowners and builders, and the best way to achieve this is to invite a public competition of plans for the area. By this means, the council will get a variety of ideas without being committed to any of them, and it will show a sincere desire to co-operate with all concerned.

Decent housing and the necessary amount of open spaces can be provided without any cost to the ratepayers, and with most satisfactory results to both landowners and builders if red tape yields to common sense.

SECOND STAGE—SECOND STEP
(b) COUNCIL DEBATE

At this stage, the first points for the council to decide are whether they will authorize the town development committee to apply for permission to prepare a scheme, and if so, what shall be its boundaries. A general outline of the scheme must be given similar to that given to the public meeting of owners explaining clearly that, except the boundaries, all the proposals are of a purely tentative character and only made with a view to showing what might be done if a scheme were made. If any provisional purchases of land have been made, these should be mentioned; but no action can be taken on them by the council, because obviously it would be ridiculous to definitely purchase land for the purposes of a scheme that has not yet been prepared.

E

If the proposal to arrange a public competition of plans has been well received at the owners' meeting, then this is the time to ask the council to approve of such a competition, subject, of course, to the Local Government Board giving permission to prepare a scheme.

SECOND STAGE—THIRD STEP
(c) APPLICATION TO THE LOCAL GOVERNMENT BOARD FOR PERMISSION TO PREPARE A SCHEME AND LOCAL GOVERNMENT BOARD INQUIRY.

Article VIII of the regulations, sub-section (a), lays it down that, with a great mass of other information, there shall also be sent '' a general description of the scheme.'' It is obviously impossible to describe a scheme that has not been prepared. On the face of it, this regulation is ridiculous.

The date of the application for permission to prepare is very important, because under section 58, sub-section (2), no compensation will be paid for any building erected after this date that turns out later on to be in contravention to the scheme. It is, therefore, advisable to make this application as soon as possible, but at the same time, it is not fair to builders nor in the interests of the ratepayers to make it too soon, because after it is made, and until the scheme is approved, development in the area will be at a standstill, since no one will know for certain what they can do and what they must not do. It is against everybody's interests to stop all development in an area for a longer period than is absolutely necessary.

We are now ready for the Local Government Board inquiry. In one instance, that of Rochester, relating to a very small area, the Board were unable to give the authority asked for, as the land was for the most part held by the Secretary of State for War and, being Crown land, could not be included in a town planning scheme. With this exception, there has never been much question as to giving permission to prepare a scheme. The only question has been as to whether any land inside the boundary prescribed by the local authority shall be excluded from the scheme. It has been ruled out of order to discuss before the Board's inspector any details of the proposed scheme, the only question at this stage being what land, if any, shall be excluded from the area. Owners who have spent money on development in the old style or have entered into contracts on those lines will not unnaturally ask to have their land excluded from the scheme, and where this can be done without in any way interfering with the objects of the scheme, it is probably the fairest and simplest thing to do, but where the exclusion of land might in any way interfere with intercommunication, or otherwise injure the rest of the scheme, then justice to these owners can be met by allowing them rather more than the general average of houses per acre, in order to compensate them for their expenditure under the by-laws. In no case should undeveloped land, on which no money has been spent, or concerning which no building or development contract has been entered into, be excluded from a scheme. The only object an owner of such land can have is to endeavour to escape from his obligations under the Act, and it is obviously unfair to give any owner preferential treatment of this sort, no matter how rich and influential he may be.

When the Board has given permission to prepare a scheme and has defined its boundaries, it will at last be possible to get to work in earnest on the preparation of the scheme, towards which, if the above suggestions have been carried out, a good deal of preliminary work will have been done.

THIRD STAGE
PREPARATION OF SCHEME

At this stage there are four important steps:
(a) Meeting of persons desiring to be heard.
(b) Settling final plan and contents of scheme.
(c) Meeting of property owners.
(d) Report to Council and Council debate on scheme.

THIRD STAGE—FIRST STEP
(a) MEETING OF PERSONS DESIRING TO BE HEARD

This should be the most important and the most useful step in the whole procedure. It gives wise local authorities an opportunity of hearing all shades of opinion on the various knotty points that are bound to arise in every scheme of any importance. This meeting is supposed to include only owners of property in the area and their agents. It should include doctors, surveyors, architects, builders, the trades council and other ratepayers interested in the subject. If there has been a competition of plans, this is the time to discuss them, not with any idea of this meeting deciding which is the best—that must be left to the assessor—but with the object of eliciting ideas and criticisms which should be extremely useful to the town development committee in the preparation of their scheme, and with this great advantage, that the committee need not, indeed should not, commit themselves to any decision. Such a meeting as this will not appeal to one type of official mind, because it means a lot of trouble, and, of course, there would be cranks present, endeavouring to take up the whole time of the meeting, who would have to be kept within reasonable bounds. But the work in hand is so complicated and so important, that no pains should be spared to collect ideas from every possible source, which ideas should after this meeting ALL be carefully considered and sifted by those responsible for preparing the scheme. It stands to reason that in large towns there must be many men unconnected with the council house, whose advice and assistance would be most useful. Their advice should be sought. It is stupid not to make use of them in the public interest.

There will be much for this meeting to discuss, such as the just apportionment of the cost of main arteries amongst the various landowners benefited. It is quite conceivable that one landowner might have the whole, or at any rate, the greater portion of his land taken up by a main artery, and an adjoining owner, who benefited quite as much from the means of communication provided by the main artery, might have land fronting on to minor roads only. It would be obviously unfair to throw the whole cost of the main artery on to the first landowner and let the second go free. This meeting might usefully discuss the " degree of benefit " obtained by each landowner with a view to deciding how to apportion the cost of the main artery between them.

Another most important point is at what date the local authority should construct main arteries. Until this is done, owners will not be able to develop their property, and the local authority will, therefore, get no increased assessable value. It would, therefore, seem wise for the main artery to the centre of the area to be constructed immediately, not in its entirety but just so much as, and no more than, is necessary to give access to the area in the manner described in Chapter IV. Other main arteries might be constructed in their turn as and when it becomes advisable to do so; but circumstances with regard to this very important question will vary so much in different schemes that no general rule can be laid down. The matter should be most thoroughly discussed at this meeting of persons desiring to be heard.

Another point is the date at which roads constructed by the landowners should be taken over and maintained by the local authority. This varies in different places, and there seems no reason on this point to depart from the local practice under the by-laws. Where there is no definite local practice to go by, it would not be unfair to take over and maintain roads and drives made by owners, when seventy to eighty per cent of them have been built up, but this is clearly a point for discussion at this meeting of persons desiring to be heard.

Another matter for discussion is the number of houses to be allowed per acre. This cannot be wisely settled without knowing the value of land in the area, and what it will cost to develop it. If plans of individual estates have been prepared and discussed as suggested earlier in this chapter, full information will be available as to the cost of estate development and it should not be very difficult for the local authority to have ascertained, before this meeting takes place, what income was being earned by land in the area before a town planning scheme was proposed. In this connexion, it must always be remembered that no town planning scheme will be worth having unless it is based on a reasonable price for the land, and a reasonable cost for estate development. The fabulous rises in the price of land that have taken place hitherto, when agricultural land has been converted into building land, must not continue if there is to be any hope of genuine improvement. They are very largely at the root of all our difficulties.

It may well arise that in designing new arteries, existing properties may be divided in two, that were previously all in one. It may also happen that, by the diversion of a road, front land is turned into back land and vice versa. This may give an unfair profit to one owner and cause unfair loss to another. It may also happen that some particular landowner badly needs a piece of land belonging to a neighbouring landowner, which this latter landowner is willing to exchange for some of the former's land. In these cases, the remedy is to arrange an exchange of land, or, as it is generally called, a re-distribution. This meeting of persons desiring to be heard provides a favourable opportunity for discussing these re-distributions, which, if arranged fairly, will benefit both owners, as well as easing the approval of the scheme. General provision number 28 (see Appendix 5) gives the local authority power to deal with this very important matter.

The following illustration shows the benefit to owners of these re-distributions:

PLAN Nº 1   PLAN Nº 2

Berliner Straße

Berliner Straße

H

H

F

F

Brook

E C K A B

THE BRIDGE
BUILDING

E C K A B

D   D

D   D

THE EFFECT OF SMALL RE-DISTRIBUTIONS*

An example by Dr Busselberg and Government Building Surveyor, A. D. Spannuth, Charlottenberg.

" The following is a striking example of the advantage that neighbouring landowners obtain from re-distribution schemes, carried out under the general supervision of the local authority.

" Plan No. 1 shows land divided into several ownerships—A, B, C, D, E, F.

" So long as the owners were left to themselves they could not agree, and among other things, the street K was originally designed to follow the dotted lines as shown on Plan No. 1, thereby seriously reducing the value of A's property. The land as a whole was kept out of the market for building purposes, owing to each individual plot not being suitable for building, and the owner F seriously injured the general lay-out by treating the whole of his land as facing on to Berlinerstrasse and leaving street K with nothing but back buildings.

" The brook, dividing property A and B, gave a very awkward boundary, and, as already mentioned, A had not sufficient building depth on his land for a long way down street K from Berlinerstrasse.

" We (Dr Busselberg and A. D. Spannuth) took the matter up, and brought the owners into agreement with each other with the following results:

" The brook was acquired by A at a very small cost, and A and B agreed on a give-and-take boundary. The position of the street K was arranged so as to give A sufficient building depth along the whole length of the street, and also some frontage on to Berlinerstrasse. The neighbouring owner B did not lose by the transaction; on the contrary, without any expenditure, he obtained a straight boundary making his land more convenient for building. The arrangement provided a more open form of building, thereby increasing the value of the buildings erected, and the increase of building land available resulted in the cost of the street works being divided among a larger number of owners, so that the cost of development per square yard of building land was reduced. In addition to the longer frontage on Berlinerstrasse, it was made possible to develop the other western parcels of land more favourably. The boundary between the lands of E and C, as it was before the re-distribution, cut through building land (see Plan No. 2) in a very awkward way. We arranged for C to acquire some land from E, which to E was only back land, but to C could be worked

* Translated from an article in " Staedtebau."

in with his front land, and the transaction was to the benefit of both parties in this way: that whilst the land was in E's possession it was only back land of very different value from that of the front land, by transferring the land to C, who could use it with his front land, it became far more valuable, and C therefore could afford to pay E more for the land than its value to E.

" Plan number 2, shows the finished scheme as arranged by us."

It will not be possible to transact all the business that ought to be transacted by those interested—and not merely left to officials—at one meeting of persons desiring to be heard, but there is nothing in the regulations to prevent several meetings being held, and it is most desirable that, where necessary, this should be done, in addition to which it will no doubt be advisable to have several private conferences with individual owners, in order to obtain their hearty co-operation with the scheme by showing them that where it is just to do so the local authority is willing to give as well as take. Local authorities will not get the best results unless they are prepared to give as well as take. On the other hand, they must not give away important concessions, such as new roads, trams or sewers, without getting something substantial in exchange.

THIRD STAGE—SECOND STEP

(b) Settling final scheme including the map and general provisions.

A model set of general provisions, of which the most important is the restriction of building density will be found in Appendix 5. These general provisions must include road cross-sections.

RESTRICTION OF BUILDING DENSITY AND CONTROL OF THE CHARACTER OF THE BUILDINGS

If a local authority is willing to provide for quick development on conditions, it should not be difficult to agree with a majority of the landowners for good development, because by this method of procedure there are very substantial concessions for landowners in return for what is wanted from them. No town planning scheme that allows an average of more than ten houses per gross acre except for a limited number of cheap cottages can be considered really satisfactory, because there will not be sufficient room for allotments, play-grounds and playing fields. Those who co-operate with progressive local authorities in the business of decent housing at reasonable rents will gain enormously from the fact that their property will be more attractive than the old-fashioned sort, and, therefore, will let or sell more readily, a very important matter to those who have not got unlimited capital to work with.

In the lay-out of small house estates, the gardens to each house should not be made too large, because the average man will not cultivate a large garden, and as he cannot afford to pay some one to do it for him large gardens to small houses will, many of them, become mere rubbish heaps. It is far better to arrange small gardens to each house and provide allotments for those who want them and will therefore cultivate them. Small houses must not be set back too far from the road. Front gardens are of little use to the poorer classes. Vegetables can be grown at the back, but are not attractive in the front.

With regard to the houses themselves, theoretical by-laws must not be allowed to interfere with the provision of proper light and air to each bedroom and sitting room. By-laws must, where necessary, be abrogated and narrow roadways and other economies allowed, so as to make building frontage cheap, and then builders will be only too glad to provide wider fronted and shallower houses. Where this is done a bedroom, 7 ft. 6 in. high will be much lighter and more airy than the by-law bedroom, 8 ft. 6 in. high, and, the building cost being less, the houses can be let at lower rents. By observing instead of ignoring economic laws it is by no means difficult to make light and airy bedrooms a better business proposition than the old-fashioned dark rooms which the speculative builder is now obliged by the regulations to provide. Regulations are made to be evaded in the spirit, if not in the letter, but if town planning is made profitable, as it can be, there will be every inducement to adopt it. Red tape is very difficult of removal, but unless local authorities do manage to free themselves from the trammels of the by-laws, they will not produce town planning schemes that are in practice successful. If we want to succeed, we must make good housing pay better than bad housing and the way to do that is to study economic laws and work with them instead of depending on stringent regulations.

The final map should provide for:

1. Adequate access to the area.
2. Public parks, play-grounds and playing fields.
3. Sites for council schools, hospitals, public baths, free libraries, churches, chapels, theatres, concert halls, police and fire stations, tramway and omnibus depots, electric supply stations and sub-stations, and, if convenient, corporation tips.

4. Sites for offices and shops.
5. Sites and facilities for works and warehouses.
6. Small holdings and allotments.

These items will not all be required in every town planning area, there will be cases where some of them are specially excluded, but it is necessary for us to consider all of them in a general way.

1. ADEQUATE ACCESS

The first essential to the success of any scheme is to provide, without delay, main arteries, sewers, and trams or motors, so as to encourage quick development, but these concessions must be made part and parcel of the scheme itself in order to protect the amenities of the area and to preserve the right of the ratepayers to one-half of the betterment due to this expenditure of public money.

The opinion has been expressed, by those who are supposed to know, that a scheme is safe as soon as application has been made for permission to prepare a scheme. This opinion is based on section 58, sub-section (2), which says that " No person shall be entitled to compensation on account of any building erected or contract made after the time at which the application for authority to prepare the scheme was made to the Board." This has been interpreted to mean that the Corporation can veto overcrowding and put a stop to the old, bad, and extravagant way of building houses, the moment there is a town planning scheme in preparation. This is an entirely mistaken opinion. As long as a builder complies with the by-laws no local authority can reject any by-law plan, until the town planning scheme is complete, and has been approved by the Local Government Board and by Parliament. All they can do is to warn the builder that if the houses he proposes to put up contravene the scheme when completed, they can, under section 58, sub-section (2), have them pulled down without being liable to the owner for compensation, and obviously no one knows what a town planning scheme will contain until it has been prepared and approved. Section 58, sub-section (2), protects the local authority from having to pay compensation, if certain events happen, but nothing can definitely prevent overcrowding or any other evil, until a town planning scheme which does this has been approved. Birmingham was grossly misled on this point with regard to her first two town planning schemes, and as these are often held up as models for other places to copy, it is necessary to warn town planners not to repeat the mistake. It was on the strength of the mistaken opinion which has just been explained and refuted, that sewers were constructed and tramways projected independently of these two town planning schemes, and before they were completed. This procedure has the two-fold disadvantage of giving concessions to landowners in town planning areas without getting any agreement from them, such as undertaking not to build too many houses per acre, and, further, of depriving the ratepayers of their claim under the 1909 Act to one-half of the betterment due to these concessions.

There is a tendency in some quarters to make light of sections 58 and 59, which deal with betterment and compensation and to use them as little as possible. This is a great mistake. These two sections can, in the hands of honest and capable administrators, be made very useful in bargaining with landowners and securing fairer terms for the ratepayers than have been obtained in the past. They are admittedly a little complicated, but the fact that they are there is a very strong card in the hands of the local authority.

Communication for a town planning area may be considered under two heads:

1. Radial access, that is, direct communication between the centre of a town and its suburbs.

2. Ring access, that is, communication between two suburbs by means of a ring or encircling road.

Radial access is, as we have seen, essential to the success of town planning schemes. Ring access is a great convenience, but its importance is not to be compared with the importance of radial access.

In Liverpool there are some very fine examples of ring roads, which are a great addition to the neighbourhood, but this idea must not be carried too far. There is a case, not in Liverpool, where radial access was not provided to a town planning area, because those responsible were spending so much on ring communication that they had nothing left for radial access.

To sum up the situation with regard to adequate access:

(a) Nothing must be done or promised except as part of a town planning scheme protecting the area from overcrowding and securing half the betterment for the ratepayers.

(b) It is better and cheaper to cut new main arteries through back land than to widen old roads.

(c) As soon as the scheme is approved sufficient money must be spent at once by the local authority on providing direct radial access to the area in order to encourage quick development.

(d) Radial access is many times more important than ring communication. Radial access is a necessity, ring communication is more or less of a luxury.

2. PUBLIC PARKS, PLAY-GROUNDS AND PLAYING FIELDS

The advocates of municipal house building are now advising the expenditure of large sums on the purchase of open spaces. They say that " Large cities must spend more and more on parks and open spaces"; they also point out that " Poor Law authorities can put something like an actual cash value on the benefits which public parks confer on an urban population in the way of improved health." The latter argument is perfectly sound, but where building density has been properly restricted very little, if any public money will be needed for parks and playing fields. It is not wise to advise large cities to spend more and more on open spaces; on the contrary it is grossly unfair that the ratepayers should spend large sums of money on the purchase and upkeep of these places in order that private individuals may overcrowd their land. There are many instances familiar to all of us where the laying out of a public park has immensely increased the value of building land adjoining it. This is neither fair nor reasonable. Private individuals should not in this way be allowed to reap the benefit of public expenditure. They should be called upon to themselves provide the amenities that increase the value of their estates.* In a well ordered town planning scheme, this will be provided for, thereby avoiding any charge on the rates. In practice, a plentiful supply of small open spaces carefully distributed is far more valuable and useful to the community than one or two large public parks, especially to the little children. The economic wisdom of providing for the healthy recreation of children of all ages and classes is becoming more and more recognized every day. At the same time, large public parks are undoubtedly an addition to any neighbourhood and where landowners are willing to give such places to the town or district they should be accepted, but the ratepayers should not spend much, if indeed any, money on their purchase, lay-out, or upkeep. The open greens or commons in the suburbs of London, with a few posts and chains round them are

* See excerpt from Marshall's " Principles of Economics," Appendix 12.

much more valuable to the health of the people and their children, and they are infinitely cheaper in lay-out and upkeep than the ornamental gardens with high, unclimbable iron railings round them that are so familiar to us in the provinces. By all means, let us have a few bright flowers here and there, but we must not overdo it. There are so many things essential to the public health for which public money is urgently needed that we cannot afford to throw away large sums on mere show. If any parks are provided, sites for hospitals should be reserved adjacent to them.

3. SITES FOR PUBLIC BUILDINGS AND LAND PURCHASE IN ADVANCE

No town planning scheme can be considered as in any way complete that does not provide sites for some at least, if not all, the public buildings that will be required when the district is fully developed. If this is arranged as part of the town plan, each building can be placed in the most convenient position for its purpose, instead of trusting to luck later on to find a piece of land in any odd place that happens to be available. Every committee at all likely to need a site should be approached as to its requirements and consulted as to what position would be most suitable. Another advantage is that by buying land before it has gone up to building value it can be got, comparatively speaking, for next to nothing. Some may object to these purchases in advance on the plea that it is not good finance to lock up public money in land that is not immediately required for the purpose for which it is bought. This objection falls to the ground if, as should be the case, the land is bought on the basis of its present earning capacity because it could then be left to its present use and would earn the interest and sinking fund on the purchase money until such time as it is required for the public building, or better still, the local authority might in some cases find it a convenience to the owner and tenant, as well as to themselves, not to purchase the land or disturb the tenant at the moment, but merely to arrange that the site shall be given up at a fixed price when required.

4. SHOPS AND OFFICES

As the population grows these business premises will arrange themselves in positions most convenient to customers and clients. All that the town planner has to do is to see that nothing in the general provisions of his scheme prevents shops and offices being built where they are needed, and also that they are not allowed to stop or impede the ventilation of dwelling-houses, nor must they take up space that is required for allotments, playgrounds, or playing fields.

5. WORKS AND WAREHOUSES

The ideal is to place these on the leeward side of the town, but in large towns it is not feasible to put all the factories in one place, the distances between dwelling-houses and workshops would be too great. At the same time, it should be possible to gather the dirty and smoky trades in that position, placing other trades in convenient areas round the towns. All areas allocated for factories should be provided with special facilities for cheap and good gas and electric light and power, and also with railway lines to the nearest goods depot. This saves wear and tear on the roads, as well as the cost of loading and unloading vans. Water communication must also be provided. With rising rates and the present congestion of railway goods traffic, canal reform has become an urgent national question.* No large industrial centre touched by a canal or navigable river should be satisfied unless its town planning schemes provide ample room for wide canals and commodious canal wharves in the manufacturing districts. The old school of municipal administrators seem to have prided themselves on putting as many difficulties as they could in the way of manufacturers. Progressive towns will see the advantage to themselves of doing all they can to encourage manufacturers to come to them and stay with them. The provision of every possible facility, including cheap power and light, as well as easy transit of goods in and out, should be recognized as one of the most important parts of town planning schemes.

The East Birmingham town planning scheme allocates land in a congested district for the use of factories ONLY. This has caused heavy claims to be made upon the Corporation and a memorial has been sent to Parliament asking for further inquiry to be made.

The contention is that the reservation of these lands for factories ONLY is a great hardship on the owners who could, it is said, make much more money by using it for housing. This complaint would not have arisen if excessive building density had not been allowed in the vicinity. At an average of ten houses per gross acre (many more are allowed in this scheme) land is not worth more for housing than for factories.

* See " Garden Cities and Canals," by J. S. Nettlefold.

Another way of avoiding claims for compensation is to allow no smoky or obnoxious factories in purely residential areas, but not to say that no houses shall be built in factory areas; at the same time the building density of small house property in factory districts should be less than in purely residential areas.

In the years to come owners of houses in smoky districts will find that their property does not let or sell so well as other property in healthier and pleasanter surroundings. This question of factory areas will be discussed further in connexion with the East Birmingham town planning scheme described in Chapter V.

6. SMALL HOLDINGS

Good cheap food is as important to the public health as good cheap housing. One of the items in the cost of food is the cost of transit, and, therefore, it should be produced as near to the consumer as possible. Belgium produces about twice as much cereals per cultivable acre as Great Britain, and she keeps almost twice as many cattle on each cultivable acre. This is due to her system of small holdings and excellent means of cheap and rapid transit.* In that small country manufacturing and agricultural districts are wisely interspersed, with the result that food is cheap and good, and, equally important, when manufacturing trades are bad and employment short, working men can earn enough to keep themselves and their families by working on the land. Another very great advantage of small holdings and allotments is that air spaces are provided without any cost to the community. On the contrary, rent is paid by the occupier, which, if small holdings are arranged in a businesslike manner, will more than cover interest and sinking fund on the purchase of the land. The old method of providing allotments is to wait until a small house district has been more than half-covered with building and the tenants are demanding allotments. The council then seeks about for cheap land that can be bought and let at a price that those wanting allotments can afford to pay, and that will not result in a loss for the ratepayers. That is to say, the council waits until land has gone up to building price or somewhere near it before thinking of allotments, with the natural result that even if it can get any land at a possible price, it cannot get nearly enough. Whereas by looking ahead and planning our suburbs as a whole at the outset, instead of in penny numbers, it is possible to satisfy the demand for small holdings and allotments

* "Fields, Factories and Workshops," by Prince Kropotkin.

without loss to the ratepayers. For instance, in the first town planning scheme, it was proposed to run a main artery right through the heart of the area which would have brought Quinton village within five miles of the centre of Birmingham (see Chapter V) thereby largely raising the value of the land at Quinton. It was ascertained that a farm of 130 acres, near the end of this artery was to be had for £60 an acre. This farm might have been cut up into small holdings and either left permanently in that state or later on used for something else. The purchase was made provisionally and as soon as it became publicly known, several offers were received to take the farm at once for small holdings at a profit to the ratepayers. This purchase was put before the Local Government Board in such a way that they felt themselves obliged to refuse it, and a most advantageous bargain was lost for the ratepayers by what a worthy councillor described as a trick (see Chapter VI). On this occasion the obstructionists won, but if town planners stick to their guns, the sins of the old school will find them out at last, and the ratepayers will come by their own.

No town is complete unless it has small holdings on its outskirts, with tongues of building running through them at various intervals. The instance quoted is only one of many cases where small holdings and allotments are quite feasible round large towns, provided the matter is considered in time.

Another advantage which should not be lost sight of is that by cutting up farms into small holdings and allotments, the assessable value is materially increased. There are great possibilities in this direction for a city like Birmingham, which has 20,000 acres of agricultural land within its borders. A farm at Northfield was being secured for small holdings by Worcestershire County Council when Birmingham decided to annex the district. The negotiations fell through, but the need remains.

THIRD STAGE—THIRD STEP
MEETING OF PROPERTY OWNERS

We are now ready for the second public meeting of owners and, if the advice given earlier in this chapter has been adopted, there should not be a great deal to discuss. The complete scheme must, of course, be explained, and questions invited on any point that has not been made clear, after which there will be a discussion. The bulk of the owners should by this time thoroughly understand how the scheme affects their pockets and, provided red tape has given way to reason, they will be satisfied that they can make a reasonable profit out of the development of their estates. There are pretty sure to be a few unreasonable owners, and these must be dealt with according to circumstances; their greed must not be allowed to injure the scheme.

THIRD STAGE—FOURTH STEP
(d) COUNCIL DEBATE

An estimate must be presented showing the total cost of the scheme, and how much it is proposed to spend during the first two or three years. The chief business on this occasion should be to show that the scheme will not be a burden on the rates. On the contrary town planning, properly administered, will effect very large economies (see Chapter IV). In some cases, it may be necessary to spend rather more at first than would have been spent under the old method in order to encourage quick development. But this outlay will be more than repaid in a very short time. Very little examination will satisfy all impartial persons that co-ordinated expenditure is, in the long run, far more economical than the old haphazard method of doing a bit here and there at any odd time, without regard to the rest of the district. The old method does not mention such large sums at any one time, but the demands come up very much oftener and, in the aggregate, they amount to a very large sum.

Attention may be directed to the fact that throughout the regulations we have been considering, most careful thought has been given to the protection of property. Owners and others have to be consulted at every turn, but at no point is it laid down that the general public must be consulted. Persons representing architectural or archæological societies are invited to make suggestions, but authorities on economics or hygiene are pointedly ignored. This is a great weakness for, although ancient monuments must not be neglected, it was in order to improve the living conditions of the poorer classes that the Housing and Town Planning, etc., Act was passed. It would, therefore, be well if at this council meeting some consideration were given to the effect which the proposed scheme is likely to have on the lives of the people. Property and rates always loom so large that too little attention is given to the great economic value of better health and rational enjoyment for the poorer classes. These improvements would not only reduce the rates, they would also result in a greater earning capacity of individuals for themselves and the community.

F

If the council pass a resolution that an order be issued under their seal formally making the scheme, and that application be made to the Local Government Board for their approval, a great mass of formalities must be attended to and maps, estimates, etc., etc., etc., sent to the Board. The council must then advertise the fact that they have submitted their scheme to the Board and that objections to the Locality's proposals as shown by the scheme may be made to the Board within one month, but these objections will not be considered unless they come from an owner of property in the area. Owners must be careful not to send in their objections too soon or they may be ruled out of order. They must also study carefully Articles XXIII, XXIV and XXVI of the Board's regulations.

FOURTH STAGE
APPROVAL OF SCHEME

At this stage, the business is more formal than real. For this reason: It is the practice of the Board to provisionally approve the scheme before they hold their inquiry. The foregoing regulations involve endless formalities, but when it comes to the inquiry, which should be an impartial tribunal, it is evident (from the fact that the scheme has already been provisionally approved) that objectors have very little chance of their proposals being really considered except on quite minor points. At the same time, it is a striking fact that in order to be heard at all at this inquiry, one must be a property owner. Who is to represent the poorer classes living in the area, and are their interests of no account? Are not healthy, cheerful and respectable surroundings for the rising generation at least as important to the community as ground rents?

There is one item in the regulations that is of paramount importance, i.e., 21 (b) (VII). '' Explanation of and reason justifying any suspension by scheme of general Act of Parliament, etc.'' That is to say an explanation of the necessity for abrogating by-laws in order to make better housing at reasonable rents a sound business proposition for landowners and builders. With regard to this explanation and reason for abrogating by-laws, the local and central authorities should satisfy themselves that:

1. The concessions in the cost of estate development are sufficient to make decent housing pay. If this is not done, the only effect of town planning schemes will be to stop development altogether in those areas where they apply and thereby create a house famine than which there is nothing more fatal to the public interest.

2. The regulations under the scheme ensure better as well as cheaper methods. That is to say, there must be sufficient light and air to every house and adequate allotments, play-grounds and playing fields.

3. Under the scheme concessions in the cost of estate development can only be granted to those landowners and builders who provide decent housing.

4. Landowners and builders willing to do their duty by their tenants cannot be harassed and obstructed as they have been in the past by antiquated officials or public men.

It is only by these safeguards that we can hope to break down prejudice and ignorance.

If the Board makes the slightest alteration or modification in the scheme submitted to them by a local authority, then their order for approval is issued under Article XXIV of the regulations. The local authority must then follow the procedure under Article XXV, i.e., advertise in a local paper or papers that the Board intend to approve the scheme, send a copy of the paper or papers to the Board and deposit the Board's draft order at a place convenient for inspection by any person interested, without payment of any fee, at all reasonable hours on any week for twenty-one days. When this period has expired and the local authority has received a copy of the order approving the scheme, it must advertise this definite approval and state that this final order of the Board may be inspected and explanation with regard thereto obtained on any weekday during three months after the date of the order. They must also transmit to the Board within fourteen days the statutory declaration and exhibits required by Article XXXI.

I have endeavoured in the foregoing pages to elucidate the procedure laid down by the Local Government Board and draw attention to the business points that need attention at every stage and step, in addition to which Appendix 4 gives an epitome of the regulations, but these regulations are so lengthy and complicated that it is advisable for local authorities to constantly consult the Board in order that they may avoid either doing anything that the Board dislikes or omitting anything that the Board requires.

" If for any reason after a town planning scheme has been completed it were to be found as the result of an appeal to the courts that the provisions of the Act had been neglected or exceeded in any way the whole scheme might be declared ineffectual."*

With regard to the regulations of the Local Government Board,

* See " Legal Aspects," by John L. Jack, Appendix 14.

it is not too much to say that they are far too complicated and throw a great deal of unnecessary expense on local authorities.

In Chapter VII proposals will be made to:

1. Put more driving force into the Act.
2. Remove brakes from the wheels of progress.
3. Give some protection to the general public.

When the scheme has been finally approved by the Board and all their formalities complied with, it has to be " laid before each House of Parliament for a period of not less than thirty days during the session of Parliament " (under section 54, sub-section (4) of the Act) " and if either of those Houses before the expiration of these thirty days presents an address to His Majesty against the draft or any part thereof, no further proceedings shall be taken thereon without prejudice to the making of any new draft scheme.''

CHAPTER IV. SAVINGS.

EVERY one is agreed that the old method of town development is most unsatisfactory, and hence the popularity of town planning or garden suburb development. But whether it can be made to pay is a question often asked by friends as well as foes of the movement. The answer is, " It has been made to pay," and what has been done once can be repeated and improved upon, but financial success depends upon town planning being controlled and administered by men who understand the work and are in hearty sympathy with it. If it is controlled or interfered with by men of the old school, failure, or at least imperfect success, is certain. There is no royal road to success in this reform any more than there is in others. Financial and general success depend upon careful attention to infinite detail; and in the preparation of town planning schemes at least as much consideration must be given to the general welfare as to private interests. In the previous chapters, references have constantly been made to the savings that can be effected for ratepayers, landowners and builders by town planning administration. In this chapter, it is proposed to make a general survey of these savings, and in the next chapter shall be given examples of successful and unsuccessful town planning schemes.

The first step necessary is to reduce the total cost of the work in hand and the second is to ensure a fair division of the cost between the public and private individuals.

The most convenient way of recapitulating the various savings that have been indicated in previous chapters will be to consider them under three heads:

1. General savings for all concerned.
2. For the ratepayers.
3. For landowners and builders.

1. GENERAL SAVINGS AND ADVANTAGES
(a) ROADS

It has been shown to be much cheaper to cut new main arteries through back land than to widen old roads or streets. It costs considerably less to construct a 100-ft. main artery with independent tram track in accordance with cross-section given in Appendix 5, than to make a 60-ft. by-law road with tram lines down the centre, and there is far more room and convenience for the traffic.

The most progressive local authorities will omit the tram track, at any rate in the first instance if not altogether; thereby effecting a further saving. In 100-ft. main arteries to new districts, 24 ft. of roadway is the maximum that should be constructed at the outset and when the traffic demands it a second roadway should be constructed. Do not widen the existing one. "Two roads of lesser width are better than one of greater width. It makes it possible to divide traffic."* A 24-ft. tar, pitch, or bitumen bound road constructed to carry the heaviest motor traffic is much cheaper in first cost and subsequent upkeep than an old-fashioned water-bound road with tram lines down the centre, and it benefits all classes of the community, not only those who ride in tram-cars.

Modern economy in road maintenance has shown that the greatest durability of surface is obtained when the traffic spreads itself over the entire width of the carriage way. Nothing keeps a road in such good order as the constant passage over it of the wheels, and the reason why the 18-ft. and 20-ft. highways of England are not in good order near the margins is simply because vehicles keep to the centre and the sides never get properly consolidated by the traffic. On a 16-ft. road, on the other hand, every time one vehicle passes another both drivers have to go close to the edge of the road, in which case, but not unless, there is plenty of room for two streams of traffic to pass each other at full speed. In some places, local officialdom may say that in purely residential roads where there is seldom more than one stream of traffic and the roadway is only 16 ft. wide, the traffic all goes down the centre, thereby wearing down the crown of the road, whereas if the roadway is wide, force of habit keeps drivers on their right side of the road. This may or may not be so in the case of 24-ft. roadways; it is certainly not so in the case of 18 or 20-ft. roadways; in the latter case, a single stream of traffic keeps on the crown of the road just as much as on the 16-ft. roadways and no sane man will assert that 24-ft. width of macadam is necessary for only one stream of traffic. Narrow roadways are a great advantage to the public, not only on the score of economy in construction and upkeep, but also from the public health point of view, because there is so much less dust, and even by modern methods of road-making it is doubtful whether this nuisance will be entirely removed. Road dust is more and more recognized as a fruitful source of many unpleasant and sometimes serious complaints. For further details on this subject see Appendix 5.

* Sir George Gibb at the International Road Congress, 1913.

The length of roadway is even more important than the width of carriage way. In spreading our populations over larger areas, we must not forget the cost of public services, such as sewers, water mains, gas mains and electric cables. The ordinary narrow-fronted by-law house is an abomination of desolation, but town planners must not go to the other extreme. The frontage to each house must, of course, be sufficient to ensure a plentiful and unobstructed supply of light and air to every window, but more than that is unnecessary and, economically speaking, most unwise. Excessively wide frontages not only seriously increase the cost of development for the land and building speculator, they also militate severely against the financial results of public services. The increased charge for interest and sinking fund on the greater length of mains and sewers, arising out of ignorant or careless planning, must result in higher rates, higher prices to the consumer, or smaller profits. An effective way of keeping down the length of roads required is to locate all parks and open spaces on back land instead of taking up valuable frontage.

Before laying down any road material the ground on which the road will rest should be well drained, levelled and rolled with a three-axle roller in such a manner that it has an equal consistency all over. It is not sufficient for road engineers to be satisfied with a foundation of so many inches of what is called hard core, they must see that, if a foundation of this nature is specified, the material used is all of equal consistency. The constantly recurring small subsidences in our road surfaces are obviously due to foundations of bad or unequal quality.

Any regulations or specifications that create a monopoly in road-making by confining road constructors to only one or two producers must put up the cost of road-making and in view of the large numbers of roads in various parts of the country that are all equally satisfactory, or, as some would say, equally unsatisfactory, it is most unreasonable to suggest that efficient roads can only be made with material from one or two sources.

(b) BRIDGES AND ARCHWAYS

The question of bridges must not be forgotten. By constructing an archway through an embankment or over a railway, it will often be found possible in town planning schemes to open up many acres of cheap land for the use of the community. The old ways of doing this work are far more expensive than modern methods. It therefore behoves all town planners to make themselves familiar, or insist that their experts shall know what there is to be known as to the use of ferro-concrete and other modern engineering methods in this and other countries.

(c) DRAINAGE

A very large saving is to be effected if only one sewer is demanded for surface water and sewage in accordance with the report of the Royal Commission on sewage disposal and Mr Watson's report on the same subject in 1912, and if these single sewers are located under the grass margins of our modern roads instead of being placed under the roadways where they have to stand the pressure of heavy traffic, further large savings can be effected in the cost of the construction and upkeep of the sewers themselves and also of the manholes, especially if British engineers will study continental methods. We are in this country much too conservative in our methods of construction. Even after satisfactory examples upon more economical lines have been available for some time in other countries, we are very slow to adopt materials and methods which are a departure from usual practice in this country. There are very substantial economies to be effected, not only in the materials of construction, but also in the careful design of sizes of sewers; even amateurs know of cases where sewers have been constructed in what is supposed to be a well managed town that have never been called upon to discharge one-half of their capacity. It is not too much to say that in many cases the capacity demanded for a sewer is mere guesswork or only based on antiquated investigations. Far too many manholes are demanded and under the present Local Government Board regulations, which were framed thirty-six years ago, an average manhole costs 35s. per foot in depth. Their number should be reduced, and by locating them in the grass margin instead of in the roadway a considerable saving in wear and tear caused by the traffic, as well as in cost of construction, can be effected, in addition to which those using the roads would be relieved from the constant jolting caused by manholes. The number of street gullies demanded by the authorities is also excessive.

Appendix 6 shows that disconnecting traps do more harm than good, and, therefore, this expenditure can and should be done away with in the interests of public health as well as for the sake of economy.

Builders should not be called upon to connect each small house independently with the main sewer; these separate connexions are very expensive and quite unnecessary; it is quite sufficient if several small houses are connected with one common shallow drain behind the houses, and this common drain connected with the sewer. It is, however, essential that where this is done, the owner should enter into an agreement with the local authority binding himself not to claim that this common drain is a public sewer and repairable by the inhabitants at large (see Chapter II). This safeguard is important. At the present time, the law on this point is very obscure and in 1896 the then Lord Chief Justice, Lord Russell of Killowen, concluding a long judgment on the meaning of " single private drain," drew attention to the " unsystematic and most confused legislation " relating to this matter, and hoped " steps would speedily be taken to reduce the existing chaos into system and order."* Up till now, nothing has been done to produce order out of chaos, and, therefore, local authorities must protect themselves by agreements under their town planning schemes. Some authorities object to the system of combined house drainage on the ground that the tenants of one house can stop up the drains to several houses. If these combined drains are made repairable by the landlord, as just suggested, he will make it his business to deal severely with tenants who put him to unnecessary expense of this sort. By allowing combined house drainage, provided it is not repairable by the inhabitants at large, and, speaking generally, by refusing to be bound any longer by antiquated by-laws or old-fashioned and discredited methods of calculation and construction, local authorities, assisted and encouraged by a well informed and practical central authority, could provide for better, as well as cheaper, drainage arrangements. For instance, the present regulations in Birmingham and other large towns where there are separate sewers for surface water and sewage give every facility for improper matter to be put down the drain. It is quite easy for the tenants, indeed the arrangements are so made as to tempt them, to throw soap suds or urine into the surface water drains by means of the gully outside the house, thereby putting sewage into surface water drains and sewers which are supposed to be innocuous to public health, and, therefore, are not dealt with in the same careful manner that is applied to those for carrying sewage.

(d) OPEN SPACES

The provision of open spaces in town planning areas presents a

* See Chapter II, also Mr Henry Vivian's Bill given in Appendix 7.

very interesting economic problem. The restriction of building density per gross acre (which gross acreage includes all roads, open spaces and allotments) instead of per net acre, makes it cost the landowner nothing to provide these amenities, because the total number of houses he may put on his land is not affected. Nor should this provision for public health and recreation put any appreciable charge on the ratepayers. If local authorities and landowners work together there will be no need for the purchase of land for this purpose by the local authority.

Some reformers who approach the problem of town planning and housing reform from the economic point of view are of opinion that part, at any rate, of any increased burdens thrown on to land-owners and builders by more stringent sanitary requirements should be borne by the local authority which makes the by-laws. This is a striking instance of how one mistake leads to others. Under the old by-law system, the sanitary requirements of local authorities have, during the last thirty or forty years, been constantly increased in severity without achieving the end in view, that is, better housing at reasonable rents. This is due to the fact that the problem has been attacked in the wrong way. Too much attention has been given to detail, and too little, or to be more correct, no attention has been given, to general results. It would be quite unsound and very dangerous for local authorities to be allowed to relieve builders of any part of the cost of burdens laid on them by sanitary requirements. This would open the door to all sorts of bribery and corruption that would be very difficult if not impossible of detection.

What ought to be done is to make the sanitary requirements reasonable, as suggested in the foregoing pages, and if this is done, the cost of estate development and house building will be so much reduced that, as has been shown in Chapter II, there will be sufficient profit on decent housing at reasonable rents to tempt plenty of landowners and builders to go into the business. Town planning properly administered should put an end to the fabulous profits that have in the past been made out of land and building speculation. These have been due, not merely to the energy and enterprise of the individual, but far more to the necessities of the helpless poor, and they have been made at the expense of the national stamina. Public opinion on this question is now aroused and it should soon be made illegal to let bad houses, just as it is already illegal to sell bad meat or run a workshop that has not been whitewashed. This makes it incumbent upon those responsible, to administer the laws governing town and estate development on the most economical lines consistent with efficiency. German towns have in this respect, with one or two brilliant exceptions, made great mistakes, and now, having realized their past errors, they are in some cases doing their best to repair the mischief.

Before considering in detail the savings to be effected for rate-payers, landowners and builders, by economical town planning methods, it will be useful to examine what the opposite policy has done for Paris.

Paris is still pointed to by many of those interested in town planning as a splendid example which every one employed in the movement should endeavour to copy. Of all the towns and cities inspected by me, from the town planning economist's point of view, no example is more instructive than Paris as showing what to avoid in the direction and control of town development. The principal streets and boulevards are very wide and handsome, providing excellent direct communication for traffic between the various parts of the city, but when one examines closer, goes into the houses, and looks at the backs, it is found that in very few instances is there a yard of land that has not at least one storey of building on it. The poorer classes are huddled very close together and piled up on top of one another in a most unnatural and un-healthy manner, which must militate most severely against their general health and stamina, and even those able to pay much higher rents are, in the great majority of cases, quite unable to obtain reasonably healthy and properly ventilated housing accommodation.

In Paris, vacant land is taxed at the same rate as occupied land adjacent to it, and this lays such a heavy charge on the owner, that he is obliged to build on it in order to get money to pay the tax, and there are no municipal regulations to prevent him from doing so, nor any relief from taxation, as there undoubtedly ought to be, in consideration of land left as a permanent open space, public or private.

The Parisian system of taxation without adequate safeguards cannot fail to encourage too intensive building at the centre and in the suburbs, but this is not the only cause of the mischief. The very high cost of town and estate development and municipal regulations which permit land sweating in the suburbs as well as at the centre of the city, are largely responsible for Paris being spoilt.

It is, therefore, to be hoped that the recently appointed town planning commission will put a stop to the destruction of amenities by:

    (a) Reducing the cost of town and estate development.

    (b) Restricting building density within reasonable limits.

2. SAVINGS FOR THE RATEPAYERS

(a) Out of the Birmingham rates of 8s. 11d. in the £ (March, 1913) no less than 2s. was spent by the Public Works Committee. A very large proportion of this amount goes in street widenings and the construction of new sewers, etc. During the last ten years no less than £800,000 has been spent on street widenings alone, which expenditure is entirely due to lack of foresight and common sense.

The expenditure of the Baths and Parks Committee (another department of town development) which has risen rapidly of late years, amounted in 1911 to a 4d. rate and the lines on which much of their work is done, are economically so unsound that they cannot possibly afford to do one tithe of what is most urgently needed; the funds at their disposal will be exhausted long before the work waiting their attention is half done.

With regard to road construction, it is necessary to go into a little more detail than has yet been given in order to show quite clearly what savings can be effected for the ratepayers in this direction by economical town planning methods. A 60-ft. by-law road with tram lines down the centre costs £23,500 per mile to construct. A 100-ft. town planning road (cross-section 1 in Appendix 5) including an independent tram track should not cost a penny more than £17,600* per mile, and ought to be done for less. Deduct from this the landowners' contribution at £6 per yard (£1 per yard less than the amount specified in the first town planning scheme approved by the Local Government Board), i.e., £10,560 per mile, a very fair bargain, and there remains a net cost to the ratepayers of £7,040 per mile for main arteries under the new system, against £23,500 per mile under the old, a saving of £16,460 per mile, in addition to which it pays the landowner when the local authority does the work promptly to give the land for the road in order to get his estate opened up at once for building. Under the old method, the ratepayers have to pay a large sum to

* A reduction in this cost can be effected, if (1) No monopoly in road material is created; (2) Rule of thumb practice is superseded by scientific methods.

the landowner, for the privilege of improving his property at the public expense.

(b) Reference has just been made to the actual cost in the pound of the town development work of the Public Works and Parks Committees in Birmingham. The expenditure of these committees on this part of their work is very largely, and quite unnecessarily, increased by the ridiculous prices paid for the land, but they are not the only committees in Birmingham and elsewhere that are constantly being caught by the old and time-honoured policy of waiting till the price goes up before buying land. At least half of the committees of an average local authority are concerned at some time or other in the purchase of land for public purposes and although in some cases the few hundreds or thousands of pounds involved may not be a large proportion of the total expenditure incurred, these sums spent on land purchase will nevertheless not be despised or ignored by careful administrators. In the aggregate the sums thrown away by not attending to the price paid for the land, when other and larger expenditure is being considered, amount to a very considerable charge on the rates, which ought to and can be avoided if aldermen and councillors will realize the situation and give the same careful attention to public business which they have no hesitation in giving to their own private affairs. The exercise of forethought and caution would reduce the price of land required for public purposes, provided always the central authority is willing to co-operate in this much needed municipal economy. Four Dwellings Farm, Quinton, might have been bought by the Birmingham Corporation for £60 per acre and at once used for small holdings without any loss to the ratepayers and with a prospect in the near future of its being advantageously and profitably adapted for decent housing, allotments and playing fields. Batchelor's Farm in East Birmingham was actually bought by the Corporation for £136 per acre, whereas £400 per acre was the ruling price for undeveloped land in the immediate neighbourhood. Batchelor's Farm, now owned by the Birmingham Corporation, could be arranged to provide sites on most economical terms for all sorts of public purposes; already it has provided the Education Committee with the cheapest site they ever got. The price charged to the Education Committee by the Town Planning sub-committee in 1911 was £200 per acre (giving the Town Planning sub-committee a profit for the ratepayers of £62 per acre). This figure of £200 per acre compares very favourably with the price of £1,000 per acre which was paid by the Birmingham Corporation in 1912 for a school site at Hall Green which is rather further from the centre of the city than Batchelor's Farm. Two Birmingham purchases of land recently approved by the Local Government Board (one for an open space and the other for a street improvement) work out respectively at £2,444 and £4,950 per acre. Ward End Park in East Birmingham (54 acres of land with one or two buildings on it, which were of very little value to the Corporation) cost the ratepayers £400 per acre, and, as usual, the reservation of this land for a permanent public open space immensely increased the value of all the building land near it, but the ratepayers did not get any compensation in consideration of the increased value that had been created by the expenditure of their money. Within a month or two of most strenuous opposition in the council chamber to the proposed purchase of Four Dwellings Farm (130 acres for the lump sum of £8,000) a proposal to spend £8,300 on the purchase of rather less than five acres of land in Harborne for public baths and other purposes was passed without a murmur. This land cost £1,729 per acre. No wonder rates are constantly rising when those who are supposed to protect the public purse, object to buying cheap land and insist upon waiting until the price goes up to an exorbitant figure before making a purchase. Such methods, if adopted by any private undertaking would very shortly result in bankruptcy.

The two following lists, supplied by the Birmingham City Treasurer, give some indication of what can be saved for the ratepayers by municipal land purchase on sound lines even under the 1909 Act as it now stands.

LIST NUMBER 1. Purchases of land by the City of Birmingham under the old method from April 1, 1905, to March 31, 1910.

Council Minute	Purpose	Purchase Price			Area Ac. sq. yds.	Cost per sq.yd.	
		£	s.	d.		s.	d.
19538	Council Schools, Sladefield Road	1,582	4	4	7,000	4	6
	Street Improvements, Alum Rock Road	20	0	0	300	1	4
19762	Fire Station, Rose Road, Harborne	615	0	0	2,461	5	0

Council Minute	Purpose	Purchase Price			Area Ac. sq. yds.	Cost per sq. yd.	
		£	s.	d.		s.	d.
19662	Fire Station, Bordesley Green	330	0	0	800	8	3
19937	Public Parks, &c., Musgrave Rd. Recreation Ground ..	2,748	0	0	9,559	5	9
19923	Council Schools, Leigh Road	2,100	0	0	7,000	6	0
20115	Wharves Depots, &c., Anthony Road ..	100	0	0	686	2	11
	Wharves Depots, &c., Anthony Road ..	1,100	0	0	5,120	4	3
20265	Public Parks, &c., Hockley Bank Recreation Ground ..	5,043	0	0	22	1	10
	Public Parks, &c., " Black Patch " ..	4,675	15	3			
20357	Council Schools, St, Benedicts Road ..	2,657	12	4	7,070	7	6
	General Property Improvement, Church Rd. and Arthur Rd.	11	0	0	55	4	0
19580	Street Improvements, Tennall Road ..	125	0	0	340	7	4
	Street Improvements, Balden Road ..	185	3	0	1,058	3	6
19945	Street Improvements, Alum Rock Road ..	24	1	0	300	1	7
	Street Improvements, Alum Rock Road ..	350	0	0	1,430	4	11

A further list might be added where the price paid by the Corporation is even higher per acre, but this list includes buildings, which in most cases had to be pulled down, but nevertheless paid for.

LIST NUMBER 2. Provisional or actual purchases under the 1909 Act.

Council Minute	Purpose	Purchase Price			Area Ac. sq. yds.		Cost per sq. yd.
		£	s.	d.			d.
21259	Batchelor's Farm ..	11,000	0	0	81	4,295	7
21264	Public Parks, Lower Quinton Farm ..	1,140	0	0	14	2,601	3¾
21285	Four Dwellings Farm, Quinton	8,000	0	0	131	3,963	3

The lowest price paid per yard under the OLD method was 1s. 4d., i.e. £320 per acre, and the highest 8s. 3d. per yard, i.e. £1,990 per acre. Under the NEW method the highest price is £140 per acre and the lowest £60.

TOTAL COST OF TOWN DEVELOPMENT UNDER THE OLD AND NEW METHODS

In the course of my town planning work in Birmingham, I was able to compare the cost of the old method and the new. I found that in one part of Birmingham during the years, 1891 to 1910, £95,737 was spent on town development which produced an increased assessable value of £91,393, that is to say, for every £1 spent by the ratepayers they got an increased assessable value of just under £1. The total estimate for Harborne and Quinton town planning scheme is £110,000 for developing 2,320 acres which cannot result in an eventual increase of assessable value of less than £1,000,000, that is nearly £10 increased assessable value for every £1 spent by the ratepayers. Similar figures with regard to East Birmingham town planning scheme are not quite so favourable. In that case, the final estimate is £69,260 for developing 1,000 acres which should produce £426,000 increased assessable value or £6 increased assessable value for every £1 of the ratepayers' money spent on development. In these figures no account is taken of public buildings which will cost more or less the same to build under both methods of development.

These savings under the 1909 Act as compared with old methods are all the more remarkable and encouraging for the future, in view of the fact, as will be seen presently, that the town planning schemes to which they refer have not been prepared on nearly such economical lines as they ought to have been. The East Birmingham results are not so good as those at Harborne and Quinton, mainly because in the former district there is in force an old agreement between the Corporation and the landowners made by one of our platform economists that is very favourable indeed to the landowners and most expensive to the ratepayers.

It is objected that the above calculations as to the increased assessable value produced in new districts by any given expenditure on development are quite misleading, because it is thought that when assessable value is increased on the outskirts a decrease follows at the centre, or in other words, if the people go to live in the suburbs there will be void houses in congested districts. The answer to this objection, which is raised purely from the rate collector's point of view without any attempt to take a wide view of the whole position is twofold.

1. Whether the rate collector likes it or not, people are moving into the suburbs, and with the help of better and cheaper means of communication will continue to do so at an increasing rate, and the sooner our financial authorities realize the position and adapt themselves to the new order of things, the better for the ratepayers whose pockets it is their duty to protect. The people will move out, which is a consummation to be desired from the health point of view, and by careful town planning it is possible to get ready to provide them a hearty welcome to the country, and at the same time effect economies for the ratepayers.

2. It is not sound economics to house the people in the centres of cities, where the land is far too expensive for the purpose. It should be used for something that will bring in a larger return and void houses at the centre gradually forcing land there into a sounder economic use will, in the long run, increase assessable value at the centre as well as in the suburbs. London proves this. The ultimate effect of people leaving the City to live further out has been to increase, many hundred times over, the assessable value of the centre. Compare the assessable value of the City of London to-day with what it was 50 or 100 years ago.

This bogey of decreased assessable value at the centre shows the fallacy of only looking at one side of the question.

The mistaken opinion held by men of this school of thought that town planning is going to cost the ratepayers very large sums of money is very largely due to the fact that under the old method estimates are presented to the council piece-meal, and when any particular piece of work is being considered no account is taken of

G

what has already been spent or of what is likely to be spent in the future. Under the new method the whole estimate is presented at one time, a much more business-like procedure, but one which is not always acceptable to a council endeavouring to appear economical. Estimates presented piece-meal do not strike the imagination as a complete estimate does. Under the piece-meal method, much more money is spent, but the ratepayers do not know it, and it is not altogether surprising that a careful regard for appearances should encourage a method of presenting estimates that do not alarm the paymaster even though in that way very much more money is actually spent. What does it matter if no one complains?

(c) There are other and very large savings to be effected by better housing at reasonable rents which cannot be expressed in figures, but which will none the less appeal very forcibly to all practical men. The Birmingham Watch Committee accounts for very nearly 6d. in the £, that is £90,000 per annum, a very large part of which is spent in seeing that people behave themselves under living conditions that drive them to misbehave. A considerable sum goes every year in the cost of administering punishment for offences which are to a very considerable extent the result of circumstances, which can and should be altered. Then there is the upkeep of our gaols. Surely the time has come for giving more attention to prevention, in order to save some of the wasted human effort and some of the time and money thrown away in attempting to cure what will continue to be an incurable disease so long as the cause of the mischief remains. Give men, women and children a reasonable chance of living clean, healthy, happy lives and the great majority will do so. Force them into slums and keep them there, as our rate collecting friend would like to do, with nothing but the public-house to help them to forget their miseries, and it is most unreasonable to complain, if some of them fall victims to the temptations around them. The Birmingham lunatic asylums cost the ratepayers £32,000 per annum, and the best authorities assert that a very large proportion of the cases dealt with in these institutions are caused by drink due to bad environment and lack of counter-attractions to the public-house. The only way to remove these evils is to spread our town populations over larger areas on sound economic lines.

Another very heavy charge on the public purse is the poor rate. This has recently been reduced by old age pensions; it can be very much further reduced by better housing.

Then there is consumption, about which so much is being said at the present time, and on which so much money is being spent in an attempt to cure the disease without removing the cause of it.

It is quite impossible for anyone to say how much these various evils cost the ratepayers, but it does not require much imagination to enable one to realize that by removing their causes enormous savings of private as well as public money would be made. Prevention is not only better, it is also much cheaper than cure.

There is one rate that needs our attention more than any other, that is the death rate. On this point a few general figures shall be given first and then some figures recently published by Liverpool.

The average expectation of life in suburban areas without slums is forty-seven years, as compared with thirty years in congested districts. The following figures taken from a publication by Dr Sykes on " Health and Housing " show how markedly death rates diminish with the reduction in building density per acre.

Density per acre	Infantile mortality.	Total death rate.	Tuberculosis death rate.
446	393	37˙4	6˙7
373	252	39˙3	4˙4
183	172	23˙1	3˙6
168	159	22˙5	2˙7

COMPARATIVE MORTALITY RATES FOR 1909:

	Infantile death rate per 1,000	Ordinary death rate per 1,000
Letchworth	31˙7	5˙2
Birmingham	134˙3	15˙4
Brighton	96	15˙3
Worthing	74	14˙5
London	107˙9	14
Manchester	134	17˙9
Liverpool	143˙6	19
Middlesbrough	157˙8	19˙1

Some people will dismiss these figures with the remark that the inhabitants of the suburbs are better off than slum dwellers and can afford better food and clothing and, therefore, the comparison is not a fair one. Reasonable reformers will admit that there is something to be said for this point of view and agree to some allowance being made for it, but to assert that lower death rates are in no way due to better living conditions and less density per acre is simply ridiculous.

G2

The figures recently published by Liverpool are not open to the above criticism, because the method there is to demolish slums and rehouse the same tenants in the same area and although the figures do not give any comparison between town districts and suburban areas, they do show the large saving to be effected for the ratepayers by better housing of the people.

In 1864, the death rate in Liverpool slums was 60 per 1,000; to-day it is 27, still very much too high and suggesting that rehousing in suburbs is better than any re-housing in congested districts no matter how well the latter may be done, but nevertheless this reduction from 60 to 27 represents a very valuable saving to the ratepayers.

Tuberculosis has declined from 4 to 1·9 per 1,000.
Typhus fever: once never absent; in 1910, not a case.
Typhoid fever: in 1896, 1,300 cases; in 1911, 200 cases.
Police prosecutions have fallen 50 per cent.

This re-housing work has thrown a charge of 2½d. in the £ on to the rates against which it is estimated that if the work had not been done, the ratepayers would be paying a rate of 5d. in the £ in order to cover the cost of increased inspection, police prosecutions, extra poor law rate and all the other charges that fall upon a city which neglects to deal with its slums. The cash saving to Liverpool under her re-housing policy is estimated at £65,000 per annum or double the cost of providing decent houses for the slum-dwellers.*

This definite saving of 2½d. in the £ is something tangible to go upon; it is also all the more remarkable in view of the fact that the Liverpool method of dealing with slum reform is about the most costly that can be found. Far greater savings should be effected by cities adopting the policy of emptying the slums into new districts properly planned beforehand. In that case not only would better results be obtained with regard to the death, poor and other rates just enumerated, but the cost to the ratepayers of town development would, as we have seen, be enormously reduced.

Mr T. C. Horsfall in the "Garden City Magazine," February, 1913, tells us that ninety years ago the Swedes were threatened with the destruction of their finest qualities by alcohol. To-day as the result of rational town planning and many other wise measures, they are a sound race, physically the finest in Europe, and their town people are even finer than those in the country. Is England too proud to learn a lesson from Sweden?

* "Garden City Magazine," April, 1913.

3. SAVINGS FOR LANDOWNERS AND BUILDERS

At first, there is sure to be a certain amount of opposition to what is called new-fangled legislation, but if local authorities will study the problem from the point of view of landowners and builders, they will find so many ways in which town planning can be made to benefit this important section of the community that by the time everything is settled, it will be found that while wise town planning benefits the community and saves the pockets of the ratepayers, it also confers great benefits on land and building developers.

(a) With regard to land, Chapter I explained how to provide builders with plenty of land at a price that will make ten houses per acre a very good business proposition for land and building developers, although admittedly not permitting the fabulous profits that have been made in the past.

It is very good business for the landowner to give the land required for main arteries and contribute £6 per yard towards the cost of construction. He loses no tangible asset by giving up this land because the area of the road is counted in the area on which he is allowed to put ten houses per gross acre. The land he keeps is worth just as much to him as was his original holding.* It is really worth more because the construction of a new main artery through his estate brings it into the market for building with no expenditure on his part until his building sites have come into rating, i.e. are bringing him in an income. He gets a 100-ft. main artery instead of a 40, 50 or 60 ft. by-law road, and the actual cost to him of the wider road is less than that of the old-fashioned narrow one. The wider road will greatly increase the value of his building sites. From the builder's point of view, it is a great advantage to have open space in front of the site. The average tenant does not like too large a garden, it costs too much to keep up, but he does like plenty of open space round his house, and he, the tenant, will be all the better pleased if some of the open space round his house is maintained at somebody else's expense. It is much better from the economic point of view not to have too large a garden to each house. Under wise town planning administration, landowners gain very materially by the quicker development of their land. They can get direct communications with railway stations and other travelling facilities, and they are

* He can put just as many houses on the land remaining to him as he could have put on his original holding.

able to plan their estates to take advantage of these improved communications, instead of, as has very often happened in the past, having their estates seriously injured and decreased in value by some tramway or motor-bus route that is quite foreign to the character of their development.

(b) If local authorities are reasonable with regard to estate development, if 16-ft. carriage ways are allowed on purely residential estates, and 8-ft. drives or pathways to groups of small houses, and if no monopoly is created in road material very large savings in the cost of estate development can be effected. Further large savings can be effected by substituting single sewers and combined house drainage for the present antiquated and discredited systems.

Under these conditions, a town planning residential road (in accordance with cross-section 3 in Appendix 5) ought not to cost more than £2 10s. per yard, and should in many places be done for a good deal less, as against £6 to £7 for the old by-law road, in addition to which in a well-ordered estate plan, the length of roads and public services will be very much reduced and the ratepayers will benefit from having much fewer square yards of roadway to maintain.

(c) Another immense advantage for landowners is that, under town planning, they are protected from having their property seriously depreciated by the erection of undesirable property next door. Many estates developed with good houses are now emptying fast, because adjoining property has been cut up for crowded cottages, other estates are seriously injured and their development delayed by a cantankerous neighbour who refuses to allow access over his land. Then again, landowners can often be very materially assisted and their property greatly increased in value by re-distributions on the lines explained in Chapter III. Footpaths can be closed without trouble or expense to the landowner.

(d) Constantly on the sale of freeholds restrictive covenants have been disregarded, thereby injuring adjacent land that has not been sold. Under the 1909 Act, the uncertainty of the power of landowners to enforce restrictive covenants will disappear. When the plan is made landowners will know exactly how their land stands and what can and cannot be done on the adjoining property. They will know for what purpose the particular district is destined and how many houses will be allowed per acre. They will be able to develop on the best lines without fear that their property will deteriorate in value or amenity.

(e) Where 100-ft. main arteries are carefully planned, and local authorities are reasonable with regard to side roads and drainage, the main arteries referred to above will open up for building at least 300 yards of land at a cost to the landowner of only £180 per acre, which includes his contribution towards the cost of constructing the main artery. These main arteries will sometimes take up an unfair proportion of some individual owner's land, and in these cases the contribution towards the cost must be fairly distributed among all the owners who benefit (see general provision 11 in Appendix 5). Land worth originally £20 per acre is, at a cost of £180, opened up and developed for building, and at ten houses per gross acre becomes worth £600 per acre, leaving a margin for landowners and building developers of £400 per acre, which will be recognized by all reasonable men as an ample sum out of which to provide professional fees, the cost of financing the undertaking and profit.

It is not suggested that these figures will prove in practice to be exactly correct in every district and every case. They are based on actual experience; and careful inquiries in different parts of the country have proved them to be fair average figures that can by practical men be adapted and corrected to the special circumstances of any particular case. One of the main principles always to be remembered by town planners is that success depends on their being able to adapt themselves to the special needs of the case they are dealing with, instead of being bound hand and foot by the by-law uniformity that has done so much mischief in the past.

CHAPTER V. EXAMPLES.

THE novelty in this country of the problem under consideration, and the way in which the expressions town planning, garden city and garden suburb are constantly being used in connexion with development schemes that have no resemblance to the real article except its name, make it necessary to give a few examples of genuine town planning schemes and others whose only usefulness is to show town planners how not to do it.

It is not possible in the space available to deal with all the schemes that would provide useful and inspiring object lessons; an attempt has therefore been made to pick out those schemes that are most instructive from the economic point of view. By doing this, it is not intended to suggest that the economic aspect of town planning is the only aspect worthy of attention. The hygienic, social and artistic aspects have their own value, they are ends to be kept in view and earnestly striven for, but, unless town planning schemes are firmly based on a sound economic foundation, the superstructure erected will not be a permanent success. That is why in this treatise most attention is given to the economic aspect, leaving it to the idealists, without whom all forward movements are barren, to deal with other aspects and ultimate aims.

It is, therefore, now our business to see to what extent those responsible for the various schemes described have availed themselves of the opportunities for economy enumerated in the last chapter. The schemes chosen are:

1. Hampstead garden suburb.
2. Harborne garden suburb.
3. Hereford garden suburb.
4. Harborne and Quinton town planning scheme.
5. East Birmingham town planning scheme.
6. Ruislip-Northwood town planning scheme.
7. Rosyth town planning scheme.

Of these seven examples, Hampstead and Harborne garden suburbs are due to private enterprise more or less assisted by public bodies. Hereford is an example of complete co-operation between all concerned in the provision and supervision of housing accommodation for the people, and the other four are the work of public bodies under the 1909 Act. Harborne and East Birmingham are the first two town planning schemes for which permission to prepare was granted by the Local Government Board. They are constantly being put forward as models for other local authorities to copy, and, therefore, must be examined with very special care. Ruislip-Northwood was the third scheme for which permission to prepare was granted, in addition to which it has been the work of a rural district council, and therefore affords an excellent opportunity of comparing results achieved in a rural area with what has been done in a great city. Rosyth is in many ways the most interesting of all; it is under the direction of the Scottish Local Government Board and therefore provides an opportunity of comparing the methods of English and Scottish Government Offices. It deals with what is practically a virgin area, which will in a very few years' time receive a large population for which housing accommodation must be found, and it, therefore, provides a unique opportunity of planning and building an entirely new town on modern lines, unhampered by mistakes of the past. The Harborne and Quinton town planning scheme is the only one that has as yet (August 1913) been finally approved by the Local Government Board responsible. The other three are still subject to detailed modifications, but are already settled to a sufficient extent to enable us to learn a good deal from them.

1. HAMPSTEAD GARDEN SUBURB

This is the first estate developed under town planning legislation in this country. By a special self-imposed Act of 1906, the Hampstead Garden Suburb Trust Limited were freed from many hampering by-laws on condition that " there shall not be built in the garden suburb on the average throughout a greater proportion of houses to the acre than eight." This Act was piloted through the House of Commons by Mr Henry Vivian, and to it is very largely due the Act of 1909. Extracts from this special Act are given in Chapter VIII of the first edition of " Practical Housing," and need not be repeated here. In the second edition of that publication, Appendix D4, are given the special provisions in building leases granted by the Trust which are designed to ensure proper development over the whole estate. The following information has been obtained from various publications kindly sent to me by Mrs Barnett.

GENESIS OF THE SUBURB

The Hampstead Heath Extension Council was formed in the summer of 1903 for the purpose of adding to Hampstead Heath 80 acres, part of the property belonging to the Eton College trustees, at North End, Hampstead, known as Wyldes. Action in the direction proposed by the Council was rendered urgent by the authorization of the Charing Cross, Euston and Hampstead Railway. This railway started from Charing Cross, and, passing through the densely populated suburbs of Camden Town and Kentish Town, was to be carried to the foot of Hampstead Heath, on the south side where there would be a station at Holly Bush Hill, and then under the Heath to North End and Golders Green, on each of which spots it was proposed to open a station. It was recognized by Mrs Barnett and her friends as long ago as 1903, that town planning must precede trams, trains and other travelling facilities to new areas if these new areas were to be efficiently and economically protected from the ravages of uncontrolled land and building speculators.

To give practical effect to the scheme the Hampstead Heath Extension Council from whose report the following information is taken, was constituted, with Mr Shaw Lefevre (now Lord Eversley) as president, the Earl of Meath as vice-president, Sir Robert Hunter, C.B., J.P., and Mr Bond, M.P., as Treasurers, and Mrs Barnett as honorary secretary. Even before the formation of this council the honorary secretary had gathered together a provisional committee which had appealed to friends for assistance, and subscriptions had begun to flow in freely. More difficulty attended the application to public bodies. The first public body approached was the Hampstead Borough Council, a substantial contribution from this body being important, not only on its own account, but as a guarantee to the London County Council of local interest in the project.* Eventually the Hampstead Borough Council, after an interesting debate, voted a contribution of £5,000. Application was then made to the London County Council, but it was only after great exertions on the part of the Extension Council that a promise of £8,000 was at length extracted. The Extension Council were thus placed in great difficulties. They had raised the unusually large sum of £17,500 from private sources and they hesitated to tax their friends further while the local bodies (Finchley, Hendon, Islington and St Pancras) showed such excessive caution in loosening their purse strings. Under these circumstances the happy thought

* This is exactly what had to be done by the Birmingham Open Spaces Society with regard to the Black Patch. The Smethwick and Handsworth local authorities each subscribed £1,000 to the purchase of this open space, and thereby made it very difficult for the Birmingham City Council to refuse to do its share in the matter.

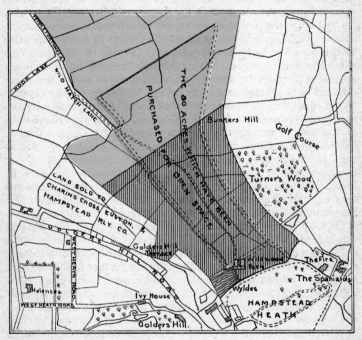

1. The portion shaded by vertical lines shows the 80 acres that it was originally proposed to purchase

2. The portion coloured green shows the 80 acres that have now been purchased.

3. The portion coloured pink represents a portion of the Hampstead Garden Suburb.

occurred of changing the position of the land to be acquired while maintaining its extent. Instead of acquiring the whole breadth of Eton College property at its southern end, it was suggested to the college authorities that they should retain a strip for building purposes on each side, and carry the proposed open space further into their estate. The result of this change (illustrated by the plan on page 91) was greatly to increase the amount of the college land which fronted on to the new open space, and which would become available for building, and thus enabled the college to reduce the price of the 80 acres to be preserved from £48,000 to £36,000. This change of plan, however, was settled with the condition that funds should be provided for the formation of roads to enable the strips retained to be utilized should the college wish to do so. The expense of the roads was at first estimated at about £3,000, and with the figures thus revised the Extension Council again applied themselves to the task of raising the necessary funds. The London County Council were induced to allow their promised grant of £8,000 to apply to the new area, the Middlesex County Council granted £2,500; Islington and St Pancras, £1,000, the trustees of the City of London Parochial Charities, £1,500, and the City Companies allowed very substantial grants to be utilized for the changed plan. By the summer of 1904 the sums promised were within about £5,000 of the total required, and on the 1st of September, 1904, Mrs Barnett was able, on behalf of the Extension Council, to write a letter to the authorities of Eton College, which preserved the option of purchase and left the council to raise only as much further money as was possible to relieve the guarantors. There were many other difficulties in connexion with the scheme, too numerous and complicated to be detailed here. Suffice it to say that they were surmounted and we now have a magnificent object lesson of what can be done by town planning methods on a sound economic basis. In the words of Sir Robert Hunter, C.B., J.P., " Had things been left to their ordinary course, if the college with the aid of the speculative builder had built merely for immediate profit, regardless of the future, and regardless of any interest but that of the ground landlord and his lessee, the prospect from Hampstead Heath would soon have changed in character. The Heath would no longer have been an outpost of crowded London, but an island in a sea of houses, but with the lands of Eton College forming the site of a garden suburb, the Heath will still command a fair view; the eye will roam over waving trees and smiling gardens, diversified rather than marred by the gables and chimneys of the homes of those who are swiftly borne from their work by tube or tramway, into pure air and agreeable surroundings. Nor is this all. The practicability of such an extension to London once proved, the character of suburb making may be expected to undergo a change. It will be realized that an estate on the outskirts of a great town may at a reasonable profit be so developed as to provide a pleasant residence, not only for the rich, but for all classes. Public opinion may well demand that town extension shall follow on some such lines, and landowners and builders, with a little help perhaps from municipal regulations or even from municipal competition will, it may be anticipated, supply what is desired. If such be the case, the growth of great cities will no longer give rise to forebodings of physical deterioration and national decay, but will be viewed as the natural and welcome outcome of the support and enterprise of the people. It would be difficult to suggest a more interesting or salutary application of a fraction of one of the great fortunes of the day than in promoting the formation of such a suburb as that designed at Hampstead. Munificent gifts are now and again made to hospitals and other charities. Here is a benefaction touching the welfare of the nation perhaps even more nearly, yet involving no sacrifice of capital but only its judicious use.''

When the first sod was cut by Mrs Barnett on May 2, 1907, the late Rt Hon. Alfred Lyttelton, K.C., M.P., president of the company, emphasized the intentions and hopes of the company in the following words: '' The great problem of suburban London was presented in all great cities. There was the rural as well as the urban problem, but the urban problem was the most instant and it was in the urban problem that they were most interested in the Hampstead Garden Suburb Trust. Their object was that on the land conveyed to them by the Eton College trustees, all classes of the community should live together under wholesome conditions. They had limited the profits to be paid on the commercial venture to 5 per cent. They hoped to plan the estate, not in the manner of speculative builders, but opening out and not breaking the vista of views in which Hampstead was so rich. They sought to gather together in natural sympathy various classes bearing each other's burdens and taking part in common duties.''

IDEALS OF HAMPSTEAD GARDEN SUBURB.

These cannot be better explained than in the following extract from a letter issued in July, 1905, by the Hampstead Garden

Suburb Trust, while it was testing public feeling before the formation of the company.

" 1. We desire to do something to meet the housing problem by putting within the reach of working people the opportunity of taking a cottage with a garden within a twopenny fare of central London and at a moderate rent. We have already evidence that the opportunity would be eagerly seized, and we believe that in cleaner air with open space near to their doors, with gardens where the family labour would produce vegetables, fruit and flowers, the people would develop a sense of home life, and an interest in nature which forms the best security against the temptations of drink and gambling.

" 2. Our aim is that the new suburb may be laid out as a whole on an orderly plan. When various plots are disposed of to different builders and each builder considers only his own interest, the result is what may be seen in the unsightly modern streets.

" 3. We desire to promote a better understanding between members of the classes who form our nation. Our object, therefore, is not merely to provide for the cottager paying from 6s. 6d. a week, but also for the richer people paying from £30 to £400 a year.

" 4. We aim at preserving natural beauty. Our intention would be so to lay out the ground that every tree may be kept, hedgerows duly considered, and the foreground of the distant view preserved, if not as open fields yet as a gardened district, the buildings kept in harmony with the surroundings."

The late Rt Hon. Alfred Lyttelton, K.C., M.P., was president of the Trust. The directors are Mrs S. A. Barnett (honorary manager), Mr Frank Denbenham, J.P., Sir Robert Hunter, K.C.B., Mr Herbert Marnham and Mr Henry Vivian, J.P. The prospectus and all other particulars can be obtained from the secretary, Mr G. W. Rousham, Central Square, Garden Suburb, Hendon, London, N.W.

The following extracts from an article by Mrs Barnett in the "Contemporary," February, 1905, explain the economic and social mistakes which this estate was designed to combat.

" When the poorer people are crowded together in mean gardenless streets, the neighbourhood becomes less desirable for those who, being blessed with more of this world's goods, or who having reached the afternoon of life, wish to live with more repose surrounded by the varied and indefinite influences known as amenities. Those, therefore, who are able to choose, seek other neighbourhoods, and thus poorer localities are deprived of the contagion of refinement which contact brings, and the richer people lose the experience which knowledge of strenuous lives and patient endurance ever provokes. Society is impoverished by class divisions, and each class loses more than it realizes. It is an essential condition of building in this suburb that the dwellings of all classes be made attractive with their own distinctive attractions, as are the cottage and the manor house of the English village, the larger gardens of the rich helping to keep the air pure and the sky view more liberal, the cottage gardens adding that cosy element which ever follows the spade when affectionately and cunningly wielded as a man's recreation. Houses are not to be put in uniform lines, nor in close relationship built regardless of each other, or without consideration for picturesque appearance. Each one is to be surrounded with its own garden and every road is to be planted with trees, and not less than 40 feet wide. Great care will be taken that houses shall not spoil each other's outlook, and that the noise of the children shall be locally limited, while the avoidance of uniformity or of an institutional aspect is to be obtained by the variety of the buildings provided. There will be play grounds for the smaller children, and rest places for the aged, who cannot walk so far as from the end of the estate to the Heath. There are to be cottages with individual gardens and cottages grouped around a quadrangle or common sward.''

The Institute forms a definite part of the work of the Trust, and has proved a brilliant success. All classes and all ages are considered. The scheme includes opportunities for learning in music, art, literature, nature study, economic and domestic science as well as classes for commercial and technical subjects, and that full advantage is taken of these facilities is shown by the fact that 1,120 students have enrolled themselves in the various societies and classes for the session 1912-13. For those who do not enroll as students, public debates, conferences, picture talks and music lectures offer a stimulating means of hearing and partaking in the discussion of some of the main questions which occupy men's minds.

AREA

The original area proposed was 243 acres. Four hundred and twelve acres have since been added by the Trust in co-operation with Co-partnership Tenants Limited, taking on lease from the Ecclesiastical Commissioners further quantities of adjoining land. The securing of these additional areas not only adds to the assets of the company, but ensures that there shall be no crowded "hinterland" to deteriorate the value of the original estate and that an area of 655 acres, or over one square mile on the north of London, will be developed with due regard to health and beauty. The estate should be further protected by the Finchley town planning scheme now in course of preparation.

The Hampstead Garden Suburb Trust Limited are the freeholders responsible for the lay out of the estate, the making of the roads and the superintendence of the erection of the buildings; land is not sold, but let on leases of 99 and 999 years for the erection of tenements and houses on co-partnership principles, to let from 3s. 3d. a week to £110 a year, and for privately owned houses costing £400 to £3,500.

DEVELOPMENT

The first centre has been given prominence by being placed at the top of the hill; the second centre will be given prominence by being placed in the centre of the hollow, like the arena of an amphitheatre. On the east of the first centre stands the Institute, on the other side are built the churches, Established and Free. The whole of this group of buildings has been designed by Mr E. L. Lutyens so as to form a unity of which the differing parts may be equally worthy and dignified. The fourth side of the great central square is left open and when the terraces are built there will be broad hill-top walks, from which an uninterrupted view of the west will be obtained, extending past Harrow to the Chilterns. The houses on the north-west corner of this square have been built by Hampstead Tenants Limited, who are also developing the southern side at rentals varying from £70 to £100 per annum. On the north of the estate on undulating ground lie the cottages and gardens of the industrial classes; on the western portion, grouped round small open spaces, stand the villas and smaller houses, while to the south are the larger houses, the occupants of which enjoy beautiful views over Hampstead Heath and its extension. The orchards and the beds of flowers, although unfenced, have remained unmolested and have shown, with the six other wall-less gardens on the estate, that although thousands of people have visited the suburb the public have, as the notice-boards request, " protected what has been planted for their pleasure." To provide accommodation for the staff engaged on the work of the estate, the Trust has built fourteen cottages. In suitable juxtaposition are motor garages, so planned by Mr Raymond Unwin as to include roomy and convenient accommodation for the drivers and their families, as well as a common washing court-yard. The Trust has also built cottage homes where those needing care, protection and assistance will live under adequate and suitable administration. All these buildings are let to return interest on the capital outlay. A haven for old people is provided by a charming quadrangle of self-contained flats built by Hampstead Tenants Limited, and let at rentals of 3s. 3d. to 4s. 6d. per week per tenement.

The rapidity with which the estate has been developed has exceeded the most hopeful expectations of those responsible. This remarkable success proves the very large demand that exists for decent housing at reasonable rents.

The value of buildings on the estate including the churches, the institute, and the club house, together with the cost of land and roads, is now more than £1,000,000.

It is estimated that after paying all interest on mortgages, debenture stock, and a 5 per cent dividend on the share capital there will be a balance of £5,000 a year, which is more than sufficient, after payment of current expenses, to allow of a larger annual outlay on the upkeep of the open spaces, and general beautifying of the estate and the promotion of public objects. The directors are of opinion that the balance over, after meeting all these charges, might be partially used for helping other similar objects.

The audited accounts of the company for the year ending March 31, 1912, show a balance on revenue account of £1,524 12s. 5d., and a dividend of 5 per cent on the ordinary shares was paid for the year ending March 31, 1909. The dividend on these ordinary shares is cumulative, and judging from the present rate of progress it should not be long before all arrears are wiped off.

The success of Hampstead garden suburb is in no small measure due to the part taken in the work by Co-partnership Tenants Limited, Hampstead Tenants Limited, and Second Hampstead Tenants Limited, working in co-operation with the Trust, who arranged to take up from the Ecclesiastical Commissioners the last 300 acres of adjoining land, thereby extending operations to East Finchley station on the Great Northern Railway.

The value of property built and owned by tenants' societies (four in number) in the suburb already amounts to £600,000, and further developments are proceeding at a rapid rate.

H

The methods of these societies, which have proved extraordinarily successful in practice, are briefly as follows:

1. To erect substantially built houses provided with good sanitary and other arrangements, for the convenience of tenants.

2. To let the societies' houses at ordinary rents, to pay a moderate rate of interest on capital, and to divide the surplus profits, after providing for expenses, repairs, sinking fund, etc., among the tenant-members in proportion to the rents paid by them.

3. Each tenant-member's share of profits is credited to him in the books of the society instead of being paid in cash.

4. This system must not be confounded with that of an ordinary building society, under which a member makes himself liable to the society for purchase money, when if he leaves the neighbourhood the house may be a burden on his hands.

5. A tenant-member if he leaves the neighbourhood can transfer shares or loan stock with less cost than a house, or if he continues to hold them can receive the interest in the ordinary way.

Ealing Tenants Limited, the first society to be started on these lines, has now been in existence for twelve years. It pays a regular dividend of 5 per cent on the ordinary shares, and also a dividend on rents, which latter amounted to 1s. 6d. in the pound for the year ending December 31, 1912.

Co-partnership Tenants Limited is the central society, and its offices are at 6 Bloomsbury Square, London, W.C. It has affiliated to it fourteen co-partnership housing societies in different parts of the country, the value of the property exceeding one million pounds sterling.

2. HARBORNE GARDEN SUBURB.

This little village is on a much smaller scale than Hampstead, but as it is built on a very awkward building site (men who understand building development were all agreed that if development at ten houses per acre could be made to pay there it could be made to pay anywhere) an account of what has been achieved there may be interesting and encouraging to town planners, especially when they come across the difficulties and discouragements inseparable from pioneer work.

The estate comprises 54 acres of land, on which there are 494 dwelling houses, three shops, a club house and a public hall. The land cost £300, and development £350 per acre, making a total cost of £650 per acre for land and development, and the building density works out at $9\frac{1}{4}$ houses per acre. The price paid for the land was very much higher than it ought to be necessary to pay now, for a similar or indeed for a much more favourable building site, because when this estate was bought there was no law to prevent forty or more houses being put to the acre. The development also cost a great deal more than should now be necessary, because the plan was settled before the 1909 Act was passed, and before economical estate development was so well understood as it is now, in addition to which there was the hilly nature of the site which has already been referred to and many other difficulties causing extra expenditure which need not and should not fall on other estates, developed in the future on similar lines.

In spite of the very heavy cost for land and development, and with an average of less than ten houses per acre, the society has, after paying interest on all loans and loan stock, earned and paid a dividend of 5 per cent on its share capital for the last four years, in addition to setting aside a sinking fund of $\frac{1}{2}$ per cent per annum accumulating at $3\frac{1}{2}$ per cent compound interest. The only time it failed to pay 5 per cent on the share capital was on its first year's working when very few houses were completed and tenanted.

Rents vary from 4s. 6d. per week including rates to £40 per annum exclusive of rates.

56 houses on the estate are let at	4s. 6d. to 6s.	per week.
114 ,, ,, ,,	6s. 3d. to 6s. 9d.	,,
100 ,, ,, ,,	7s. 6d. to 9s.	,,
224 ,, ,, ,,	over 9s.	,,

These financial results in the face of £650 per acre for land and development prove conclusively what an easy task it is for builders (under reasonable town planning administration) to provide decent housing accommodation in the suburbs for those now living in congested districts at rents that these people can afford to pay, and at the same time make a good profit for themselves. A very large proportion of the houses in congested districts in Birmingham are let at rents of 4s. 6d. or more per week.

The practical example of Harborne Tenants answers the question raised at the beginning of Chapter IV, viz., " Can garden suburb development be made to pay? " It not only can be made to pay, it has been made to pay, and at house rents about 2s. per week lower than the new houses provided for many years past under the old extravagant by-law methods. This being the case, it is most earnestly to be hoped that the general public will no longer allow themselves to be misled by the pretences and fairy tales of the land-jobbers' party, but will insist upon the adoption of business-like methods, and the achievement of practical results, so that the very large proportion of those living in congested areas who would move further out if they could afford it shall be able to do so.

It is not reasonable or fair, nor is it sound economics, to keep these people in the slums, merely because if they moved out there might be some temporary depreciation in the value of property in the centre of the city.

As Harborne Tenants' Moor Pool estate is the only estate in Birmingham developed upon anything approaching economical town planning lines, it is not altogether surprising that the general public is not yet aware of what can be done in the way of better housing at reasonable rents. What has been done at Harborne is on the basis of £650 an acre for land and development, a very high price, but it should be realized that a practically unlimited supply of building estates within easy reach of the centre of the city could be brought into the market on the basis of £300 per acre for land and development on town planning lines, and public opinion ought to insist upon the necessary steps being taken by the powers that be to carry out what has been proved by actual experiment to be a thoroughly practical suggestion, that is, garden suburbs all round Birmingham.

The roadways at Harborne are 16 feet wide with grass margins and gravel footpaths, and have recently been made up to the satisfaction of the local authority, and taken over by them. Four years' practical experience shows that 16 feet of roadway is ample width for two streams of traffic. There is across the middle of the estate a 50-ft. by-law road connecting two narrow lanes, which was certainly not needed for the traffic it carries. This relic of the old methods was insisted upon by the local authority, and has added considerably to the cost of development. There are two sewers instead of only one for surface water and sewerage, and in many cases these are laid under the roadways instead of under the grass margins, or at the backs of the houses. The drainage of several houses is collected into one common drain before discharging into the sewer, thereby saving a good deal of money, but there are disconnecting traps to street gullies which in the opinion of the Local Government Board are unnecessary, and also many other items of expenditure which ought not to be insisted upon.

The success of Harborne Tenants, in spite of the adverse circumstances mentioned above and many other difficulties which need not be mentioned here, is the strongest possible testimony as to the economic possibilities of town planning, when it comes to be better understood by the public, and more efficiently administered by those whose duty it is to protect the interests of the ratepayers. At the same time it is only fair to state that this success is by no means entirely due to economical town planning estate development. It is also in no small measure due to the system of co-partnership in Housing invented and carried to a successful issue by Mr Henry Vivian, under which system many savings are effected as compared with housing under the ordinary speculative system. In these co-partnership societies the members are shareholders as well as tenants, that is to say, they are, to the extent of their shares, their own landlords, and the dividend on their shares comes after the interest on Government loans, loan stock and all other charges. It is, therefore, to the interest of the tenants to take care of the property. There are, practically speaking, no voids on estates under this system, and the sum needed for repairs is very much smaller than where landlord and tenant are not one and the same person. For these and other reasons co-partnership housing will always give tenants better value for their money, but it is quite open to the ordinary landlord to give his tenants an interest in the property on lines similar to those laid down by Miss Octavia Hill, and put into practice with such marked success in London and other cities.

The vital statistics of Moor Pool, Harborne, are very remarkable, especially in view of the fact that it is less than three miles from the centre of a population of over 1,000,000. The total death-rate for five years is five per 1,000, and the infantile mortality is six. There have already been several hundred births. One hundred per 1,000 is generally considered a very low infantile mortality; at Moor Pool the results are sixteen times better, without any expense having been thrown on to the ratepayers. On the contrary the society have until quite recently, in addition to paying the same rates as other property owners, maintained and lighted their roads at their own expense and done their own policing.

The hygienic and economic results achieved at Moor Pool, Harborne, have caused very grave dissatisfaction, and uneasiness in landjobbing circles, because it has been shown that land sweating is by no means an economic necessity. This is the first step to getting rid of land sweating, and when that is done the landjobbers' occupation will be gone. No wonder then that they miss no opportunity of endeavouring to discredit a successful

competitor, but surely the time must come when the public will
see through these misrepresentations.

The high rate of infantile mortality is only one of many social
evils, it is only one of many disgraces to the big cities; but here
is a small corner of the city where it has been successfully fought
and routed—and without expense to the ratepayers. Should not
this point a way to better things and along town planning lines?

3. HEREFORD GARDEN SUBURB.

This is up to the present the only example in this country where
there has been complete co-operation between the local authority,
landowner and builder engaged in the provision and supervision of
housing accommodation for the poorer classes. It is also the only
case where the whole problem of town planning and housing reform, otherwise known as slum reform and slum prevention, has
been considered and treated methodically and fully.

The problem that came before the Hereford Town Council was
as follows: In the centre of the town were some very bad houses
quite unfit for human habitation and quite incapable of being made
fit to live in. Under the Act of 1903, which has since been most unwisely repealed by the Act of 1909, the Hereford Corporation had
powers which they wished to exercise to call upon the owners of
this wretched property to demolish it, but already there was a
shortage of housing accommodation in the town, and to demolish
these places without providing or arranging for the provision of
decent houses to replace them would have accentuated the house
famine, and, therefore, injured the very people whom the corporation wanted to help. It was, therefore, decided that new houses
must be provided "pari passu" with the demolition of old ones. It was
also decided that these new houses should be provided on the outskirts of the town, on an estate planned on modern economical
lines, instead of as in other places, under orders from the Local
Government Board, re-housing the people where land is much too
dear to make it possible to do the work properly, and where a
totally inadequate supply of fresh air and unimpeded sunlight is
available. A less enlightened local authority would have jumped
to the conclusion that municipal house building was the best
policy to adopt, but Hereford Corporation, who had carefully
studied the pros and cons of this and other methods, decided to
adopt the policy of encouraging and assisting private enterprise
to do the actual work of house building and house letting (the
success of which depends upon very careful attention to innumer-

able personal details), and very wisely confined themselves to their proper function of supervising what was done, thereby ensuring far better financial and other results than are achieved when local authorities themselves undertake the building and letting of houses, for which work they are, owing to circumstances inseparable from their position as a local authority, entirely unsuited.

The wise and comprehensive policy adopted by Hereford, and most ably and energetically carried out by Alderman E. F. Bulmer, who was then Mayor of Hereford, has resulted in one of the best examples, if not the very best example, in this country of garden suburb development on economical town planning lines. It may be much smaller than some of the other and better known ventures, but it is the most complete and best adapted to the needs of the case.

Hereford was fortunate in launching her town planning scheme before the 1909 Act was passed, otherwise it would have been delayed for three or more years by the complicated regulations referred to in other chapters. She was also most fortunate in her mayor and corporation, who dealt with the rather difficult and complicated problem submitted to them in a thoroughly business-like and common-sense manner.

Before dealing with the slum prevention part of their work, it will be interesting and useful to explain what happened in the more congested parts of the town.

It was found in Hereford, as in other places, that it was not possible to house the families who are actually displaced from the slums in the new houses in the garden suburb. But the medical officer for the city (Dr Miller) conducted a personal investigation into the movements of the displaced families. The result was to prove that a general move-up was brought about. The houses in the garden suburb were occupied to some extent by people who were previously paying rather lower rents, but vacated their houses voluntarily in order to move into better houses with better surroundings, regarding the new houses as worth to them the extra money. The houses vacated by these persons were occupied similarly by a class below them, and in this way the previous slum-dwellers were enabled to get houses of a better quality than those previously occupied, and at rents not much above those they had previously paid.

The total area of the garden suburb is $9\frac{1}{2}$ acres, which includes $1\frac{1}{2}$ acres of open space used as play grounds and allotments for those requiring gardens larger than the average, the total number of houses is eighty-six, making an average of nine houses per gross acre. Land and development cost £242 per gross acre, in spite of the fact that the land cost £158 per acre, a higher figure than it will be necessary to pay in future where cheap land is opened up for building. The cost of development and law expenses was only £84 per acre, which shows what can be done in the way of economical and efficient development where the true intent of town planning is understood, and when the local authority, landowner and builder work together in perfect harmony for the common good and on the basis of reasonable, but not excessive, profits.

The land was purchased and the roads constructed by the town council. The estate, exclusive of the roads which are maintained by the corporation, is leased to Hereford Co-operative Housing Ltd. on terms under which the society pays the town council a sum equal to the interest and sinking fund on their loans. When these loans are paid off the land becomes the freehold property of the society. The corporation spent £2,300 on land and roads and they have the security of £17,000 worth of buildings.

Eight out of the eighty-six houses on the estate are let as high as 7s. 9d. per week, and of the remainder nearly half are let at 4s. 9d. including rates, with a garden and three bedrooms to each house, the other rents varying from 5s. 6d. to 6s. and 6s. 6d. for houses with four bedrooms for exceptionally large families.

The year 1912 was the first financial year in which there had been no unproductive capital on which to pay interest. The profit earned, £261 15s. 6d., was sufficient to pay 5 per cent on the £2,528 of ordinary shares, but it was considered wiser to only pay 2½ per cent dividend, which amounted to £59 0s. 5d., writing £100 3s. 5d. off the property, putting £100 to reserve, and carrying forward £71 4s. 5d., which was slightly more than the carry-forward for the previous year. It is most satisfactory to notice that although the rents were over £1,200 for the year, the ascertained bad debts were less than ten shillings.

The results may be summarized as follows:

1. Better town development and better housing for the people at reasonable rents.

2. A dividend for the shareholders (2½ per cent was paid in 1912 and 1913).

3. No charge on the rates, which is very different from what often happens with municipal house building schemes.

This shows what can be done in the way of housing reform

where there is a true spirit of co-operation between all concerned in the provision and supervision of housing accommodation for the people, not merely with a view to protecting property which, although deserving of consideration, is certainly not the only thing to be thought of, but also with a fixed determination to ensure fair play and common justice for those who have neither the knowledge nor the influence necessary to enable them to deliver themselves and their children from the bad influences and insanitary living conditions that have been engendered in the past by selfish greed, ill-considered regulations and haphazard methods.

The provision of healthy housing accommodation on the outskirts enabled Hereford to do away with bad housing at the centre without creating a house famine. The total result of her combined schemes and comprehensive policy has been to empty slums, and to house people with low wages in real country instead of driving them into another slum. Every one interested in town planning and housing reform should visit Hereford and study the policy and methods that have been so successful there, with a view to adapting them to their own district.

It may be said that Hereford is, comparatively speaking, quite a small place, and, therefore, what has been done there cannot be done in larger towns or cities. It is true that Hereford is a small place, but then also her resources are small compared with those of larger places. The general principles remain the same, and can be adapted to meet any individual case. In the case of Hereford, there were plenty of difficulties to overcome, and so there will be in every other place, large or small, where good, sound, solid work of this nature is attempted, but all these difficulties were overcome at Hereford, and so they will be elsewhere, provided those responsible for the administration of local affairs really mean business, and are not satisfied with a mere pretence of doing something.

4. HARBORNE AND QUINTON TOWN PLANNING SCHEME.

This scheme is now complete, and has been finally approved by the Local Government Board. The area presented unique opportunities to earnest and well-informed town planners. There is an abundant supply of cheap land, providing excellent building sites for all classes of the community, within easy distance of the centre of the city, and development has only been retarded by lack of adequate communication. Back land is available for the cutting of new main arteries with easy gradients.

The scheme that has been approved must be examined together with the map, in regard to a variety of points:

1. Adequate access in order to encourage quick development.
2. Protection against exorbitant rises in land values.
3. Economical development.
4. Open spaces.
5. Sites for public buildings.
6. Small holdings.
7. General provisions.

1. ADEQUATE ACCESS

On the accompanying map X is the centre of the town planning area, where development should come first ⚹ is Five Ways, Edgbaston.

Existing roads are shown thus ———. Roads designed by the Corporation thus — — — —. Roads omitted by the Corporation, but nevertheless necessary to make the scheme worth having, are shown thus — · — · —. The present access from X to ⚹ is by way of Lordswood Road and Hagley Road marked A or by way of Lordswood Road, High Street, Harborne, and Harborne Road marked B on map. The new access proposed by the Corporation is marked C on map, leading from X to Hagley Road Station and entering Hagley Road opposite a brick wall at right angles to the traffic in the old road. This new road C was advocated on the ground that further access was urgently needed between the areas north and south of Hagley Road. As a matter of fact there are already two means of access (Norfolk Road and Lordswood Road), and a third could be provided without any cost to the ratepayers by a road marked K on map. The advantages of road K over road C are:

1. It would cost the ratepayers nothing, because it would be a landowner's road opening up his land for building.

2. It follows the natural lie of the land, and involves no heavy expenditure on embankments or cuttings, whereas C is to cost the ratepayers £16,000.

3. It would encourage building development, thereby increasing assessable value, whereas road C will, by reason of its high embankment, entirely block building development for a considerable distance on either side of it.

The most important point of all is that radial access is vastly more important than ring access, and to propose a means of improving ring access round the town without thinking of radial access into

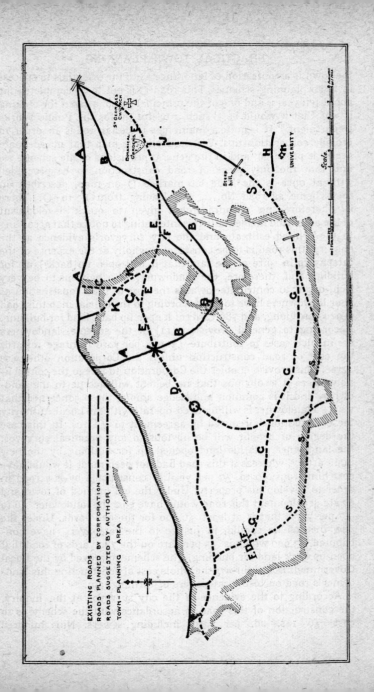

EXISTING ROADS
ROADS PLANNED BY CORPORATION
ROADS SUGGESTED BY AUTHOR
TOWN-PLANNING AREA

Scale

St. George's Church
BOTANICAL GARDENS
Steep hill
UNIVERSITY

the town is a confession of ignorance as to the essentials to success in town planning schemes. This road C is not to be completed for about ten years, and one of the principal reasons given for making it was that it would be " such a useful tip for the Public Works Department." It is quite a quaint idea to design roads in order to provide corporation tips. We see from the map that no adequate access is proposed, and in the general provisions of the scheme we find that the only piece of road construction to be proceeded with at once is the little bit marked D on map, described in the scheme as road No. 2, and leading from X to O. There is, therefore, no encouragement given to quick development of the area. And incidentally it is interesting to notice that according to the printed estimate and the city surveyor's evidence at the enquiry, this road is to be constructed wholly at the expense of the ratepayers in spite of the fact that it will open up back land for building and, therefore, the landowner, who happens to be very rich, ought to contribute towards the cost of road construction as poor landowners have to do. According to the official map this road is 920 yards long, and 780 yards of it open up back land for building. According to general provision (11) of the scheme, landowners are in such cases to contribute £3 10s. per yard frontage towards the cost of road construction unless the Corporation otherwise agree. This proviso enables the Corporation to forego the contribution where it is obvious that no benefit will accrue to the landowner, and it is common knowledge among those concerned that where a landowner is willing to co-operate with the Local Authority the contribution is reduced by agreement to £2 10s. In this case the degree of benefit will be obvious to any practical surveyor, the landowner gets his land opened up for building by the new main artery, whereas if this road had not been made it would have cost him from £6 to £7 per yard to construct a by-law road in order to develop his property. Under the old method of town and estate development this road would have cost the landowner £6 to £7 per yard, that is at least £6,000 for the 920 yards. Under the new method he should, in justice to the ratepayers, have contributed £3,900 which is £5 per yard on the 780 yards of road that open up back land for building. The scheme approved by the Local Government Board throws the whole cost of constructing this landowner's road on to the ratepayers of Birmingham.

According to the evidence of the city surveyor at the inquiry, the construction of this road in accordance with the scheme is to cost £6 14s. 2d. per yard, including sewers. Nine hundred and twenty yards at this price come to £6,171 13s. 4d., as the total cost of constructing the road. The total cost given in the official estimate is £6,981. This discrepancy between the surveyor's evidence, and the official estimate is probably accounted for by the expenditure incurred in forming the road and other sundries. We need not trouble ourselves about this discrepancy, but it is important to notice that the official information and figures prove conclusively that there is to be no contribution from the landowner towards the cost of road No. 2 in the scheme, marked D on Map, which is to be constructed at once, and which will increase the value of a considerable quantity of privately owned land. In previous chapters it has been shown that under intelligent town planning administration the cost of town and estate development can be more equitably divided between owners and ratepayers with great advantage to both parties, the total result being that town development should in the future cost the ratepayers very much less than it has done in the past. In this case not only has no saving been effected for the ratepayers, an actual charge has been thrown on to them for estate development which, without the intervention of the Corporation, would have cost the owner, not the ratepayers, about £6,000. It would obviously have been very good business for him to get off with £3,900 the degree of benefit settled by the scheme in those cases where owners co-operate with the Corporation. This subsidy to a rich landowner represents a dead loss to the ratepayers of £3,900.

What ought to have been done was to construct at once the new main artery marked E on map from X to ✠ indicated on the map by — · — · — with a short branch to Gordon Road marked F on the map. Figures given in Appendix 1 show this to be a far more economical proposal than the Corporation method.

The road marked G on map in the southern part of the area, known locally as the ridge road, cuts right through the middle of two golf courses, and not unnaturally aroused great opposition from those in possession, because no matter what modifications in construction are made, in order to minimize the disturbance caused, it will, if it is ever made, very seriously interfere with the comfort and enjoyment of the players. This fact will be obvious to any golfer who has played on Malvern or other courses where public roads run across the links. This road shows no imagination. It merely follows as far as possible existing accommodation roads and footpaths, which is just what the best modern road designers avoid doing; it is, in fact, merely something to look at, and will not stand the test of any examination from the points of view of public convenience, general amenities, economics or hygiene. To seriously injure if not destroy, these two golf courses, thereby encouraging, if not actually causing, their development as building estates is an offence against all the principles and objects of town planning, which ought not to be passed over lightly. The preservation of these open spaces, although not free to the general public, will be of inestimable importance to that part of the city, when the land in their immediate vicinity is developed for building, as it could and should be in the near future under able and energetic administration of the 1909 Act. By no means the least attractive point concerning these open spaces is that no expense for their maintenance falls on the ratepayers.

The inclusion of this road G in the scheme aroused great and justifiable opposition, which might all have been avoided if a little expert knowledge and practical common sense had been exercised. Any practical man surveying the land and studying the ownerships, and present user of the land will come to the conclusion that a new road cut along line S would:

1. Cost less to construct than road G.
2. Open up more land for building.
3. Avoid friction with the landowners.

Road S would also open up Four Dwellings S Farm marked F D F on map for immediate building and other uses. Road G is most obnoxious to the owners through whose land it passes, whereas S should, and no doubt would, be welcomed by the owners through whose land it passes, because it would convert their cheap agricultural land into what is technically described as "red hot building land," especially if, as should be done, a service of motor-buses were run along it in return for an undertaking from the landowners to provide the necessary amenities, viz., ten houses per gross acre, one acre in every ten open space, etc., etc.

Another objection to road G as designed by the Corporation is that it ends nowhere, or, to be more exact, ends with a right-angle turn into a steep narrow lane, whereas it ought to be connected with Farquhar Road marked I, and University Road H, as shown on map, and Farquhar Road ought to have been connected by means of a road marked J on map, with the Botanical Gardens, and if the negotiations with the landowners had been properly conducted these communications would have cost the ratepayers little or nothing. But people who construct sewers in a town planning area and project tramways into it before any bargains have been concluded with the landowners, are obviously not much good at protecting the interests of the ratepayers. Economy is important to those who have to pay the bill and so is efficiency. It is most annoying to be called upon to pay a heavy bill, and find that one has only got a very inferior article. This will be the position of the Birmingham ratepayers with regard to roads G and C. In both cases it is proposed to finish off a fine wide road through a narrow neck round a right-angle corner, which is indeed a curious way of providing access to the area. It is a misnomer to call this town planning.

It may be objected that roads EE, J, and S, could not be satisfactorily carried out without extending the town planning area. This raises an important point in procedure which has already been dealt with in Chapter III, where it was pointed out that before settling the boundaries of an area to be town planned, it is necessary to make quite certain what new main arteries will be required to open up the area for quick development, so that the land through which these arteries pass may be included, no matter whether it is or is not already developed.

The omission in this instance to include sufficient land to provide adequate access to the area is a fatal blot on the whole scheme.

2. PROTECTION AGAINST EXORBITANT RISES IN LAND VALUES

According to the official report of the town clerk and the city surveyor, land in this area is worth from £60 to £100 per acre, and according to the president of the Property Owners' Association, land on which not more than ten houses per acre may be built becomes worth more than £200* per acre, from which it follows that, according to these gentlemen, if ten houses per acre had been the number fixed for this area, there would have been a profit for the landowners of more than £100 to £140 per acre, a very nice, comfortable percentage; but this profit was not considered large enough, and, therefore, the number was fixed at twelve houses per acre, thereby increasing land values in this area by a further 20 per cent.

* The author takes no responsibility for this opinion which was given in a letter to the City Council.

3. ECONOMICAL DEVELOPMENT.

In Section A2 primary of the road sections prescribed by the scheme the width of roadway shown is 35 feet. This is far more than is necessary in the first instance, and only adds to the cost. It is by heavy and unnecessary expenditures such as this that other members of the council not on the town planning committee are frightened out of providing at once the adequate access essential to quick development. Even in the ultimate section 35 feet is an unreasonable width. It is too much for four streams of traffic, and not enough for five. Another grave objection to the ultimate section is the fact that houses on the left-hand side of the road are cut off from the roadway by the independent tram track, a most inconvenient arrangement that must seriously hinder development on that side of the road.

Section B3 for side roads on residential estates shows 18 feet width of roadway. This is as unreasonable as the 35 feet in A2. It is neither one thing nor the other; it is too wide for two streams of traffic and not wide enough for three. The roadways on Harborne Tenants', Moor Pool estate, are 16 feet wide, and experience has proved conclusively that there is ample room for two streams of traffic to pass each other at full speed. The extra 2 feet is a mere fad. It may be said that it adds very little to the cost, but why add to the cost of estate development when no good object is achieved thereby? It all goes on to the rents of the houses.

Section B5 allows 8 feet roadways to small groups of houses; but these roadways must not exceed 100 feet in length. This length does not admit of sufficient air and garden space for the houses to which these roadways lead; it should be increased to at least 500 feet, in order to provide for adequate ventilation to the houses.

Only four out of the twelve cross-sections laid down by the Birmingham Corporation have been reproduced here. The remarks on these four apply also to the other eight. It is most inadvisable to lay down a lot of road cross-sections that must be rigidly adhered to. Elasticity is vital to the success of town planning; conditions are bound to vary on different estates, and these varying conditions should be met by adapting one or other of the general cross-sections to the needs of each case, instead of, by cast-iron regulations, making it impossible to do the work properly.

The Birmingham Corporation have ignored the report of the Royal Commission on sewage disposal. If the recommendation in this report had been adopted very large savings could have been effected. No mention is made in the scheme of laying the sewers

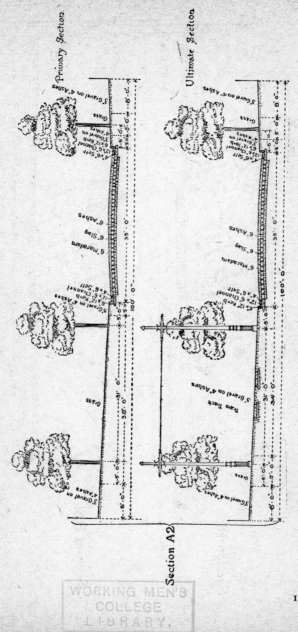

Primary Section.

Ultimate Section

3' Gravel on 4" Ashes

3' Gravel on 4" Ashes

Grass

Grass

6"×12" Channel
1½"×6" Kerb
3" Gravel on
4" Ashes

12½"×6" Kerb
3" Gravel on
4" Ashes

1'4"×6" Self

1'4"×6" Self

6" Ashes

6" Ashes

6" Slag

6" Slag

6" Macadam

6" Macadam

1'4"×6" Self

6"×12" Channel
1½"×6" Kerb

3" Gravel on 4" Ashes

3" Gravel on
4" Ashes

Grass

3" Gravel on 4" Ashes

Tram Track

3" Gravel on 4" Ashes

Grass

Section A2

I

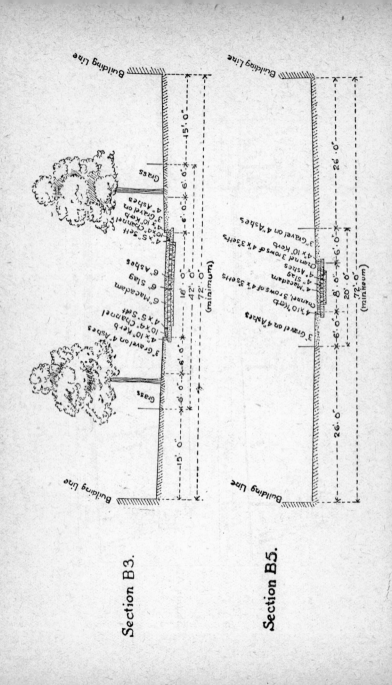

Section B3.

Section B5.

under the grass margins, and drains at the backs of the houses, instead of under the roadways, which is another means of saving expenditure, and at the same time increasing efficiency.

In the Birmingham area a monopoly has been created in the supply of road material and kerbs and gutters. Under economical town planning methods this monopoly would have been destroyed. This has not been done. During the last twenty years or so the cost of making a by-law road in Birmingham has been increased from £2 to £3 per yard forward to nearly £7. Part of this increase was necessary, the old style of road making not being good enough, but a great deal of it is due to the monopoly in road materials, increased charges for connexions to the main sewer, and other official requirements which are not reasonable. Town planning presented an excellent opportunity of correcting these mistakes which opportunity has unfortunately been missed.

In view of its great importance to the builders and the tenants of small house property I have worked out the cost of estate development on actual estates in this area in two ways:

1. Under the general provisions and cross-sections of the Harborne and Quinton town planning scheme.

2. On methods approved by the Royal Commission on sewage and other leading authorities.

Under the Harborne and Quinton town planning scheme the cost per acre averages more than £300 as against £180 per acre under more enlightened regulations. At twelve houses per acre, this extra cost amounts to £10 per house, which at 6 per cent (speculative builders pay more than this for their money) is 12s. per annum, i.e. 2¾d. per week, to which must be added the extra rates levied on the extra rent, viz., 1⅜d. per week, making a total of 4⅛d. extra per house per week, due to official fads. The tenants will probably have to pay an extra 6d. per week, without getting anything in return that will benefit their health or increase their enjoyment of life.

4. OPEN SPACES

Very little land has been reserved in this area for public open spaces, and this feature of the scheme has been severely criticized by some town planners. By careful administration of the Act it is possible to provide for sufficient open space without actually reserving any special plots of land for the purpose* and where

* Civic centres are an exception to this rule.

this is done economy is effected. It may be that the Corporation intends to adopt this policy, but if so why reserve any public open spaces at all? The little bits reserved in the plan, 10·4 acres, 8 acres, 5 acres and 7½ acres, are neither one thing nor the other. If they are needed at all they are not nearly big enough and if they are not needed, then why waste the ratepayers' money?

5. SITES FOR PUBLIC BUILDINGS

No land is reserved for this purpose, from which it would appear that the intention is to wait until the price goes up before allowing the ratepayers to buy what they must have.

6. SMALL HOLDINGS

This scheme presented a unique opportunity of providing small holdings within easy reach of an important market which would have been a great boon to the community, and need have put no burden on the rates. The opportunity has been missed.

7. GENERAL PROVISIONS

Appendix 5 gives a model set of general provisions; it is, there-fore, unnecessary to take up much space with comments on the general provisions of this particular scheme; suffice it to say that the general provision enacting that all claims for compensation or betterment shall be made within twelve months from the date of the approval of the scheme is an obvious contravention of the intentions of Parliament under Sections 58 and 59 of the Act. It is quite impossible to make a claim within twelve months, in respect of a matter which may not arise for twenty years. This general provision, therefore, rules out betterment altogether, and therefore is dead against the interests of the ratepayers, who ought to get, and under the Act are expressly given, a share of the increment due to the expenditure of public money.

The only general conclusions that can be come to with regard to this the first town planning scheme under the 1909 Act are:

1. The rate of development will be very slow. It was evidently not realized that it is not enough to stop bad development, and that it is of paramount importance to expedite development as well as arranging that this work shall be well done.

2. The saving to the ratepayers will not be nearly so much as it ought to have been.

3. The cost of estate development is very much too high.

4. The provision for amenities is quite inadequate. Twelve

6s. 6d. houses per acre does not leave enough room for open spaces, play grounds and allotments.

The town planning idea is thoroughly sound from the economic as well as the hygienic and æsthetic point of view, but it will not give satisfactory results unless it is carefully and intelligently carried out. Old-fashioned ways must be discarded for up-to-date methods and above all the public welfare must have preference over private interests. Is the rise in rates nothing? Is the death-rate in the slums nothing? Is the prevention of tuberculosis nothing?

Town planning properly administered can very materially assist in the solution of all these problems, but those responsible for this particular town planning scheme have only hindered matters.

5. EAST BIRMINGHAM TOWN PLANNING SCHEME

(a) Adequate Access.

In this case, with the exception of one short piece of road across Batchelor's Farm, to which reference has already been made, there was no need for cutting new main arteries in order to encourage quick development. Development was already proceeding at a great pace on the old lines, and the problem was how to direct it into new and better channels with the least possible cost to the ratepayers and without depriving those who had spent money, or entered into contracts, of their just return on any expenditure that had been incurred or commitments entered into.

(b) Protection Against Exorbitant Rises in Land Values.

Some of the land in the area had already been sold or leased on exorbitant terms on the assumption that development would be allowed to continue in the old way. This state of affairs presented several difficult cases in areas immediately adjacent to existing building, each of which called for special treatment. By careful thought it was found possible in some cases to give such benefits under the Act as to induce the landowner to agree to development on modern lines, because in view of the concessions accorded to him it paid him to do so. In other cases owing to expenditure actually incurred or commitments entered into there was no alternative but to allow more than the proper number of houses per acre. On the whole the apparently hopeless task of at once improving the method of development even on what is technically known as " red hot building land," without hindering it for a longer time than that insisted upon by the Local Government Board, turned out in practice to be much easier than was at first anticipated provided sufficient time and care were given to the work and provided, of course, that the owners and builders concerned were met in a reasonable spirit.

At a very short distance from this " red hot building land " the problem was comparatively simple, because in these cases no expenditure had been incurred and no commitments entered into, and above all the land had been in its then ownership for many years, that is to say, none of those with whom the Corporation were called upon to negotiate had been misled into paying extravagant prices for their land, by the assumption that they would be allowed to develop it on land sweating lines. In no case had the land in question cost its present owner more than agricultural value. For this land, therefore, it was quite easy and strictly in accordance with the intentions of Parliament to prepare a town planning scheme, restricting building density in such a way as to ensure reasonable amenities for future residents.

The Corporation's unwise omission to restrict building to a reasonable density, coupled with their wise reservation of certain areas for factory purposes, has involved them in a claim of £10,000 for compensation. The claimant objects to what he describes as the arbitrary selection of his land for factories and workshops on the ground that, in a neighbourhood where there is a big demand for house accommodation, the sites for factories are likely to " ripen " much later than sites for houses. This problem was referred to in Chapter III. It must also be considered here.

Business men needing factory sites are better able to protect their own interests than the tenants of small house property and, therefore, unless special facilities are provided in the way of railway sidings, sheds and other works, owners of factory land will not be able to realize as quickly as owners of housing land. Another reason for providing these facilities is that considerable savings would be effected for the ratepayers by avoiding the wear and tear of roads caused by heavy vans and lorries. In this scheme the Corporation of Birmingham asked for powers to provide these facilities, but the Local Government Board ruled that they did not come within the scope of the 1909 Act.

Town planners are agreed that it is advisable wherever possible to confine smoky and obnoxious factories to certain districts, but narrow-minded officialism has done its best to prevent this idea being put into practice. It will not be possible by the old methods to provide nearly such complete arrangements in the way of railway sidings, sheds and other works; in addition to which the facilities that are eventually provided will cost the ratepayers and manufacturers very much more than would have been the case under the 1909 Act wisely administered. Under the conditions of this scheme as approved by the Board, landowners, manufacturers and ratepayers all have strong grounds for complaint.

(c) Economical Development.

The road cross-sections and other regulations for development laid down by this scheme are almost exactly identical with those laid down in the Harborne and Quinton scheme. The remarks on that scheme concerning economical development apply with equal force to this one, and, therefore, need not be repeated here, but there are two important points peculiar to this scheme.

The first of these, the purchase of Batchelor's Farm, has already been dealt with.

The other is the improvement of the River Cole. This river, which runs along the eastern boundary, is constantly overflowing its banks, and, therefore, the land adjoining is of little or no value until this flooding has been stopped and a sewer laid down. The old method is to pay the landowner for the right to run a sewer across his land, and to construct a sewer at the public expense. The landowner benefits twice over; he is paid for the right to run a sewer, for which easement he often gets more than his land is worth, and at the expense of the ratepayers his land is provided with drainage, thereby very largely increasing its value. Under town planning it is possible to buy land of this character at its real value, and secure for the ratepayers the increment due to the expenditure of public money. In the case of the River Cole the right thing to do in the interests of the ratepayers was to buy a strip of land along the river about 400 acres in extent, of which 100 acres is to-day subject to constantly recurring floods, and, therefore, of very little value to the owner, straighten the course of the river, and construct a sewer alongside. An ornamental walk might have been made along the river bank, and the land next to this reserved for allotments and playing fields. By buying the land outright, at once it would have been possible in this instance, with careful management, to provide the river improvement, ornamental walk, allotments and playing fields at a profit to the ratepayers, because the increased value of the higher land would have more than paid the cost of amenities on the low-lying land. No mention is made of this matter in the scheme now under consideration, but as some of the land adjoining the River Cole is left uncoloured on the map it is just possible that the committee may have something in their minds for the future; at the same time, their scheme, as published, makes it impossible to secure sufficient land at a price that would make it possible to provide the amenities described above without very considerable expense to the ratepayers. The scheme does provide for an expensive and unnecessary new road parallel with the river, cutting through land which is badly needed for allotments and playing fields. This new road is to have 32 feet width of macadam—one more example of how to spend the greatest possible amount of money, and get the least possible value in return.

(d) Open Spaces.

When work was commenced on this scheme the first thing done was to ascertain the total acreage of existing allotments, belonging to the Corporation or private individuals, and also the total acreage of playing fields, bowling greens, etc., under private as well as public ownership. The figures supplied to the author of this book were 49½ acres of publicly owned allotments and playing fields and 148¾ acres under private ownership, which latter were liable at any moment to be cut up for building (18 acres are already being dealt with in this way). It was also found that the total supply of allotments and playing fields then in existence did not nearly meet the demand. The district was already more than 150 acres short of what it needed in the way of permanent open spaces, and to this had to be added the further 140 acres of permanent open spaces that will be needed when the 1,400 acres that comprise this town planning area are fully developed. Even the most courageous town planners will admit that this was a very difficult task, but with a little care and forethought it might have been accomplished without cost to the ratepayers. At least half of the amount required might have been provided along the River Cole, in the manner described above, and the remainder could have been arranged for in the development plans of individual estates if reasonable concessions had been made to landowners in the cost of estate development. The Corporation scheme only provides an additional 64 acres out of the 290 acres required, that is to say, all the time and money spent upon this so-called town planning scheme will result in the area being far worse provided with amenities when the work is completed than when the work was first started.

The demand for allotments in Birmingham is far greater than

the supply, and a very large proportion of those in existence are only held on annual tenancies—a most unsatisfactory arrangement for the cultivators. This state of affairs is by no means peculiar to Birmingham and, therefore, it behoves town planners to leave no stone unturned to increase the supply of these necessary amenities and ensure that they shall be on a more permanent basis.

Mr Streetly, secretary of the Birmingham and District Allotments and Small Holdings, pointed out the other day that " There is danger in assuming that the problem is solved by the gardens which town planning prescribes. . . . There is evidence of a large unsatisfied demand for allotments, but, so far from helping, the Birmingham town planning schemes may defeat our object by jeopardizing allotments which already exist." He also drew attention to the fact that the leases of a number of the Birmingham allotments expire within a few years and tenants subject to a month's notice to quit are very chary about putting money and labour into property of which they may be dispossessed before they can gather the fruits.

(e) Sites for Public Buildings.

These have been very scantily provided in this scheme. In 1911 the Education Committee was provided with the cheapest school site they have ever bought, and it is possible that one or two other public buildings may be located on Batchelor's Farm, which cost the ratepayers only £136 per acre, whereas adjacent land was valued at £400 per acre, but there is no sign in the scheme of any general comprehensive policy of providing sites for public buildings before the land has risen to building value.

(f) Small Holdings.

There is no land in this area suitable for small holdings.

(g) General.

Speaking of the scheme as a whole it can only be described as a mere pretence of town planning, and is in fact a complete failure from the ratepayers' point of view. They are called upon for a much larger expenditure (the official estimate is £69,260 0s. 0d.) than would have been necessary if economical town planning methods had been adopted by the Corporation and approved by the Local Government Board. They will when the area is fully developed have far fewer open spaces in proportion to the population than they have at present, and last, but by no means least, the Board will not allow them to provide railway sidings, etc., that would save wear and tear of roads and induce manufacturers to come to the district, thereby increasing assessable value.

It may be said that motor vans on properly constructed roads provide adequate and economical means for collection, and delivery of goods, and this is true in the case of small consignments, but large consignments comprising several truck loads could be more conveniently and economically dealt with, if factories and warehouses were connected by rail with the central goods yard.

The Local Government Board's approval of ridiculous proposals like the right angle corners at the end of new main arteries and the £16,000 Corporation tip in the Harborne scheme, and their rejection of thoroughly sound schemes like the Birkenhead purchase of Storeton estate (see Appendix 1) and railway sidings, etc., in East Birmingham, will be further considered in chapter VI. These decisions are quite unintelligible to any practical town planner, and their effect is to throw on to the ratepayers very heavy expenditure that might have been avoided, as well as hindering town and estate development, and ensuring that what work is done will not be nearly as well done as it should have been.

In the early days of the preparation of this scheme great pains were taken to ascertain the views of land agents concerned, and to consider how far these could be met without neglecting the Corporation's duty to its ratepayers, and before these negotiations were terminated one very satisfactory agreement was arrived at which provided for only ten houses per acre, with allotments at the back on land next door to existing buildings, without any cost to the ratepayers, and the owners expressed themselves as quite satisfied. This success was achieved by granting concessions with regard to building lines and other details. There was a certain small loss in the amenities, but it was in no way commensurate with the very great advantage of only ten houses per acre, with allotments at the back on land ripe for building, and, therefore, the Corporation, like the owners, had every reason to be satisfied with their bargain. Other difficulties were under consideration, and might have been adjusted. For instance, one estate in this area had for some years past been very seriously depreciated in value by cantankerous neighbours, who refused access across their land, in spite of the fact that this access might have been provided without any injury to the opposing owners. If the agent of the estate requiring access had been reasonable in other matters, very valuable assistance might have been given to him in the development of his client's property, and reasonable amenities provided for the people. This agent admitted that the long back additions to houses built under the by-laws are very unhealthy and seriously obstruct the supply of light and air to living rooms and bedrooms; he also admitted that in a majority of cases large individual gardens to each house soon become rubbish heaps emitting bad smells, whereas allotments not only produce a little extra income for the owner, but are much appreciated and carefully cultivated by those who rent them.

In this East Birmingham scheme, as in the Harborne scheme, there is no apparent attempt to ensure quick and economical development so as to expedite the emptying of the slums into the country, which is so urgently needed at the present time in the interests of public health, but which would obviously depreciate the value of small house property in congested districts. It is sometimes said by sympathetic people who have not carefully ascertained facts, that generally speaking the dwellers in the slums have to live there in order to be close to their work. The best authorities who have ascertained facts all agree that, except in very special circumstances which do not apply in Birmingham, at least one-half of our slum dwellers could and would move further out if only they were given some little encouragement to do so, instead of being kept in the centre as they are at present, in order that house property in congested districts shall not depreciate in value.

Neither of these Birmingham town planning schemes are in the least degree likely to help those people who so badly need assistance, if only for the sake of their children. These will be the citizens of to-morrow, and on their health and character the future prosperity of our city will very largely depend. These two schemes are a veritable triumph of the lawyer's skill in dealing with detail, the letters, forms and notices drawn up to meet the complicated and confused regulations of the Local Government Board are most admirably worded and deserve the highest praise. The only thing that seems lacking is a true appreciation of the real meaning of town planning. What is the position of Birmingham to-day? A rapidly approaching house famine with nothing being done by the local or central authority to meet it, in spite of constantly increasing rates, rising rents and unsuitable accommodation. It is true the rate collector is quite happy because in the slums of Birmingham there are fewer void houses than has been the case for many years past, and this means another £8,000 per annum collected in rates. It would be far better for the ratepayers, from the economic as well as other points of view, to collect this extra

£8,000 in rates from the new suburbs which ought to, and would very soon be built if the 1909 Act were administered with energy and ability.

One local land agent tells us that '' Since November, 1912, the erection of only seven houses has been arranged for in the East Birmingham area, whereas to meet the demand some hundreds of houses should have been put up. Present circumstances prevent surveyors advising expenditure on new roads, etc. Rents in East Birmingham have gone up in many cases from 3d. to 1s. per week and there are numerous instances of two families occupying one house on account of the lack of proper housing accommodation. What has happened in East Birmingham will happen elsewhere unless the Town Planning Committee agree to be more reasonable in their demands.''

Another land agent says: '' The general effect of the scheme is to discourage the building of smaller working men's houses, especially in the developed areas, exactly where the houses are so urgently wanted. Rents are much higher in the district already, the area having been shut up from building operations for nearly three years. I have only leased land for six houses within the area since the scheme was projected.''

And in the autumn of 1913, at the Meeting of the British Association, Mr George Cadbury, Junior, himself a member of the Town Planning Committee, told us that '' in Birmingham there is now a backward flow into the old areas and the number of un-inhabited houses in the central areas is getting less.''

6. RUISLIP-NORTHWOOD TOWN PLANNING SCHEME

In this district a penny rate only produces about £200, whereas in Birmingham it produces £15,000, and yet the smaller place has dealt much more thoroughly and effectively with the various problems at issue than has been the case in Birmingham. This scheme comprises about 6,000 acres of land, as against less than 4,000 acres in the two first Birmingham schemes combined. The Ruislip-Northwood scheme was started at practically the same time as the Birmingham schemes just described, and with no more knowledge and experience at their disposal, but they put what knowledge and experience were available to much better use. Ruislip-Northwood took care to include sufficient land in her town planning area; Birmingham did not.

Another example of the foresight of Ruislip-Northwood was the inclusion in their area for the protection of their scheme of land situated in an adjoining rural district. This was strenuously opposed by the Watford Rural District Council, in whose area the land was situated. They feared that Ruislip-Northwood was going to confiscate the land, and did not see that it was to the advantage of their ratepayers to get even a small part of their area planned on modern lines without having to go through all the trouble and expense of preparing a town planning scheme. This objection was supported by the Hertfordshire County Council on the ground that :

" 1. The overlapping of a portion of land under a town planning scheme into two counties was in every sense undesirable.

" 2. There had to be a limit somewhere and the county boundary was the natural limit.

" 3. The Local Government Act of 1894 stated that the county boundary should be the controlling boundary for all public health and local government purposes, and express provision was made in that Act, that not only each rural district but each parish should lie wholly within the county of which it was a part, and where necessary for that end, the boundaries should be rectified by order of the County Council.

" It would be most inconvenient to set up in effect a separate authority for dealing with such matters as building regulations, sewerage and water supply."*

They forgot that:

1. Town planning was not known in this country when the Local Government Act of 1894 was passed, and that the Act of 1909 expressly provided for the inclusion of land in adjoining districts, where this is essential to the success of a town planning scheme as in the case of Ruislip-Northwood.

2. That Ruislip-Northwood is already draining an area which is outside the county in which it is situated.†

To quote Mr E. R. Abbott, Clerk to the Ruislip-Northwood Urban District Council, " This idea of a boundary was a beautiful idea, but not a fact."

It was urged by the neighbouring authority that if developments were required, they were quite prepared to consider a scheme

* Vide " Middlesex and Buckinghamshire Advertiser," February 18, 1911.

† This is just the sort of thing that is constantly happening all over the country, due to the fact that these county and other administrative boundaries are quite out of date. They were settled many years ago, long before there was any possibility of knowing what modern requirements would be, and with little or no regard to drainage and other practical problems that are constantly coming before local authorities at the present day.

themselves, but as they gave no undertaking to this effect at the inquiry, it was not possible to take them seriously.

The land in question was needed for access as well as protection, and was eventually included in the scheme.

A few small pieces of land situated within the area were excluded from the scheme; but as the total area of these small patches is a negligible proportion of the total area, it is not necessary to go into the reasons for their exclusion.

With regard to the scheme itself.

1. Adequate access has been provided not only with regard to roads, but also in the arrangements made with the railway company, and it is interesting to notice that adjoining districts will benefit from these roads when they are made, without having to contribute towards the cost of making them. The Ruislip-Northwood District Council, therefore, deserved every support, and not opposition, from adjoining authorities.

2. Certain areas have been allocated for special uses or different classes of buildings, such as shops, private dwelling houses, factories and other purposes so as to protect the residential amenities.

3. One hundred acres have been reserved as private open spaces, and 150 acres of public open spaces have been acquired without cost to the ratepayers.

4. The area is divided into districts where respectively not more than twelve, eight, six and four houses to the acre averaged over each land unit are allowed, twenty being the maximum number of dwelling houses allowed on any single acre. The Ruislip Manor Company's plan divides their estate into four main areas intended for different classes of houses from the most expensive in the north, to medium sized villas in the centre, and workmen's dwellings in the south. This plan provides for the largest possible proportion of houses to have an approximately southern aspect. It also provides for open spaces, sites for churches and schools and other public buildings, as well as the grouping together of dwelling houses for those who are likely to have common tastes and interests, while every effort will be made for the preservation of objects of interest and natural beauty.

It has been possible by a system of give and take to provide necessary communication across the company's land for adjacent owners and occupiers, and in one or two cases access will be afforded to the company through lands of other owners to roads and railway stations.

At the southern end of the town planning area, land had been plotted out before the preparation of this scheme for development on the old lines. To meet this difficulty an agreement was made between the local authority and the owners of the property, by which the number of houses to be put per acre was considerably reduced, and various open spaces were arranged for. In return for these amenities the owners obtained valuable concessions in the cost of estate development, and the total result is highly satisfactory to all concerned.

Thanks to the wise and conciliatory methods adopted by Ruislip-Northwood, it may be confidently expected that her scheme will lead owners in the future to lay out their lands in such a way as will provide amenities in themselves, and it is satisfactory to notice that the local authority has done everything in its power to facilitate and encourage quick development of the area.

All through this scheme it is evident that the first consideration has been given to sanitary conditions, and old fashioned habits have not, so far as the local authority is concerned, been allowed to interfere with economic and hygienic necessities. A proper sense of proportion has been maintained by those preparing the plan, and everything possible under the circumstances has been done by them to prevent the perpetuation of old methods from frustrating the main object of town planning.

By-laws have been relaxed, and the local authority has obtained by agreement the restriction of building density it desired, in return for which the landowners have obtained (1) Through communication, (2) Protection from the bad development of neighbouring land, and many other advantages.

In connexion with these agreements there is a very interesting point that is of inestimable value to landowners. Under the old method of selling freehold land with restrictive covenants upon it, there is no guarantee that these covenants will be observed by all the future owners. As a matter of fact, they are often broken by unscrupulous men with serious detriment to honourable men who have bought on the strength of the restrictive covenants. By means of town planning schemes and agreements thereunder, it is possible to give landowners permanent protection against this injury to their property.

The Ruislip Manor Company's estate comprises 1,300 acres of land, with three miles of frontage to existing roads, and their first step was to invite a town planning competition and appoint as assessors Sir Aston Webb, C.B., R.A., and Mr Raymond Unwin.

The winning plan was that submitted by Messrs A. & J. Soutar and its principal features were:

1. Convenience of access to all parts of the estate and to adjoining estates.

2. Economy in road making and careful consideration of contours.

3. The planning of as many roads as possible running north and south so as to secure an ideal orientation for the houses.

4. Ample opportunity for architectural treatment and interesting effects without injuring the commercial prospects of the scheme.

Messrs. Soutar's plan has been adopted by the company.

Twelve houses have been built in Manor Way grouped round a lawn 170 feet long by 50 feet wide, each containing three bedrooms, bathroom, two living rooms and scullery, and let at 10s. to 11s. per week exclusive of rates. Similar houses on adjacent sites are sold freehold at £325 to £425 and leasehold at £300. Further schemes have been approved for building 150 small houses and cottages at rents varying from 6s. to 15s. per week.

The total estimate for the whole scheme is £29,000 for 6,000 acres against Birmingham's two estimates taken together of £179,100 for less than 4,000 acres.

GENERAL PROVISIONS

In general terms these seem, like the town planning map of the area, a little too elaborate. They go into more detail than is advisable. Town planners should aim for simplicity of regulations and elasticity in detail, and so far as the map is concerned it is wiser not to fix beforehand more than is absolutely necessary with regard to main arteries and connecting roads, because even the cleverest and most experienced designers cannot foresee all the points that will arise in the process of actually developing a town planning area, or even an individual estate. Unforeseen difficulties and opportunities of improving in detail upon the original conception are sure to arise as the work proceeds, and if those responsible are too tightly bound by the original plan and regulations, opportunities of improvement will have to be ignored. A skeleton plan, leaving details to be filled in as the work proceeds, is the safest and most efficient method, and the general provisions of a scheme should be so worded as to ensure general amenities and economy without going into more detail than is absolutely necessary. Simplicity and elasticity in the preparation of town planning schemes are the only way of ultimately achieving the best and most economical results.

ROADS

The types of road in this scheme are varied according to the weight of traffic, lighter construction being allowed in the case of purely residential districts in exchange for the giving up of certain areas of land for open spaces, either public or private. This arrangement suits all parties; the ratepayers get the open spaces that are needed without any charge on the rates, and the tenants of houses fronting on to these cheaper roadways do not, as under extravagant by-law or town planning schemes, have to pay extra in their rents for useless expenditure. In this matter of narrow inexpensive roadways in purely residential districts, there are two very important matters of economic detail which should not be forgotten. These narrow roads should be so planned as to give no inducement to general traffic to make use of them, that is to say they must not provide a short cut between two points where general traffic passes; great care and thought should also be exercised to arrange open spaces on back land, in such a way that the shortest possible length of roadway is required. If this point is successfully attended to great savings will be effected in the development of individual estates and also in the cost of public services for the ratepayers. These services are responsible for a very large proportion of the public expenditure on town development.

LAND UNITS

General provision 65 of this scheme lays it down that no land unit shall be greater than seven acres in extent. This seems to me to be a mistake and to ignore some of the main objects of town planning, e.g., proper intercommunication between adjoining estates and the planning of new districts on comprehensive lines, instead of in penny numbers. It also seems to ignore the practical fact that for various reasons it will often occur that on certain individual seven-acre plots, it will not be convenient or desirable to arrange for any appreciable amount of open space, and in these cases it may be well that more than the average number of houses per gross acre will have to be allowed, the balance being adjusted by arranging for more than the average amount of open space on an adjoining seven-acre plot. The land unit system is a cumbersome method of dealing with the question of building density, and in Appendix 5 the alternative general provision 17 suggests a simpler way of meeting the point. Where it is considered necessary to adopt the land unit system, each unit should be as large as possible.

General provision 93 of this scheme is framed with the intention of destroying the present system of land purchase by local authorities under which the exact purpose for which the land is required has to be specified and which results in public bodies nearly always paying more for land than it is worth. With the law of the land as it now stands this is a very difficult point to deal with in a town planning scheme. The general provision mentioned above is one way of getting over the difficulty, and general provision 37 in Appendix 5 is another way of attempting to do the same thing. There will be differences of opinion as to which of these general provisions is most likely to achieve the object in view, but there will be no difference of opinion as to the necessity for an intelligent sympathetic and determined central authority who will not allow forms and ceremonies to increase the burdens of the ratepayers.

On the question of procedure under the Act, Ruislip-Northwood's experience suggests that there should be a notice informing owners of the deposit of the scheme when modified by the Local Government Board, but that of the various notices ordered by the Board, the first and third are needed and all the others might be dispensed with. On this it may be said that the regulations do not provide for any more notices than are demanded by the Act. If this is so, then the sooner the Act is amended in this, as well as many other respects, the better for the whole country. England badly needs effective town planning untrammelled by meticulous regulations and dilatory administration.

The protection of unspoilt neighbourhoods from land sweating is at least as important in smaller places as in large towns, and the success of Ruislip-Northwood, where a penny rate only produces £200, proves conclusively that town planning is not beyond the financial resources of these smaller places where it is so urgently needed.

7. ROSYTH

I am indebted to Mr J. E. Wilkes, A.M.I.C.E., town planning engineer to the Royal Burgh of Dunfermline, for the following description of this scheme.

"The work is divided into four town planning schemes, viz., Dunfermline Rosyth, Inverkeithing, North Queensferry and Brucehaven, which taken together cover a total area of 6,200 acres, or very nearly ten square miles.

"The Rosyth area is planned chiefly to accommodate the population coming to the district as a result of the establishment therein of H.M. Dockyard and Naval Base. The incoming population is estimated at 35,000; in addition to which 25,000 men are to be based on the port. The main idea has been to secure conditions which will allow of the erection of workmen's houses to let at a reasonable rent.

"As the land is very undulating it was decided to make an altitude survey of the entire district, showing differences of level of 5 feet by contour lines; this survey was made entirely by means of the tacheometer to ensure exactitude. On the survey, all streets, sewers, stream regulations, etc., were designed.

"At the outset negotiations with landowners were entered into, with a view to arranging the price of building land; also with a view to securing the necessary land for road widenings, and for contributions towards the requisite works.

"Now that the principal negotiations have been concluded the writer would, with great respect, pay a tribute to the principal landowner, the Rt. Hon. The Earl of Elgin and Kincardine, K.G., who has taken great personal interest in the scheme and made valuable suggestions as to its preparation. His Lordship has put enough building land into the market at about half the local rate to suffice, with the Admiralty building land, for Rosyth for many years. Further he has agreed to contribute liberally towards the cost of road widenings; his action has influenced other landowners to do the same.

"For Rosyth proper, it will be noticed that a somewhat formal design has been adopted, the ground here permitting this; where possible the writer prefers to follow the direct methods of the formal school.

"Sites are provided for public buildings.

"The immediate tramways route to Dunfermline will be on a main artery 100 feet wide, as also the principal tramway route to Inverkeithing. The tramways are to be double track with pressed steel sleepers laid on ballast. No cast-iron sewer manhole or other covers are to be placed in the carriage-ways, which will be for the most part of tarred stone; subsidiary sewers will be behind the houses, where possible.

"In one place a steel arch under-bridge and in another place a reinforced concrete over-bridge is provided, in order to open up back land.

"Each building in the town centre and sub-centres is to form part of a uniform design, whilst elevations of all buildings are to be controlled.

" Districts are set aside for workmen's houses. The cottages here will be suitably grouped, and must conform generally to type designs. The present building and road-making regulations are to be much modified, so as to permit of more economical construction.

" The Rosyth area is very fertile and well wooded. It is also well sheltered from the prevailing south-westerly winds.

" Subsidiary roads have been planned in detail in the Dunfermline area north of St Margaret's, in order to settle properly the main roads and sewers, which alone will be included in the town plan.

" The passenger station occupies a position well between business and residential areas, and the goods station has been kept well away for the sake of amenity. The railway company's estimated cost of these stations is £42,000, and they are the subject of a bill now before Parliament.

" Street terminals have been arranged so that each serves as many streets as possible, some doing duty in nine directions; but as regards the amenity of the new town, it is sufficient to point out that Rosyth is in the Royal Burgh of Dunfermline, the birthplace of Mr Carnegie, who has endowed it with an income of £40,000 per annum to be spent in public work of utility and beauty.

" The public are to have access to much of the land in the Naval Base.

" With regard to the areas of Inverkeithing and Brucehaven, the sewer outfall at East Ness will be tide controlled by means of an air lock, a line of fine old trees will be preserved and some of the foreshore will be reclaimed.

" The whole of the roads in North Queensferry are perforce on land very hilly and broken up, but they will command beautiful views of the Estuary of the Forth.

" A new access to North Queensferry, to avoid the somewhat squalid district of Jamestown, is to be provided by spanning the Great North Road, the low level railway and the Admiralty railway by a bridge, 100-feet span."

At the Edinburgh Town Planning Conference, Mr Wilkes explained in further detail his negotiations with landowners and others:

" 1. The railway company originally intended to provide a station that would only cost £6,000, and they were told that if they did not give a decent station they would be left in a slum. It would obviously not be worth the while of the Burgh of Dunfermline to provide a handsome road to an insignificant station. On these representations the railway company have agreed to provide a station costing £42,000 and to give a new bridge.

"2. Over 1,500 acres of land for the new town have been arranged at an average feu duty of £10 per acre, whereas on the old lines £40 per acre has been obtained for the poorest land. This has assured development in Rosyth. The argument used was that the Burgh would spend money if they were sure of something to rate, on which they could get a return.

"3. Land has been given free for widening four miles of road to 100 feet, and the landowners have undertaken to contribute two-thirds of the cost of widening.

"The cost of preparing the scheme including contours will be £750, and the total Corporation outlay on development will be less than £4,000 by 1923 and not more than £11,000 in the end."

The plan published by Mr Wilkes, but not yet (December, 1913) approved by the Scottish Local Government Board, goes into a great deal too much detail and there is far too much of the chess-board method.

Exact information is not yet available as to what cross-sections of roadways will be required or how many houses will be allowed per acre, nor have the general provisions been settled, but so far as the scheme has gone it shows great promise.

Adequate access has been provided for, wherever it is required, and back land is to be opened up for building. The land has been carefully contoured with the most modern appliances. Antiquated systems of drainage have been rejected, and modern methods adopted. The tramways, where needed, will be laid on independent tracks and no cast-iron sewer manhole or other covers will be placed in roadways. Subsidiary sewers will be behind the houses wherever possible. In addition to which it should be a great advantage that the Admiralty, who will be very large employers of labour in the district, are also large owners of land in the area. Negotiations with other large landowners have produced results which are described as most satisfactory to all concerned; but those familiar with the economics of town planning and decent housing at reasonable rents will recognize that £10 feu duty is too high a price to pay for land to be developed on genuine town planning lines.

Open spaces have been reserved before the land has risen to exorbitant prices, and also sites for public buildings.

It yet remains to determine upon a reasonable number of houses per acre, and in view of the fact that by far the greater part of the land in the area was purely agricultural, before the Naval Base was inaugurated, and the town planning schemes projected; both of which events are obviously entirely due to public enterprise and the expenditure of public money, cheap land (i.e. land at somewhere near its agricultural value), the first essential to satisfactory town planning, should in this area be available in practically unlimited quantities, leaving only economical development, the second essential, to be put into practice.

The population eventually to be provided for will amount to 60,000 people, a town in itself. Here is indeed a unique opportunity for doing something really good. At the same time the housing problem to be solved is by no means an easy one.

The eventual population is to be 60,000; that means at least 12,000 houses, of which about 3,000 will be needed in a year or two. A considerable proportion of these 3,000 houses will be tenanted by men who ought not to pay more than 5s. per week in house rent including rates. It will not be an easy matter to provide decent housing accommodation at this figure, especially as the rates and taxes on such a house in this district amount to 1s. 4¼d. per week.

Some experts are of opinion that the only possible way to provide housing accommodation on a sound commercial basis at 5s. per week including rates is to adopt the tenement system: this is a mistake. Cottages have been provided at Moor Pool, Harborne, for 4s. 6d. per week, including rates, where land and development cost £650 per acre, and although nearly all the local conditions at Rosyth differ from those at Harborne, house rents need not be any higher at Rosyth than at Harborne provided only that those responsible for the development of Rosyth understand their business, and arrange for (1) cheap land, (2) rational development, and (3) cheap capital.

It is most earnestly to be hoped that Dunfermline will not allow the tenement system; that would indeed be a retrograde step, and would only raise land values to a quite unreasonable extent, without keeping down house rents. That is the experience of Germany and other countries where the tenement system has been in vogue for a very long time. The best informed town planners in Germany are now straining every nerve to prevent the erection of any more tenement buildings, and to get adopted instead the English custom of self-contained houses for working people.

It must not be forgotten that a very large proportion of the population shortly to be housed at Rosyth will come from south of the Border, and are not accustomed to living in flats. These men will not live in flats if they can avoid it, and people who erect this class of property will run grave risk of finding themselves without tenants.

Rosyth presents a unique opportunity for the building of a new town on modern lines.

CHAPTER VI. DELAY AND ITS CAUSES.

A SHORT survey of the housing progress since the passing of the 1909 Act is the necessary preliminary to an examination into the causes of the delay which has so unfortunately supervened. Up to the present the 1909 Act has not improved matters with regard to housing, but rather has made things worse than before, for while it has pulled down many houses, it has built few or none to replace them in accordance with modern ideas. Immediate action of some sort is needed to set the almost arrested tide of house building flowing again. Landowners are willing to adopt better methods of developing their estates with or without the formalities of town planning schemes, but several such schemes for housing the people in accordance with modern ideas, have been held back and others altogether stopped by the stupidity, or something worse, of public bodies.

The immediate effect of the 1909 Act as administered by the Local Government Board has been to stop building in areas where a scheme is under consideration, and to drive builders into other areas not yet protected. The total tendency to date has been to assist in creating a house famine. The Board's regulations are all for delay and against progress, and this is especially the case with regard to schemes brought forward by private enterprise. Nothing has done more to delay housing reform in England than this strong tendency on the part of public bodies to take everything upon themselves instead of first considering how far existing organizations and private individuals can be encouraged to assist so that as far as possible central and local authorities may be confined to their legitimate and proper function of supervision and control.

On March 17, 1913, Mr John Burns, addressing a labour deputation, boasted that whereas " in 1910 twelve local authorities spent £108,000 on municipal house building, in 1912 ninety-six local authorities spent £650,000 "; also, " the housing question should be left to local authorities, guided, advised and even compelled to take action where necessary by the central authority." He urged the Labour Party through their branches to extend their influence upon these authorities, which is sound advice, because it is from members of the Labour Party, who personally feel the pinch of bad and expensive housing, that the strongest driving force for reform is to be hoped for, but the policy here advocated of relegating all housing work to public bodies—municipal house building, in fact—is one that has been tried for twenty years and found wanting. What is wanted is co-operation between the public authority and respectable private enterprise; the actual work of housing the people being carried out by the latter and supervised and controlled in the interests of hygiene, sanitation, etc., by the former. Mr Burns was for many years a member of the London County Council, and no one knows better than he the disastrous results of municipal house building under Part I of the 1890 Act, into which the County Council were driven by the supposed difficulty of working Part II of the same Act, under which the cost of mending or ending insanitary houses falls on the right shoulders, that is on the owners of houses unfit for human habitation, and not on the general body of ratepayers.

Mr G. H. Roberts, M.P., at the Trade Union Congress, 1913, stated that: " There was an admitted scarcity of 100,000 houses in our rural areas, and many of the houses that did exist were quite unfit for decent human beings. It was a question of the investment of State money for an urgent public purpose. Some people thought State invested money in rural houses would have the effect of subsidizing wages (during the Corn Law agitations Protectionists averred that cheaper food would mean lower wages; the opposite has been the result). In Ireland millions had been spent on rehousing the Irish labourer; wages had risen in those districts 25 per cent to 50 per cent because the Irish labourer had been imbued with a sense of freedom and given a new outlook so that he is no longer willing to live in the beastly conditions that previously existed."

There are in these remarks not only true statements of fact, but also quite a good suggestion, viz., that it would be quite wise of the State to invest some of its money in decent housing, provided that adequate guarantees (see chapter VII) are given by those to whom the money is lent; but Mr Roberts has not had so much time at his disposal for the study of the housing problem as other men whose motives are as honest and sincere as his, and therefore he does not know that municipal house building schemes have:

1. Thrown enormous expenditure on to the ratepayers.

2. Handsomely rewarded owners of insanitary houses for neglecting their property.

3. Kept people in congested districts, instead of encouraging them to move into the suburbs.

The best authorities on town planning and housing reform are of opinion that the first business of central and local authorities should have been the amendment and co-ordination of building by-laws and other regulations for the control of town and estate development. During the last five years or so England has constantly been promised by her most prominent town planning administrator that this urgent need should be attended to, but up to the present nothing has been done. If this promise had been kept, town planning or garden suburb development would not now have been hampered in the way it has been, and it would be possible by now to form a reliable opinion as to what further steps, if any, were necessary to cope with the urgent need for better housing. To modernize the by-laws is the simplest and most natural remedy to apply, as well as being the cheapest and most direct, and until it has been fully and fairly tried it is madness to attempt other and more expensive methods. Municipal house building makes a brave show but it is not practical, and in spite of the most determined efforts by really able and energetic men, it has failed to meet the needs of the cities to any appreciable extent. Anyone who visits Liverpool, the Mecca of municipal house building, and notices the miles of mean streets and jerry-built houses in that city, cannot fail to come to the conclusion that Liverpool, while providing a certain number of model flats in the centre of the city, has entirely failed in the larger and more important field of general supervision and control.

The total population of England, Scotland and Wales in 1911 was nearly forty-one millions, of which at least one-fourth are living under most insanitary conditions either in houses thoroughly bad in themselves and shockingly crowded, or, still worse, are living far too many in one house, because there is nowhere else to go to. On the lowest computation, taking five persons to a house, 2,000,000 houses are urgently needed to house or rehouse these people according to modern ideas.

The average cost of each house for land, development and building cannot safely be put at less than £200, that is to say, if through the Board's love of show and their omission to amend their by-laws we are forced into meeting present needs by public bodies undertaking work for which they are entirely unsuited, the ratepayers of the United Kingdom will have to spend £400,000,000, whereas if less showy but more practical methods are adopted the work can be better done without any charge being thrown on to the ratepayers or taxpayers of this country.

Suggestions have from time to time been thrown out by the Local Government Board that " local authorities should review the requirements of their by-laws," but no practical step has been taken to " compel " them to do so, and the progress of the garden suburb movement is continually hampered by inane by-laws.

It is a most instructive fact, to which attention was drawn the other day at Coventry by a Local Government Board inspector, that where municipal trading is most active there the rates are always highest. Birmingham is promised this year (1913) £152,000 from her municipal trading concerns, and her rates are 8s. 11d. in the £. The coincidence of high rates and large municipal trading profits which puzzles the average ratepayer is easily explained by the way in which municipal accounts are " arranged." For instance, it is well known to every one who has studied the subject with an unbiassed mind that motor-buses will, on any given width of road, carry at least twice as many passengers as trams, and yet, when street widenings are required for trams, the usual practice is to charge a large part, if not all, of the cost to the public works department, and not to the tramway department, in spite of the fact that if motor buses were adopted instead of trams, not only could more traffic be carried on existing roads, but it could be carried quicker. It is by no means uncommon in London and elsewhere to charge land to municipal house building schemes at what is called its " housing value," that is, far below what it cost; the remainder of the cost being tucked away in some other account. In Birmingham, a credit balance is shown on the Corporation housing schemes by the simple process of charging nothing for the land. It is owing to methods of this sort that large municipal trading profits are coincident with rising rates.

The only advantage that public bodies have over private enterprise in the matter of house building, is that they can at present borrow from Government on better terms, but even this great advantage does not enable them to produce such good results.

In a memorandum issued by the Local Government Board in March, 1913, it is said that houses for better paid workers are more likely to be provided by private enterprise than houses at the low rents necessary for the poorer classes. At Hereford garden suburb where there are only nine houses per gross acre, all built by private enterprise, the majority are let at 4s. 9d. per week, including rates, whereas at Yeovil, a municipal house building scheme very highly praised by Mr John Burns,* there are twenty

* Mr Burns opening the Yeovil Corporation Housing Scheme, said " If the local authorities in the country followed the example of the Yeovil Council, the back of the housing problem would soon be broken."

houses per acre and 132 out of a total of 158 are let at 5s. per week.

In "Practical Housing" considerable space was given to explaining why municipal house building has failed to solve the problem, and my experience of the last five years more than confirms the opinion previously held.

One of the many objections to municipal house building is that every petty detail must be definitely settled before a loan can be obtained, and, therefore, if mistakes are made (and they always are made, "humanum est errare") it is impossible to correct them. If Harborne garden suburb had been planned and developed on those methods it would have been very different from what it is, because as the work proceeded mistakes and possibilities of improvement were continually being discovered and dealt with in the light of fresh experience. This could not have been done under a public body with its hard and fast rules and regulations. Public bodies will never house the people as they should be housed; they have neither the time nor the interest to attend to the thousand and one little details that go to making a house pleasant and comfortable to live in; their houses must of necessity be all of one pattern, thereby producing the monotony so strongly condemned in the Board's own memorandum of March, 1913. In work done by public bodies there is no elasticity, and without elasticity housing schemes are bound to fail. In this same memorandum the Board deprecate overcrowding, and yet, there are only one or two municipal house building schemes in this country that are not overcrowded. The Board advocate economy in the cost of estate development "where by-laws admit," but in spite of all their promises to reform they have not yet taken any practical steps to make their so called "model by-laws" more reasonable. If only they would attend to their first duty, i.e., the making of sensible by-laws, instead of rushing into house building, for which they are in no way suited, it would be much better for all concerned. They advocate wider frontages, a most important matter, but they take no steps to reduce the cost of frontage, so as to make it economically possible to build wider and shallower houses, without those insanitary and obstructive long back additions which are forced on builders by extravagant by-laws.

The Housing and Town Planning, etc., Act, 1909, gave the Local Government Board a splendid opportunity of adopting a new policy, but they have remained intrenched behind their "local by-laws and statutory provisions" which every expert knows have harassed and hindered respectable builders and played into the hands of land-jobbers and jerry-builders. If the Board would attend to the duties laid upon them by the 1909 Act, viz., to encourage and assist local authorities to plan out new districts economically, and to allow them to buy land for public purposes at a reasonable price, enormous sums would be saved for the ratepayers and a sound solution of the housing problem much nearer than it is at present.

Municipal house building always has been, and from the very nature of the circumstances surrounding it, always must be more or less eleemosynary in its results, and very often these doles reach quite the wrong people, such as owners of houses unfit for human habitation. One of the principles of modern social reform is to give the people their rights, not charity, and this great principle ought to be applied to housing. Surely respectable private enterprise has a right to reasonable building by-laws, and surely it is better to grant that right than to insist upon giving charity by way of municipal house building.

For many years past the attempts of municipal house builders to grapple with the problem have been carefully watched, and the results achieved by respectable private enterprise in face of the most determined and persistent opposition and obstruction from public bodies have also been noted. The foregoing opinions are based on this information, but in order to ascertain whether these opinions were correct, a comprehensive inquiry was instituted in the autumn of 1912, and one of the two following questionnaires was sent to every local authority said to be engaged upon a town planning scheme, and to every known garden city, suburb or village.

TOWN PLANNING QUESTIONNAIRE

1. Have you a special town planning committee? If so, what other committees of your council are represented on it? If not, by whom is your town planning scheme being prepared?
2. How many acres does your scheme comprise?
3. Is it an urban or a rural district?
4. How many houses will be allowed per acre? Does this include roads and all other open spaces? What concessions will you make to landowners in order to make fewer houses per acre pay the builder?
5. Do you expect quick development? If so, why?
6. How many acres do you propose to reserve for playgrounds, playing fields, parks, allotments and small holdings?

7. What is the value per acre of the cheapest and of the dearest land in the town planning area which, if opened up, would be suitable for building?

Give the budget valuation if possible.

8. What will it cost per acre to develop it? Roads, sewers, fencing and lay-out of open spaces, etc.?

(a) Under your by-laws?

(b) Under your town planning scheme?

9. What do you estimate the land will be worth per acre when developed?

10. What expenditure will your town planning scheme throw on the rates?

11. What increased assessable value will your scheme produce?

12. What is the present population upon the area, and what is the total number of houses your scheme will provide for?

13. What is the average ground rent per week or per annum in the whole district under your control on a house let at:

From 6s. 6d. to 6s. od. per week gross rent?

6s. od. to 5s. 6d. ,,   ,,   ,,   ,,

5s. 6d. to 5s. od. ,,   ,,   ,,   ,,

5s. od. to 4s. 6d. ,,   ,,   ,,   ,,

How many years' purchase can this ground rent be sold at?

14. What are the actual rates per week or per annum on a house let at:

From 6s. 6d. to 6s. od. gross rental per week ?

6s. od. to 5s. 6d. ,,   ,,   ,,   ,,

5s. 6d. to 5s. od. ,,   ,,   ,,   ,,

15. Is there any land in the area of your municipality which being back land is not being developed? Would such land be developed if under a town planning scheme concessions were made in the cost of road making and drainage facilities?

16. Is there any cheap land suitable for building which is not being utilized:

(a) Through lack of capital to develop it?

(b) Through lack of suitable communication by road, tram or rail?

(c) Through lack of main drainage facilities?

17. Is there any land which is suitable for building, but which the owner is holding:

(a) For increased value?

(b) To prevent the neighbourhood being spoilt?

18. What is the cheapest land which could be bought:
    (a) Within the urban area?
    (b) Within reasonable distance of the town, if better transit facilities were created?
    Give the budget valuation of such land if possible.
19. What is your infant mortality?
    What is your total death-rate?
20. General remarks.

GARDEN CITY AND GARDEN SUBURB QUESTIONNAIRE

1. How many acres does your scheme comprise?
2. Is it an urban or a rural district?
3. How many houses are or will be allowed per acre? Does this include roads and all other open spaces?
4. Do you expect quick development? If so, why?
5. How many acres do you propose to reserve for playgrounds, playing fields, parks, allotments and small holdings?
6. What did your land cost per acre?
7. What will it or has it cost per acre to develop it for roads, sewers, fencing and lay-out of open spaces, etc.?
8. What do you estimate to be the present value of your developed land per acre? Has it gone up in price since the time of purchase?
   Give budget valuation if possible.
9. What is the total number of houses you
   (a) Have built?
   (b) Propose to build?
10. What ground rent do you charge on a house let at:

    From 6s. 6d. to 6s. od. per week gross rental?
          6s. od. to 5s. 6d. ,,   ,,   ,,   ,,
          5s. 6d. to 5s. od. ,,   ,,   ,,   ,,
          5s. od. to 4s. 6d. ,,   ,,   ,,   ,,

11. What are the actual rates per week or per annum on a house let at:

    From 6s. 6d. to 6s. od. per week gross rental?
          6s. od. to 5s. 6d. ,,   ,,   ,,   ,,
          5s. 6d. to 5s. od. ,,   ,,   ,,   ,,
          5s. od. to 4s. 6d. ,,   ,,   ,,   ,,

12. What is your infant mortality?
    What is your total death rate?
13. General remarks.

The written and verbal replies to these questions contain an immense amount of information invaluable to the initiated, not only as to the comparative practical results achieved to date by public bodies and private enterprise in town planning and housing reform, but also as to future possibilities if intelligent measures are adopted by central and local authorities. The information was obtained partly by personal interviews, and as a great deal of it was given on the understanding that strict confidence would be observed, it is not possible to publish details, but a general summary is admissible and will, it is hoped, be useful to those studying present conditions and considering future possibilities.

At the end of 1912, that is, just three years since the passing of the Housing and Town Planning, etc., Act, 147 local authorities were reported to be engaged upon 164 town planning schemes.

CO-ORDINATION OF THE WORK

Only 5 authorities had appointed representative committees.

23 authorities had appointed special town planning committees.

And 10 authorities had referred the question to some independent committee or sub-committee.

—

38

PROGRESS MADE WITH TOWN PLANNING UP TO JANUARY 1, 1913

2 schemes had been approved by the Board but not yet submitted to Parliament.

2 other schemes had been submitted to the Board for approval.

In 20 cases authority had been given to prepare a scheme.

,, 1 case permission to prepare had been refused.

,, 13 cases applications had been made for permission to prepare a scheme.

—

38

,, 23 cases notices had been given with a view to application for permission to prepare.

,, 35 cases it had been informally decided to proceed.

,, 68 cases the matter was under consideration.

—

164 was the total number of schemes in progress.

The thirty-eight schemes that had got as far as application being made to prepare a scheme comprise about 70,000 acres, but in many cases the boundaries were not definitely settled.

NUMBER OF HOUSES PER ACRE

Information on this point was available in the case of only seventeen schemes, and in only two or three cases was the number actually settled.

In 1 case the proposed number of houses per acre varied from: 4 to 12
,, 9 cases ,, ,, ,, ,, ,, 12 to 18
,, 7 ,, ,, ,, ,, ,, 20 to 24

In garden cities, suburbs and villages there were:

4 cases where the number of houses per acre varied from 5 to 6
6 ,, ,, ,, ,, ,, ,, ,, 7 to $9\frac{1}{4}$
9 ,, ,, ,, ,, ,, ,, ,, 10 to 12
2 ,, ,, ,, ,, ,, ,, ,, 13 to 14

As no town planning scheme had been approved on January 1, 1913, it is obvious that no houses had been built in accordance with a town planning scheme, but that is not the worst. Building operations that were going on (not always on the best lines, but nevertheless providing houses of a sort) had been held up in town planning areas for two or three years, thereby creating a house famine, than which there is nothing worse for the tenants, and nothing better for the owners of small house property. In garden cities, suburbs and villages, on the other hand, 15,000 houses had been built and 50,000 more were in contemplation, making a total of 65,000 houses built or planned by private enterprise, in spite of the most strenuous opposition and obstruction from many public bodies. This achievement gives some indication as to what could be done by respectable private enterprise reasonably encouraged instead of obstructed.

It may be pleaded in defence of public bodies that the garden city and suburb movement started before the Town Planning Act was passed; but this fact admitted by public bodies is obviously another argument in favour of respectable private enterprise against public bodies.

In order to meet cases where decent housing at reasonable rents is made impossible by obsolete by-laws and where public bodies stand in the way of progress, the Act provides for a right of appeal from an obstructive local authority to the central authority, but in practice this right of appeal is inoperative, because the

Board will not listen to any proposal for the revocation of by-laws under clause 44, unless the local authority supports the application of the landowner or builder, and this being the attitude of the Board, no private individual would be so rash as to undertake all the trouble and expense of preparing and presenting a town planning scheme with his local authority in opposition to him. It is difficult to realize that any court of appeal could possibly refuse to hear an appellant unless he is supported by the person or persons against whose decision he is appealing, but that is nevertheless the attitude adopted by the Local Government Board.

COST OF LAND AND DEVELOPMENT

In town planning areas the value of the land varies from	£50 to £3,000 per acre.
In garden cities, suburbs and villages the price paid for land varies from	£40 to £600 ,, ,,
Cost of development under the by-laws varies from	£400 to £1,000 ,, ,,
Cost of development under town planning schemes is estimated at	£200 to £500 ,, ,,
Cost of development actually incurred in garden cities, suburbs and villages varies from	£174 to £500 ,, ,,

LAND HELD UP FOR VARIOUS REASONS.—CAUSE

    In 8 replies out of 12, Cost of development too expensive.
    In 7 replies out of 13, Lack of capital.
    In 13 replies out of 19, Lack of communications.
    In 10 replies out of 18, Lack of drainage facilities.
               Other places did not reply.

    In twelve replies out of eighteen, land was being held up for a higher price or to protect the neighbourhood from being spoilt.

	Infantile Mortality. (average)	Death rate. (average)
Old method of town development	127	15
Garden cities and suburbs	37	6.4

In view of all the talk there has been about housing reform during the last twenty or thirty years these results are very disappointing. 15,000 houses built on decent lines by private enterprise with another 50,000 in contemplation, as against none under

town planning schemes prepared by public bodies, is the strongest
possible argument in favour of applying the voluntary system to the
solution of the housing problem, especially when it is remembered
that a great deal more would have been done by respectable private
enterprise if it had not been for the obstruction of public bodies.
At the same time, it must be admitted that the existing supply and
that in contemplation are quite inadequate to meet the needs of the
case, and although at Hereford and Harborne and elsewhere respectable private enterprise under common sense methods has done
better than public bodies and other persons under obsolete by-laws
in the way of providing for the poorer classes, what has been done
up to the present only serves to show what could be done under
the voluntary system if only public bodies would be more reasonable in their regulations, and more progressive in their ideas. The
only alternative to this policy is a wholesale scheme of providing
houses at charity rents by public bodies, for those who cannot
afford more than 4s. or 5s. per week, and even the English Local
Government Board will hardly advocate such a rash proposal
without first giving a fair trial to the voluntary system. It may be
pleaded that the Act has only been in force three years, but that
reason is insufficient. The causes of delay lie deeper and deserve
investigation.

This inquiry must be confined to England, where evidence from
all over the country goes to prove that the Local Government
Board has been a drag on the wheels of progress instead of the
driving force that it ought to be.

The causes of delay may be classified under six heads:

1. The Local Government Board.
2. Ignorance and apathy of local authorities.
3. The by-law rut. Expensive estate development and extravagant building regulations.
4. Dear land.—The land-jobbing interest.
5. Dear capital.
6. Constant increases in the rates on improvements, but not
on land.

1. THE LOCAL GOVERNMENT BOARD

The Act itself is the first attempt in this country to solve the
problems of housing reform and town development on rational
lines, and, therefore, was never looked upon by the best informed
town planners as anything more than a sort of trial trip. A very
serious defect in it is that Parliament left a great deal too much

in the hands of a government department, without first making quite sure that the department in question understood the work that was required of it and had time to attend to it. The result of this mistake has been the issue of regulations by the Local Government Board that would have entirely killed almost any other movement for reform, but fortunately the town planning movement had so strong a force of public opinion behind it that although very seriously hampered and hindered it has not been killed. When these regulations first appeared many ardent town planners expressed the opinion, by no means unjustified, that they were unworkable, The more patient men pointed out that only practical experience could show what is really needed. That experience has now been gained, and in the next chapter will be found a series of suggestions for amending the Act and simplifying the regulations. This chapter must be devoted to explaining the inadequacies and shortcomings of the existing regulations which, speaking generally, contain too many safeguards and too little driving force. There is inadequate control over opposition landowners and too little support to those landowners who want to help the movement forward. The Act provides full protection for the interests of the ratepayers; the regulations do not. For the convenience of officials and others who have to study and carry out the innumerable formalities required, an epitome of these regulations and also the regulations themselves will be found in Appendices 4 and 9.

They contain thirty-six articles, some very lengthy, which are designed to protect property at every turn and which insist upon interminable delay; it is not too much to say the Board recognizes no other interests than those of property. The Board was evidently so obsessed by the rights of property that it had no time to think of the duties of property nor of the public welfare, nor of the pockets of the ratepayers. There are no less than seven opportunities given by the regulations for property owners to object:

1. At the public meeting of owners.
2. At the first Local Government Board inquiry.
3. When the Board has given permission to prepare the scheme.
4. When the scheme has been prepared, a draft printed and the map deposited.
5. If the Board approve of the scheme with modifications.
6. When the final approval of the Board is given.
7. During the thirty days that the scheme lies before Parliament.

In addition to these seven special opportunities, property owners have many other opportunities of bringing pressure to bear through political organizations, and by other means.

Eight different maps are specified, but in practice this number can be reduced.

Three resolutions have to be passed by the local authority.

Two applications made to the Local Government Board containing an immense amount of information, some of which is quite useless. For instance, estimates have to be given based on present prices for work that will probably not be done for twenty years, when present prices will be obsolete and the proposals pretty sure to be modified.

Two inquiries held by the Local Government Board.

Eight notices sent to owners and others.

Eight advertisements in the newspapers.

Three meetings of owners.

And there are specified periods of waiting between the various processes.

It has been computed that if everything went without a hitch a scheme might possibly be got through in nine months. In practice it has taken 3½ years from the passing of the Act to get the first scheme approved by the Local Government Board. Careful inquiries all over the country have elicited the information that small places, where town planning is often most urgently needed, and where it is at least as much needed as anywhere, are afraid to undertake it, because of the great labour and expense involved. Some authorities give £500* as the minimum cost of preparing a scheme of any importance under these regulations. It is said that none of these regulations could be omitted without contravening the Act. If this statement refers to the fact that full power is given to the Local Government Board to make what regulations it likes, then, of course, it is strictly correct, but no town planner can find in the Act any justification for many of the regulations laid down by the Board, and there is already quite enough local opposition from slum owners and land-jobbers, without the Board adding to the difficulties of those who really want to improve the living conditions of the poorer classes. In the Act there are fourteen clauses relating to town planning, and in the regulations there are thirty-six articles, many of which are considerably longer than any clause in the Act. To put it shortly, every town planner who reads these

* This estimate is based on the experience of a rather elaborate scheme; where simple methods are adopted and only the general lines of development laid down the cost ought to be very much less.

regulations cannot help feeling that if those responsible for them had intended to make the Act unworkable, they could not have adopted a more effective method. It almost looks as if the Board resented the fact that town planning legislation was forced upon them by the Association of Municipal Corporations, and are determined that nothing useful shall result from it. If simplification of the regulations is objected to for fear of contravening the Act, then I venture to suggest that the Local Government Board have already committed that sin. In the first town planning scheme approved by the Board there is a general provision which enacts that all claims for betterment and compensation shall be made within twelve months from the date of the approval of the scheme by the Board. It is obviously impossible during the first twelve months to ascertain with any approach to accuracy what will be the ultimate effects of the scheme, and, therefore, this general provision is nothing more nor less than a deliberate reversal of the intentions of Parliament concerning betterment and compensation when Sections 58 and 59 were approved and passed by both Houses.

There are two fatal defects in the administration of the Act. The Board makes such a strong point of local authorities coming to an agreement with owners in the preparation of town planning schemes that concessions have to be made to recalcitrant people which are not in the public interest, and which are a great deal more than the owners have a right to. Examples of this have been given in the descriptions of the Birmingham schemes. On the other hand, there are many landowners in the country genuinely desirous of providing better housing at the old or lower rents, but this cannot be done on a business basis without concessions being obtained in the cost of estate development and house building.

The Act gives landowners needing these concessions a right of appeal from obstructive local authorities to the central authority, but in practice, the Local Government Board will not listen to them, unless the local authority comes with them and supports their application, which means, of course, that the right of appeal is null and void, another direct contravention of the wishes of Parliament and incidentally a great obstacle in the way of progress.

Another thing needed is simplicity in the regulations; for instance, it is most unwise to insist, as has been done in more than one case familiar to town planners, that in residential districts there shall be cross roads every 300 yards, regardless of the fact that the object of this regulation, viz., a plentiful supply of light and air to the houses and reasonable facilities for traffic, can be provided for far better and much more cheaply in other ways. This regulation has seriously hindered town planning development, and increased house rents without any advantage to the tenants. Many other examples could be given to show the urgent need for greater simplicity in the regulations, but it is quite evident that there is nothing to be hoped for in this direction from the Local Government Board.

The expense incurred in the preparation of town planning schemes is a great deterrent to the work being undertaken, especially by small places; this cause could be removed by a simplification of the regulations which need not in any way interfere with the efficiency of the work; on the contrary improved regulations will improve the ultimate results.

The main cause of delay is due to the work having been delegated to a government department which is so steeped in old and out-of-date methods that it has entirely failed to grasp the new situation created by town planning legislation. They have hedged themselves in with endless regulations and spent immense time on seeing that these regulations are observed in every detail, but when it comes to practical results, they are not interested. For example, Birmingham's bad scheme has been approved, and that of Birkenhead, which presented great possibilities for emptying the slums into the country, was rejected without even holding an inquiry. The general impression is that the Birmingham scheme was approved, because it had been carried in the Council Chamber by ninety votes to five. There is little else to recommend these unpractical and extravagant proposals. The Town Clerk of Birmingham, speaking of a suggested modification of the scheme, said " The Board were asked to do an unheard-of thing—deliberately to set on one side the considered judgment of the City Council." The approval of the local council evidently carried great weight in this instance; why was it ignored in the case of Birkenhead ? Only one member of that council voted against the proposal, which was strongly supported not only by the chairman of the finance committee, in a clear and convincing financial statement, but also by every other member of the Corporation who had held that position since Birkenhead's incorporation thirty years ago. City councils are not always given complete and accurate data on which to form an opinion, but the Birkenhead Council was given this information and only decided to buy the Storeton estate after most careful and detailed consideration of all the points at issue.

Birkenhead has spent many thousands of pounds on slum reform on the old lines, and at last had to give it up. Sir William Lever, a great housing reformer, to whom we owe Port Sunlight, is of opinion that there is no better way of dealing with the twin problems of slum reform and slum prevention, than by municipalities acquiring land in large quantities at reasonable prices, so as to enable them to offer facilities for the erection of better houses in suburban districts. He backed his opinion by buying the necessary land himself, and then offering it to Birkenhead, without any profit to himself, thus giving Birkenhead a unique opportunity of doing something practical, and at the same time effecting large savings for the ratepayers. The English Local Government Board rejected the proposal without even holding an inquiry, and the principal reason given was that insufficient details were supplied by the Corporation of Birkenhead. That plea explains the failure of the Local Government Board to deal with the housing question. They are all for details, and quite unable to take a general view of the situation, and deal with housing difficulties on comprehensive lines. Their recent attitude at Coventry illustrates this very clearly. Central improvements are urgently needed in that city, and one of the Board's chief stipulations is that any people dishoused by the improvement scheme shall be rehoused within a mile of the area affected. No wonder such little progress is made with town planning and housing reform, when they are administered by such an antiquated central authority, whose chief object seems to be to protect property but not the ratepayers.

Every one who has taken any serious interest in town planning is aware that tramway extension is part and parcel of town development, and cannot wisely be separated from it, and yet tramway extensions have been deliberately excluded from town planning schemes, thereby depriving the ratepayers of their right to one-half of the betterment that would accrue to them if tramway extensions were included, and thereby brought under the betterment and compensation clauses of the Housing and Town Planning etc. Act, 1909.

It is said that tramways come under another government department, and, therefore, the Local Government Board cannot give authority for their construction. If this is good law then the difficulty could be very easily surmounted by inserting in town planning schemes, a general provision that the local authority undertakes to " exert all due diligence and despatch in obtaining powers for trams or motor buses along any specified route, and further in the exercise of those powers when obtained." This would secure half the betterment for the ratepayers, but the English Local Government Board does not appear to concern itself with the interests of the ratepayers.

No Act, however good it may be, is of the slightest use unless it is administered with understanding, and the Local Government Board have shown that they do not understand the meaning and the objects of their own Act. It is suggested that the creation of a special housing department at the Local Government Board would get over the difficulty; but this is gravely to be doubted, for it is hardly to be supposed there would be any radical change in the policy and methods preferred.

2. IGNORANCE AND APATHY OF LOCAL AUTHORITIES

It is often the case that a landowner is more willing to develop his estate reasonably than the local authority is inclined to support him. One of these authorities told a progressive landowner that " they could not see their way to apply for authority to carry out his scheme in its present form, because it did not comply with the by-laws, but if he would submit a scheme showing conformity with the by-laws they would endeavour to get it sanctioned by the Local Government Board." This sapient reply is thoroughly typical of the attitude towards town planning, that is adopted by a great many local authorities in this country. On one occasion I was invited to be one of the judges of a so-called town planning competition, and the first condition of the competition was that plans submitted must be in accordance with the by-laws. In another instance that came before me, progressive landowners and builders asked the local authority for alterations in the local by-laws in order to enable them to provide better housing at reasonable rents on a sound economic basis, and the local land-jobbers and jerry-builders strenuously opposed any alteration in the by-laws. They had found out how to make " pots of money " under the existing by-laws, and they did not want their business interfered with. The local authority took their instructions from the land-jobbers, and nothing was done.

Town planning is still very imperfectly understood, and in this country literature upon the subject is strictly limited. One author explains the architectural point of view, another the legal aspect, and so on, but none of them take a comprehensive view of the whole situation, and the surveyors on whom has fallen the pre-

paration of town planning schemes are not interested in the economic effect of the proposals; that is not their business, but it is the economic aspect of the question that is most important of all, and on it depends ultimate success or failure.

The by-law system has utterly failed because it is economically unsound, too much attention is given to technical details, and no attention is given to economic laws. What we have to do is to try and persuade the authorities to study economic laws and work with them, instead of against them. If this is done, ignorance will give way to intelligent appreciation of the great possibilities presented by town planning, and apathy will be replaced by eagerness to adopt the new method in its entirety—not merely with the least possible modification of the old methods. As things stand to-day, local authorities are discouraged rather than encouraged to do anything. When they ask for practical information and advice how best to prepare a town planning scheme, most of the time is taken up in warning them to be very careful to carry out to the letter the Local Government Board's regulations, and they are told that if in this respect they make a slip they may have to go back to the beginning. No wonder they are alarmed at the immense trouble and expense involved, and no wonder that under these conditions three years' work has produced no tangible result!

With this, as with every other reform, there is the innate prejudice against new ideas. Old-fashioned aldermen, councillors and officials cannot, or will not, see the advantage of spending a few pence to-day in order to save the expenditure of many pounds a few years hence. The expense of preparing a town planning scheme is admittedly far too high, especially for small places and immense harm has been done by a statement very widely circulated that a town planning scheme cannot be prepared for less than £500. That figure was based on a very ambitious scheme. If the methods advocated in Chapter III are adopted the cost of ordinary schemes should not exceed £200, and in small places well managed the work ought to be done for less, especially if the central authority would help local authorities on this most important point, instead of doing their best to increase expenditure.

The next difficulty on the score of expense is that the success of town planning very largely depends on a little immediate expenditure, in order to encourage quick development of new districts, and thereby make town and estate development a thoroughly sound, and not merely speculative, business proposition. This very wise policy of a "stitch in time" is strongly objected to by friends of the old haphazard methods, which have produced large fortunes for a few individuals (not as a rule the builders, but generally those financing the builders) and at the same time have resulted in wretched housing for the people. The Act applies to undeveloped districts, and it is the land and building speculators who are chiefly interested in such districts. It is worth their while to spend money and take trouble to obtain influence on the local councils. Even in larger places they have great weight and this accounts in no small degree for the very inadequate results achieved up to the present. They are looked upon as experts, and doubtless they are experts in the old discredited method of estate development, but they do not understand, and do not want to understand, the new method. When proposals are brought forward for dealing with this problem under the new method they talk very loud, and the public seldom realizes that they are financially interested in the questions at issue. Their quiet influence behind the scenes and their loud talk in public have up to the present been most successful from their point of view. Local officials have long been accustomed to working with men of this stamp and their influence is too often seen in a number of arrangements in the interests of property, plausibly presented and supported, whereas the interests of health and right living, having no recognized money value, are neglected by those who should be their jealous guardians.

There is what may be called a rate-collecting spirit in all public bodies, that is, a blind desire to secure and maintain assessable value in a municipality. The influence of this party goes to reinforce the land speculators, and is unfortunately in inverse ratio to their breadth of view, and intelligent grasp of the situation. They do not realize that the human assets of a community are of far greater economic value than mere material assets, no matter how many million pounds sterling these may represent. They see that decent housing will by fair competition depreciate the value of slum property, and thereby reduce the rate income from bad property, but they do not see that any temporary loss from this cause will soon be more than recouped by increased assessable value on the outskirts of the city as well as at the centre, and by the public saving due to lower rates. There is also the greater economic efficiency of the working population, which must ensue from better living conditions.

The interests of property and the opinion of short-sighted rate-collectors are not the only obstacles to reform to be met with on public bodies. Much disinterested labour is wasted in wrong directions, notably in that of municipal house building, or to be more correct municipal barracks. This policy has perpetuated congestion in slums, instead of relieving it. The advocates of this policy forget the improvements that have been made in traffic facilities, thereby rendering very much larger areas of land available for building purposes. A proportion of those who live in congested districts are obliged to, or actually want to, live there, but in no case is this proportion more than half the population of congested districts. The other half are able and want to move further out if only they were given a chance of doing so. It is therefore clear that the only sound policy is to encourage and assist town populations to spread themselves OUTWARDS over larger areas, and NOT UPWARDS in tenement buildings, but this does not suit the property owners nor the rate-collectors, and up till now municipal house builders have done little or nothing to help it forward.

Speaking generally, careful investigations all over the country have disclosed the fact that local authorities are averse to reform, and the central authority instead of exercising the powers they have to push them forward, has done everything in its power to delay progress by pinning its faith to the " model " by-laws and municipal house building (see Local Government Board memorandum, March, 1913).

3. THE BY-LAW RUT

The thoroughly English objection to giving up old methods and adopting newer and cheaper ones presents one of the greatest obstacles in the way of town planning. Some authorities are of opinion that expensive estate development does more to cause bad housing at exorbitant rents, than the high price of land. This is overstating the case (see Chapter II), but it is an undeniable fact that Ruislip-Northwood and other places have obtained for their ratepayers, without any expenditure of public money, concessions as to the number of houses per acre, and a considerable area of open spaces and other amenities, by co-operation with landowners and builders on the lines of reduction in the cost of estate development. This wise and economical policy has unfortunately not been adopted in other places, and in one case, where the local authority was willing, Whitehall insisted upon the landowner submitting to a whole paraphernalia of unnecessary regulations. This circumlocution might have destroyed the scheme altogether; it did cause great delay and unnecessary expense. In this case 50-ft. roads were demanded where they were quite unnecessary, and cross roads every 300 feet, and these demands were only withdrawn after many interviews, much correspondence and considerable waste of time and money, both public and private.

In another case a 50-ft. by-law road was insisted upon right across a town planning estate, thereby increasing expenditure and destroying amenities; the folly of this official fad is proved by the fact that there is seldom more than one vehicle to be seen on this road.

The difficulty in getting out of the by-law rut is due to the fact that central and local authorities are composed of men and advised by officials who are wedded to the use of antiquated laws and by-laws. Custom continues their use in spite of their unsatisfactory results as regards housing and economy; novelties are suspect and in spite of the fact that every one of account in municipal circles has been obliged to profess adherence to the town planning movement, men who have spent their lives carrying out the old policy do not in practice look with favour on the new. All their inclinations are to keep in their old groove, with the result that they only slightly modify their old way of doing things. They put the new wine into old bottles, and we get the old ideas presented under a new name; a mere pretence of progress and improvement, where very little, if any, real improvement is effected. Men of this type are far more dangerous to a new movement than those who openly declare themselves against it. They call themselves town planners and describe what they produce as a town planning scheme, and the general public is very slow to realize that they are not being given the real article. It all looks so pretty and sounds so nice, and is called town planning. How should the public realize, until they find their rates still going up, that it is nothing of the kind?

Another reason, already referred to, for maintaining the " model by-laws " unaltered is because they suit the land-jobbers and jerry-builders. Compliance with the by-laws has become a science. There are people who know to an inch what they can do without getting their wretched property condemned on inspection, and yet the squalor of this property which just passes the by-laws is a crying scandal, whereas these same by-laws which do not stop jerrybuilding, have always delayed, and often killed, genuine efforts to provide decent housing at reasonable rents. The land-jobbers and jerry-builders do not want the competition of decent housing, and they will not have it if they can help it. This is just where the Local Government Board ought to step in and insist upon the reform of local regulations in the interests of efficiency and economy. They at any rate are not influenced by the land-jobbers, and they must know from their wide experience how pressing is the need for more and better housing in both town and country, but in spite of all their opportunities for seeing the disastrous results of a cast-iron by-law system they are the worst offenders of all in this blind adherence to old and discredited methods.

In previous chapters it has been seen how important a part the cost of estate development plays in the provision of better housing. We have also seen how the by-laws increase the cost of building, and at the same time produce dark and unhealthy living rooms and bedrooms. " By-law road " has already become a term of contempt, and " by-law bedrooms " should soon follow. A leading surveyor, who was appealed to for his opinion on this evil, said that if the authorities would be more reasonable in their by-laws, he and his colleagues would be only too pleased to provide better housing at reasonable rents. He pointed out how the heavy unnecessary expenditure on roads, drainage and other matters forces land and building speculators into overcrowding their land in order to get their money back.

4. DEAR LAND

In the Local Government Board's memorandum of March 25, 1913, on the Housing of the Working Classes Acts, 1890 to 1909, it is stated that the cost of the site in most cases constitutes a comparatively small proportion of the cost of providing houses, and this opinion is based on the fact that the " loan charges in respect of a loan spread over the maximum period of eighty years, on the basis of ten houses to the acre and land at £100 per acre, would be less than 2d. per week per house."

There are very few, if any, municipal house building schemes in this country for which the land only cost £100 per acre, or indeed anything like so low a figure. Not so many years ago Birmingham paid £350 per acre for land required for a municipal housing scheme under Part III of the 1890 Act, and this is much more like the average price paid for land for housing purposes. In many cases a great deal more than £350 per acre was paid for the land. The 1909 Act makes it possible by restricting building density to keep land values within more reasonable bounds, but the Board has itself in more than one instance unnecessarily increased land values by allowing more houses per acre than was suggested by the local authority; one example must suffice. A rural district council proposed to allow ten houses per acre, which would have left a very handsome profit to the landowners; the Board insisted upon twelve houses per acre where there ought not to have been more than eight.

The statement that the cost of the land is not worth considering in relation to the total cost of providing houses—a statement which is persistently repeated by the opponents of land and housing reform—discloses a complete misunderstanding of the situation on the part of those who make it. It is one of those half truths that obstruct progress far more than a hundred straight-forward lies. It is quite true that out of a 6s. 6d. weekly house rent 7d. per week is a fair average of the amount due to the cost of the land plus land-jobbers' profits, and professional fees, the other 5d. per week that makes up the average weekly ground rent of 1s. being due to interest on the cost of development, and this 7d. per week may be considered by some people a small proportion of the total rent, but it must not be forgotten that the charge for land per week per house is only kept as low as 7d. by crowding forty or more houses on to every acre.

If cheap land were opened up and protected as suggested in Chapters I and II, the author of the Board's memorandum quoted above would be quite justified in his remarks; but this has not yet been done, and, therefore, town planning and better housing has been, and still is, very seriously delayed by dear land. This applies quite as much to small places as to large ones, indeed land monopoly and its consequent famine prices for building land, is often stronger in rural and semi-rural districts than it is in larger towns. The opinion so often expressed by the opponents of land and housing reform, that the cost of the site is a negligible quantity and too often accepted by unobservant people, is a fallacy.

Plenty of land can be provided at a reasonable price for town and estate development if:

1. Cheap land is opened up and protected against land sweating.
2. Land required for public purposes is bought in advance before it has risen to an excessive price.

But this policy is bitterly resented by the land-jobbers, and up to the present time, force of habit and lack of insight and foresight on the part of public bodies have enabled their opposition to block the way. The land-jobbers say that ten houses per acre is a financial impossibility, and bound to fail, and they are supposed to know what they are talking about. Public bodies believe them, land values are preserved by land sweating, and dear land blocks reasonable town and estate development.

The slum owners and land-jobbers foresee that better housing will upset their business and, therefore, leave no stone unturned to prevent anything really useful and practical being done, and, speaking generally, some of our representative bodies are permeated by this sinister influence to a degree that is very inadequately realized by the general public. These interests find it profitable to be actively represented on the local governing body, and they are supported in their endeavours to obstruct progress by our English dislike and suspicion of changes, as well as by the cautious attitude always adopted by the legal profession on questions affecting real property. Sound caution is an excellent quality, but excessive caution is often the most ruinous procedure that can be adopted. The enormous sums of public money that have been wasted by the policy of waiting till the price goes up before effecting any public improvement are familiar to every one who has studied this great and interesting problem, and yet even to-day there is a solid coterie of public men and public officials who always resist every proposal to spend 1d. to-day in order to save £1 to-morrow. The slum owners and land-jobbers understand exactly how to make use of this misplaced hesitation in order to continue their own policy. They do not declare themselves as opposed to town planning; on the contrary, they speak of it in the most sympathetic terms, but when it comes to getting something done, all sorts of plausible reasons are brought forward for not doing anything that might possibly make bad housing unprofitable. Sewers are constructed in a town planning area and trams are projected long before the area has been protected from overcrowding by the preparation and approval of a town planning scheme. The fact of the matter is that, as we have seen in previous chapters, the local authorities have long found the capital required for town development, such as better communications, council schools, free libraries, public baths, police and fire stations, parks and other amenities, and the land-jobbers have by land speculation taken the profits due to this expenditure. This privilege has been so long enjoyed by private individuals that they will not give it up without a mighty struggle. When the general public realizes, as sooner or later it will realize, how severely it is being bled by a few private individuals there will be a reaction in favour of a fairer division between ratepayers and land-jobbers. Vested interests are very difficult to move, their ways are devious and the wealth at their disposal for "business purposes" is very great, but when the victory is won a vast waste of public money will be stopped. Ratepayers will get better value for their money, and rates will go down instead of constantly increasing, as has been the case all over England for many years past.

The following examples of how the law as it now stands encourages and indeed forces public bodies to pay far too much for land are interesting and instructive.

(a) The Staffordshire County Council spent about a quarter of a million on an asylum which expenditure of public money sent up the value of the surrounding land. It became necessary in order, among other reasons, to obtain a better water supply for the district to buy more land. The land required was only being used for agricultural purposes, but the public had to pay £722 per acre for it. If the County Council had been able to foresee its requirements, and allowed to buy the land a little in advance of actual requirements (that is before the asylum was built instead of afterwards) this landowner would not have been able to bleed the public to the same extent, because in that case there would have been other sites to choose from instead of the County Council being tied to this particular piece.

(b) Another striking example is the claim of £43,707 made by the Duke of Devonshire in respect of alleged damage to a park (which is earning nothing) by the laying of pipes for carrying water for the supply of Sheffield, Derby, Nottingham and Leicester. Mr Balfour Browne, K.C., on behalf of the Duke, admitted that dual ownership was the real cause of the difficulty. This difficulty of dual ownership could be got over if public bodies had reasonable powers for the purchase of land, and if, in cases like Chatsworth Park, they had the right to take the land they pay for, instead of leaving it in the possession of a private individual who has charged the public for mere easement as much as, and in many cases a great deal more than, the land is worth. Another way of putting things on a fairer basis is to reform our system of rating (see Section 6 of this chapter).

(c) The first town planning scheme in this country provided a very instructive example of how the 1909 Act enables public bodies to foresee future requirements with absolute certainty, and, without running the slightest risk, save large sums for the ratepayers.

In the early stages of the preparation of the Harborne and Quinton town planning scheme, it was seen that the construction of a new main artery as proposed by the scheme would bring a

M

large quantity of very cheap land within easy distance of the centre of the city. Inquiries were made, and it was ascertained that a farm of 130 odd acres could be purchased by the Corporation for £60 an acre (see Chapters III and IV). The position was explained to the General Purposes Committee of the old Birmingham City Council, who unanimously, and indeed with enthusiasm, authorized the purchase, subject, of course, to the approval of the Council and the Local Government Board. This land is admirably suited for the following purposes:

1. Part of it for a model housing estate.
2. Part of it for allotments.
3. And the remainder for playing fields.

The originator of the idea to buy this land wanted the purchase laid before the Council and the Board on these straightforward lines under Section 60 of the 1909 Act, but legal advisers in their wisdom insisted upon ALLOTMENTS ONLY being given as the purpose for which the land was required. This was, on the face of it, absurd, and the landjobbers' party did not fail to make the most of the blunder. Later on, when it was too late, endeavours were made to retrieve the error.

The result of this intentional or unintentional blunder was that although the Birmingham City Council approved the purchase of this land by twenty-eight votes to nineteen, the Local Government Board refused to sanction it on the ground that 130 acres were not yet needed for allotments in this part of Birmingham. In spite of the fact that the Board were clearly informed as to the actual use this land would be put to, they, as usual, adhered strictly to the letter of the law and ignored its spirit. This purchase would have shown a very good profit for the ratepayers and at the same time helped forward town planning ideas. On the other hand there was no question of robbing the landowner. He was well satisfied with his bargain; £60 an acre showed him a very handsome profit.

The chief causes of the loss of this most advantageous bargain for the ratepayers were:

1. The antiquated law (it dates back to the reign of Edward III) that prevents public bodies from buying and holding land unless they specify the exact purpose they are going to use it for.

2. The fixed determination of a small body of very influential people not to allow public bodies to buy land cheap for fear that this might interfere with private land speculation, which it undoubtedly would.

(d) Some years ago, in a small country town, land suitable for building was on the market at a very favourable price, and the local council took the opportunity and bought it. Some of this land has been used for a housing scheme. Other portions have been sold off at a profit. The whole transaction has been most satisfactory to the ratepayers, and the fact that this land was controlled by the local authority has enabled them to ensure a much better lay-out than would have been the case if the estate had been dealt with by the ordinary land and building speculator. Owing to the fact that the council could not say exactly what purpose the land was bought for, they have not yet (1912) dared to apply to the Local Government Board for a loan. The land has not yet been paid for, nor a conveyance taken, but interest is being paid on the purchase money. If the Local Government Board refuse their sanction, as judging from past experience they are very likely to do, and if the loan is refused, then the ratepayers will have to find the purchase money for this land out of revenue, or they will have to sell their remaining unused land in a hurry and, therefore, not on the best terms for the ratepayers, in order to mitigate the undue immediate burden on the rates that would be caused by having to pay for this land out of revenue. It may be said that under the 1909 Act the local authority might have achieved the end in view, viz., better lay-out, etc., etc., by making a town planning scheme for this land. Here comes one of the great objections to the way the 1909 Act is administered by the Local Government Board. The Board insists that town planning schemes must meet with the approval of all the landowners. In this case, the landowners would not have agreed to such a good lay-out as the council have arranged for, and therefore, in accordance with the Board's principle enunciated above, the best possible town planning scheme would not have been approved by the Board.

In this case, it will be seen that a considerable sum of money has been saved for the ratepayers and much better housing provided for the people than would otherwise have been the case, but this has only been done by running some risk—not of having paid too much for the land, quite the reverse—but of having to pay for the land too quickly. Objection is constantly raised to giving wider powers of land purchase on the plausible ground that it might lead to all sorts of land jobbery and corruption. It is a little difficult to see how buying land cheap for public purposes is going to encourage jobbery and corruption, whereas every expert knows that the present procedure at Local Government Board inquiries into public land purchases does tend to corruption and has resulted in the public being very badly bled. Immense stress is laid upon the question as to whether the land in question is really required for the purpose specified, and little or no interest is shown in the price paid. The most perfunctory evidence on this all-important point is accepted without demur. The way to stop jobbery and corruption is for the Board to examine most carefully the present " user " of the land, and judge from that its real value. The Board's inspectors should go still further, and take some pains to ascertain whether there is not other land suitable for the purpose that can be bought at a lower figure. PRICE NOT PURPOSE SHOULD BE THE GOVERNING FACTOR IN PUBLIC LAND PURCHASE. This is the policy of any well-managed business, and surely it is not unreasonable to suggest that public bodies, whose business transactions are rapidly increasing every year, should apply ordinary business methods to the management of public affairs. Small holdings and allotments fare very badly under the present system, especially near large towns. Local authorities are not allowed to buy land for allotments until it is all actually wanted for that purpose, and by the time it is so required the price has risen to a figure that makes it impossible to let the land to the workers at a rent they can afford to pay without making a loss on the transaction. The Allotments Act does not permit schemes that do not pay their way, and, therefore, the working classes in large towns have to go without the allotments they so badly want, and are driven to other and unprofitable forms of amusement. This difficulty is sometimes got over temporarily by local authorities taking a lease of land for allotments and sub-letting it, but the method is very far from satisfactory, because there is no security of tenure, and just when the allotments are most badly needed the land is cut up for building.

If public bodies were able and willing to exercise foresight and practise economy by purchasing land for allotments a few years in advance, this vicious circle would be broken. There would be an ample supply of allotments without any charge on the rates, and their existence would greatly facilitate open estate development on modern lines.

Some reformers are of opinion that nothing short of a wholesale scheme of public land purchase will get over the difficulty. A sudden large demand of this nature would put up the price of land against the ratepayers and taxpayers as in the case of Ireland, and as in the case of housing schemes under Part I of the 1890 Act. The policy of going to work quietly and buying a little here and there, where it is certain that the land will be needed and its price will rise, if not bought at once by the local authority, is much more likely to keep down land values than any wholesale scheme of land purchase. The latter method would be more showy, it would also be much more expensive and pretty sure to do harm instead of good. By all means buy where the price is right, but not unless, and if the central authority were to turn their thoughts in this direction and make proper use of the powers given to them by the 1909 Act, the obstruction of dear land would soon be removed.

(e) Some reformers are of opinion that town planning, unaided by other legislation, can surmount the difficulty of dear land. The following example shows the fallacy of this idea.

A very attractive little seaside place was being utterly ruined by land sweating of the worst description. A few active people stirred up the local authority and persuaded them to mark out an area for protection by a town planning scheme. This area was none too large for the purpose intended, but it was considered too large by those who supported local landed interests, and therefore, a smaller area was proposed. This smaller area was then objected to on the grounds that it would deal with one or two landowners and let others go on with their unrestricted development. It was, in fact, the same old story, the obstructionists were too clever to openly object to town planning. Direct and straightforward opposition to town planning could not have stood against public opinion. The land-jobbers, therefore, professed sympathy with town planning, but always found the most plausible objections to every practical suggestion that was made. The first area was said to be too large and the next one too small; the real reason being that land was selling at about £650 per acre, and the land-jobbers did not want their profits interfered with.

Small houses with the narrowest of frontages and crowded together in a disgraceful manner are now being built and plans for further development on the old lines constantly being passed. The rate-collecting element on the local council are congratulating themselves on the rapid increase in rateable value and do not realize, or at any rate do not care, that by their stupidity they are killing the goose that lays the golden eggs for them. The natural beauty of the place is being rapidly destroyed, which means that sooner or later the visitors, on whom the prosperity of the place very largely depends, will leave off coming to what is rapidly becoming a slum.

There is plenty of cheap agricultural land within easy reach that should be available for town extension on modern lines, but this is held up for the ridiculous price of £400 per acre (on its present earning capacity it is not worth more than £20 an acre) and one of the landowners responsible professes to be in hearty sympathy with the town planning movement, but when it comes to business, £400 per acre is his price, and he refuses to consider a profit of only 100 per cent, that is to say, he laughs at the idea of selling or leasing his land on the basis of a capital value of £40 per acre, which would make genuine town planning a feasible proposition, whereas £400 per acre makes it impossible. With cases like this all over the country, it is difficult to understand how anyone with the slightest common sense or self-respect can dare to assert that dear land does not delay town planning and better housing. Where the conditions are like those just stated, there is only one way of overcoming obstruction, and that is to rate a man on the value he puts upon his property and not merely on the income he is getting from it at the moment; let him if he likes wait until he can get his price before selling or leasing his land, but charge him for waiting; that is to say, assess his property at his own valuation and make him pay rates on it in the same proportion as that paid by other property owners in the district. It is neither fair nor reasonable that he who is injuring the whole district by hemming in development and forcing land sweating on the community should get off with an infinitesimal contribution per acre towards local expenditure, when others are rated heavily for their enterprise in improving the neighbourhood. Doubtless, they do it for their own purposes, but the whole community benefits with them. Our present rating system punishes industry and rewards idleness, but that is not the worst of it. Under our present rating system, a selfish and short-sighted landowner has it all his own way in negotiating with a possible purchaser or lessee; he can afford to wait because until his land is developed the rates charged on it are very small indeed, whereas the intending purchaser or lessee cannot wait, he must have land somewhere for private or business purposes and, therefore, he has to pay the monopoly price. If the land monopolist is made to pay rates on his own assessment of the value of his property in the same proportion as other property owners, the relative positions of buyer and seller, lessee and lessor, will be much fairer than they are at present. The rating of land values on an equitable basis is badly needed in order to relieve town planning and better housing from the obstruction of dear land.

The question of rating land values has already been touched

upon in previous chapters, and will be more fully dealt with in the last section of this chapter and in Chapter VII.

5. DEAR CAPITAL

In spite of the fact that dear land has in many places delayed town planning and better housing, there are nevertheless in other places a considerable number of landowners willing to take a reasonable price for their land in order to make it economically possible to develop their estates on modern lines, provided always that the local and central authorities are moderate in their requirements, but up till now comparatively little has been done for lack of the necessary capital.

A plentiful supply of cheap capital is essential to the success of any policy of land and housing reform. Every 1 per cent on the capital employed represents at least 8d. per week in the rent of a 6s. 6d. house, and, therefore, it is neither prudent nor possible for those who are determined to do the work properly or leave it alone altogether to pay more than 4 per cent or 5 per cent for the capital they employ. It is this lack of cheap capital for a thoroughly safe and sound undertaking that has prevented the development of a large number of estates on up-to-date lines. The landowners were willing to take a reasonable price for their land in order to have their tenants decently provided for at ten houses per acre, and by one means or another the prejudice of by-law officials might have been overcome by offering to the public a liberal amount of open spaces and allotments without charge to the ratepayers, but the necessary capital was not forthcoming at 4 or 5 per cent interest.

The capital required for providing housing accommodation for the poorer classes is obtained:

   (a) From the small investor.
   (b) By means of mortgages.
   (c) By the sale of ground rents.
   (d) By Government loans.

The first three of these methods provide a great deal of employment for the professional classes, who, therefore, not unnaturally resent any proposal for interfering with present arrangements, because they do not feel quite certain that they will do as well out of any new arrangements as they are doing under present conditions. There are a great many professional men whose chief income is derived from town and estate development. There is no valid reason why the new methods should not provide reasonable employment for these gentlemen on lines which will please the best of them far better than present methods. It is true that the disgraceful inflation of ground rents and the sale or mortgage of rotten property to unsuspecting persons must be stopped if the nation is to be properly housed and our towns developed on reasonable lines, but under the new methods there will be plenty of honest work to be done which should provide employment for the professional classes, and they should be well paid. The commission on the sale of twelve acres at £100 per acre (see Chapter II) should be larger than the commission on one acre at £400.

Chapter II explained the very large profits that are got from the creation of ground rents, that is, by the development of land for small house property, and the hope was expressed there that when the small investor sees how he is being fleeced under the old methods he will turn his attention to other investments where the cream has not been taken off the milk and a large quantity of water added before it reaches him. It was also explained that mortgages on real property are, according to law, trustee investments, no matter how badly the houses may be built and let. The small investor who buys a house built on the old methods gets a higher rate of interest, at least for a year or two, than if he decides to support the new, and herein lies one of the greatest obstacles to town planning and better housing. When the small investors (it is they who chiefly finance the old method of town development) are offered property which shows a return of 6, 7 or more per cent instead of only 4 per cent or 5 per cent on well built and well let property, it is not surprising that they take the 6, 7 or more per cent regardless of the future. Hence, there is a great shortage in the supply of cheap capital for housing the people on modern lines, and without cheap capital it is impossible to do this work properly.

Freehold ground rents and mortgages on house property are considered safe investments because there is always the small investor's money behind them, and, as has just been explained, the preparation of the various deeds and documents required provides an immense amount of employment for the professional classes. Some awakening has, however, taken place. Investors are beginning to realize that it is necessary in their own interests to ascertain what condition house property is in before putting their money into it, and this has made it much more difficult than it used to be to dispose of rotten property. Very bitter complaints used to be brought against the old Birmingham Corporation Housing Committee because their insistence that owners of small house property should make their houses fit for human habitation, or else close and demolish them, made it extremely difficult to sell bad property, and these complaints from those interested in slum property had considerable effect on the minds of men who wanted to support slum reform, but felt they could not do so if it interfered with business. It was not realized that unless the Housing Committee's work did result in making rotten property unsaleable, it would mean that they were not really doing their duty to the city, but only making a certain show before the public. Their work, properly done, was bound to damage the interests of slum owners, of men who had a vested interest in human misery. When these men began to feel the effects of the new policy, they began to cry out, and they made their voices heard, which is what the dwellers in the slums never did. However, the result of the Birmingham Housing Committee's work has been to make people a good deal more chary about investing in slum property, and that is a step in the right direction.

Another sign of the times, which, although producing temporary trouble in the shape of a house famine, is nevertheless most encouraging to those who look ahead, is the fact that the creators of the ordinary by-law suburb do not find it quite so easy as they used to do to gull the small investor into financing their undertakings for them. The step from refusing to invest in bad house property to deciding to invest in good house property will probably take some time; but public confidence will come with a few years of regular half-yearly payments of dividends and interest; and in spite of unfortunate experiences with jerrybuilt houses, the small investor will eventually realize that for him there is no better nor safer investment than well built, well let house property.

The position as regards the large investor is even more difficult. The interest obtainable on thoroughly sound and liquid securities has risen considerably the last few years, and, therefore, the ordinary large investor conversant with the money market is no longer satisfied with 4 per cent or 5 per cent, he wants 5 per cent or 6 per cent and has no difficulty in getting it. A considerable sum of money has been put into garden cities, suburbs and villages at a low rate of interest and these large investors insist upon careful business management of the housing schemes in which they are interested, but their action is due to public spirit rather than a pure commercial instinct and they are not typical of the general public.

In time, no doubt, when the general rate of interest goes down again, money will be put into town planning and garden suburb development on purely commerical business grounds, and those who want their money to be in something safe will, as a matter of course, put it into well built, well let house property. When that time comes there will be plenty of cheap capital available for town planning and housing work. At present, the movement is being very seriously delayed by the great lack of sufficient cheap capital, and, therefore, some means must be found of supplying the want.

Private enterprise has nobly shown the way to better housing of the people; it now rests with Government to take up the work and push it forward. The new methods do not provide a sufficient rate of interest to induce landjobbers to undertake the work and the Act does not provide adequate capital for respectable landowners and builders who are willing and anxious to house the people decently. It has to a certain extent stopped bad development; it has not promoted good development and housing because, among other reasons, it does not offer adequate financial support to respectable private enterprise. In order to get the best out of human nature there must be a driving force behind and some inducement in front. The 1909 Act fails in both respects; there is not enough driving force and very inadequate inducements. The recent offer of the Duke of Marlborough, the Earls Fitzwilliam, Leicester, Selborne, Shaftesbury, the Marquess of Salisbury and others to sell land for housing purposes at its agricultural and not its building value, for the purpose of the erection of cottages, shows that considerable progress could be made if only there were sufficient cheap capital available. This provides a unique opportunity for the Government to offer inducements to private enterprise to provide decent housing accommodation on modern lines, and if this were done on safe lines town planning administration would be made very much easier than it is at present. When a public body can only forbid and not encourage, the results are never as good as when a serious economic advantage can be offered for doing what is required.

It may be said that the Government already gives very great financial facilities to local authorities undertaking housing schemes, and that the time allowed for repayment of loans was considerably increased by the 1909 Act. This is quite true, but it is also true that public bodies have done little worth doing. With the exception of the Hereford Town Council, who assisted private enterprise by buying the land and making the roads, and Shrewsbury Town Council, who are considering a housing scheme at an average of twelve houses per gross acre, there is not, as far as I know, a single municipal house building scheme in this country which provides for less than twenty houses per gross acre.

Under the 1909 Act public bodies can borrow the whole of the capital required at $3\frac{1}{2}$ per cent with repayment in 80 years for land, 60 years for building, 30 years for sewers, and 20 years for street works, but when private enterprise proposes a scheme with only ten houses or less per acre and plenty of open spaces, it can only borrow two-thirds of the money at $3\frac{1}{2}$ per cent, and has to repay the loan in 30 years, which on the annuity principle brings up the annual charge to nearly $5\frac{1}{2}$ per cent as against 4 per cent paid by a local authority which puts 20 or more houses to the acre. This extra $1\frac{1}{2}$ per cent represents 1s. in the weekly rent of a 6s. 6d. house. That is a heavy penalty to pay for doing the work properly and is very seriously retarding the progress of town planning and better housing because for the reasons already given it is quite impossible as yet to raise the remaining third from the public for more than a very small part of the work that urgently needs doing. The Insurance Act provides that housing shall have first call on any funds at the disposal of the Insurance Commissioners for investment. This is a most wise and far-sighted provision because better housing will reduce the demand for sickness and unemployment benefits under the Insurance Act. In the next chapter, a scheme shall be outlined for making such investments quite safe.

The Local Government Board memorandum of March 25, 1913, deprecates overcrowding, but every practical town planner knows that an average of 20 houses per acre is overcrowding, because there is not nearly sufficient room left for the necessary amenities, such as allotments, play grounds, and playing fields. Yet this is the number of houses sanctioned by the Board for municipal schemes which they prefer to the work of private enterprise. The Board says that " the housing question should be left to local authorities." It not only says this, but it does its best to ensure that this policy shall prevail. The whole of the capital required is lent on easy terms with long periods of repayment for grossly overcrowded municipal house building schemes, whereas private enterprise, working on the most approved up-to-date lines, can barely get two-thirds of their expenditure, and then often only after immense trouble and many interviews. Surely the time has come to settle what loans shall be granted and on what terms according to the quality of the work that is proposed, without reference to who does it!

Of course, some private enterprise has been very far from satisfactory, but the best private enterprise has done infinitely better than any public body with the one exception of Hereford, who got private enterprise to help them. Fifteen thousand houses built by private enterprise on town planning or garden suburb lines with another 50,000 in prospect, as against 86 provided for by public bodies are the strongest possible argument in favour of Government giving fairer treatment to respectable private enterprise in this matter of cheap capital.

Putting humanity quite on one side, and considering only the economic position, now that the taxpayers are committed to finding many millions per annum for sick and unemployment benefits under the Insurance Act, it would pay the nation very handsomely indeed to finance approved housing schemes on genuine town planning lines, because the health of the tenants on these estates and their general outlook on life would be so much improved that their calls on the Insurance Act funds for sick and unemployment benefits would be very much less than if they are left to live in slums and congested districts. If the Government does not see its way to be more liberal in its financial support of respectable private enterprise the many landowners and builders not only willing but anxious to provide decent housing at reasonable rents will be thrown back on the landjobbers, and so long as this is the case town planning and better housing will be interminably delayed by dear capital.

It may be said that garden cities and suburbs have only provided for the better paid working classes, and do not deserve State help. The facts are that in spite of public bodies having an advantage over private enterprise of 1s. per week on a 6s. 6d. house in cost of capital, the latter has provided cottages ten to the acre at 4s. 6d. and 4s. 9d. per week (see Chapter V) as against 5s. per week for cottages provided by a public body with an average building density of 20 per gross acre. Surely this achievement justifies the statement that private enterprise adequately assisted and controlled by Government is much more likely to solve the housing problem than public bodies bound down as they are by red tape and hampered by ancient precedents. Experience shows that by far the most hopeful solution of our problem is for Government to lend State money much more liberally than they do at present to approved land and housing schemes under adequate safeguards.

There is a school of thought, by no means confined to any one political party in the State, that persistently advocates eleemosynary methods of dealing with the land and housing problem. This means the ignoring of economic laws, a procedure which is sure to lead to trouble. State aid to private enterprise in the form of cheap capital is urgently needed to assist in the solution of the problem before us, but this cheap capital should be provided on careful business lines and not in any sense in an eleemosynary or even semi-eleemosynary manner.

6. CONSTANT INCREASES IN THE RATES ON IMPROVEMENTS BUT NOT ON LAND

In section 4 of this chapter, examples were given of how dear land has very seriously delayed better town development and better housing. Take the first: the case of the Staffordshire lunatic asylum. The County Council was in a hole and the landowner knew it. It was a case of an anxious buyer and an unwilling seller and the buyer had to pay very heavily. Chatsworth Park (example b, section 4) is another useful illustration. Private parks in congested districts benefit the community, but this is not so in the country. They are for private enjoyment, they earn no money and therefore pay no rates worth mentioning. It is often claimed that a man may do what he likes with his own, but surely rich men should pay rates in at least the same proportion as poor men.

Now, if in these two cases the land had been assessed at the price charged for necessary public improvements and the unwilling sellers rated in the same proportion as other property owners, the public would have been on a fairer footing in their negotiations with them, and even if the public improvements had been delayed by the exorbitant prices demanded, the rate income from the land would have helped to pay for public improvements in other parts of the districts concerned, instead of the whole cost of these improvements being levied in such a way as to discourage town and estate development. Exactly the same remarks apply to the very large number of landowners who are preventing the preparation of genuine town planning schemes at the present time by demanding the ridiculous price of £400 to £600 per acre for agricultural land on which the rates now being paid are a negligible amount. This means that it costs the landowner nothing to hold up his land, whereas he ought in common justice to pay heavily for the privilege of being allowed to create and perpetuate unhealthy towns.

The following typical example of how our rating system works in practice is most illuminating. A Welsh landowner in a bare and sparsely populated district demolished the cottages on his estate in order to avoid paying rates on them and a farmer tenant of his is now obliged to employ only single men and board and lodge them, because all the cottages have been destroyed. There ought to be an economic incentive to landowners to provide or arrange for the provision of adequate housing accommodation for the workers on their land, but as things are at present the economic incentive is all the wrong way. The landlord gains by destroying cottages instead of building them.*

In order to substantiate my assertion that under our present rating system " the economic incentive is all the wrong way," I cannot do better than quote Mr Asquith and Mr Lloyd George:

Speaking at Tayport, East Fife, on October 14, 1898, Mr Asquith said: " All these great improvements in our social and municipal life have been effected by the representatives of the ratepayers, and they have been carried out at the cost of the occupiers of houses. But, gentlemen, who in the long run has benefited, and will continue to benefit by them? Those who have contributed little or nothing to the cost—the owners of the ground. I am convinced that the next great step in the direction of a larger and better municipal life will be in a form of taxation which no one can assert to be inequitable, because it simply imposes the burden upon those with whom the benefit will ultimately rest. I trust, therefore, that we may be able to submit to Parliament a well-considered scheme which will free our municipalities from the trammels under which they at present act, and which will open an avenue to a new source of social and industrial development."

Speaking in the House of Commons on February 19, 1908, Mr Asquith said: " For the local expenditure which is ultimately to be chargeable locally you will have to rely first on an improved system of rating, and secondly upon some system of taxation of site values."

Speaking to the National Liberal Federation at Birmingham on June 19, 1908, Mr Asquith referred to the Housing and Town Planning Bill, and said: " I agree with those who think that its necessary complement is a complete reconstruction of our valuation and rating systems."

Mr Lloyd George in the House of Commons said: " The moment a landlord put up a good building up went the rates."

Mr Arthur Balfour and Lord Robert Cecil have also spoken in public to the effect that under our present rating system the economic incentive makes for bad housing instead of good.

In the same way public bodies have not sufficient economic

* See excerpt from Marshall's " Principles of Economics," Appendix 12.

incentive under the present rating system to induce them to spread their people over larger areas instead of keeping them cooped up in congested districts in order to preserve existing assessable value. One reason for this is that the cost of town development falls wholly on buildings and other improvements, instead of, as it ought to do, partly at any rate, on the land whose value is increased by the expenditure of public money.

The 1909 Act (sections 58 and 59) gives very valuable powers in this direction, but they have not been used. The only town planning scheme as yet approved distinctly deprives the ratepayers of their right under the Act to one-half the betterment caused by the scheme. The excuse given for this peculiar procedure is the assertion that it is not possible in practice to keep accounts for betterment and compensation open, pending the actual development of the area, and the result is to rob the ratepayers as well as to deliberately contravene the obvious intentions of Parliament. The simplest and only certain method of ensuring that some part, at any rate, of the betterment due to public expenditure shall come to the ratepayers, is to assess land on its value and not merely on its use; and when this is done there will be a direct economic incentive to public bodies in the right direction instead of the wrong.

When land values are rated upon the full site value, whether used or not, in the same proportion as other property, the opening up and protection of cheap land will automatically and immediately produce increased assessable value on the outskirts of existing towns and urban districts, and with the assistance of the precautions advocated in this treatise, this method of rating will more than recoup any slight temporary decrease in assessment at the centre that may result from emptying the slums into the country. Our present rating system is seriously delaying town planning and better housing; the rating of land values on an equitable basis would greatly expedite the movement, provided there are proper safeguards against land sweating (see Chapter VII).

In those places where town extension on rational lines is made impossible by the land monopoly no local or central authority, however able and energetic, can get over the difficulty unless town planning administration is supported by the rating of land values.

It may be said that so long as there are any void houses in a district, the empty land in the neighbourhood is not required for building and the owner cannot be accused of holding it up. It is first necessary to ascertain what the void houses are like and what rent is being asked for them. Are they fit for human habitation, or are they so crowded together that the supply of light and air is inadequate ? Is this congestion due to the exorbitant prices demanded for land, and are the rents reasonable compared with the wages paid in the district ?

There is, as has already been mentioned, a great deal of cheap land that might and would be used for housing if adequate access were provided and if the policy already advocated were adopted this could rapidly be thrown into the market for building, thereby increasing the supply of land, and to that extent breaking the land monopoly. Where land suitable for building is not used for that purpose owing to lack of proper communication, it is obviously unfair to accuse the owner of holding it up, but it is not unfair to point out that under our present rating system and under the Housing and Town Planning, etc., Act as at present administered there is not sufficient economic incentive to landowners to take any steps to provide the necessary roads. So long as undeveloped land pays no rates worth mentioning the owners of such land can afford to wait, but if land values were rated in the same proportion as other property the situation would be very different. In that event the owners of land capable of being used for building would have a very strong economic incentive to get it opened up.

The rating of land values is an essential part of any sound policy for land and housing reform.

If land is assessed on the valuations of " full site value " as fixed under the Finance Act, 1910, this will in many cases be a great hardship on the owners, because these valuations have been arrived at on the assumption that 40 or more houses will be allowed per acre. For instance, land in a town planning area where there are to be only 12 houses per acre has been valued under the Finance Act at £500 to £550 per acre, which is very much more than can possibly be realized on this building density. This excessive valuation was agreed upon before it was generally understood that town planning means much fewer houses per acre than heretofore and therefore much lower land values. It would obviously be unfair to rate the owners of this land on a valuation arrived at under a misapprehension. It would also produce a result exactly opposite to that which is hoped for from the rating of land values, viz., a plentiful supply of cheap land for housing and other purposes; because people who are made to pay rates and taxes on excessive land valuations will have a very strong claim to be allowed to sweat their land in order to meet the rates and taxes on it. This state of affairs would merely perpetuate the old vicious circle—dear land, land sweating—land sweating, dear land. It is, therefore, necessary in the public interest, as well as in order to be fair to individuals, to allow landowners to reconsider their position before these excessive valuations are taken as the assessment on which their land is to be rated. It must not be forgotten that the true reformer's policy is not to punish individuals for past misdeeds, due largely to a faulty system, but rather to amend the law in such a way that individuals shall have an economic incentive to act in the public interest instead of against it.

Fewer houses per acre means lower land values and reformers who hope to reduce land values by rating them must be careful to do this on a fair but not excessive land valuation, or they will defeat their own ends. In several cases, the fact that duties have been paid on excessive valuations has been used as a lever to get permission to erect too many houses per acre. The simplest and fairest way of remedying the evil of over valuation is to arrange for annual revisions as in New York.

It is the tenants of small house property who are, in proportion to their income and expenditure, most severely hit by the present system of raising rates and taxes. These people do not, in England, pay rates direct, but they do pay them indirectly in their weekly rent. The landlords of small house property pay the rate collector, but unless they in their turn collected an equal amount (it is in practice generally rather more than they pay out) from their tenants, it is obvious that they would very soon become bankrupt. Indirect taxation is always unsound, and in this particular case it conceals a great injustice, The rates and taxes on a 6s. 6d. house are 1s. 6d. per week; this is borne by the tenant, and is a very heavy burden on his very limited exchequer. The poor man, like the rich man, has to live somewhere, but he can very seldom afford to pay for enough space for health, and yet the anomaly is that the yard or two of land he gets is of the dearest, and he must pay the heaviest tax. The rich man who will not sell or lease his land for building except at exorbitant prices, who is actually the cause of the poor man's position, pays no rates at all worth speaking of on the land he holds up. If this rich man were rated on the value he puts upon his property in the same ratio as other property owners, he would have less incentive to starve his neighbours in the matter of land, and more incentive to do his duty by them, in addition to which the intolerable burden now laid on the poor man's back would be considerably lightened.

N

Reform of our obsolescent rating system is essential to a successful solution of our land and housing problem, but without proper safeguards there is grave danger that harm will ensue.

One reformer thinks that town planning will effect all that is required, another thinks public land purchase is the sovereign remedy, a third still believes in municipal house building in spite of all its many failures, a fourth is convinced that the rating or taxation of land values, unaided and unprotected by any other measures, will accomplish the end. An attempt will be made in the next chapter to show that all these remedies, with the exception of municipal house building, must be employed and properly co-ordinated if there is to be any reasonable hope of better towns, lower rents, and decent housing for all classes of the community.

CHAPTER VII. THE NEED FOR FURTHER LEGISLATION AND BETTER ADMINISTRATION.

THE object of this chapter is to show that no one of the various remedies offered can alone solve the land and housing problem, and to suggest a way of co-ordinating them into a complete policy. What is wanted is to ensure:

1. Rational town and estate development.
2. A plentiful supply of cheap land.
3. Sufficient capital at a reasonable rate of interest and on reasonable terms of repayment.
4. The abolition of unfair and unwise financial burdens on people who are increasing the wealth of the country.

The legislation needed to attain these ends may be divided into three classes:

1. The amendment of existing laws.
2. The repeal of antiquated legislation.
3. The enactment of new measures to meet modern needs.

1. THE AMENDMENT OF EXISTING LAWS

The first law claiming our attention is the Housing and Town Planning, etc., Act, 1909. Eight years ago, when consideration was first given to town planning legislation for the United Kingdom, the main object was to make a start in order to get practical experience, and four years later, when this Act was passed, it was recognized as only a trial trip for the purpose of finding out the weak spots in local government with regard to town and estate development so that effective remedies might be later on devised. It has now been in operation three and a half years, and those who have worked it in a sympathetic spirit and at the same time with a critical mind, have seen where it has failed and how to improve it, but no legislation is of any practical use unless provision is made for sympathetic and effective administration.

The Local Government Board has shown itself to be so entirely out of sympathy with the main objectives of town planning legislation that any amendments to the Act of 1909 will be merely waste paper, unless they include the appointment of a special government department to deal with this matter, which department must not be under the control of or in any way subject to interference from the Local Government Board. It may be said that it is neither fair

nor reasonable to take this work away from the Local Government
Board after only three and a half years' trial. The Local Government Board were in 1906 presented with a new idea, which, without
any assistance from them, rapidly became extremely popular.
They resisted the innovation as long as they dared, and did nothing
until the Association of Municipal Corporations obliged them
to take it up. The Board may say that the action of this Association
had nothing to do with subsequent developments, but the fact
remains that no town planning Bill was laid before Parliament
until after the Association of Municipal Corporations had waited
on the late Prime Minister, Sir Henry Campbell-Bannerman, and
Mr Burns, and asked for legislation on this subject. Having been
forced into Parliamentary action against their will, the Local
Government Board insisted upon putting a provision into the
Act that no local authority should prepare a town planning scheme
without first obtaining permission from the Board to do so, and
this, as was foreseen by those who had studied the subject, has
proved not only a quite unnecessary and very expensive precaution,
but also most detrimental to genuine and effective town planning.
The Board is in fact the greatest obstruction of all to genuine and
effective town planning. Their public utterances and official mem-
oranda all harp on adherence to the by-laws and municipal house
building. Municipal house building has been tried for twenty or
thirty years, and we are as far off as ever from a satis actory solution of the housing problem. With regard to the by-laws, every one
who has made the smallest practical attempt to provide better
housing at reasonable rents, condemns unreservedly the so-called
model by-laws of the Local Government Board, and there are
innumerable practical examples of the utter failure of these petty
regulations to stop bad housing, whereas there are almost as many
cases in which they have obstructed or altogether prevented the
provision of good housing. The Board have not only deliberately
ignored the very strong public opinion concerning their wretched
" model by-laws," they have in addition openly flouted the intentions of Parliament with regard to betterment and other very
important points in town planning administration, and, worst of
all, they have played into the hands of the landjobbers and jerry-
builders. The membership of local authorities is decided by popular
election, and this too often turns on political issues which have
nothing whatever to do with municipal business. The ability to
profess some particular political belief whether one believes it or
not is no qualification whatever for dealing with and controlling

such a highly technical and complicated business as town and estate development on modern lines, and, therefore, the interference of politics with municipal business is very liable to result in town development committees being very largely comprised of men who have had no practical experience, and indeed know nothing whatever about the work. Where this occurs the real control rests entirely with the officials and they are proverbially slow to take up any new idea. They not unnaturally prefer to stick to their old ways because so long as an official does nothing new he is very highly respected by all around him. Those who are financially interested in maintaining the "status quo" make it their business to be well represented both directly and indirectly on public bodies. The officials are perfectly well aware of this fact, and it is not surprising that some of them find it easier to leave things as they are rather than carry out the wishes and look after the interests of the general public, which is a very vague and nebulous entity, especially when it comes to filling official positions and voting salaries. Under all these circumstances, it is obvious that a new idea like town planning which, if sincerely administered, will seriously interfere with landjobbing, needs the driving force of a strong central authority that will take pains to educate public opinion as to the main points to be examined in town planning schemes, and which will itself refuse to approve proposals made by local authorities unless they are in accord with the public interest. Private interests must be considered, but they must not be allowed (as they have been in the past) to destroy the public health or rob the public purse, and the only way to ensure this is to appoint a special government department sufficiently well informed and with sufficient time to attend to the work. Housing and town planning is a special branch of work, and has wider issues than any involved in local building by-laws so dear to the hearts of existing authorities, both central and local. A new department is urgently needed to deal with the new work in hand on the new lines instead of nullifying new ideas by insisting upon the perpetuation of old methods. One of the most useful functions of this new department should be to organize a scheme for explaining to local authorities and the general public what town planning really means, and what are its possibilities, thereby helping the movement forward by the dissemination of information instead of holding it back by innumerable rules and regulations, and the key-note of all their work should be to make bad housing unprofitable and good housing a thoroughly sound business proposition.

The land and housing problem is first and foremost an economic question, and in the last chapter it was explained that town planning and better housing have been most seriously retarded by lack of an adequate supply of cheap capital. The economic and financial aspects of our problem connect it very closely indeed with the Treasury, and great advantage might be obtained by placing the new government department in the closest possible touch with the Treasury, if not actually under it. The old school will say that this proposal is contrary to all precedent, that the proper function of the Treasury is to check as far as it can the expenditure of public money, and not to trouble itself as to whether or not public money is wisely spent. Their idea is that supervision and control of public expenditure are outside the province of the Treasury and this time-honoured idea largely accounts for the constant increases in our rates and taxes.

Another reason for putting town planning under the Treasury is that land included in a town planning scheme becomes liable for undeveloped land duty. Government valuers under the Finance Act, 1910, have valued land in town planning areas at prices far above what it is worth for development on modern lines. If taxation and town planning were co-ordinated this injustice could be avoided. Another injustice that needs attention is the collecting of undeveloped land duty on land the development of which is delayed two or three years by the preparation of a town planning scheme.

The Road Board and the Development Commission are already under the Treasury. The designing of new main arteries (see Chapter I) is the first business that has to be attended to in the preparation of a town planning scheme. The Road Board has powers in this direction, that, if used in conjunction with town planning powers, might very materially assist in the successful solution of many knotty questions of detail, on which the practical efficacy of town planning schemes very largely depends. For instance, clause 11 of the Development and Road Improvement Act, 1909, gives the Road Board, subject to the approval of the Treasury, power to acquire land for new roads and in addition "land on either side of the proposed road within two hundred and twenty yards from the middle of the proposed road." If this power had been put into force in the case of the new main artery through Edgbaston to Harborne (see Appendix 1) the ratepayers of Harborne would have been greatly benefited and the profit on back land converted into valuable building sites would have gone a long way towards paying for the road. Town planning is at the present time no part of the Road Board's work, but the following extracts show that already they understand the problem better than the Local Government Board.

Extracts from circular issued by the Road Board, November 28, 1912:

" 1. They [the Road Board] do not encourage proposals relating to the widening of streets, in fully built areas, which are crowded and congested mainly with local traffic, as they do not consider that such works are fairly within the scope of the Road Improvement Act.

" 2. They will favourably consider proposals which will facilitate the execution of town planning schemes so far as these contain provision for the improvement of through road communications.

" 3. They will give special consideration to proposals for the acquisition of vacant land required or likely to be required for widenings of important roads in cases where it can be shown that the prospect of building is imminent."

It is outside the province of this book to presume to say how the policy advocated should be carried out in practice; but it is not unreasonable to draw attention to the great economies and improvements in administration that might be effected if the central land and housing department were under the Treasury. A central authority that controlled the purse strings and had power (like the Road Board, for instance) to contribute towards the cost of new roads of general utility would be able to lead local authorities on the right way and not merely drive them.

Power should be given to the central land and housing authority to obtain from all local authorities information under the following heads:

URBAN

1. The number of void houses to let at 6s. 6d. or less per week including rates.

2. The standard and minimum rates of wages in the district.

3. The total number of houses in the district let at 6s. 6d. or less per week and their condition as regards:

    (a) General ventilation and arrangement.

    (b) Cleanliness and damp.

4. The extent of the demand for good cheap houses.

5. The amount of empty land in the district and its price.

6. Means of communication between empty land and the centre of population.

RURAL

1. The ruling wages of the district and what labourers can afford to pay for a cottage and one-eighth of an acre of land.

2. The condition of existing housing accommodation and the demand for more.

3. The ruling rent for farm land.

AMENDMENTS TO THE ACT

Assuming that arrangements have been made for cautious and energetic administration the next step is to consider what amendments are necessary to the Housing and Town Planning Act of 1909, in order to remove the obstructions that have been set up and thereby save money for the ratepayers. Amendments are urgently needed with a view to:

(a) Simplifying the regulations.

(b) Making the Act apply to existing towns as well as to undeveloped districts.

(c) Facilitating the construction of new main arteries.

(d) Securing betterment for the ratepayers.

(e) Reducing the present exorbitant prices paid for land for public purposes.

(f) Ensuring a restriction of building density that renders possible reasonable amenities.

(g) Giving respectable private enterprise a real right of appeal from an obstructive local authority in place of the present inadequate safeguard.

(h) Providing an adequate supply of cheap capital for approved housing schemes.

(i) Giving architects and other local experts a proper "locus standi" in the preparation of town planning schemes.

(a) SIMPLIFICATION OF THE REGULATIONS

The most effective way of doing this is to abolish the obligation to obtain permission to prepare a town planning scheme. The law as it stands and the regulations have created a ridiculous and impossible position. It is directly opposed to the interests of the ratepayers for a local authority to give the slightest indication of its intentions until a good deal of work has been done and various steps taken to guard against private land speculation at the public expense, and yet local authorities are not supposed to do anything practical before showing their hand to the landjobbers. The reason given for putting this brake on the wheel was the statement that local authorities could not be trusted to safeguard the pockets of their ratepayers; it was said that enthusiasts would rush into all sorts of mad expenditure without first considering whether the district could afford to meet it. The practical results of this alleged safeguard against over enthusiastic local authorities have been:

1. Ridiculous regulations.

2. Interminable delay.

3. Increased cost.

4. An unfair advantage to greedy and cantankerous property owners.

This so-called safeguard has in fact utterly failed in its alleged purpose of protecting the pockets of the ratepayers. On the contrary, it has so increased the cost of putting the Act into force that a very large number of localities have been deprived of the protection they so badly need. It cost one local authority no less than £500 to make out a prima facie case for permission to prepare a town planning scheme in a rural district where the vested interests so dear to the hearts of the old school cannot possibly have been of any serious account, and where therefore the procedure ought to have been quite simple and cheap.

The preparation of the Harborne and Quinton town planning scheme cost £2,743. Under reasonable regulations a competent local authority could have done the work for £1,000 or less.

The present unconscionable delay in the preparation of town planning schemes is most unfair to landowners. The inclusion of their land in a town planning area makes them liable for undeveloped land duty and they have to pay this tax for the three or four years required to complete the scheme without being able to get any adequate return on their land.

In applying for permission to prepare a scheme, local authorities are called upon to describe a scheme which they have not yet received permission to prepare (article VIII (a)) and they are also expected to supply an estimate of its cost. As a matter of fact local authorities do not want holding back in this urgent matter of town planning and better housing, they sorely need pushing forward, and the sooner the obligation to apply for permission before getting to work is removed the better for all concerned.

This obligation involves:

2 debates in the Council Chamber, where property is always well represented;

4 notices to owners;

3 advertisements in the newspapers;

2 maps;

1 meeting of owners;

1 letter of application to the Board with most voluminous information;

1 Local Government Board inquiry.

If the above formalities were dispensed with, there would still be:

1 debate in the Council Chamber;

4 notices to owners;

5 advertisements;

6 maps;

2 meetings of owners, one public and one private;

1 letter of application to the Board with most exhaustive information;

1 Local Government Board inquiry;

4 opportunities for objections from property owners.

Surely this is enough to restrain the ardour of enthusiasts and surely the cost of all this remaining procedure will be a sufficient charge on the ratepayers for endeavouring to protect their district from overcrowding and themselves from an undue toll to the landjobbers.

A competent central authority would insist that every local authority should have a town planning scheme instead of making them apply for permission to do so.

In Holland the Law of 1902 forces municipalities to prepare plans of extension. Large towns are compelled to include permanent open spaces in their extension plans.

In Italy the Law of June 25, 1865, says that " If in carrying out a town extension plan the corporation has to cut new roads, landowners affected are obliged to give the land free for the purpose, and all neighbouring owners have to hand increment over to the community.

In Sweden the Law of 1874 imposes on towns the obligation to have an extension plan and to reserve open spaces.

In Switzerland the towns of Geneva, Lausanne, Fribourg, Berne and Zurich are obliged to have extension plans.

Unless our English towns are allowed to direct their own

development subject only to an appeal on the final plan to an independent central authority the " PARASITES " will merely use town planning schemes to bleed the community at least as thoroughly as they did under the old system.

The abolition of the obligation to apply for " permission to prepare " would at one stroke greatly simplify the regulations by cutting out notices, advertisements, applications, maps, etc., etc., some of which are extremely foolish.

A land and housing department that understood its business, and was attending to main issues instead of bewildering itself with endless petty details, would soon find many other ways of simplifying the regulations, and thereby remove one of the main obstacles to the progress of town planning in this country.

This great subject of land and housing needs the WHOLE TIME of first-rate men who will give every consideration to the rights of property, but not allow the rights of the people to be ignored. When the work is entrusted to men of this stamp pettifogging regulations will be abolished and main principles, such as adequate access to cheap land and reasonable building density, will be insisted upon.

(b) ACT TO APPLY TO COMPLETE DISTRICTS

To call the Act of 1909 a Housing and Town Planning Act is a ridiculous misnomer. It gives no power whatever for the planning of existing towns; on the contrary, it specifically restricts the powers under the Act to the planning of " land in course of development or likely to be used for building purposes " or " land so situated with respect to any land likely to be used for building purposes that it ought to be included in any town planning scheme made with respect to the last-mentioned land." This limitation of town planning schemes to " land likely to be used for building purposes " is on the face of it absurd. Who can say what land is or is not likely to be used for building? For instance, what rational human being nowadays would commit himself to the opinion that any land within 20 or 25 miles of London or ten miles of any large town is not likely to be used for building purposes, during the next thirty or fifty years ? Those responsible for this definition must have been asleep for many years. They cannot have noticed the rapid developments of means of transit that have been achieved during the last few years nor have given a moment's thought to the possibilities of the next ten years, or they would never have suggested such an obviously unintelligent restriction.

The 1909 Act is in fact merely a measure for the protection of suburbs and, therefore, entirely defeats the first object of town planners, which is to deal with towns as a complete whole instead of in the old extravagant piecemeal fashion. It is quite futile to provide for 100-ft. main arteries in the suburbs leading into narrow central streets where the traffic is greatest and where, therefore, the streets should be wider—not narrower—than they are further out. To quote from " Practical Housing," which was first published in 1908: " The first principle of town planning is to consider beforehand the constituent parts of a modern town and then to arrange them in such a way that the result shall show an ordered harmony. If we had the power to consider first how existing towns ought to have been planned and then year by year to make our improvements in accordance with that plan, we might by degrees correct past mistakes, and, on systematic, economical lines, gradually bring our centres of population up to the standard required by modern conditions of life.

" A town extension plan contemplates and provides for the development AS A WHOLE of every urban, suburban or rural area likely to be built upon during the next thirty or fifty years."

The policy, stated briefly, is to prepare a skeleton plan of the existing town providing improved communications between the centre and its suburbs, the provision as far as possible for proper communication with other towns by road, rail or water, and the protection of new districts against overcrowding. The 1909 Act gives no power to deal with anything beyond the last item in this programme, whereas the first thing that should claim the attention of town planners is the map of their own town and of adjoining districts as they exist to-day with a view to designing proper means of communication in every direction and also through the centre.

The scope of the 1909 Act needs widening and the restriction to land likely to be used for building must be abolished if the work is to be done properly. There is no need to insist upon a complete, fixed, and exact plan of the whole neighbourhood. That would be a great mistake. But it is essential to success that the local authority should have in its mind a skeleton plan of its whole district, and this is the only foundation on which can be based town planning schemes for particular areas that will be in any way permanently satisfactory. These little schemes for individual areas must form part of a carefully considered and harmonious whole.

The best way to get ideas for a general plan of the whole district is to institute a town planning competition, as was done in the case of Greater Berlin, Chicago and other places.   The general skeleton plan should be published when completed as a general guide as to what may be done during the next fifty years, and as a help in the preparation of town planning schemes for individual areas; but it must be clearly explained that the local authority does not bind itself to carry out all or any of the improvements indicated, and that anyone speculating on their execution would do so entirely at his own risk. The local authority must be carefully safeguarded against any claim for compensation on the ground that some anticipated improvement has not been carried out, and they must hold themselves perfectly free to alter or modify the skeleton plan as and when required. The experience of Dusseldorf and other town planning authorities emphasizes the need for conditions and safeguards of this nature.

(c) MAIN ARTERIES

Far stronger powers are needed for the cutting of new main arteries through back land in order to throw cheap land into the market for building purposes. The Road Board has fairly strong powers in this direction, but even these are scarcely strong enough. Where it can be proved that a new main artery is needed in the interests of the community, no landowner should be allowed to block it nor should he be allowed to charge the community for the privilege granted to him of increasing the value of his land by turning back land into front, as has so often happened in the past. Road improvement and town planning are so closely allied that they should be under one head. Those responsible for these branches of what is really all one business could help each other enormously not only with regard to the designing but also in the carrying out of the work.

(d) BETTERMENT

Section 58, sub-section (3), gives the ratepayers one-half of the betterment due to a town planning scheme. In Birmingham and other places this clause has been nullified by projecting and carrying out public improvements in town planning areas independently of the town planning scheme. This is most disloyal to the ratepayers, but where private interests are concerned the pockets of the ratepayers are often forgotten. The above sub-section should be strengthened so as to include any public improvement made in a town planning area no matter whether it be part of the town planning scheme or not. It must be made impossible for any member of a local authority to sacrifice the interests of the ratepayers in order to gratify a personal whim or oblige a friend.

Another way in which betterment has been deliberately thrown away by the authorities was explained in connexion with the first town planning scheme approved by the Local Government Board. The method adopted was to enact that all claims for betterment must be made within twelve months of the date of approval of the scheme, and this makes the betterment clause absolutely inoperative.

If land were rated on its value and not merely on its use it would be impossible for any local or central authority, however incompetent or corrupt it might be, to evade the law.

(e) LAND PURCHASE

Wider powers of land purchase are badly needed in order to protect the ratepayers against the disgraceful way in which they have been bled in the past. Section 2 of the 1909 Act, subsection (3), enables local authorities to buy land for housing, notwithstanding that the land is not immediately required for that purpose, but it must eventually be used for housing under Part III of the 1890 Act or resold. Section 60 of the 1909 Act enables a local authority to purchase land by agreement for the purpose of a town planning scheme, but the Board has ruled that the exact purpose for which the land is bought must be specified. The object of this reservation is alleged to be to protect the ratepayers against jobbery, the effect of it in practice is to make local authorities always pay more for land than any private individual. Section 60 of the 1890 Act provided an opportunity of doing away with this plan for bleeding the ratepayers, but the Board decreed otherwise. This is a striking example of one of the dangers of modern methods of legislation. A great deal of power is left in the hands of some board or department. The results are excellent when the board or department is in sympathy with the legislation passed, but when it is not, the intentions of Parliament are, as in this case, frustrated by administration. It is a public scandal that the ratepayers should not be allowed to buy land cheap and section 60 needs strengthening so that our administrators both local and central shall be obliged to carry out the intentions of Parliament, and in order to make the ratepayers quite safe general legislation is advisable. The question of land purchase will be returned to in a later section of this chapter.

(f) BUILDING DENSITY

It was seen in Chapter II that a restriction of the number of houses per acre will not increase house rents. House owners are already getting out of their tenants as much as they can afford, or rather manage, to pay and therefore the effect of restricting building density will be to keep land values within reasonable bounds, not to increase house rents. As the Act and its administration now stand the onus is put on to the local authority to justify a building density that will leave sufficient room for the necessary amenities. This is most unreasonable. What ought to be done, and what must be done if any real progress is to be made, is to put the onus on landowners to prove their right to more than ten houses per acre. Evidence should be produced showing the present income from the land and what it can be made to earn under economical town planning methods at ten houses per acre. The landowner should be satisfied with 25 years' purchase of the present income plus 50 per cent profit. This profit will sound very extravagant to some housing reformers, and so perhaps it is when the question is considered in the abstract, but it must not be forgotten that up to now the profits on land and building speculation have been very much larger.

Having restricted building density to a reasonable number of houses per acre, the necessity for a certain proportion of cheap cottages must be attended to. Unless there is some elasticity, no houses will be provided in town planning areas below the average standard rent in the district, which in urban districts is 6s. 6d. per week including rates. It is, therefore, necessary to allow those land and building developers who are willing to provide cheap cottages to put rather more per acre so that they can realize the same price per acre for their land. The numbers suggested in Chapter II are 12 houses per acre at a net rent of 4s. 3d. per week, and 15 at a net rent of 3s. 6d. per week. There are well-known objections to inserting exact figures for wages or house rents in an Act of Parliament, but there is no objection to giving public bodies power to insert such a condition in the general provisions of their town planning schemes, and it is of vital importance to the poorest classes who most need help that the legislature should do everything in its power to increase the supply of good cheap houses on a sound economic basis.

(g) LANDOWNER'S APPEAL TO CENTRAL AUTHORITY

In Chapter VI it was shown that whereas garden cities and garden suburbs have done something towards better housing, the Town

Planning Act has in three years and a half achieved absolutely
no tangible results. It was also mentioned that private enterprise
would have done a great deal more, if it had not been for the opposition and obstruction of local authorities. In " Practical Housing,"
great emphasis was laid upon the necessity for an appeal from the
local authority to the central authority in cases of this sort. That
appeal has been put into the Act but it is administered in such a
way as to make it far too cumbersome and costly for practical
use. Section 44 enacts that if the Local Government Board is
satisfied that housing is unreasonably impeded by by-laws, then
it may require the local authority to revoke such by-laws. This
seems quite simple and straightforward, but in practice the Local
Government Board will do nothing under this section, unless
the local authority is in agreement with the landowner and comes
with him to the Board. This method of administration entirely
nullifies any virtue there might be in this apparent provision for
appeal. Public-spirited individuals or societies are, therefore, thrown
back on section 61, sub-section (b), which enables the Local Government Board to order the local authority to adopt a scheme prepared
by the owners. This involves all the paraphernalia explained in
Chapter III, endless maps, notices, advertisements, etc., etc., which
mean very great expense and delay, and it is not surprising that
owners opposed by their local authorities have not thought it
worth their while to take all this trouble and spend all this money
with the strong possibility of losing their appeal—public bodies
generally hang together. It is most urgent and important that the
landowners' right of appeal to the central authority should be a
real appeal and also be made quite simple and cheap.

Gratitude is often described as a sense of favours to come, and
if the State hopes to receive as much help from private enterprise
in the future as it has in the past, it might not unreasonably show
its gratitude by giving private enterprise a fairer field and more
favour.

(h) ADEQUATE SUPPLY OF CHEAP CAPITAL FOR APPROVED
SCHEMES—STATE LOANS

The first impulse of idealists is that evils must be remedied no
matter how, and the tendency is to eleemosynary methods because
these seem to be the quickest and most direct. It is often not
realized that although eleemosynary or semi-eleemosynary methods
may apparently do good at the moment, in the long run they seldom
if ever fail to do more harm than good. One of the greatest mistakes

in the mismanagement of Ireland has been the way in which England has administered doles whilst robbing the people of their just rights. This policy broke Ireland's spirit and destroyed her self-dependence. The only safe way to help an individual or a nation is to help them to help themselves, and it is sincerely to be hoped that that method will be applied to the solution of our land and housing problem. We really require an entire economic revolution in order to make it a natural process, beneficial to landlord and tenant alike, to provide better housing, and the process most likely to produce the desired result is to:

1. Take advantage of the landowners' offer of cheap land.

2. Support housing enterprise with adequate State loans on careful business lines.

3. Organize co-partnership housing societies.

The offer of Earl Fitzwilliam and other landowners " to lease or sell land which has only an agricultural value at its agricultural value to local authorities and public utility societies working either on co-operative or co-partnership lines" opens up great possibilities. This offer may not look much, coming as it does from only ten landowners, but it is a first step in the right direction, and as such has a capital significance. It shows the fundamental identity between human rights and property rights. The " Times " of March 15, 1913, draws attention to the fact that " cottages are as much the furniture of farms as farmers' dwelling-houses, barns, etc. A farm with good cottages lets for more rent than a farm without such accommodation. It is the business of the landowner to provide decent cottages and his interest to do so. His return will be in an increased rent for his farm." It is quite true that the erection of cottages improves the value of an estate, but it must not be forgotten that an adequate supply of decent cottages is not being provided at the present time. Benefits as well as injuries to one class of the community sooner or later react on the whole body. The policy suggested above would immediately profit landowners because the sale of land on these terms will benefit the seller, but it would also benefit the tenants, and by enlisting voluntary effort in the service of better housing help forward the whole movement. The great interest taken by employers and others in the Territorials in some parts of the country shows the desire of Britishers to do their duty by the nation against foreign foes, and in the matter of town planning and better housing the landowners' offer just mentioned shows that there is the same readiness to adopt similar methods in fighting the enemies within our gates—bad housing, vested interests and extravagant administration. It would indeed be a thousand pities if this genuine patriotism in the form of private enterprise were not taken full advantage of. " One volunteer is worth ten pressed men."

Clause 54 (3) of the Insurance Act, first paragraph, concludes as as follows: " those Commissioners shall in making the investment give preference to stock or bonds . . . for the purposes of the Housing of the Working Classes Acts 1890 and 1909." This provision presents great possibilities. Public money specially ear-marked for housing loans could do as much as anything towards town planning and better housing, because it would remove one of the chief obstacles to progress at the present time that is the very inadequate supply of cheap capital available for up-to-date housing schemes.

At the same time precautions must be taken to ensure that the benefits to be obtained by co-operation between landowners, landlord and tenants shall be fairly divided between all parties (see later).

Section 3 of the 1909 Act authorizes loans to local authorities of the whole of the capital needed for housing schemes for periods not exceeding 80 years, and no condition whatever is made as to the lay-out of the estate or the number of houses put per acre. The chief point of interest seems to be to get as many houses or tenements on to the land as the by-laws allow. Those responsible for these schemes lack imagination, they do not recognize the value of light and air, and they waste money on useless regulations. On pages 195 and 196 will be found:

1. A local authority's idea of developing an estate.

2. The same estate as dealt with by enlightened private enterprise.

No money should be lent to local authorities for housing unless the houses are limited to a reasonable number per acre.

In the case of loans to private enterprise only two-thirds of the capital required for housing schemes is lent (see section 4, 1909 Act) and the period for repayment is only 30 or 40 years as against 60 or 80 years granted to local authorities. It is not reasonable to expect property of this sort to be written off in 30 or 40 years. It will last at least 60; probably a great deal longer, and by hastening repayment of the Government loans in this unreasonable way an unfair burden is put upon present tenants for the benefit of their successors. Private enterprise has done all that has been done towards better housing on modern lines, and in the public interest

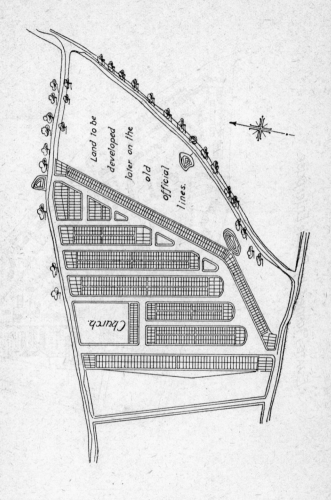

ESTATE - Planned by a Local Authority.

Land to be developed later on the old official lines.

Church.

Estate–Planned by Private Enterprise.

Recreation Ground.

Church.

it is high time that greater monetary support should be given to housing schemes of this nature, but this must be done on careful business lines, not in the form of doles. The money should be lent at a rate of interest that will ensure no loss to the Treasury. The security must be real, and no financial support should be given to schemes that do not provide for decent living conditions with reasonable amenities. The following general terms on which State loans might be granted should ensure the ends in view:

1. Building density not to exceed an average of ten houses per gross acre, except for houses let at 4s. 3d. and 3s. 6d. per week net, in which case building density may be slightly increased (see Chapter II), 10 per cent of the estate to be set aside for allotments and other open spaces.

2. The landowner to sell his land at a price that makes the above form of development a sound business proposition and to accept payment in loan stock or loan stock debentures of the society, which shall rank after the Government loan and have a claim on the assets of the society prior to that of the shareholders. Government should ascertain what the land is earning at the time of sale before approving the price paid to the landowner.

3. The cost of development must not exceed the amount necessary for reasonable means of communication and adequate sanitation.

4. The tenants to subscribe for shares in the society at the rate of 1d. for every 1s. of rent paid or to take up loan stock debentures to an equivalent amount, whichever they prefer.

5. A certain proportion of the houses on the estate to be let at rents suitable for the poorest classes and at least one-third of the total should be within the compound or where there is no compound at a rate commensurate with the ruling wages of the district, always provided that the general policy should be to encourage a rise in wages by providing better housing rather than to build down to low wages.

6. Loans to be granted on larger houses provided their number does not exceed a certain proportion of the total. Reasonable provision of accommodation for public meetings and social intercourse should be encouraged and also an adequate but not excessive supply of shops, by granting loans on these assets as well as on houses.

7. In rural districts, the rents guaranteed exclusive of rates must be sufficiently low to meet the current wages of the district, and each cottage should have sufficient land to render the labourer more or less independent of his employer so that he may be able to gradually get his wages increased. Tenants must not be liable

to be turned out of their cottages because they leave or are dismissed by their employers. When a tenant member is turned out of the society or out of his house for misconduct, he should have a right of appeal to the central authority who should send down an inspector to inquire into the circumstances on the spot.

8. The Government department granting the loan should satisfy itself that the rents to be charged show a reasonable return on the expenditure involved.

9. The whole of the capital required for development and building must be advanced by the State and the annual charges for interest and sinking fund should not exceed 4 or $4\frac{1}{2}$ per cent.

No business, however sound it may be in theory, is likely to succeed unless it is carefully managed. The object of calling upon the landowner to accept payment for his land in loan stock and of insisting upon share subscriptions from the tenants is to ensure careful management of the society's affairs. If all the money were found by Government and no financial responsibility laid upon local individuals there would be no local interest in the financial success of the undertaking, and it is obviously out of the question for Government to attempt the day-by-day detailed management of such ventures as these. They would be almost sure to fail and, even if they did succeed, it would be very bad indeed for the societies concerned to have all responsibility taken out of their hands. Nothing could be worse.

Practical experience shows that share subscriptions at 1d. in every 1s. of rent added to the rent would make the total weekly payment on these co-partnership estates no more (in many cases less) than the rent now charged for equivalent accommodation on estates developed on the old lines at 30, 40, or more houses per acre, and, therefore, it would be no hardship to insist upon share subscriptions being paid with the rent. On the contrary, it would be a distinct advantage for the tenants as compared with existing conditions, because whereas under the old system a tenant often pays for every brick in his house without owning one of them, under the system suggested above 1d. out of every thirteen pennies paid by him would be put to the credit of his share account, and there is this inestimable advantage to the society as a whole: the tenants are all landlords as well as tenants. None of them can say, "This house is mine;" they can all say "These houses are ours," and the result of this feeling of ownership is that the cost of repairs and losses due to voids are less than one-third of what they

are on ordinary estates. Voids and repairs are a very heavy item
in the current accounts of small house property.

The third condition is also important. It protects Government
against granting loans on estates where money is wasted through
extravagant by-law regulations.

Condition 7 provides for the security of tenure, so essential to
the worker, and protects him against individual caprice.

The policy of adequate State loans, with reasonable periods for
repayment on some such conditions as those enumerated above,
presents great possibilities for housing reform both urban and rural.
Co-partnership Tenants Limited, 6, Bloomsbury Square, London,
has already been referred to (see also " Practical Housing ").
The same methods have been adopted by the Rural Co-partnership
Housing and Land Council, 4, Tavistock Square, London, W.C.,
presided over by Lord Henry Bentinck, M.P., and under their
auspices six societies have already been formed (December 31,
1912). If the landowners' offer of cheap land already mentioned
in this chapter were supplemented by adequate State loans progress
on sound lines could be greatly expedited.

There is no more attractive method than this for dealing with the
actual business of house building and house letting. The surplus
profits after paying 4 per cent or 5 per cent on capital, go to the
tenant members, thereby getting over one of the greatest obstacles
to housing reform, namely, the conflicting interests between
landlord and tenant. Under co-partnership housing, the landlord
and tenant become one and the same person, so that the better the
concern is managed and the higher the charges made for rent and
amenities the more the surplus profits for tenant members. At
the same time there is an important point, which, if neglected, may
cause ruin to the society and the loss of hard-earned savings.
In any community of 100 or more persons there are sure to be a
few who will endeavour to get more than they have a right to at
the expense of their neighbours. It is, therefore, essential to success
to have strong men in command of the society's affairs until the
tenants have acquired a responsible stake in the concern and have
had time to study and understand the working of the system that
has been inaugurated for their benefit and for that of no one else.
There is a case where the tenants got control before they understood the system and nearly ruined the society and themselves by
charging too low rents, thereby destroying their credit and depriving themselves of the surplus profits that would have come to
them under well-instructed and careful management. The growth

of co-partnership housing in urban districts has been phenomenal, although it is still hampered by difficulties inseparable from pioneer work. There is undoubtedly a very large future before it, because it is a thoroughly wise and well-balanced mixture of self-interest and communal interest. The surplus profits all go to the tenants and if any tenant acts against the communal interests of his fellow members, they have the power by a two-thirds majority of the shareholders to turn him out of the society. Where the co-partnership idea is properly carried out nothing is given for nothing, but very good value is given for the money spent, as is proved by the fact that on co-partnership estates void houses are a negligible quantity.

The great advantage of co-partnership housing over municipal house building is that in the former case people are helped to help themselves, whereas in the latter everything is done for them, than which there is nothing worse for human nature.

The policy of adequate State loans to co-partnership housing societies at 4 or $4\frac{1}{2}$ per cent with reasonable terms for repayment may be criticized in two ways.

1. Can the financial terms that are proposed be defended from the Treasury point of view?

2. Is the co-partnership housing movement, even when supported by adequate State loans, likely to grow big enough to cover the whole problem ?

1. The State is borrowing from working men through the Post Office savings bank at $2\frac{1}{2}$ per cent, and, therefore, it would be very good business for the State to relend it at 4 or $4\frac{1}{2}$ per cent, and if further moneys are required a well organized State whose housing conditions are being rapidly improved should have no difficulty whatever in obtaining at $3\frac{1}{2}$ per cent or 4 per cent as much money as they require for reproductive work of this nature. This should provide an ample margin for administration expenses. The security given to the Treasury would be ample. They would have:

(a) A first charge on the land, buildings and all other assets belonging to the societies and landowners having taken payment for land in loan stock there would be a substantial margin between the money lent for development and building and the total value of the estates when developed.

(b) An assurance that no unnecessary or unproductive expenditure would be made on estate development or building.

(c) A steadily increasing share capital coming into societies and ranking after State loans, thereby constantly improving the security.

(d) A certainty that the property on which State money was lent would be well developed and well built, and further, that it would be well taken care of, because the tenants being shareholders, would have the pride of possession and consequently every inducement to protect the property.

2. No one can say authoritatively at the present moment that any one method is equal to the task of housing decently all our fellow countrymen who need it, but past results justify the statement that none of the methods yet suggested present greater prospects of success than the co-operative movement. Its field of activities is only limited to the question of finance and adequate State loans would open up to it the whole country-side.

Co-partnership housing is a method of work, its principles can be applied by any body of people. It need not and should not be confined to any one body of men.

(i) CO-OPERATION OF ALL THE ARTS AND SCIENCES

Under the present régime the preparation of town planning schemes is very largely in the hands of men obsessed with the old ideas and the old methods. The by-law official, the rate collector and the old-fashioned lawyer or the mere politician are the very last people who should be entrusted with new and important work of this nature. No good will be obtained from town planning until it is put into the hands of men who already understand its meaning or are willing to learn. The work involves not merely a consideration of roads and sewers, it also involves attention to public health, public buildings, tramways, motor-buses, open spaces and housing, and cannot be done properly without the assistance of experts in all these branches of town development and administration. The medical officer of health ought to have a strong voice in the preparation of town planning schemes, and so should the architectural profession. A town planning scheme that does not provide advantageous sites for good architectural effects, sanitary and economical housing, a sufficiency of open spaces and proper facilities for traffic, is a failure. It is, therefore, essential to secure the co-operation of all the arts and sciences, as is done in other countries where town planning is attempted. It is not reasonable to expect one man, the local borough surveyor, in whose hands up till now town planning in this country has generally been left, to be an expert on all these questions.

A sound knowledge of social economics is of first-rate importance in the preparation of town planning schemes, and that is the last thing to be expected from a borough surveyor—it is not his business.

2. REPEAL OF ANTIQUATED LEGISLATION

(a) Mortmain.

The necessity for wider powers of land purchase and administration has been more than once referred to and explained. The exorbitant prices paid for land for public purposes is due to various laws and customs built up on the Statute of Mortmain, which was passed in the reign of Edward III to restrain the power of the Church. These laws and customs enable old-fashioned administrators to hinder and hamper in every possible way the purchase of land for the ratepayers on equitable terms. The older part of the Statute of Mortmain forbidding a corporation to hold land has to be negatived whenever a company or a corporation is created whether by Royal Charter, private Act of Parliament, or under a general Act, in order to enable the company or corporation to hold land, and even when this has been done public bodies have to use the land they buy for the purpose specified and no other.

Those who uphold this grossly extravagant system are of opinion that public bodies ought to be forced to live from hand to mouth, and so be continually under the control of the electors; the alleged object being to prevent jobbery and speculation. The electors would find it much easier to check the land operations of their representatives if their attention were directed to the price paid rather than to the purpose for which the land is required, and a simple way of achieving this would be to repeal Mortmain, thereby destroying unwise laws and customs built up on it, but if for any reason this is considered objectionable the case might be met by some such provision as this: " Notwithstanding any law or custom to the contrary, it shall be lawful for any municipal corporation to acquire any quantity of land and to use the same for any purposes whatever PROVIDED THE PRICE PAID IS FAIR TO THE RATEPAYERS."

(b) Entail.

Public-spirited landowners willing to develop their land on modern lines are often hindered by lawyers and trustees. These gentlemen not unreasonably consider it their duty to get the most possible out of the estate for the sake of future beneficiaries, and as the present owner is only a tenant for life, he is not allowed to interfere. The old system allows 40 or more houses to the acre, and as this produces the best return per acre, reasonable building density is resisted.

There are at present all sorts of elaborate methods for keeping together estates which have various charges and mortgages upon them. There are often several mortgagees, each one of whom after the first must see that the last penny is screwed out, and at the same time it is not unusually quite impossible to raise cash that might with great profit be spent on the estate, and yet trustees seldom want to sell unless all the beneficiaries agree. If mortgaged land is sold, the mortgagee not unusually nor unreasonably insists that the cash realized shall go in reduction of the amount lent on mortgage, and, therefore, no money is obtained to spend upon improving the rest of the estate, which means that in these cases there is no economic incentive to sell land and allow it to pass into the hands of those who can use it properly.

The present system of, at all costs, " keeping estates together " is thoroughly bad for the nation and for individuals, owners as well as tenants. It is not for a layman to say how best to abolish this pernicious system, but that its abolition is essential to our future national prosperity is apparent to every economist.

3. NEW LEGISLATION

(a) Land Purchase.

In the Birmingham Housing Committee's report of July 3, 1906, which was approved by the City Council by 30 votes to 16, the opinion is expressed that "a corporation cannot own too much land, provided that it is judiciously purchased. Municipal land could be laid out with open spaces and all other essentials to a healthy, happy community, with the additional advantage that any future rise in the value of the land would directly or indirectly go to the rate-payers . . . The policy of buying land and encouraging other people to build the houses would enable the Corporation to give a great stimulus to the supply of good cheap houses on the outskirts of the city and would thereby benefit a very large number of people." In the speech (see Appendix 10) moving the approval of this report it was pointed out that " £1 spent in land goes at least seven times as far as £1 spent in house building towards the solution of the housing problem." Attention was also drawn to the fact that the

Corporation of Ulm, whose housing successes are familiar to all experts, had during the few years previous to the date of this report increased its ownership of land by 33⅓ per cent with highly satisfactory financial results, and it was further mentioned that "In Baden, there are 121 local authorities which have no rates whatever owing to their income from land. In Bavaria there are no fewer than 526 in a similar position and one local authority in Germany not only has no ratepayers at all but is actually paying a dividend of £15 a year to those who in other cities would be ratepayers." These remarkable facts explain the enthusiasm of those who want to see all the land of this country in public ownership. It must, however, not be forgotten that the highly satisfactory results of municipal land purchase by the Corporation of Ulm are quite as much due to the very careful management of an exceptionally able man, Herr Oberbürgermeister Wagner, as to reasonable laws, and it is too much to expect that more than a very few other localities could possibly secure the services of so able and energetic an administrator. The profits secured for the ratepayers in other localities owning large tracts of land are largely due to the fact that it has been in public ownership from time immemorial, from which it follows that the increment in land values due to the increase of population and to the expenditure of public money has automatically gone into the public purse instead of, as with us, into the pockets of private individuals. It is true that in 1870 the German Imperial Legislature sent round instructions to all local authorities to buy as much land as they could at a reasonable price, and never to sell a yard except with very stringent conditions giving the local authority power to repurchase at the price that was paid for it in cases where the purchaser was proposing to sell the land to a third party. The public ownership of land, dating back to very early times and the instructions of 1870 have been of inestimable value to the ratepayers of Germany, but in this matter England is at least fifty years behind the times. Wider powers of land purchase are urgently needed by local authorities in order to enable public bodies to buy land judiciously, but the wholesale purchase of land by public bodies would only put up the price against them.

Public bodies might with perfect safety be allowed to buy land provided they can show that it will earn sufficient to pay interest on the loan required plus a sinking fund spread over 100 years, and if public bodies were allowed to buy land as opportunity offered they could purchase on much better terms than under the present ridiculous régime. The old school will object that land purchase on these lines would lead to all sorts of jobbery. Under the present system of land purchase for public purposes there is already a considerable amount of jobbery and every one admits that public bodies pay far more for land than private individuals. It is in fact a recognized rule with land agents to charge public bodies a bigger price than they would ever think of asking from a private individual. No laws and no system will suddenly do away with this, but obviously a system based on careful examination of the price paid for land by public bodies compared with its earning capacity at the time of purchase will tend towards lower prices and less corruption than now exist under the present methods.

One of the greatest objections raised to the Housing and Town Planning Act is what opponents describe as arbitrary interference with the liberty of the subject to do what he likes with his own, whereas what reformers want to do is to break the arbitrary control exercised by landowners, and at a recent meeting of the Building Societies' Association of Great Britain and Ireland, the chairman, Mr Edward Wood, a well-known Liberal, speaking of the undeveloped land duty, objected to " taxing land that was not required and where the owner was quite willing to sell at a reasonable price." If public bodies had power to buy land at a " reasonable price " without being obliged to specify beforehand exactly what it would be used for, the differences of opinion between those who object to arbitrary interference with the management of private estates and those who object to arbitrary control by the landowners could be easily settled by public bodies purchasing land at a reasonable price; but the question arises: What is a reasonable price? The Acquisition of Land Bill, February 19, 1912, says that " the price to be paid shall be the total value of the land as ascertained for the purposes of the Finance Act, 1910." There is plenty of land in this country which is to-day earning only £2 to £5 an acre which has been valued under the Finance Act at sums varying from £500 to £1,000 per acre. This is called prospective value and this prospective value is based on the anticipation of land sweating being permitted. Section 59, sub-section (2), of the 1909 Act, denying landowners any right to compensation in respect of a limitation of the number of houses per acre, has altered all that, and as the Act is now nearly four years old it can be justly held that landowners have had due notice of the change. That is the position in equity, but the landowners and the Government valuers do not seem to have realized it and, therefore, to purchase land at the Budget valuation would be a very bad bargain for the ratepayers. For instance, in a town planning area where the number of houses per acre is not to exceed twelve, which means a land value of £150 to £200 per acre, undeveloped land has been valued at £500 and £550 per acre.

The promoters of the Acquisition of Land Bill are of opinion that " the public ownership of land would enable local authorities to:

" 1. Secure more effectively the proper development of their acres.

" 2. Diminish the evils of land speculation and the withholding of land from use.

" 3. Provide communities with an asset of the highest value and correspondingly reduce the burden of rates.

" 4. Give security of tenure to tenants of public land."

This is quite sound in theory, but in practice our officials as a whole have not taken kindly to the idea of proper development of land, and past experience shows that as a rule sudden large purchases of land by municipalities might easily result in public lands being administered merely with a view to making the greatest possible profit in order that the rate-collecting element on local authorities might be able to pose before the public as good men of business.

It is certainly wise to buy land cheap as opportunity offers, but it would be most unwise to try to buy too much all at once. Public land purchase at a reasonable price is quite sound; public land speculation is very dangerous and due caution must be exercised. Cheap land is essential to economical and efficient town and estate development, but over-enthusiastic public purchase is not the way to achieve the end in view.

Public land purchase without a reform of our rating system might very easily land the ratepayers in very large unprofitable expenditure. To quote an opponent of land and housing reform: " As long as we recognize private property in land, we must allow each private owner to determine for himself without pressure from the State at what price he will sell to another private person. If, on the other hand, the land is required for public purposes then the public must pay for it at a fair value." There is something to be said for this point of view, but it is not reasonable that a man should pay rates on a land value of £20 an acre and sell the same land to the rating authority at £1,000 an acre. Until landowners are rated on the full site value there is no security that the public will be able to acquire land at a fair value.

At the Labour Party Conference, February 1, 1913, instructions were given to the Parliamentary Labour Party to introduce a Bill to empower all local authorities to:

" 1. Impose and levy for local purposes a rate on all land values, such valuation to be declared by the landowners.

" 2. Acquire land at the valuation for rating purposes declared by the owners.

" 3. Deprive the Local Government Board of the power, which it now exercises, to compel local authorities to satisfy it as to the purpose for which the land is required.

This programme goes to the root of the matter, but half-hearted measures will do more harm than good.

(b) A General Law to Stop Land Sweating.

The failure of the by-law system to solve the problem of better housing for the people at reasonable rents calls for a new set of town planning regulations or general provisions governing town and estate development that shall be applicable to the whole country, one set for rural districts and another set for urban districts. But this would need considerable time and thought, and it might quite reasonably be urged that town planning is not yet sufficiently well understood in this country to make such an undertaking a safe procedure in the interests of the community.

Experience shows that town planning as at present administered cannot be relied upon to prevent land sweating, and even with an amended town planning act administered by a competent central authority local interests would make it very difficult to prevent its continuance. During the preparation of the second town planning scheme in this country a land agent actually increased his demands as to the number of houses to be allowed per acre on the pleas that:

1. Large works had recently been erected in the neighbourhood.

2. His client had paid undeveloped land duty.

He enlisted very considerable local sympathy. The only way to deal with cases of this sort, which are bound to be constantly arising, is to make land sweating and bad housing illegal, just as it is already illegal to sell bad food.

To destroy a man's health is far worse than to steal his purse. The latter crime is punished by a long term of imprisonment. The former crime is often rewarded by a seat on the aldermanic bench.

The only way to ensure that the whole country shall benefit from town planning legislation is to pass a general law forbidding the erection of more than ten houses per gross acre in any new district and at the same time allowing local authorities, subject to the approval of an independent central authority, to make concessions to landowners in the cost of estate development, and if this law were accompanied by a law for rating land values, and by energetic action in the provision of better means of communication, building development would be enormously encouraged.

In this connexion the following interview with Mr Lloyd George, which was reported in the " Daily Chronicle " of January 29, 1912, is very important. He expressed the opinion that " around the towns there was greater waste in parsimony than prodigality as regards the land. A virile and contented population would never be got until the land in the neighbourhood of the great towns is measured out on a more generous scale for the homes of the people. Social well-being must be secured through improved housing, the release of the land and the betterment of the children. The slum child is a great national asset. We must carve out for him a brighter future."

The Finance Act, 1910, has prepared the way for a reform of our rating system; but unless there is co-ordination in our land legislation and administration there is grave danger that the object in view will not be achieved.

If land is rated on the full site value without any safeguards, experience shows that there is a strong tendency to induce land sweating (see Chapters II and IV) and even if this did not occur it would not be fair to let an owner pay rates on £1,000 per acre for a year or two and then introduce a town planning scheme forbidding the erection of more than ten houses per gross acre; which restriction would at once reduce the value of his land to £100 or £150 per acre. It would be much fairer and more statesmanlike to deal with both aspects of the problem at one and the same time, that is to say, pass a law to prevent land sweating at the same time as the law for rating land values. Advocates of the policy of rating land on its full site value are of opinion that this alone will so increase the supply of land thrown on to the market for building, as to break the land monopoly and enable builders to obtain what land they need at a price that will enable them to make reasonable housing pay; but this opinion is not supported by the actual results of rating land values in New Zealand, Canada or Paris.

(c) The Rating of Land Values.

Taking the country as a whole, from 1884 to 1908 rates have risen from 3s. 6d. to 6s. 8d. in the pound, and in spite of the fact that Imperial contributions to local expenses have increased at an even greater rate, the suggestion is continually being made that these increases in local rates are due to the niggardliness of the Imperial Government. This complaint made against Government by local spendthrifts is a convenient way of withdrawing attention from local extravagance and the gross injustice of our present rating system.

Discontent is justifiably growing with the way in which local rates are constantly rising, and yet our educational system and the condition of our public roads (two causes of large expenditure) are both very far from being what they ought to be. Our technical education is much inferior to that of Germany, which places a very serious handicap on British trade, and our main roads are not so good as those of France. The position, therefore, is that although local rates now constitute a very heavy burden, especially on the poorest classes, public expenditure on necessary public services is not sufficient to make these services as efficient as they ought to be, and must be, if we are to hold our own in commercial competition with other nations.

There is a constantly recurring agitation for larger "grants in aid" from the national exchequer for local needs. This is a roundabout method of meeting the difficulty. It is only a palliative and not a remedy. In the words of the Chancellor of the Exchequer "such a policy merely means that local authorities would spend more, and ask for more," and they would have less inducement than ever to see that they got good value for the money spent, because they would not have the responsibility for raising it, and would, therefore, avoid the odium that always attaches to the tax gatherer and rate collector. On this ground alone it is essential to public economy and efficiency that those who spend public money should themselves bear the odium of raising it, and not be allowed to throw it off on to somebody else's shoulders. At the same time there are some public services paid for locally, such as education, poor relief, main roads, and asylums which are predominantly national in character. Contributions to these services might justly be made out of national funds raised by a uniform national tax on land values that have been created and maintained by these and other public services and franchises, but these contributions would not sufficiently relieve local rates. We must go deeper. Some

P

reformers are of opinion that a wholesale scheme of public land purchase would meet the ever-growing financial needs of local administration, but for reasons given (see section 3, sub-section a, of this chapter) such a policy unless very carefully handled, and except in special cases, might in England easily result in more loss than profit, and in even more serious holding up of land. We are fifty years behind the times in this matter of public landownership, and cannot at once make it good even if we tried.

There is, however, a simple and equitable way of meeting the difficulty, and that is to rate land on its full site value. The most equitable system of raising money for local purposes is to rate property according to the benefits received by its owners. The presence, the increase, the industry and the expenditure of the population are responsible for the rapid creation of land values so familiar to every student of this subject, and it is only fair that a reasonable share of the cost of public improvements should be borne by those who so largely benefit from them.* The constant rises in rates already referred to are very largely due to expenditure on education, public works and baths and parks (see Chapter V), all of which public expenditure immensely increases the value of land in the vicinity. This can best be realized by imagining what would be the result if any of these services were removed or abolished. Under our present rating system the landowners who reap such large profits from town improvements and extensions pay little or nothing towards the cost of this work. On the contrary they put up the price of land on those whose expenditure has benefited them. When in 1878 the toll across Waterloo Bridge was abolished at a cost of nearly half a million to the London rates, the rents of small houses south of the Thames were raised 6d. per week. The whole of the saving which ought to have gone to the general public was swallowed up in rent; at first in increased house rent, and later on in higher ground rents. The people of London pay directly or indirectly seventeen millions a year to make and keep the land valuable, and then pay twenty millions a year to the landlords because it is valuable. If land were rated on its full site value in the same proportion as other property in order to help pay for the public improvements, parks, etc., etc., which increase its value it would be possible to provide the better education, better main roads, and other urgent needs of a civilized community, without putting any undue financial burden on those who work.

The city BEAUTIFUL will never be really beautiful until it has

*See excerpt from Marshall's " Principles of Economics," Appendix 12.

become the city EQUITABLE, and this can only be brought about by making land contribute fairly to an expenditure that increases its value. The only sure way of permanently raising the wages of agricultural or any other labourers is to make more accessible the source of all production—the land—and reduce its cost. The rating of land values carefully safeguarded will do both of these things. Another result would be to remove taxes from industry. The enormous discrepancy between market value and rateable value especially of vacant land makes rating reform a very urgent question. The land around a village or small town which, while assessed at a few shillings per acre, is charged for building purposes at four hundred or more pounds per acre, and the farm land that can only be procured for allotments or small holdings at a prohibitive price constitutes as great a national loss as the withholding of land near large centres of population. An urgently needed step towards the completion of our English system of " FREE IMPORTS " is a reduction of the internal tariff which assessment committees now impose upon houses, workshops and enterprise.

It is contrary to all equity as well as being economically unsound to treat one class of property owners (the landowners) more favourably than others. Landowners own a privilege, not property created by labour, they are really only tax collectors; they must remain tax collectors, but there is no reason for giving them specially favourable treatment. It might be considered to be interfering with the liberty of the subject to say that these men shall not eat unless they work (although that is exactly what is in practice said to the poorer classes); but it cannot justly be maintained that it is economically sound to reward men for being idle or keeping their land idle, by relieving them of taxation and throwing it on to the industrious classes, thereby fining them for working. Mr Harold Cox is of opinion that " if rates are high, smaller houses will be built, or inferior work put in " and further that " high rates on buildings in any district will tend to depreciate the value of the land because it will discourage people from building in that district." High rates on buildings do most assuredly discourage building and, therefore, the rating of land values and consequent reduction in the burden on improvements is the best possible way of encouraging the building trade. In the words of the late Sir Henry Campbell-Bannerman: " Our present rating system operates as a hostile tariff on our industries. The rating of land according to its market value whether used or not would induce those who hold land without using it either to use it themselves or pass it on to others. The present system of rating gives every facility for holding land back from use, narrows the available supply of land, and forces up the rents of land in use."

Sir C. A. Cripps, Unionist Member for Wycombe, Bucks., is in favour of a special rating of site values for local purposes. "There is a great volume of agreement among economists and skilled administrators in favour of throwing the main burden of taxation upon general incomes and inheritances graded according to their size and upon site values and certain other properties of the nature of monopolies. These are the bodies of wealth possessing the true ABILITY TO PAY and increasing sums can be taken from them without impairing the incentive of their owners to employ them usefully. The thorough comprehension of the operative principles of the incidence of taxation is thus the first condition of a successful solution to those problems of local government, which constitute one of the largest and most urgent tasks of domestic policy in the near future." Professor Marshall in his evidence before the Royal Commission on local taxation said: "The tax on that part of the annual value of land which arises from its position, its extension, and its yearly income of sunlight, heat, rain and air, cannot settle anywhere except on the landlord."

In 1900 the rental of Edinburgh was £2,648,000 and the area 8,800 acres, of which 2,300 acres were unfeued, the value being £10,394. The total assessment of the city was about £300,000 and the proportion of that borne by unfeued land £325. The Edinburgh Gas Corporation had to pay £1,180 an acre for 105 acres of land rated at £5 10s.

Mr Trustram Eve estimates the capital value of the land of Great Britain at £2,400,000,000. Others put it at £6,000,000,000 The land value of the city of New York alone is £1,000,000,000, and therefore the larger figure given above as the value of the land of Great Britain would seem to be nearer the mark than the lower one.

Mr Charles Bathurst, Unionist Member for South Wilts., is of opinion " That there is some scope for rating capital values of land in the neighbourhood of towns where there is an increasing capital value, but that is to be found to a very small extent in rural areas." This admission from a member of the Unionist Party that there is some scope for rating land values in urban districts is very important, and if it is correct that no serious income will be obtained from rating land values in rural areas then there is no ground for the owners of agricultural land objecting to the proposal.

In the old city of Bradford, whose area is 10,776 acres, there are 4,512 acres unbuilt upon. The value of these 4,512 acres is estimated at £3,821,644, but they stand in the rate books at only £180,480, and thus escape their fair share of public burdens while houses are overtaxed. If these idle acres were rated on their value in the same proportion as other property, the " general rate " would be enormously reduced, and they would be opened up to industry and public improvements.

Out of the 43,537 acres comprising Greater Birmingham, about 20,000 are rated at only £2 per acre. If this land was rated at the market value put on it by its owners for selling or leasing purposes the total assessment of the city would be so much increased that local rates could be very materially reduced.

Those administering the Housing and Town Planning Act have, in the only scheme finally approved (August, 1913), destroyed the betterment clauses of that Act and, therefore, general legislation is most urgently needed to protect the interests of the ratepayers.

Urgently needed municipal improvements are very often delayed, and sometimes prevented altogether by their excessive cost. Under our present rating system the ratepayers have to find the money for the improvements, and the owners of frontages take the profits. If there were a rate of only 8d. in the £ on land values, that means that two-thirds of the whole annual land value would go into the local treasury each year, and in the same way two-thirds of any increase in land values due to the making of public parks, etc., etc., would also go back to the local treasury. By rating land on its value, and not merely on its use, and rating it separately from the building on it we should automatically secure for the public a large share of the betterment due to the expenditure of their money. In addition to which trade would benefit by the reduction of taxes on industry and houses would be better and cheaper.

Other forms of property contribute their share to rates and taxes; why should land be " excused "? It is because the town is lighted, paved and drained that people will pay so much more for land in towns than for land in the country.

It is acknowledged that " the housing problem in town and country—the physical and moral health of our poorer classes—lies at the very root of our social and economic well-being." The simplest and fairest way of reducing house rent and improving the quality of the accommodation provided is to take unjust rates off houses and put the burden on to the land which is increased in value by the expenditure of public money. When this is done there will be no more talk of the necessity for housing the people at charity rents. Members of all political parties are agreed that the industrial classes are not getting their fair share of the enormous prosperity of the country at the present time. Here is a simple and direct way of doing something to adjust the balance, and at the same time giving a tremendous impetus to the trade of the country by freeing it from the land monopoly.

Public opinion is growing very rapidly in favour of a minimum wage. Under our existing fiscal arrangements land and capital always manage to shift their burdens on to labour by increasing the price of commodities. The best way to bring about an increase in wages is to increase the demand for labour, and impose taxation that cannot be passed on to labour.

Some say that the rating of land on its full site value will increase its price. This statement will not hold water. Land is a monopoly and, therefore, the price is fixed by the ability of the consumer to pay for it. Customers are already made to pay as much as they can afford, and cannot be made to pay more; the rate must, therefore, come out of the seller's pocket. Land is not made by human hands and, therefore, the cost of production does not enter into the calculation. Land has no cost of production. The price is fixed by (1) the demand for it, (2) the degree of intensity to which it can be used. The rating of land values will force a certain amount of land into the market, and to that extent reduce, not increase, the price, and a restriction of building density, if adopted will still further reduce the price, thereby easing our housing difficulties.

There is much talk of " broadening the basis " of taxation which is only another way of making the poorer classes pay even more than they do at present. The fairer and sounder method is to put taxation on to the shoulders of those who get most benefit from it. They have the "broadest back." Heavy taxation for the poor man means doing without some necessities for him or his children. For the rich man it only means a cutting down of luxuries, the loss of which does not in any way impair his economic value to the nation. In the rent of a 6s. 6d. weekly house, 1s. 6d. is due to rates, and 1s. due to ground rent, leaving the tenant only 4s. out of 6s. 6d. per week for housing himself and his children. The reduction of even 6d. per week in the weekly charge of 2s. 6d. for rates and ground rent would be a great boon to a man getting only 25s. a week. An extra 6d. for food is no small item in a weekly budget of

25s. The economic position between the poor man who is over-heavily rated, and the rich man who confines him to a small back yard by refusing to sell or lease land below a certain price, is that whereas the poor man is not able to afford the bare necessaries of wholesome living for himself and his family, it costs the rich man nothing to hold up his land because the poor man is paying rates which he (the rich man) ought to pay, and would be called upon to pay in any well-ordered state. Our present rating system not only enables, it actually encourages, landowners and land-jobbers to hold up their land, which action on their part perpetuates over-crowding and causes ill-health. The longer they wait, the more population increases and the more urgently their land is needed and, therefore, the higher the price they can get for it, and the less land or garden space those who purchase it can afford for each house. Let them wait for their price if they really think it wise in their own interests to do so, but it is only fair to charge them something for the pleasure of perpetuating overcrowding, and caus-ing ill-health, and the least charge that can be put upon them is to rate their land on its full site value. There are scores of places in England at the present time that badly need a town extension plan, but they are land locked. All the land in the neighbourhood is held up for £400 an acre or thereabouts, a price which makes town planning or garden suburb development for low rented houses a financial impossibility, and the only way to break this disastrous monopoly is to rate land values, which policy would only be the barest justice to the general body of ratepayers. Land that has not been increased in value by the expenditure of public money would pay a very small sum to the local exchequer, whereas land that has been increased in value by the expenditure of other people's money would make something like a reasonable contribu-tion to the public purse. In the first town planning scheme in this country a rich landowner is going to get a road made at the public expense, that will turn his back land into front land, thereby greatly increasing its value, which increment will all go into his pocket. The rating of land values would do something to correct anomalies of this kind.

There is another kind of expenditure which must not be for-gotten. That is the expenditure by railway companies and others which puts up the price of land. The following extract from a land speculation advertisement is instructive: "The recorded increase in value of London freehold during the past eight years is over £10,000,000. Every £10 invested now at Golders Green may double, treble and further multiply itself in the coming months, and investors who select their plots now will secure this increase of cash values.

"THE NEW TUBE STATION WILL ABUT ON TO THE ESTATE, and when it is built PRICES WILL GO UP WITH A JUMP."

This increment will go to those who have done no work. Surely it is not unreasonable to suggest that they should hand over to the State or the locality a part of their profits, in order that those who do work shall not be fined quite so heavily for benefiting those who do not work!

All that is advocated here is a more equitable distribution of rating and taxation between those who produce wealth and those who do not, with a view to securing for the ratepayers some of the betterment which was allotted to them by the Housing and Town Planning Act, 1909, but which has been denied to them by those administering this Act.

Mr Harold Cox tells us that " ground rent has no necessary relation to the economic rent of the ground. It is merely a device for raising money, and is commonly fixed at one-fifth of the letting value of the house."

Assuming this to be correct, and there is no ground for thinking otherwise, Mr Cox has provided one of the strongest possible arguments for rating ground rents. If ground rents have no necessary relation to the economic rent of the ground, which is only another way of saying that they are inflated, then it is only just that the State or locality should take their toll on them, especially in view of the fact that " improved ground rents," or to be more correct " inflated ground rents," are nothing more or less than land speculation, and nothing has done more than land speculation to produce the wretched housing conditions which all thoughtful men deplore.

Overcrowded and insanitary housing accommodation is not the only evil arising out of our present irrational rating system. When farm land assessed at £20 or less for rating purposes is required for small holdings or allotments, very much higher prices are demanded. The result of this is that respectable and industrious working men are not given a fair chance of adding to their meagre earnings by honest labour, and the land in question is not put to its best use. In this respect, as in so many others, our present rating system encourages speculation and discourages honest work.

Our present system of tenure by which the owner of land can rent his tenant on what the tenant has made his premises worth, and our system of rating which penalizes an occupier in proportion as he expends capital and enterprise in increasing his holding are quite unsound. Thousands of hardworking men in all ranks of commerce look forward with dread to the termination of their leases, and to a repetition of the Gorringe case. Rating land values, fixity of tenure and compensation for improvements are vital questions to many business men.

The present system of assessing land and building together is most unfair, it is impossible under these conditions to maintain a fair assessment as between the two distinct classes of property. In the case of town land the relative values of building sites, and the buildings on them are constantly changing in the course of a ninety-nine years' lease. To put this statement into figures: At the beginning of a lease the site value may be £200 and the value of the building £800, total assessment £1,000, whereas at the end of the lease the positions will be reversed, site £800, building £200. During the period of the lease rising rates all fall on the lessee, whereas the landowner is reaping the benefit in unearned increment. This state of affairs falls very hard on shop-keepers. They start with being obliged to pay a rack rent for their premises and all increases in rates fall on them; they are caught both ways; whereas the landowner gets all the benefit due to his tenants' exertions without spending or risking anything. The only fair system of assessment is to separate the site from the building, and let each party pay its own share of the rates.

Opponents of rating reform draw attention to the fact that " at present there is much land round all towns used for market gardens, etc., and rated on the basis of the actual yearly income." They admit that " in many cases the capital value of this land is increased by the anticipation that it may be some day used as building land," but they contend that " the only fair method of taxation is to tax a man on what he actually has now, not on what somebody imagines he may have in the future." In their opinion, " a special tax on land with the object of compelling the holder to sell it at a lower price than he could otherwise have obtained, would rob the seller for the benefit of the buyer. . . The only result would be that while a first holder would be penalized, a second would be able to continue to hold the land up from use. A worse result might be brought about, and if they did not take care builders would reduce the size of gardens and build skyscrapers so as to have less land on which to pay tax."

The objection that rating land values would "rob the seller for the benefit of the buyer"* will not disturb those who have had dealings in land. As things stand to-day the seller has it all his own way, he can wait because it costs him nothing to do so, whereas the buyer cannot wait; the supply of land suitable for his purpose is severely restricted and, therefore, he is obliged to pay a fancy price in order to be able to get on with his work. The idea that the "buyer" or, as he is described above, "the second holder" would be able to "continue to hold the land up for use" is based on a misunderstanding. This second holder would have to pay rates just the same as the first, which means that he would have just the same economic incentive as any other landowner to put his land to its proper use or else sell it. The argument that "the only fair method of taxation is to tax a man on what he actually has now, not on what somebody else imagines he may have in the future," would be very simply met by allowing landowners who take this view to fix their own assessments provided they undertake to sell their land to the locality or the State at the price they themselves have put upon it; the question of other people's imaginations would not then arise.

The following account given by Mr Harry S. Gullett in the "Daily News and Leader" of April 17, 1913, is interesting. "Australia's Federal Land Tax became law in 1910. Every unbiassed Australian recognized the folly of shutting up grand farm areas in holdings of from 20,000 to 100,000 acres, carrying a sheep to the acre, and worked by a handful of squatters' servants. The State Government had vainly attacked the land monopoly with powers of compulsory resumption, but these largely defeated themselves by raising the price of all land against the farmers.

"Despite the good demand for land at prices well above the grazing value, the wealthy squatters were indifferent sellers. Living a pleasant life, they preferred their acres to the trouble of investment. The Act makes no charge on properties of an unimproved value of less than £5,000. The tax begins at 1d. in the £, and rises with the value of the total. Between £30,000 and £45,000 it is 3d.; above £75,000 it is 6d. The Act promises to be an unqualified success. It throws the responsibility of valuation upon landowners, who returned a total unimproved value of £207,547,540 which was reduced by the department to £178,446,698. It only cost £17,121

* For "buyer" read "user" or "worker."

to collect £1,367,177 in taxes. The cost of collection was 1·25 per cent of the receipts. Immediately prior to the first collection many landowners sold largely. During the first four months of the tax £2,712,775 worth of land was disposed of, and during the next nine months taxpayers sold more than £18,000,000 worth of land in 18,288 separate transactions, and other taxpayers, or in some instances, the same taxpayers, bought over £9,000,000 worth of land in 2,874 transactions. The buyers of land as a rule are those who are subject to the lower rates of taxation. Little or no depression of the value of taxed lands is reported. Doubtless some of the estates which are already put to their proper use will suffer, but if we except city building sites, this remark applies to very little land in Australia. The trouble with the Australian landholders is that they have too much land, and as a consequence nearly all rural industry is marked by slipshod methods. The land tax is paid by those who are rich in unearned increment, and its success is not to be judged by the money raised, but by the fact that landowners are in self-defence being FORCED TO PUT THEIR LAND TO ITS PROPER USE."*

Australia and New Zealand have fought the land monopolists instead of accepting the situation. The policy has been that land monopolists must adjust themselves to the needs of the people. It is not only unjust, but thoroughly unsound to attempt to adjust economic conditions to vested interests in land. The war against land monopoly has greatly benefited the business community. One result of rating land values has been to increase wages, which gives increased spending power to the people. Better wages create a demand for better housing. Increased wages have produced improved housing conditions, and got rid of bad habits, which is one of the obstacles in the way of housing reform. The effect of an increase of wages is to break up the environment which continually reproduces these bad habits. That result is very encouraging, but it must not be forgotten that rating reform unaided by other reforms has encouraged land sweating (see Chapters II and IV) and, therefore, it must not be accepted as a sovereign remedy.

* The federal tax exempts all estates below a certain value. This has caused the subdivision of estates and given the poorer classes more encouragement to work, thereby increasing the wealth of the community. At the same time it must be remembered that exemptions are very dangerous. The love of speculation is by no means confined to the richer classes, and there is grave danger that exemptions in favour of small estates might encourage land speculation among the poorer classes. Land speculation is equally bad for the community whether it is indulged in by rich men or poor men.

Some town planners are very nervous as to the effect on their work likely to be produced by the rating of land values, and they have suggested that " local authorities should have power to waive the rate on vacant sites if the possessor is willing to dedicate it to the public for a play ground, or for any similar use until he can obtain a customer for it." Great care must be exercised here. City lungs should be protected by exemption from excessive taxation no matter whether they are in public or in private ownership provided they are of a permanent nature, but safeguards must be inserted to avoid enabling landjobbers to dodge the rate collector, by pretending that their " red hot building land " is only intended for market gardens, play grounds, or playing fields.

In making valuations due regard should be taken to every restriction validly imposed on the land and legally binding at the date of valuation. Permanent gardens and other open spaces in towns should be exempted from excessive taxation so as to preserve them as lungs by valuing them on the income derived from using them for that purpose, but there should be no exemption from taxation, except where it can be shown that the open spaces in question are for the general benefit of public health, and are of a permanent nature.

Another safeguard which is absolutely necessary in the interests of both landowners and public bodies is to arrange for an annual revision of all assessments. In New York revaluation takes place every year, and is a comparatively simple matter when the old valuation is there to go upon. This is the only way to ensure just treatment for all concerned, viz., landlord, tenant, and public body (see Appendix 12, excerpt from Marshall's " Principles of Economics ").

If these safeguards were adopted the rating of land on its full site value would not injure town planning. On the contrary it would greatly expedite it.

The experience of the past $3\frac{1}{2}$ years shows that town planning legislation by itself can effect very little. Experience also shows that the policy of rating land values by itself might also fail, but if these two policies were joined together and supported by reasonable town planning and adequate State loans, great things should be achieved for the nation without inflicting any genuine hardship upon individuals. Concessions in the cost of estate development and adequate State loans to approved housing schemes could more than recoup private landowners for any apparent temporary loss they may incur through not being allowed to put as many houses per acre as the by-laws would have allowed, and as for the rating of land values, it must not be forgotten that any laws or regulations restricting building density will reduce the rates and taxes t at will have to be paid on land if our rating system is reformed.

GENERAL

The above attempt to set forth a complete co-ordinated programme of legislation and administration for dealing with the land and housing problem is respectfully offered for the consideration of reformers of all shades of political opinion. The natural tendency will be for advocates of the various remedies offered to adopt those which suit their views and ignore the others. It is, therefore, necessary to explain that so far as the author is concerned his position is that the policy set forth above is offered as a whole, and in his opinion some of the remedies suggested, if adopted without the assistance and safeguards provided by other items in the programme are more likely to do harm than good. The land and housing problem is many sided, and, unless it is dealt with on every point needing attention, failure, or at any rate only partial success, is inevitable.

These problems are fortunately now of such burning interest to a large section of the British public, that no matter what party is in office some attempt is bound to be made to solve them. Experience shows that administration is at least as important as legislation. The Housing and Town Planning Act is most imperfect; it has been killed by faulty administration.

The Finance Act, 1910, and the Insurance Act have, on the other hand, been administered by men who believed in their work. No reasonable man expected that these would work quite smoothly all at once, but in spite of enormous difficulties, some inseparable from pioneer work of this magnitude, and some created by malicious opponents, these great reforms have already conferred lasting benefits upon the poorer classes, and, what is even more important, those who drafted these measures showed a remarkable prescience as to what is needed to help forward land and housing reform.

Land valuation under the Finance Act will be completed in a year or two, and being uniform smooths away anomalies as between one rating area and another. It rectifies inequalities between one ratepayer and another, and enables local authorities to levy rates on site only, on annual value, or on capital value as desired. This prepares the way for the rating of land values, and if perchance the valuations are too high or too low, errors can be corrected by annual revisions. Out of 4½ million valuations, 3½ millions are already settled, and the number of appeals has only been 1 in 833. The net cost to the nation of this invaluable piece of work has been £64,913, against which there is a very large number of land taxes not yet collected. Section 54 (3) of the Insurance Act enacts that the Commissioners shall, when investing insurance funds, give preference to housing loans.

These two Acts of Parliament are an excellent foundation on which to build up a land and housing reform policy which shall at one and the same time provide the driving force and also the economic incentive essential to success.

At the same time it must not be forgotten that the path of a reformer is never easy. Vested interests are very powerful and very plausible. They have already done their best to prevent the nation knowing what the land of the country is worth; they will no doubt now do their best to prevent this knowledge being put to any practical use. It is to be hoped that the proletariat will not be beguiled by self-interested witnesses into selling their BIRTH-RIGHT for a MESS OF POTTAGE.

The land laws of England were made by the landlords, and no doubt they thought that what benefited them would benefit the nation, but it is not surprising that decisions arrived at by so one-sided a body of men have proved very detrimental to the nation as a whole.

The advent of the Labour Party to the House of Commons and the Parliament Act have made it less impossible to solve the land and housing problem than it used to be, and it is to be hoped that some day Capital will to some extent see how severely British industry is handicapped by one-sided land laws; but there are reasons why too much must not be expected from this quarter. If the land is freed from the curse of monopoly and Labour is given a fairer chance of earning an honest living, with less dependence for employment on the goodwill of other classes, it will be in a much stronger position to bargain with Capital for a living wage, and therefore those who depend on Labour for their profits will have to pay higher wages.

Many capitalists do not see that higher wages, duly earned, mean higher profits. They fear the onward march of a fairer division of profits between Capital and Labour, and they think the only way to defend themselves against what they think would be detrimental to their interests, is to stand by the landowners in the hope that when it comes to their turn to be attacked by Labour and asked for a more equitable division of profits between Capital and Labour the landowners will stand by them.

Economists are of opinion that higher wages mean higher profits, and that a fairer division of profits between Capital and Labour would increase the general prosperity of the nation. They think that the prosperity of a nation lies in the cottage, but most business men do not, in practice, at any rate recognize economic laws and, therefore, we must be prepared to see a large body of capitalists joining hands with Land in opposition to the reform of our antiquated land laws.

This alliance is similar to that of Beer and the Bible which resulted in the Church, many of whose members belong to the Church of England Temperance Society, enabling the Brewers to convert what had for 400 years been recognised as an annual tenancy* into a freehold (see Licensing Act, 1904) and thereby delay Licensing Reform for many years.

This subversion of law and order could not have been achieved except by a very powerful combination. Land and Capital are at least as powerful as Beer and the Bible, by whom no doubt they will be supported. Organized Labour, on the other hand, is even more powerful than Land, Capital, Beer and the Bible. It should have no hesitation about joining the movement to break the land monopoly, which monopoly is the root cause of the present cutthroat competition for employment that enables rich men to exploit their poorer neighbours. "Nil sine magno Vita labore dedit mortalibus." The object to be achieved is of vital importance to the future health and strength of our race, and therefore it is to be hoped that the Labour Party in Parliament will choose the Straight and Narrow Path.

Those who claim a vested interest in human misery will fight to the last ditch, and offer all sorts of palliatives with the object of putting Labour off the scent of real remedies, but unless these vested interests are unmasked, fought and beaten, Britain will not get land and housing legislation and administration, capable of remedying the evils which disinterested men of all parties agree need an immediate and practical remedy.

Sound land and housing reform will no doubt be described as socialistic. It is just the reverse. It will help the poorer classes to help

* "It is a new licence for the new year." "It is not a renewal of the licence, it is another licence for another year." Lord Halsbury in the Boulter case, 1897.

themselves, than which there is nothing better for the nation and less socialistic. A few individuals who talk most eloquently about the lazy working man may themselves not have so much to waste on idleness and luxury, and others who are perfectly genuine may have less superfluous wealth to give away in charity, both of which results would be quite good for the community as a whole. Charity without self-denial does little good to the giver, and seldom fails to more or less sap the independence of those who receive it. Justice, not charity, is the only sound basis on which to build up a prosperous and contented nation. How often it is said of the poorer classes that they do not properly appreciate what is given to them, and how true it is that those who live on other people's charity tend to become more and more discontented.

For these and other reasons it is most unwise of Land and Capital to join hands against the just demands of Labour for a fairer share of the profits of industry. The present artificial and quite unreasonable distribution of wealth is bad for individuals, rich as well as poor, and for the nation it is disastrous. No legislation will suddenly readjust anomalies and injustices that have arisen from many years of haphazard and selfish methods. Public land purchase, for instance, and the minimum living wage may have to be brought into play in order to mitigate as soon as possible evils needing an immediate remedy, but it must never be forgotten that these are only palliatives. As with physical diseases, so with social evils, root causes must be discovered and sound economic remedies applied; we must discover the germ and destroy it. One of the germs of social and economic evils is the land monopoly, and the best way of attacking our land and housing evils is to rate or tax land on its full market value in the same proportion as other property. That would be evolution, not revolution, and Capital will be most unwise if it opposes this remedy for fear that rating land values may result in higher wages. Past experience shows that when evolution is prevented revolution sooner or later comes in its stead. Capital has always been able to adjust itself to economic evolution, but no man can say what revolution will bring forth.

CHAPTER VIII. TOWN PLANNING AND CITY EXTENSION.

WHAT we in this country describe as town planning schemes are known in Germany as " stadterweiterungesplane " the literal translation of which is " town extension plans." England has taken the town planning idea from Germany without fully understanding what it means. In spite of the Housing and Town Planning, etc., Act of 1909, and in spite of the enormous strides that have been made of late years in the means of transit for local traffic (carrying the people quickly and cheaply over much longer distances than were even thought of for local traffic a few years ago) proposals for extending borough boundaries are still considered with little reference to town planning, and mainly decided by Parliament on the two questions, (1) Is the district to be annexed urban in character? (2) and has it any community of interest with the city ?

Improved means of communication have automatically enlarged the areas over which community of interest can be proved to the satisfaction of those conversant with the modern trend of events, and efficient town planning demands that every town, city or urban district shall have within its boundaries plenty of cheap agricultural land, so that the population shall be spread outwards instead of being squeezed upwards into narrow tenement buildings, and so that there shall be plenty of room for small buildings and allotments on a sound economic basis.

This great truth has been partially recognized in the passing of the 1909 Act, but it is not yet fully recognized by Parliamentary committees when city and borough extensions are under consideration.

A plentiful supply of small holdings, allotments, play grounds and playing fields is essential to a well-ordered, healthy town, and extension schemes that do not provide for this should be rejected on the ground that insufficient empty land has been included. Parliament, on the contrary, constantly rejects extension proposals because the district to be annexed is not considered sufficiently urban in character; in spite of the fact that when a new district has become urban, the mischief has been done, and little real good can be achieved by putting it under the ægis of the mother city. What the city and the suburbs round it need is that they should be unified and town planned before the amenities of the country have been destroyed, and before land values have risen to a figure that makes efficient town planning economically impossible.

In 1902 a large tract of land which was threatened with immediate development in the old way, was offered as a free gift to the City of Birmingham on the sole condition that it should be laid out and maintained by the Corporation. It was recognized that the preservation of this land as a permanent open space would be of enormous value to Birmingham, but unfortunately it was outside the city boundaries, although adjacent to a densely populated centre, and in spite of the fact that the neighbouring councils of Smethwick and Oldbury had contributed £1,500 out of £11,500 needed for the purchase of the estate there was considerable hesitation in the Birmingham Council Chamber about accepting this valuable gift. The old school wanted to leave it entirely to the neighbouring local authorities in whose districts the land was situated to deal with the matter, but these local authorities were not nearly strong enough financially to grapple with so large an undertaking.

A few years later the Birmingham Open Spaces Society secured the option of several small pieces of land in central parts of the city, and also of 20 acres of land known as the "Black Patch," and situated as to one-third in the county borough of Smethwick, one-third in the urban district of Handsworth and the remainder in Birmingham. Smethwick and Handsworth contributed £1,000 each, and with the help of voluntary contributions the land, which is in a very congested neighbourhood, that badly needed a breathing space and recreation ground, was offered to Birmingham at rather less than £187 per acre on the sole condition that she should "consult Smethwick and Handsworth as to the laying out of the land." This proposal was strenuously opposed by the Lord Mayor of the day on the pleas that:

1. Handsworth and Smethwick had not paid their fair share.

2. It would cost a large sum to prepare and fence the land, culvert the stream and build a house for the park-keeper.

3. Birmingham could not afford to spend money for the benefit of other districts.

The final result was a victory in the Council Chamber by fifty-two votes to eight, but this was not achieved without an enormous amount of hard work, and a considerable expenditure of money on propagandist work which ought not to have been necessary.

The objection of local authorities to spending money in adjoining districts not under their control is by no means peculiar to Birmingham. The same attitude is to be found wherever there is multiple control. The difficulties in connexion with the extension of Hampstead Heath (see Chapter V) are another striking example of the grave objections to multiple control. When the London County Council was asked to help they pointed out that the land to be acquired was outside the county of London, and it was said that Hampstead is a rich suburb, and already well supplied with open spaces. The platform economists on the London County Council entirely ignored the fact that thousands of Londoners go out to the Heath for fresh air and by this means, to a certain extent, mitigate the evils under which they suffer from bad housing conditions in the county of London. There could not be a clearer case for financial assistance from a local authority, but it was only after very great exertions that a promise of £8,000 was at length extracted. Other and poorer public bodies did not see why they should bear more than a small share of the cost of an open space so largely used by Londoners. They did not consider that they could afford it, and the existing open spaces seemed to them ample for the needs of their own inhabitants. It was only by the great energy, ability and generosity of private individuals that this invaluable open space was preserved for the benefit of Greater London. Out of the £36,000 required the public bodies that were benefited only subscribed £11,500, a beggarly amount compared with the huge sums spent on hospitals, gaols, asylums and work-houses; which expenditure would be very largely reduced if there were an adequate supply of open spaces, and other amenities essential to public health and rational enjoyment.

The fact may be mentioned that, under wise town planning administration, large open spaces no longer so necessary as they were, should not be provided unless the whole of the land or the whole of the money is given by private individuals, and, therefore, these examples prove nothing. They were chosen because they illustrate in the simplest possible way the practical impossibility of properly town planning any district that is under multiple control. Open spaces are only one of many things to be considered in the preparation of a town planning scheme, which cannot be adequately dealt with unless the area is all under one control.

Another reason why city extension is essential to the success of town planning is the fact that genuine town planning means spreading rateable value over a large area, and when the Housing Committee first laid their ideas before the City Council some capable administrators objected to Birmingham's adoption of town planning methods unless at the same time the boundaries were extended so that spreading the population over a larger area should not decrease the total assessments of the city. To put it shortly, the two first essentials to successful treatment of the housing problem are town planning and city extension, and these are the considerations that were at the root of the Greater Birmingham scheme. The contention was that Birmingham had outgrown its old boundaries and that the suburban districts it was proposed to incorporate really belonged to the city in character and interests rather than to the counties, also that without administrative powers over these surburbs, Birmingham could not control her own necessary development, and further that it would be for the public advantage that " Greater Birmingham," the population both inside and outside the boundaries, should be under one local authority.

When large centres of population are administered by several different local authorities there is much antagonism of local interests, besides diversity of administration. Single control should be more economical as well as more efficient than multiple control.

Under multiple control difficulties constantly arise as to which authority shall bear the expense of necessary public services. For instance, old boundaries often run along brooks and water courses, thereby involving constant disputes on questions of drainage, whereas the only scientific method is to plan boundaries as far as possible along ridges, so as to bring what is all one drainage area under one local authority. A city and its suburbs are interdependent, but in practice the suburban districts are not able, unaided by the centre, to make sufficient provision for the needs of a large population, such as means of transit, adequate supply of open spaces, etc., etc. Divided authority in the matter of tramways, gas, electric supply, etc., etc., causes great inconvenience to the general public, as well as unnecessary expenditure of public money. Under multiple control the administration of public health is much more difficult and far less efficient than under single control. In order to stamp out infectious disease it is necessary to take general action on a concerted plan.

As long as suburbs remain for certain purposes under the control of county councils sitting twenty or thirty miles away, a considerable portion of the rates levied in these districts is spent outside instead of in the districts where the money is raised, and this seriously hampers the development of the city. The county authorities cannot be expected to understand urban problems, and it must not be forgotten that "a town extension plan contemplates and provides for the development AS A WHOLE of every urban, suburban and rural area likely to be built upon during the next thirty or fifty years." (See Practical Housing, Chapter V.)

It is obviously impossible to plan out "as a whole" districts that are controlled by several different local authorities, and further it is quite contrary to the spirit of the 1909 Act to wait until rural districts have become urban before allowing them to be planned and protected against land sweating. It is no use locking the stable door when the horse has been stolen. Provision is made in the Town Planning Act for a "responsible authority" to prepare a town planning scheme for land under the jurisdiction of another authority, but this method is not at all satisfactory in practice. The actual work of preparing a town planning scheme is in itself quite complicated enough, and when the difficulties are increased by the conflicting interests of neighbouring authorities, efficiency becomes well nigh unattainable.

The problems we have to consider are: Whether or no it is easier and better to direct the development of a city by means of single or multiple control, and whether or not it is advisable to plan out rural districts round centres of population, as part of the town or city to which they ought to belong before they have been spoilt by the speculator. None of these outlying districts have a centre of their own, they all very largely depend upon the central district for their prosperity and also for many of the amenities of life.

The general principles that should govern town or city extensions may be briefly cited as follows:

1. Rural areas likely to become urban during the next fifty years should be included so that they may be protected from land sweating, and so that the central district may have ample room to expand on modern lines, with an adequate supply of open spaces, allotments, and small holdings. The main objective of town planners is to bring the town to the country, and the country to the town; to spread population outwards and not force it upwards.

2. The extent of the area to be included should depend upon what is locally a convenient distance for cheap quick means of transit for local traffic. Tubes, motor buses and trams have made the radius of Greater London very big, and in the larger provincial towns and cities the convenient radius may be put at least at five miles.

3. Consideration should be given to the places of residence

adopted by those earning their living in the town. It is not fair that these citizens should escape their financial obligations by living outside the boundaries of the town from which they benefit.

4. For the sake of convenience and economy in the matter of drainage, boundaries should run along ridges, and old parish or other administrative boundaries should be ignored. These were settled in a more or less haphazard way long before the problems of modern civilization had arisen, and undue consideration of ancient precedents always produces bad results.

5. Great care should be taken to reconcile the conflicting interests of interdependent communities by unifying them into one co-ordinated whole.

The Birmingham city extension scheme to a certain extent complied with these conditions but not entirely. It will be seen from the map opposite that there are three indentations, two of which reach to within two and a half miles of the centre of the city. The reason for not taking in the indentation on the west was that this district is a county borough. The other two indentations represent land rural in character, which as has just been seen is the strongest possible reason for its inclusion in order that it may be protected against the depredations of the speculator, but it was feared that Parliament would refuse to include them. With these exceptions the five-mile radius was fairly well observed, and it is satisfactory to note that to a very large extent the boundaries run along ridges.

The district now controlled by the City Council of Greater Birmingham was formerly governed by six local authorities and three county councils. The following figures may be of interest.

	Old Birmingham	Greater Birmingham
Area in Acres	13,477	43,537
Population	526,000	867,000
	£	£
Rateable Value	2,970,553	4,340,017
Produce of a Penny Rate	10,875	15,000

This extension scheme cannot be described as perfect, but compared with the very disappointing way in which Glasgow was treated by Parliament, it is correct to look upon it as reasonably successful. This success is very largely due to the fact that owing to a fortunate concatenation of circumstances, Birmingham was able to proceed by the scientific experimental method instead

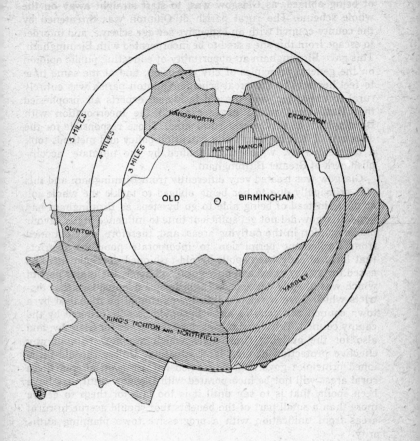

of being obliged, as Glasgow was, to start straight away on the whole scheme. The rural parish of Quinton was threatened by the county council with an expensive sewage scheme, and in order to escape from this she asked to be incorporated with Birmingham. This gave Birmingham an opportunity of educating public opinion on the general principles of city extension, and at the same time to feel her way to the great scheme. Quinton parish was entirely rural in character, and the old-fashioned experts all prophesied that Parliament would never sanction the incorporation with Birmingham of this purely rural area. Those responsible for the direction of Birmingham's city extension policy and methods took a different view, which was justified by the ultimate accomplishment of Greater Birmingham.

Glasgow was treated very differently from Birmingham and this was principally due to her being obliged to tackle the whole job at once, instead of being able to go by steps as Birmingham had gone. Glasgow did not get sufficient time to influence in her favour public opinion in the outlying areas, and, therefore, only obtained from Parliament permission to incorporate populous districts that have already been spoilt by old-fashioned development. She asked for 20,027 acres and only got 6,208 acres, the major part of which was already developed. The principle adopted was that districts which have developed into towns should be managed by a town council and country districts should be administered by the county council. This decision was most disastrous for Glasgow, and also for the outlying rural areas which are now without any effective protection against land sweating. Unless the old-fashioned principles governing city extension are soon altered these rural areas will not be incorporated with Glasgow until they have been spoilt, that is to say until it is too late for them to derive more than a small part of the benefits that should accrue to rural areas from unification with a progressive town planning authority.

London municipal administration is a striking example of the absolute necessity for single instead of multiple control, with regard to town planning, means of transit and housing. It is immensely difficult to bring a large number of different authorities into line on a town planning scheme—what suits one public body will not suit another—and yet it will be apparent that independent town planning schemes by each of the innumerable local authorities that govern Greater London are directly contra to the first principles of town planning which depends on harmony and co-ordination. The London County Council which is expected to exercise general control over Greater London has no general highways powers. It is under statutory obligation to maintain its tramway tracks, and has certain other very limited powers and obligations with regard to a few streets and bridges, but the Borough Councils are in practice the highways authorities for London. It is difficult to imagine anything more absurd than putting the means of communication between the centre of London and its suburbs under an endless number of different authorities, each with its own interests to serve and none of them with the slightest economic or other incentive to consider London traffic as a whole. No wonder vast sums of public money are spent every year in providing policemen on point duty, and no wonder that anyone using the streets of London in the busy season spends more time in being held up at street crossings than in actually moving from one place to another. Englishmen are apt to be extremely proud of the way in which London traffic is regulated by policemen on point duty. Is it not the admiration of all foreign visitors to London? If we Englishmen were really as practical as we think we are, we should be thoroughly ashamed of the fact that London streets are so badly planned, that thousands of pounds per annum have to be spent on policemen on point duty in order to make it possible to use them at all.

The tramway system of Greater London is recognized by both friends and foes of this means of transit to be as a whole thoroughly unsatisfactory. There are no through routes worth mentioning, and the number of missing links is astounding to anyone not aware of the fact that the tramway authority (i.e., the London County Council) cannot lay down trams anywhere without the consent of the Borough Councils through whose districts they have to pass. The first essential to success of any system of transit for large or small towns is that the problem should be dealt with as a whole, and the interests or supposed interests of individual localities subordinated to the greatest good of the greatest number, which is just the opposite of what now takes place in London. Satisfactory town planning with a view to encouraging the population to spread itself over a larger area depends first and foremost on a complete system of quick cheap means of transit, which in the case of tramways is just what London is denied by the system of multiple control. Some authorities are of opinion that tramways will soon be superseded by motor-buses, and it is most certainly a fact that the weekly traffic returns for London show constant increases for buses against constant decreases on the trams. Tramway advocates* say that " wherever the bus goes, the road repairer follows, and the ratepayer foots the bill. Meanwhile the tram which is the property of the ratepayer is burdened with the cost of making and widening the roads, which the bus, which contributes nothing to the rates, destroys." Friends† of the motor-bus on the other hand say that where roads are properly constructed there is no increase of maintenance charges due to the use of rubber-tyred motorbuses, and with regard to road widening, " The London County Council tramcars have been charged with only £500,000 of a total which exceeds £10,000,000. Very large sums are charged by the London County Council to improvement account, and whilst the whole of the £10,000,000 has not been spent upon, or in connexion with, tramway routes, we are satisfied that the trams have escaped at least £2,500,000 of such capital expenditure." It is also pointed out that " London motor-buses, by the yield of the petrol tax, may be held to contribute practically the whole of the £250,000 which the Road Board recently set aside for specific allocation to London Borough Councils."

Dispassionate observers will probably conclude that motor-buses will for many reasons (greater flexibility, etc., etc.) eventually supersede tramways but that tram cars will run in our streets for many years to come because of the enormous sums of public money that have been sunk in them. Whatever view may be taken as to the relative commercial and other merits of trams and motor-buses, there can be no doubt as to the very heavy direct and indirect loss thrown on to the ratepayers by the present inadequate control of London traffic, and the only way to cure this evil is to sub-stitute single for multiple control.

London tramways are severely handicapped through not being able on many routes to carry passengers to their desired destina-tion. If the traffic of Greater London were all under one control, present termini could be linked up with one another, and tramways extended to better recognized traffic points. Schemes for linking up and other extensions were recently submitted to Parliament amounting altogether to an estimated cost of £420,000, but only £33,000 worth of work has been approved. Opinions may differ as to the relative merits of trams and motorbuses, but even if trams were immeasurably superior to motorbuses, they could not prosper under the present power of veto exercised by the Borough Councils. The other means of transit provided for Londoners are run purely for private profit without any regard to the problems and

* " Daily News and Leader." † " The Commercial Motor."

difficulties of town development, and the total result of this chaos is that the town planning of Greater London cannot be carried out as efficiently and economically as should be the case if traffic and town planning were all under one authority. The policy of slum prevention by means of town planning is, therefore, most seriously hampered and delayed.

The problem of slum reform, already in itself quite complicated enough, is in London still further complicated by the conflicting interests of different local authorities. If Part I of the Housing of the Working Classes Act, 1890 is adopted the cost falls on the County Council, whereas if Part II is adopted the Borough Council pays. The natural tendency, therefore, is for each authority to prefer the method which throws the responsibility for spending public money on to some one else, and for neither authority to give as much consideration as should be given to the main point at issue, viz., which is the more efficient method, and which throws the lesser burden on to the ratepayers. Both authorities have to raise their funds from the same ratepayers. The only safe way to deal with slum reform is to call upon owners of insanitary property to mend it or end it at their own expense. It is not fair to the ratepayers at their expense to reward the owners of houses unfit for human habitation for neglecting their property, as has invariably been the case when insanitary areas have been dealt with under Part I of the 1890 Act. These men should not be rewarded for neglecting their duty to their tenants. They should be reasoned with and treated as lightly as is consistent with the sanitary obligations of the local authority, and where this is done good results are obtained at a very small cost to the ratepayers. When landlords are treated reasonably most of them will co-operate; there are always a few recalcitrants; the law provides ample power for dealing with them. Part II of the 1890 Act is infinitely better from every point of view than Part I, but the Borough Councils of London whose object should be to save the pockets of the ratepayers are almost invariably in favour of Part I, which puts a far heavier charge on the ratepayers than Part II, because when Part I is adopted instead of Part II it is the County Council and not the Borough Council that has to spend the same ratepayers' money.

In the matter of housing, single control of Greater London is far better than multiple control on the score of public economy. It would also be far more effective. Careful students of this problem are aware of the fact that of the people living in congested districts, not more than one half are obliged by their employment to

live there. If cheap, quick, means of transit were provided to suburbs where decent houses were obtainable at moderate rents,
50 per cent of our existing city populations would move further
out, where land is cheaper and the air fresher. Under the present
administrative conditions of Greater London, it is to the rate collecting interest of each borough council to keep its population in
the borough, so as to maintain its rateable value. If for housing,
town planning, traffic and rating purposes Greater London were
unified and one uniform rate levied over the whole city, this
economic incentive to public bodies to do the wrong thing would
disappear, and the policy of spreading town populations outwards
instead of forcing them upwards would have a better chance of
being put into practice.

City extension is sometimes objected to on the ground that the
outlying districts to be taken in are better governed than the
centre. Where this is the case the only safe method is to unify a
sufficient number of suburbs, so as to make it possible for them to
have a real voice in the government of the new city, and not
merely be swallowed up by the old school of thought at the centre.
If this is not done the full benefit that should arise from unification
will not be secured and, amongst other things, there is pretty sure
to be a serious rise in rates.

Another point that needs most serious consideration on the
part of those responsible for city extension schemes is the question
of differential rating. The present practice is for the mother city
to promise differential rating to the outlying districts for a number
of years in order to induce them to come in by agreement, and this
practice is not only approved but actually insisted upon by the
Local Government Board. It is most unsound economically, and
quite unjust to the ratepayers at the centre. Lower rates in suburbs
not yet unified are due to the fact that these suburbs obtain many
benefits from the centre for which they do not pay, and one of the
main objects of unification should be to adjust this anomaly, not
to continue it. The granting of differential rating to outlying
districts and the promise of all sorts of improvements on condition
that they come in by agreement, are the principal cause of the
higher rates that nearly always follow city extension. The only
right and fair basis on which to arrange for unification is for both
parties to the bargain to recognize the mutual benefits to be
obtained from single instead of multiple control, and for neither
party to demand or accept any money payment from the other.
Outlying districts who accept differential rating put themselves

in an entirely false position. When unification has taken place they pay lower rates than the centre of the city and, therefore, have less claim for expenditure on improvements than other rate-payers paying full rates. The only sound method is to levy a uniform rate over the whole city, so that any proposal for improving any part of it may be considered purely on its merits, and not be prejudiced by the fact that less rate income is being derived from the district affected than from other parts of the city. Another inestimable advantage of a uniform rate would be that equal payments should carry equal rights in the government of the city, that is to say, the representatives of outlying districts should not allow themselves to be swallowed up by the old school at the centre, as is so often the case at present. Where this happens unification becomes merely annexation and the result is higher rates and bad administration.

CHAPTER IX.

Summary of town planning policy with notes on kindred subjects
—Improvement in living conditions—House famine—Slum reform
—Habits of the tenants and the drink question—Incentives to
landlords—Municipal house building—Rural housing—Epilogue.

THE policy and methods enunciated in the foregoing chapters
may be very briefly summarized as follows:

1. Open up cheap land for building and other purposes
by means of new roads and improved waterways.*

2. Protect it from excessive rises in value by forbidding land
sweating.

3. Protect the ratepayers against exorbitant prices for land
required for public purposes by making price, not purpose, the
governing factor in State or municipal land purchase.

4. Lease land (not sell it) to the workers for housing, allotments
and small holdings at a price to cover cost plus a small margin of
safety.

5. Reform the rating system so as to relieve industry and put
a reasonable charge on those who allow land to lie idle.

6. Repeal antiquated legislation such as mortmain and entail.

7. Put town planning administration in good hands, and not
in the charge of men who have axes of their own to grind, or too
many friends in land-jobbing circles.

8. Appoint a strong central authority not steeped in the old
methods, but fully conversant with town planning on modern
lines armed with sufficient powers, and endowed with the necessary
courage to reject bad schemes.

9. Give this central authority an adequate staff to cope with
the work and compel local authorities to attend to their business
instead of neglecting it.

If these canons are observed town planning will result in lower
rates, better towns, better health and better trade.

To improve the living conditions of the people is the great aim
of town planning, but it needs the co-operation of many other
agencies before this can be brought about. What those conditions
are may perhaps be seen in the most striking way by looking out
of a railway carriage window on leaving a large town. The railway
is often on a raised embankment; one has, as it were, a bird's-eye

* Vide " Garden Cities and Canals," by the same author.

view into the squalid, airless, dingy, back courts where the poor live. Then follow the interminable rows of dingy houses, packed together without light or air, and stretching out after the green fields and pure skys which they never succeed in reaching. The public is just awakening to one of the evils directly due to our town life, namely consumption. Enormous sums are now being spent by the State and by municipalities on its cure. This scourge and many other social evils could be very much reduced, if not prevented altogether, by adopting wiser methods of town and estate development, and prevention is not only better, but also very much cheaper than cure. It has been said " The business of the State is not merely to cure, but to prevent disease if it can. . . . It is cheaper to teach a man how to keep well than to drug, doctor and maintain him whilst he is ill. . . . The next function of Insurance Committees is to inquire into social and industrial conditions which might account for excessive sickness, to report upon them in the proper quarters and insist that adequate remedies are applied."

From the purely business point of view it is simply ridiculous to spend all the money we do without taking means to ensure that these human beings, on whom so much time and money is spent, shall have a reasonable opportunity of becoming healthy, happy, useful citizens. Infinite pains, care and wealth are expended on the upbringing and education of the population; innumerable statistics are prepared and published concerning death rates and infantile mortality, but the most efficacious and most economical means of improving the race are at present adopted to a very limited extent. A plentiful supply of light and air to the living rooms and bedrooms of the people is more important than anything else to public health and well-being; and a lack of it is responsible for more disease and mental depression than any other single cause, and yet this free gift of nature is denied to many millions of our fellow citizens because there are no precedents in its favour, so far as public bodies and land and building speculators are concerned. The astonishingly low death rates in garden cities, suburbs and villages show the great possibilities of genuine town planning in the direction of prevention.

There are at least three essentials to the achievement of reasonable living conditions for the poorer classes.

1. Higher wages.
2. A reformed system of rating and taxation.
3. Better housing at the old or lower rents.

1. HIGHER WAGES

One way of securing better living conditions for the poorer classes is to give them higher wages, but although some good results both for employer and employed even where this is done in a piece-meal fashion, experience shows that the tendency is for any general rise in wages to be cancelled by an equal or even greater rise in the cost of living. During the last ten or fifteen years wages have risen in England and in Germany, but the increase in the cost of the necessaries of life has been greater than the rise in money wages, with the result that during a period of exceptional prosperity Labour has obtained an even smaller share of the profits of industry than it did in less prosperous times. This state of affairs is most unsatisfactory and most unsound economically. It is explained by the fact that under our present fiscal system (land monopoly) Land and Capital pass on to their customers every increase in the cost of production, and in passing it on, add to it a little more profit for themselves. The same economic law applies to charges put upon trade by the Employer's Liability for Accident Act, the Insurance Act, free education, etc., etc. All of these items sooner or later find their way into the cost of production and are paid for by the customer. They gradually filter through the different trades until at last they eventually fall on the working classes, in the form of an increase in the cost of living. The meaning of all this is that remedies of the nature mentioned above are in reality only palliatives, and those who are looking for an effective and permanent remedy for existing social and economic evils must go deeper.

Most owners of horse flesh recognize that it is good business for them to house and feed their horses properly. It is really equally good business for an employer to pay his men sufficient wages to enable them to house and feed themselves decently, so that they may be fit for their work, because where this is the case working men earn more, not only for themselves but also for their employers. The other day a manufacturer friend of mine told me how one of his workmen who was only getting 18s. per week came to him for a rise in wages, on the plea that he could not on that wage afford the food necessary to keep him in decent health. When my friend asked his foreman how much the man was worth he was informed that at 18s. per week the man was a very bad bargain for the firm. In spite of this the man was raised to 22s., and on inquiries being made a few weeks later as to how the man was getting on my friend's foreman told him that whereas at 18s. per week the man had not earned what he was getting, now that he was getting 22s. per week, he was able to feed himself properly and the work he did showed a profit for his employer over and above the wages paid to him, instead of the loss it showed when he was only getting 18s. Instances of this kind could be multiplied; suffice it to say that sweated labour is thoroughly bad business for employers as well as employed. It results in worse work, more accidents, and a smaller output from the capital invested in land, buildings and plant, than when labour is paid enough to house and feed itself properly. " The workman who obtains an advance in wages is a benefactor to his country and his kind.*

It is said that British trade will not stand higher wages than those now paid, and the Census of Production is quoted in support of this theory. This census shows that the value added to materials by about 7,000,000 industrial workers reported upon is as nearly as possible £700,000,000 giving a net output per worker of £100 per annum. Rent, interest, profit, etc., have to come out of this £100 per worker, which fact has led many people to the conclusion that the payment of even a thirty shilling minimum wage to the adult male worker is in practice impossible. The fallacy of this conclusion lies in the fact that out of these 7,000,000 industrial workers only just over 4,000,000† are men, the rest being women, boys and girls, from which it follows that the net average output per adult male worker is considerably more than £100—statistics do not tell us how much. There is, therefore, nothing in the Census of Production to justify the statement that British trade will not stand a living wage for the workers.* On the contrary experience shows that reasonable wages pay employers far better than sweated labour, provided they are duly earned. This proviso is of vital importance, because unless wages are earned it is impossible to maintain them, no matter whether they be high or low. It is essential to the economic success and, therefore, to the permanency of higher wages, that those who receive them should do more and better work than lower paid workers. Some trade union leaders are of opinion that if a man does more work or if the efficiency of his labour is increased by the introduction of machinery (which is only another way of putting the same point) other workmen will be done out of a job. Experience shows that this is not so; on the contrary, the lower the cost of production due to greater

* Mr L. G. Chiozza Money.
† Mr A. W. Flux, Director of the Census.

R

industry on the part of the worker or to improved methods of manufacture, the cheaper can the goods be sold and, therefore, the greater the number of people who can afford to buy them. That is to say, the more employment there will be for those who make them. When screws were made by hand there were infinitely fewer people employed in the trade than to-day when, thanks to the introduction of machinery and other improvements, the output per worker is many times greater than it used to be—and wages were very much lower than they are now. Fifty odd years ago it was a matter of course to strike against the introduction of machinery, because it would increase the output per worker and would, therefore, it was thought, reduce the number of workers required. The fallacy of opposing the introduction of machinery has now been recognized and, therefore, it is to be hoped that the opposition to an honest day's work for an honest day's pay may also some day disappear. Economic laws are inexorable, and unless they are obeyed will always sooner or later punish those who ignore them. Higher wages, which are one of the essentials to our national prosperity and social well-being, will not be maintained unless employed as well as employers understand economic laws and observe them. On the one hand, it is true that British trade could and should stand a living wage for the workers; it is also true that decent wages, provided they are earned, are good business for employers, but unless they are earned as well as paid those who pay them will sooner or later be driven out of business by home or foreign competition. This is an economic law which no amount of sophistry or sentiment can possibly upset. There is no need for labour to overdo its physical strength; on the contrary, it is bad for all concerned when this happens; but unless it gives reasonable work in return for reasonable pay, increased cost of production will kill the trade in which it is employed. Decent wages fairly earned is the only sound policy not only for the individuals who pay them and receive them, but also for the nation. Higher wages mean greater purchasing power for the proletariat and there is nothing so good for trade as a prosperous proletariat. The purchases of any single working man are as nothing compared with the purchases of a rich man, but the total number of working men is so very much greater than the number of rich men or even well-to-do people, that in the aggregate the total amount of trade dependent on the demand of the workers far outweighs the rest of the trade done in any country. There is no money power greater than the power of the pence, and in no case is it more powerful than with respect to the general trade of the country; nothing would be better for British trade than higher wages.

2. A REFORMED SYSTEM OF RATING AND TAXATION

If better money wages for the workers are accompanied by higher cost of living and increased taxation, their condition is not materially improved. Indirect taxation bears far more heavily on poor men than on rich men. No man, however rich he may be, can consume more than a certain amount of food, drink and tobacco, and as he pays indirect taxes in exactly the same proportion as every one else, the burden on him in proportion to his income is very much less than that borne by the poorer classes. Indirect taxes on food and other necessaries certainly broaden the basis of taxation, but they place the burden on the weakest back, which is most unjust and, therefore, economically most unsound. Our revenue from taxes on food for the year 1912-13 was approximately £10,000,000 and until some other tax is found to supply the revenue now collected in a most expensive way from the food of the people it cannot be truly said that England is a free trade country. Thanks to our policy of not taxing imports except for revenue purposes, the prices of commodities have not during the last ten or fifteen years risen as much in England as in other countries. The figures are (see " Gold and Prices," by Professor W. J. Ashley):

England	a rise of		13	per cent.
France and Japan	,,		18	,, ,,
Canada and Australia	,,	21 to 25		,, ,,
Germany	,,		28	,, ,,
United States	,,		32	,, ,,

This is satisfactory as far as it goes but Free Traders should not rest satisfied until all taxes on food have been abolished, and other revenue found to take their place.

Another direction in which steps should be taken to complete our Free Trade system is to free the land from monopoly, and the best way of doing this is to rate or tax land at its full market value in the same proportion as other property. This is a tax which cannot be passed on to anyone else (see Professor Marshall), which means that Capital could not recoup itself from Labour by charging higher prices for its goods, as has been done in the case of the Employers' Liability Act and other measures passed for the benefit of the poorer classes. Rating land values would in addition have the inestimable advantage of giving Labour freer access to the land, thereby enabling it to earn something for itself without the interference of Capital and, therefore, rendering it more independent and better able to bargain for a fair wage, a far more satisfactory way of doing things than passing a general law enacting a minimum living wage. It is always better and sounder to help people to help themselves than to treat them like children and do everything for them.

This proposal will no doubt be described as interfering with the liberty of the subject. That is what is always said of any proposal to give the poorer classes a fairer chance in life. This idea of the liberty of the subject should be applied to the poor as well as to the rich; the poorer classes have just as much right to live in decency and comfort, provided they do an honest day's work, as the richer classes have to do what they like with their own, and under our present rating system the vast majority of our working classes are denied the right to decent housing at reasonable rents.

3. BETTER HOUSING AT THE OLD OR LOWER RENTS

Of all the remedies for our social and economic evils better housing at the old or lower rents seems the one whose benefits are most likely to stay with those for whom they are meant instead of being filched from them, as has been the case with so many other well-meant reforms whose promoters were absolutely sincere in their intentions. Previous chapters have been devoted to explaining how this object can be achieved on economical town planning lines without really injuring the landowning class as a whole, but nothing useful can be done without interfering with what the " Law Times " of September 16, 1911, described as " private rights." No man has a right to destroy his neighbour's health or property, and yet this is exactly what has taken place under the old system of town and estate development; each owner being allowed (subject to petty by-law regulations which have done at least as much harm as good) to develop his own estate without any regard to neighbouring estates or the public health and convenience. The Housing and Town Planning, etc., Act of 1909 was passed to remedy this, and the " Law Times " is most laudatory of the reasonable and conciliatory spirit shown by the Local Government Board in its administration. It is quite true that this department has been most considerate to "private rights," but unfortunately it has entirely ignored the intentions of Parliament, the public health, and the pockets of the ratepayers, and that is the principal reason why the Housing and Town Planning, etc., Act, 1909, has proved so ineffective. If the "private rights" of poor men had been considered as well as those of property, much more might have been done even with this very imperfect Act.

In Chapter I et seq., a policy and methods have been described that would, if adopted, make it commercially possible to provide every new working-man's house that is built with an adequate supply of light and air without any increase of rent; on the contrary where it is necessary and economically sound to do so (as in the case of widows, etc.), much cheaper houses could be provided than have been built of late years under the old by-law system. In the garden suburb at Harborne, Birmingham, houses let at 4s. 6d. per week including rates, show a very satisfactory return on the outlay in spite of rates at 8s. 11d. in the £, whereas under the old method of town and estate development no speculative builder has provided anything at less than 6s. 6d. per week. This result is due not only to economical town planning estate development and the co-partnership system, but also to strict economy in the building of the house itself and subsequent management. It is no use economizing in site values unless equal care is taken in the planning and building of the house itself. There are many instances all over the country where the efforts of generous landlords to provide decent housing accommodation for the poorer classes at reasonable rents on a sound commercial basis have been frustrated by extravagant architects and builders. The popular idea is that cottages in garden suburbs must be fanciful or they will not be attractive. No greater mistake could possibly be made. Simplicity, not elaboration, is the truest form of art, and although no doubt the architect who depends upon good lines for the beauty of his elevation has to take more trouble than those who are satisfied with the sugar cake style of decoration, the result of those who aim for simplicity and even severity, is infinitely more pleasing to the artistic eye as well as being much more economical for the landlord and far more useful to the tenant.

This brings us to the items that make up the weekly rent of a working-man's house. The following figures are the result of careful investigations in several different localities; they are based on information obtained from several different places and from several different men working under varying conditions. The average results are as follows:

On a 6s. 6d. weekly house in towns and urban districts.

	per week	
	s.	d.
Ground rent	1	0
Rates and taxes (including water rate and w.c.)	1	6
Voids and repairs		7
Management and insurance		4
Interest and sinking fund on the cost of building	3	1
	6	6

From these figures and from the facts given in previous chapters, it will be seen that decent housing with reasonable amenities at rents within the means of the poorer classes is a sound business proposition, provided land values are kept within reasonable bounds, and money is not wasted on extravagant, unnecessary, and insanitary estate development as ordered by the '' model by-laws,'' and also provided money is not wasted on æstheticism and fussiness with regard to the architecture of working-men's houses, or the general arrangement of estates on which they are erected.

It will also be seen from these figures that if our present unsound rating system were reformed, and landowners were called upon to pay their fair share of the public expenditure which increases the value of their property, the rents of houses tenanted by people of small means could be materially reduced or still better from the point of view of social and political economy, average house rents might be left where they are to-day and better value given for the money paid.

If land was assessed on a fair basis, and rated in the same proportion as other property the tenants of 6s. 6d. weekly houses would no longer have to pay 1s. 6d. per week, in rates and taxes, in order that rich men may be able to dole out their land in driblets, and thereby force their poorer neighbours into houses which no man with or without a growing family ought to be asked to live in.

HOUSE FAMINE

At the present time there is more or less of a house famine all over the country. This is often attributed to the Finance Act, 1910, and perhaps this opinion is not altogether incorrect owing, not to anything in the Act itself, whose economic tendency is all in the direction of encouraging building enterprise, not retarding it, but owing to the uncertainty in the minds of property owners as to what is going to happen next. Every genuine reform carries with it a certain amount of unsettlement during the first few years of its working; as this clears away and when property owners realize that it is very unwise of them to allow political prejudices to interfere with the management of their business affairs, they will soon awake to the fact that the Finance Act, 1910, while charging speculators for gambling with the lives of the people, is at the same time all in favour of honest industry and enterprise. When this awakening takes place, the temporary set-back in the provision of small house accommodation will, so far as the Finance Act is concerned, be replaced by a greater activity than ever before.

There are, however, other causes for the house famine, which do not at present show any signs of being overcome. The Housing and Town Planning, etc., Act, 1909, laid down various new principles concerning the mending or ending of small houses unfit for human habitation, and the provision of new housing accommodation for the poorer classes which are far more revolutionary than anything contained in the Finance Act.

The Torrens Act of 1868 gave local authorities the power to call upon owners of insanitary property to repair it at their own expense (see Section 8) or shut it up and demolish it (see Section 18), and the only appeal was to Quarter Sessions. The Housing of the Working Classes Act, 1890, took away from local authorities the power of making closing and demolition orders, and put it into the hands of local magistrates at Petty Sessions, and for years little or nothing was done in the way of slum reform, except for some pioneer work in Hull, and later in Birmingham. The Act of 1909 (see Sections 15, 17 and 18) restored to local authorities the power of making closing and demolition orders which had been taken from them by the 1890 Act, and this has greatly expedited and improved the work of slum reform, but it has also unsettled the minds of property owners; they do not quite know where they are or what is going to happen next.

Another great upset which is no doubt the main cause of the house famine that exists to-day, is the way in which the town planning sections of the 1909 Act have been administered. Adequate access to cheap land has not been provided, thereby retarding the development of new areas and even worse still, the old discredited by-law system has been perpetuated wherever possible, in spite of repeated promises of reform. A third reason for the present unsatisfactory state of affairs is the unconscionable delay due to the regulations of the Local Government Board. During the preparation of a town planning scheme ordinary builders dare not erect houses on the old lines for fear they will be demolished without compensation (Section 58 (2)) and they have not built houses on modern lines, because sufficient economic incentive has not been given to them to do so (see Chapters I, II, and III).

There is another cause for the delay in providing adequate and suitable housing accommodation for the poorer classes which must not be forgotten. It is the unscrupulous opposition and obstruction of local landjobbers and slum owners. They see that better housing at reasonable rents with adequate access to the centre will knock out their rotten property and, therefore, they leave no stone unturned to prevent any decent property from being built.

The existence of this house famine is even more serious than it appears on the surface, because it prevents a large number of localities from dealing as they know they ought to with the insanitary property in their district. Those who excuse themselves from reforming their slums " because there are no houses for the people to go to " should visit Hereford (see Chapter V) and copy her methods. She has dealt with slum reform and slum prevention in a most comprehensive and thorough manner, and what she has done other localities should be able to do as well, or better.

Some reformers are of opinion that in new suburbs no houses should be built to let at less than 6s. 6d. per week, because in their opinion cheaper houses will only reduce wages, and this is quite true if the provision of cheap cottages is not made with very great care, but it must not be forgotten that there are people who cannot and never will be able to earn more than a small wage, and unless these people are provided for in garden suburbs they will have to live in a slum or crowd two or more families into a house, which is thoroughly bad for themselves and their children. The bottom dog has at least as much claim on our consideration as any other class of the community.

SLUM REFORM

During the early months of this year (1913) comparisons were instituted between the Liverpool policy of demolishing and reconstructing slum areas under Part I of the 1890 Act, at the expense of the ratepayers, and the Birmingham policy of having this work done under Part II of the same Act, at the expense of the owners, compensation being paid under Section 38 for obstructive buildings that have to be removed in order to let in light and air to the houses that remain. This subject was discussed at some length in " Practical Housing " and also in " A Housing Policy." In " Practical Housing " it was pointed out that the Liverpool method cost the ratepayers £56 per head of the population benefited, whereas the Birmingham method only cost them 15s.* per head, and it was further explained that whereas under Birmingham's economical method the city could well afford to deal with all the slums needing attention, the available funds of even a rich city like Liverpool will be exhausted long before she has dealt with one quarter of the cattle pens in which so many of her people are hovelled, not housed. This is not all—the housing question is not merely a mathematical problem, it has many aspects and the most important is that owners of small house property should have every incentive to keep their property in good order, and no temptation to neglect it. Under Part I it pays slum owners very handsomely to let their houses fall into decay, in which case they are bought up by the corporation at a big profit to the owners and a huge loss to the ratepayers, that is to say, the economic incentive is all the wrong way, bad housing pays much better than good housing, and therefore, bad housing predominates.

The complaint is sometimes made that Birmingham is not spending enough on slum reform. This complaint could be very easily met. There are said to be 6,000 courts in Birmingham, and certainly it is a fact that very few, if any, of these courts are really fit for human habitation. If 1,000 of these courts were opened up to the street every year, it would take six years to make Birmingham a reasonably healthy city, and judging from past experience should not cost the ratepayers more than £20,000 per annum. This expenditure should satisfy those who want to see more work being done, and yet at the same time it is a very small figure compared with the huge sums spent, or rather wasted, every year on curing diseases and disorders which need not and should not exist to anything like the present extent.

Slum reform under Part II is, however, only a palliative, the only real remedy is to move the people out into garden suburbs where they can have houses at 4s. 6d. per week (see Harborne garden suburb, Birmingham) or perhaps even less, when our land and

* This figure has now increased, owing to the removal of more obstructive buildings, which is well worth the extra money, but it is still well under £5.

housing system has been reformed; but practical men are aware that for many years to come a considerable proportion of our town populations (the best authorities say 50 per cent) will have to be provided for at the centre. The question, therefore, arises how best to do this. The municipal house builders are not quite so fond of their corporation barracks as they used to be, but they have not yet all come to see that back-to-back houses are in crowded neighbourhoods the only possible alternative to flats, or that unsatisfactory as this system is, it is nevertheless infinitely preferable to the tenement system under which small children are not able to get out and run about so freely as is necessary to keep them in good health.

I do not advocate the erection of new back-to-back houses, but I do say that for the accommodation of poor people who must or will live in towns back-to-back houses in terraces, with a good current of air in front, are much better for the people from every point of view than barrack buildings. Some reformers are strenuously opposed to the perpetuation of back-to-back houses. They would like to destroy them all as quickly as possible, and substitute self-contained through houses built in accordance with the model by-laws. This has recently been tried in Birmingham, and has not proved satisfactory. The rents are 6s. 6d. per week, which under all the circumstances cannot in this case leave much profit for the builder, but which is far beyond the means of the ordinary slum dweller and the houses are very much too close together.

One of the main principles of slum reform should be the preservation of low-rented houses, and the increase of the supply of good cheap houses (see first edition of " Practical Housing," page 16) and unless this is done great hardship will be inflicted on the very people whom it is desired to help. The wholesale demolition of existing back-to-back houses would create a shortage in the supply of houses. Rents would jump up and any sudden large rise in house rent would hit the tenants very hard, because although the general tendency is for wages to follow rents, these poor people could not suddenly get a rise in wages to meet the rise in rent. A small rise in rent for a sanitary house instead of the former insanitary hovel, such as results from the patient but persistent Birmingham policy, has been found by the tenants to pay them very soon. In a good home there is not the same temptation to go out in the evening and spend their money.

Experience shows that the rearrangement and thorough repair of existing houses is by far the best policy in the interests of tenants of small house property in congested districts, and the only wise way of adding to the supply of good cheap houses is to encourage and assist their erection in the suburbs. This two-fold policy, if carefully carried out, will make it impossible for landlords to charge tenants more than a fair rent.

The main objective of all housing reformers should be to get the people out into the suburbs, and for this reason those responsible for slum prevention (i.e., town planning) should be in the closest possible touch with those responsible for slum reform. Every inducement should be given to slum dwellers in the form of adequate access to cheap land, and decent cottages with proper amenities at reasonable rents, to leave their wretched dwellings in the centre and give their children a fair chance of growing up into healthy, cheerful, useful citizens, by taking them to live in the country; but provision must be made for those who remain behind. No method of housing the people in congested districts can be anything but a palliative. The preservation and reformation of existing back-to-back houses is perhaps the least showy policy; it is nevertheless the least objectionable and, therefore, can justly be described as making the best of a bad job.

It has been suggested that nothing will meet the evil but wholesale demolition of existing small houses and wholesale concentration in flats. There are some fatal objections to flats for working men:

1. No dust shoot has been nor can be devised that in practice is air-tight top or bottom; dust shoots must, therefore, be distributors of germs and breeding places for flies.

2. The many flights of stairs confine small children to the house, whereas it is essential to their health and strength that they should spend as much time as possible playing about out of doors.

3. Intensive building of this nature puts up land values, whereas the first essential to a successful land and housing reform policy is that land values should be reduced.

4. Buildings of this height obstruct the supply of light and air to tenements situated on any but the top floors.

Compare these conditions with those which exist in a back-to-back house and the latter, although far from perfect, is infinitely better than the former.

HABITS OF THE TENANTS AND THE DRINK QUESTION

A very common cry is: " What is the use of repairing small houses? They will soon be dirtied and destroyed again by the tenants." The London Agenda Club has inaugurated a "Vigorous crusade against the ignorance, bad habits, and other conditions which constitute a standing menace to health." In 1912 it succeeded in inducing about fifty municipalities to extend facilities for a Health Week, in the areas under their jurisdiction, and in 1913 the same thing was done in even more cities and towns, of which Birmingham was one. It is said that: " Notwithstanding all sanitary science has achieved during the last half century, the health of the people is far below what it might be. Thoughtful observers see very clearly that, working on present lines, we cannot get much further. THE NEXT ADVANCE MUST COME FROM THE MASSES THEMSELVES," and these "thoughtful observers " are of opinion that " each person's health is mainly in his own hands." This may be true of people who can afford to live in decent surroundings; it is very far from the whole truth concerning those who are herded into slums or let out grudgingly into by-law suburbs which are only one degree better than the slums from which they have escaped, with the inevitable result that bad habits and demoralizing tastes are engendered in them. If the 150 sermons preached in Birmingham during the Health Week had been directed against the ignorance, apathy and sometimes corruption of public bodies, as well as against the bad habits of the tenants this " concerted attack against evil conditions and bad habits " would have been more effective. The ruling classes, like other human beings, are more ready to see the failings of others than to correct their own. If aldermen and councillors would first cast out the beam from their own eyes, they would then see clearly to cast out the mote from their neighbour's eyes. No housing reformer of any experience will deny that there are faults on both sides, on the side of the tenant, as well as on the side of the landlord, but it is most unjust to blame slum dwellers for their bad habits, unless and until they are given a fair chance of living decently, and experience shows that when they are given this chance most of them avail themselves of it vide Liverpool. " A higher moral tone is at once observable, self-respect rises and a keener love of home springs up; the mother takes an interest in the welfare of her children, they are, therefore, better clothed and better fed, and the very fact that their environment is better makes for their lasting social and physical good." To put the question in a nutshell—During the Birmingham Health Week a worthy councillor explained that " the corporation could not go round washing the children's teeth." This is quite true, but the corporation can, and it ought to insist upon there being at least one water tap in every house, and when this has been done, but not before, will it be reasonable for the ruling classes to complain of the "dirty habits of the tenants."

Another thing that corporations might do is to encourage by their example the management of small house property on more sympathetic lines. A wider application of Miss Octavia Hill's system of rent collecting to corporation property is badly needed, but the influence of the house agents has prevented the movement from spreading as it should. The Manchester Housing Reform Company is doing excellent work on these lines (see Appendix 13), but very few public bodies seem to take any interest in the human aspect of the housing problem.

Another aspect of this question of the bad habits of the tenants is the drink question, but when a man comes forward determined to effect genuine reform, vested interests move heaven and earth to drive him out of office, and too often they succeed. So long as there is a redundancy of public-houses in any neighbourhood, so long will the tenants or managers of these houses be forced by their masters, the rich brewers, into tempting poor people to drink more than is good for them, and so long as these poor people are kept in slums in order that vested interests may not be interfered with, so long will they be tempted to get drunk in order to forget their miseries. What wonder then that there is the vicious circle—slum-land drink, drink slum-land! This circle must be cut at two points if any lasting good is to be effected. Better living conditions must be provided and public-houses must be reduced to a number that is sufficient for and not in excess of, the legitimate needs of the neighbourhood.

The evidence given before the Glasgow Municipal Commission on the Housing of the Poor 1903, contains many striking statements on this subject. Space does not admit of mentioning more than four.

1. Miss K. V. Bannatyne and Mr A. M. M'Craken, Charity Organization Society:
   "Drink to a very large extent causes the housing problem."
2. Miss M. B. Blackie, Kyrle Society:
   "Drink is at the root of the housing problem. If we had less public-houses we should require less police."
3. Rev. Canon Mackintosh, Archdiocese of Glasgow:
   "The multiplicity of public-houses, especially in slum districts, has a most deleterious effect on the population."

4. Rev. G. Lawrie:

"Drink is very largely responsible for the housing problem. It is sometimes a cause and sometimes an effect."

The Birmingham Housing Committee during their inquiry, the results of which were reported to the City Council on October 20, 1903, were given exactly similar information; one quotation must suffice:

Messrs Reynolds and Pritchard, School attendance officers:

"The great difficulty is that there is nothing to counteract the inducements to spend so much money in drink. The public-houses are always full, and the tenants seem always able to pay for drink, even when they say they have no money to pay the rent."

In the opinion of the Rt. Hon. John Burns, M.P., "The one supreme remedy immediately at hand is for the overcrowded to drink less and to think more." This is quite sound doctrine, but really it is not reasonable to expect ordinary human beings to think more and drink less so long as they are packed into slums, with one public-house to every twenty or thirty houses, and only allowed to get out of their misery when it seems to suit vested interests that they should do so. When wiser and juster counsel prevails, the result is very different.

A Unionist working-man member of the Birmingham Housing Committee informed me many years ago, that in those particular small areas where the number of licensed houses had been reduced to a reasonable number by the wisdom and business capacity of Mr Arthur Chamberlain, there had been an immediate improvement in the way the people lived; their houses were cleaner and more sanitary in every respect, in spite of the fact that the Housing Committee had given no special attention to these spots. This practical result proves conclusively that Licensing reform must go hand in hand with Housing reform, if the best results are to be obtained.

There is an answer to those who complain of the dirty and destructive habits of the tenants of slum property. Give them a chance of living decently, do not tempt them to do evil, but encourage and assist them to do well before condemning them to the miseries and degradation of slum life. Give the good side of human nature a fair chance of coming out even when dealing with the bottom dogs who live in slums. Well-to-do people living in comfortable homes, who know nothing of the temptations to which the poor are subjected, will dismiss this advice as poetical.

In addition to removing temptations to the tenants of small house property to be dirty and destructive, there are also ways, which have stood the test of experience, of giving them an inducement to take care of their homes. Miss Hill's system of management for small house property and Mr Henry Vivian's system of co-partnership in housing give a direct economic incentive to the tenants to be clean and careful.

INCENTIVE TO LANDLORDS

A way should be found of giving social and economic incentive to landlords to do their duty by their tenants, and this is supplied by persuading public bodies to carry out slum reform under Part II of the 1890 Act, instead of Part I as explained earlier in this chapter. Another method which would be even more effective if adopted in this country, because it is preventive and not merely curative, is the system adopted by Stuttgart and other German cities. This is to have a municipal housing bureau whose duties are:

" 1. To keep in constant touch with the housing market so that in the event of a house famine being threatened immediate steps shall be taken to prevent it.

" 2. To take preventive measures against unwholesome dwellings, especially with regard to overcrowding, by a regular system of house inspection.

" 3. To publish a house directory for general use giving information concerning houses to let as well as houses actually let.

" The organization of this bureau comprises two municipal officials who collect and collate the information from which are compiled the necessary records. These officials get their information from 120 voluntary inspectors elected by their fellow citizens or appointed by the city council.

" The advantages of this system are:

" 1. The local authority has complete information as to the condition of all house property in its district, and can, therefore, deal with it comprehensively and systematically.

" 2. House owners and agents find that they can earn as much as, if not more than, before, and tenants find it much easier to satisfy their needs. Repairs are done systematically.

" 3. When complaints are made that there is a house famine the bureau can ascertain at once the facts and also exactly for what type of house, if any, there is a demand. They are also able with the information at their disposal to explain the reasons for any shortage that may exist and how best to meet it.''*

It must be admitted that minute and meticulous regulations that are suitable to the German temperament are quite unsuitable to the English temperament, and therefore it is not suggested that this German municipal house building bureau system should be transplanted wholesale into this country; but in the minds of all disinterested people who have given any serious thought to the subject, it is unquestionable that a municipal register of small house property is most desirable in every town, city and urban district.

It is by no means an uncommon occurrence to meet single ladies and other benevolent people whose incomes are largely derived from small house property, the condition of which they know nothing about; the management of their property is in the hands of their agents, whose business and duty it is to make as much as they can out of it. These benevolent people, who give away a large part of their incomes in charity, would be horrified if they knew the condition of the property from which they derive their incomes. A municipal housing register giving the number of small houses in every district, the condition of each house, and the name of the owner, ground landlord, etc., would undoubtedly provide one of the greatest social and economic incentives to property owners to insist upon their houses being kept in a state fit for human habitation.

MUNICIPAL HOUSE BUILDING

The failure of this method of attacking the house problem has been referred to in '' A Housing Policy '' in '' Practical Housing,'' and also in earlier parts of this treatise, and therefore it is not necessary to add much here.

In the Local Government Board Memorandum of March 25, 1913, on '' The Housing of the Working Classes Acts, 1890 to 1900 '' it is stated : '' As a general rule, experience shows that houses suitable for the accommodation of persons of the better paid working class community (who can afford to pay a rent which will provide a fair return on the capital employed) are more likely to be provided by private enterprise than houses at low rents which are necessary for the accommodation of the poorer classes. It will, therefore, frequently be the case that the efforts of the local authority will be directed mainly to the provision of houses of the

* For a more complete account of the Stuttgart Housing Bureau, see first edition of '' Practical Housing,'' pp. 120-31.

latter class," and at the end of this memorandum is the plan of a two-story cottage, three rooms and a scullery, the estimated cost of which is £110. In urban districts where land is dear and rates are ever increasing these cottages would not show a reasonable return at a rent of less than 4s. 6d. per week.

This plan provides a total air space in the rooms of only 3,792 cubic feet, and the Liverpool municipal flats let at 4s. 6d., which are admitted to be a charge on the rates, only contain 4,120 cubic feet of air space in the rooms, whereas the 4s. 6d. cottages at Harborne contain 4,258 cubic feet of air space in the rooms, and the Hereford cottages let at 4s. 9d. per week contain 4,640 cubic feet of air space in the rooms.

These facts show that in the matter of inside accommodation, as well as with regard to outside amenities, respectable private enterprise can do better than public bodies.

It is quite true that up to the present ordinary private enterprise has not, of recent years, provided to any great extent for the lower paid working classes, but this is not because under rational legislation and administration it is impossible to earn a reasonable profit on this class of property. It is because those responsible for our existing land and housing laws, and their administration have not given any attention to the economic laws that govern the problem with which they have to deal. Measures have been suggested in the foregoing chapters which, if adopted, would make 4s. 6d. houses as good a paying proposition as 6s. 6d. houses, and when this is done there will be no need to talk of charity rents for the poorer classes.

Public bodies have one, and only one, advantage over private enterprise, and that is cheap money, but this advantage is more than swallowed up by extravagant administration. It would be far wiser, as well as much more economical to give private enterprise a fair chance, and see what it can do under reasonable legislation and administration, instead of rejecting its offers of assistance without trial.

RURAL HOUSING

I cannot claim any practical personal experience of this branch of the problem, but perhaps a few remarks from a very interested spectator may not prove quite useless. It is generally agreed that bad housing in the country drives people into the towns, thereby accentuating urban evils and, therefore, urban housing reformers are obliged to take some interest in the rural problem.

s

The rural housing problem is first and foremost a wages question. Unless the money wages of rural labourers are increased, they will not be able to pay an economic house rent. It is often given as an excuse for the low wages paid in agricultural districts that the labourers get all sorts of perquisites in kind—a cottage below its market value, etc., etc. This system is thoroughly unsound and seems to many to be a breach of the Truck Act. If this is correct, then the sooner the Truck Act is put into force in country districts the better for all concerned, and if the present Truck Act does not apply then Parliament had better pass one that does apply.

Just as the old system of out-door relief acted as a subsidy towards wages and therefore lowered them, so the present rural system of paying a man so much a week and a cottage has undoubtedly kept down wages, and this has been a very great misfortune for all concerned.

Some years ago it was my privilege to discuss the problem of rural housing with a leading land agent in the South of England. He told me he had often laid before his principals proposals for building decent cottages, but with few exceptions his efforts towards better housing had been unsuccessful, because as cottages were thrown in with the farms, no adequate increase in rent could be obtained for the new cottages if they were provided. I ventured to suggest to him that what was needed was a reform in book-keeping and that the Truck Act should be applied to agricultural wages and house rents, making it illegal to pay wages in kind, in the form of reduced house rent. He agreed that my theory was quite sound, but foresaw, as every one would do, great difficulty in introducing such a reform. Englishmen are such creatures of habit, and, especially in the country, object strongly to moving out of their old ruts. It is, therefore, very interesting and encouraging to hear that Mr W. C. D. Whetham, F.R.S., a Fellow of Trinity College, Cambridge, has put this idea into practice on a small estate in Devonshire, with most satisfactory results. To quote Mr Whetham's explanation of his scheme: "If landowners would let their cottages either through the farmers or preferably as far as possible direct to the labourers, at rents which represent a fair return on the value of the buildings and covenant with the farmers to pay increased wages to householding labourers in proportion, the landowners would get the same total sum per annum for their property, but the rent would be equitably divided between land, farm buildings and cottages. What landowners lost on the rent of their farms, they would recover in the increased returns from the cottages. The labourer would pay more rent for his cottage, but would make up his loss in increased wages, and would learn that the value of a cottage is more than 1s. per week. The farmer might lose somewhat if non-householders were able to bargain effectively for the new rate of wages, but as at the present time he is usually paying a rent for his farm lower than circumstances warrant, he will generally be found willing to try the experiment. The system makes little, if any, change in the net monetary position of landowner, farmer or labourer, but it has the great advantage of placing the returns from farms and cottages on their true relative footing and does something to make new building possible by raising the standard rents of rural cottages generally.''

If this method successfully carried out by Mr Whetham, were adopted as a general custom by other landowners a step would be made towards the solution of the housing problem, for, as the general standard of cottage rents rose throughout the whole country, cottages would once more be built freely as an economic investment, and as the supply of cottages became greater the choice of homes would give the labourer more economic freedom, tend to increase his real earnings as the state of agricultural industry allowed, and thus help to raise the whole standard of rural life.

Mr Seebohm Rowntree, in his extremely valuable book '' How the Labourer lives,''* shows that the weekly minimum expenditure for a family of two adults and three children is 20s. 6d., which sum includes 2s. for rent. He also shows that in 1907 the weekly earnings of ordinary agricultural labourers in England averaged 17s. 6d. From these two facts, it is obvious that the existing standard of agricultural wages does not admit of anything being paid for house rent; on the contrary, even if nothing had to be paid for rent, the rural labourer getting 17s. 6d. per week would nevertheless, according to Mr Rowntree's calculations, be 1s. per week below the poverty line—Mr Rowntree is justly recognized as a great authority on these subjects. Three shillings per week is about as low as the average economic rent for rural cottages can be put, even under more favourable circumstances than now exist; 21s. 6d. is therefore the minimum living wage for agricultural labourers.

The question now arises how to provide sanitary cottages in rural districts on a sound economic basis at 3s. per week. In the first place, it is necessary to let the cottages separately from the farms under the system successfully carried out by Mr Whetham. We must also assume that the landowner's offer mentioned in

* Nelson and Sons, 2s. net.

Chapter VII has been accepted and that State loans for road-making (where necessary), drainage and building will be granted to private individuals on the lines suggested in the same chapter at 4½ per cent per annum to cover interest and sinking fund. On these assumptions the following is a fair average calculation:

		Per house		
Land £20 per acre divided by 8 houses per acre=		£2	10	0
Roads and drains £12 per acre divided by 8 houses per acre=		£1	10	0
		£4	0	0
Total cost of building including dead charges		£126	0	0

	Per house per week	
	s.	d.
4½ per cent on £4, the cost per house of land and development = 3s. 7¼d. per annum, divided by 52 weeks, gives us a ground rent of		1
Rates and taxes		5
Voids and repairs		3
Management and insurance		1
Interest and sinking fund at 4½ per cent on cost of building	2	2
	3	0

The ground rent of 1d. per house per week explains itself. Rates and taxes are taken at one-seventh of the gross rent, which should be enough in rural districts. In urban districts for this size cottage it is only one-sixth. Voids and repairs are taken at 7½ per cent on the gross rent. In well managed co-partnership housing societies they are only 2½ per cent. Management and insurance is taken at 2½ per cent on the gross rent which should be enough. Interest and sinking fund at 4½ per cent should be ample to write off the whole cost of building in 60 years.

The committee of the Parliamentary Labour Party are in favour of State-aided rural housing pending the elevation of wage rates to a standard at which the payment of economic rent becomes possible. Every reformer must wish to see rural labourers living in decent houses at rents they can afford without having to starve themselves and their children, but experience shows that charity rents to meet low wages always tend to perpetuate low wages. The only safe method is to raise wages to meet rents.

Another, and to many minds more efficacious, way of raising rural wages is to give the labourer freer access to the land. If this is done he will be able to earn something for himself independently of any employer and thereby place himself in a stronger position to bargain with his employer for a living wage.

In 1881 there were 1,592,520 persons employed in agriculture in Great Britain, whereas in 1901 there were only 1,396,350. It ought to be just the other way about. Our total population has increased, which means a larger demand for food, and we are now importing vast quantities of food which could be and would be produced in this country if the policy of small holdings and allotments were more generally supported by those who have the land to let.

EPILOGUE

The City of Health and Beauty is our objective, but Public and Private Economy must be our guiding principle or town planning and garden suburb and city development will never be more than a rich man's hobby. It is only by studying economic laws, and working with them, that we can ever hope to get this system generally applied all over the United Kingdom. Bad town and estate development must be made unprofitable and genuine town planning and better housing must be made a sound business proposition for the individuals who undertake it. John Bright once said, " The nation in every country dwells in the cottage. The rich find everything just as they like . . . If a class has failed let us try the nation . . . trust to numbers not to intellect, least of all to the scholarly intellect." He regarded statesmanship not as a mere executive function, but as a means of guiding and stimulating the better mind and judgment of the nation.

APPENDIX I

Showing how to provide adequate access to cheap land.

ILLUSTRATION NO. 1

Harborne and Quinton town planning scheme.

In this case there were two problems to solve:

I. The provision of adequate access to the town planning area in such a manner as to:

(1) Encourage building development in the area itself and also along the line of route.

(2) Produce increased assessable value.

(3) Provide a road of sufficient width to accommodate present and future traffic.

(4) Save money for the ratepayers.

II. The provision of trams or motor-buses to Harborne:

(1) At the least possible expense to the ratepayers.

(2) With the least possible injury to the adjoining suburb of Edgbaston so that there should be the least possible decrease in assessable value.

(3) On a road with reasonable gradients.

(4) By the shortest possible route.

These two problems are closely connected with each other and the only satisfactory solution is by means of a joint scheme. The Corporation of Birmingham made the very grave initial mistake of attempting to solve them independently of one another.

The accompanying map shows:

1. The town planning area whose boundary is hatched thus: ⲙⲙⲙⲙⲙ

2. The centre of that part of this area which will develop first marked with a X. The development of the southern part of the area will be delayed for many years by two existing golf links.

3. The ✳ in the right-hand top corner of the map is Five Ways,* Edgbaston, from which one main thoroughfare without tram lines and running north-west leads to the Town Hall and another thoroughfare with tram lines on it runs east and west.

4. OO mark High Street, Harborne, to which trams or motor-buses must run. F is a well-graded street running through a thickly populated district.

* I am not responsible for this meeting of six roads, being known locally as Five Ways.

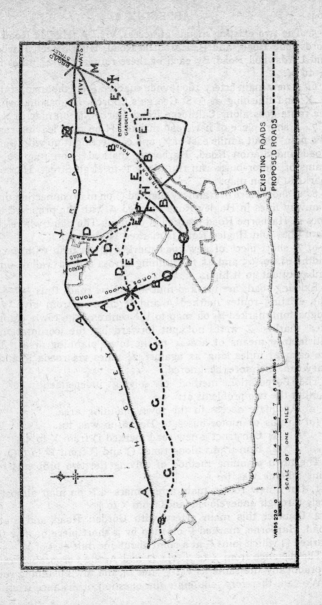

EXISTING ROADS

PROPOSED ROADS

YARDS 220 0 1 2 3 4 5 6 7 8 FURLONGS

SCALE OF ONE MILE

5. The two existing means of access, viz., A, Hagley Road and Lordswood Road, and B, Harborne Road, High Street, Harborne and Lordswood Road. By each of these routes it is 2¾ miles from ✳ to X.

6. A new main artery 100 ft wide marked E on the map, starting at X and finishing at ⚹ St George's Church, Edgbaston, whence the route goes along Calthorpe Road marked M on map to ✳.

7. A short piece of new road marked H on map leaving road E at a point about a mile east of X, and connecting it up with Gordon Road and Station Road, Harborne, marked F on map so that trams or motor-buses can run along it to High Street, Harborne, marked OO on map.

8. A short piece of tramway marked C on map connecting up the tramway lines in Hagley Road marked A with the proposed tram lines in Harborne Road marked B on map. The point where these tram lines join Hagley Road is marked ⊠ on map.

9. A short piece of new road marked D on map with varying widths of 60, 65 and 45 ft. running across a deep valley on an embankment 40 ft high.

Existing roads are marked thus ——. New roads thus — —— —
The existing routes marked A and B on map from Five Ways, Edgbaston, marked ✳ on map to the centre of the town planning area marked X were not put forward by the corporation as satisfactory means of access to the town planning area. They are each 2¾ miles long as against 2¼ miles via roads E and M. They can, therefore, be ignored.

The Corporation method of solving independently of one another the two problems of:

(a) Adequate access to the town planning area.
(b) Trams or motor-buses to Harborne was to:
    (1) Construct a new road marked D from X to ⚹
    (2) Run trams along roads C and B from ⊠ to OO.

The town planning method of solving the two problems by a joint scheme was to:

1. Cut a new 100-ft. main artery marked E on map almost entirely through undeveloped lands from X to ⚹.

2. Connect this main artery with Gordon Road and Station Road, Harborne, marked F on map by a short piece of new road marked H which joins E at a point about one mile east of X.

The distance from X to ✳ via D and A, the Corporation route, is practically the same as via E and M, the town planning route. We can, therefore, eliminate the question of distance from our consideration of the comparative advantages and disadvantages of the rival methods of solving the problem.

The first point to consider is the question of expense. The Corporation's estimate for road D after deducting owners' contributions, etc., etc., is £16,190, to which must be added £410 for rounding off the very dangerous corner at ↓, vide city surveyor's evidence at the Local Government Board inquiry, making a total net cost to the ratepayers of £16,600. When the tramway scheme was before the House of Commons £77,643 was sworn to as the cost of running trams from ✗ along C to a point rather less than 1¼ miles beyond OO. In order to make a fair comparison with the town planning method this 1¼ miles must be deducted from the Corporation estimate of £77,643. Take the cost of constructing this tramway at £16,000 per mile, an excessive price, and, therefore, in favour of the Corporation, because it is deducted from their estimate, and we have to deduct £20,000 from £77,643, leaving £57,643 for tramways and £16,600 for road D. Add these two figures together and we get a total net cost to the ratepayers of £74,243 for the Corporation method of solving the two problems of access and trams. Under the town planning method the new 100-ft. main artery included in the town planning method and marked E is 3,380 yards long, which according to the city surveyor (vide evidence at inquiry) would cost without tram lines £6 14s. 2d. per yard to construct; it ought to cost much less, but take his figure.

3,380 yards at £6 14s. 2d.	£22,660
Digging and levelling 50,000 cubic yards at 1s. 6d.	3,750
Firm quotation for railway arch	3,600*
Compensation, etc., to railway company	1,400*
New road H and demolition of buildings ..	1,590
	£33,000
Add 10 per cent for contingencies	3,300
	£36,300

* It was suggested at the Local Government Board inquiry that as the Corporation had recently paid a higher price for a much smaller bridge, therefore, it was ridiculous to say that this bridge could be built for £3,600; it was also suggested that the railway company would prevent it being built at a reasonable cost. These misconceptions make it necessary to explain that the above figures are based on the assumption that the work would be carried out under the supervision of competent technical advisers who understand the powers conferred on local authorities by the 1909 Act and the use of ferro-concrete and other modern engineering methods.

The Harborne and Quinton town planning scheme
    says owners shall contribute £7 per yard towards
    the cost of main arteries through their property.
    Take this at £5 instead of £7 and assume it
    would not be got on more than 2,000 yards out of
    the total 3,380 yards   10,000

                                    £26,300
Compensation, less betterment   3,700

                                    £30,000

This is essentially a case where motor-buses are far more suitable than trams.

1. They would give far less annoyance to Edgbaston, through which they must pass, thereby avoiding a decrease in assessable value as well as removing the opposition that proposals for trams through Edgbaston have always met with in Parliament and which has cost the ratepayers of Birmingham a great deal of money.

2. Passengers could be taken down Broad Street, which is where they want to go, but which has no tram lines,* instead of being forced down Islington Row, where the majority do not want to go.

3. In new districts like Harborne, which under careful management ought to develop very rapidly, it is very unwise for the ratepayers to be bound to any particular route by the fact that a large capital outlay has been made on tram lines. A motor-bus can, if necessary, alter its route to meet the changing needs of a new district. When public money has been spent on tram lines it cannot be recovered. The loan has to be repaid by the ratepayers whether or not their tram lines are remunerative.

So far as cost is concerned, it is, therefore, clear that provided a cautious policy is followed and motor-buses adopted, the town planning method of solving our problem would only cost £30,000 against £74,243 for the Corporation method. If, on the other hand, trams are unwisely insisted upon, then £42,000 must be added to the town planning total, leaving it still £2,243 less than the Corporation total.

These figures have been carefully checked and re-checked.

---

* When the proposal for trams to Harborne was before Parliament it was said on behalf of the Birmingham Corporation that tram lines down Broad Street were impracticable; since then the City Council has decided to run trams down this street in spite of the congestion of traffic that already exists at the lower end.

The result will not surprise practical surveyors who have carefully studied the best town planning methods. The loss to the ratepayers caused by the Corporation method is really much greater than from these figures it appears to be. When trams are dealt with independently of town planning the ratepayers are deprived of their right under the 1909 Act to one-half of the betterment due to this expenditure of public money. Some years ago, the price per acre of a small building estate of thirty-six acres, with which I am very familiar, went up more than £100 per acre on the promise of trams to Harborne, and went down again by the same amount when the application for permission to construct these trams was refused by Parliament. On this little estate alone the ratepayers' share of betterment would have been £1,800. From this hard fact it is not difficult to see that the betterment due to trams would in the Harborne and Quinton town planning area of 2,320 acres have amounted to a very large sum, which would have greatly increased the saving effected by town planning methods as compared with the Corporation method even if trams had been insisted upon. If, on the other hand, the more cautious and efficient policy of making a beginning with motor-buses had been adopted, there would have been a saving for the ratepayers of £44,243, plus half the betterment due to motor-buses.

So far as quick development of the town planning area is concerned the town planning method of providing access is far preferable to the Corporation method in three respects not yet mentioned:

1. It could be completed in a year or two, whereas the Corporation tell us it will take ten years to complete road D.

2. Road D by the height of its embankment blocks building development on either side of it, whereas if the town planning method were adopted the landowners interested could make a road, marked K on map, from Meadow Road across main artery E to an existing road, marked P on map, thereby opening up the whole of the valley for building, and at the same time providing the new access between Harborne village and the district lying north of this map, which was said to be needed and which was given as one of the reasons for spending £16,600 on road D.

3. About a quarter of a mile south of the Botanical Gardens is a blind-end road that has lain fallow for many years. The cutting of main artery E would enable the landowner to join up with it this blind-end road by means of a new road, marked L on map, thereby opening up several acres of land.

The other advantages of the town planning method are much wider roads and much better gradients. The following table summarizes the comparisons:

	Corporation method	Town planning method. Motor-buses	Trams
Comparative costs	£74,243	£30,000	£72,000
Length of road along which building development is blocked	700 yards	Nil	
Do. along which assessable value is decreased	1,100 yards	Nil	
Area of land along line of route opened up for building ..	13 acres	108 acres	
Length of road less than 23 ft. wide	60 yards	Nil	
Greatest width on tram or bus route	45 ft	100 ft	
Length of route with gradient 1 in 20 or worse	558 yards	Nil	
Worst gradients ..	1 in 16·1; 1 in 17·3 1 in 18·9; 1 in 19·2	1 in 22·5	

The total increased assessable value produced by the town planning 100-ft. main artery along its route is at the lowest £14,520, to say nothing of the building development further out that would be encouraged and expedited by it. The Corporation method, on the other hand, will not produce more than £1,760 increased assessable value.

It is only fair to mention that the Corporation gave as one of their principal reasons for road D that its embankment would provide a very valuable corporation tip (vide speech by chairman of public works committee at council debate and city surveyor's evidence at the inquiry). This seems hardly a sufficient reason for adopting a very extravagant corporation scheme with a mean approach to Hagley Road or for emptying traffic into an existing road that has already as much traffic as it can comfortably carry, rather than adopt a most economical town planning scheme which would provide a dignified approach to the town planning area and, incidentally, expedite its development. There is nothing more valuable to the health of a city than radial parks such as road E would be. By the time this radial park was completed (thereby providing adequate access to the town planning area) an intelligent local authority would no doubt see the financial wisdom of constructing the 100-ft. main artery, marked G on the map, and running from X westwards to Quinton village, marked Q on map. As this road runs through very cheap agricultural land, the financial results to the ratepayers should be even more favourable than in the case of road E. When this 100-ft. main artery, marked E and G on map, is completed, the distance from Quinton village, marked Q on map, to St George's Church, Edgbaston, will be just under four miles and if motor-buses are run along it the journey from Quinton village to the centre of Birmingham should be performed quite easily in about twenty minutes. Under these conditions, and with the large supply of cheap land available, building development should be very rapid. That is to say, the main objective of town planners to empty the slums into real country would in this area be achieved and at the same time very large sums saved for the ratepayers, but it must not be forgotten that these results would not please the land-jobbers or their friends.

The chief objections to the town planning method of providing adequate access to the town planning area and trams or motor-buses to Harborne that were raised by the Corporation and the chief arguments (beyond those already mentioned) adduced by them in favour of their own method shall now be dealt with "seriatim":

CORPORATION'S OBJECTIONS TO TOWN PLANNING METHOD

1. The gradient in one part was alleged to be too steep and the cutting there was said to be deep; exception was also taken to a short embankment $12\frac{1}{2}$ ft. high.

An embankment $12\frac{1}{2}$ ft. high is obviously easier to deal with than an embankment 40 ft. high, and as a matter of fact by setting the building line a little further back, which can be done without financial loss where town planning methods are adopted, building land abutting on to an embankment not more than $12\frac{1}{2}$ ft. high can be satisfactorily utilized. This has been done with very pleasant effects and quite satisfactory economic results on Harborne Tenants' Moor Pool estate. The same remarks apply to the short cutting, the depth of which was objected to.

With regard to gradients, one of the Corporation's technical advisers suggested as an alternative to the town planning road from Ravenhurst Farm in Ravenhurst Road to the railway, i.e. part of road E, a route via Ravenhurst Road and Margaret Grove. In this route, there is a gradient of 1 in 11·2 and an awkward right-angle corner; whereas the gradient objected to in the town planning road is 1 in $22\frac{1}{2}$. It seems a little inconsistent to object to a gradient of 1 in $22\frac{1}{2}$ and advocate in its place a gradient of 1 in $11\frac{1}{2}$.

2. It was suggested that it was not necessary to include this road in the town planning scheme because it could be made by agreement between the corporation and the landowners independently of the town planning scheme.

This suggestion ignored the powers, conferred on local authorities by the 1909 Act, to protect the interests of the ratepayers in dealing with owners, which Act would also greatly assist the Corporation in dealing with the railway company. The road might possibly be carried out by agreement but the ratepayers would in that case undoubtedly pay much more for it than they would have to pay if the Corporation's town planning powers were enforced.

3. It was further suggested that it would be to the interests of the landowners through which this road passes to make it themselves.

That is a good reason for getting a substantial contribution from the owners towards the cost of the road, but it is not a valid reason for leaving the matter entirely in their hands. If this road were made merely as a road for developing a building estate, it should in the proper interests of the owners be constructed on very different lines to those needed for a main arterial road; from which it follows that there would not be adequate accommodation for through traffic; and it must not be forgotten that in the city surveyor's evidence he estimated that there will be a population of 50,000 in this town planning area when it is fully developed, to say nothing of the existing population in Harborne that would use this road.

4. An objection that carried great weight in the council chamber was the fact that this road, if made, would benefit Harborne Tenants Limited. This objection, or rather admission, gives away the whole Corporation case. Harborne Tenants' Moor Pool estate is situated almost in the centre of that part of the town planning area which will develop first. To admit that this road would benefit Harborne Tenants is to admit that it would benefit the town planning area.

5. It was also said that existing roads were quite adequate for motor-buses to Harborne and the fact was mentioned that motor-buses are now running along Harborne Road. In this route there

are gradients of 1 in 16, and 1 in 17·3. Is it not a little inconsistent to assert that such gradients are quite satisfactory and then object to road E because for a short distance there is a gradient of 1 in 22½ ?

6. Another objection was that there would be very little pick-up for trams or motor-buses along the route.

This objection applies to any tram or motor-bus route through Edgbaston; many of the residents in that suburb keep their own carriages or motor-cars and do not want to be annoyed by trams or motor-buses, and as they do not want to use them they do not see why their poorer fellow citizens should be considered. In this respect, the new road has two advantages over the present route along Harborne Road.

(a) It would tap the Botanical Gardens, thereby popularizing this desirable resort and creating a new pick-up that does not at present exist.

(b) As most of the land through which the new road would pass is at present unbuilt upon, the people who went to live on it would go there with the full knowledge that trams or motor-buses were going along it. Most of them would go there for that very reason; whereas the Edgbaston residents on the existing Harborne Road (which has twice been rejected by Parliament as a tramway route) strongly object to trams and have not hesitated to say so at Westminster and elsewhere. There is no doubt in the minds of practical surveyors that if this new road were cut and provided with a tram or motor-bus service, moderate sized houses or villas would very quickly spring up along it, thereby providing a much larger pick-up along its route than can possibly be expected for trams or motor-buses along any existing road through Edgbaston from the centre of the city to Harborne.

The town planning method was rejected and the Corporation method adopted by the Birmingham City Council by 90 votes to 5.

This is the strongest possible argument for the appointment of a special and well-informed Government department for this new, extremely technical, and very complicated work of town development on economical modern lines with a view to providing decent housing for all classes of the community at reasonable rents and at the same time protecting the interests of the ratepayers.

If the city council of Greater Birmingham, which is sometimes described as the Mecca of town planning, can make a mistake like this, what is to be expected from other and smaller local authorities, without a strong and efficient central authority to assist, and where necessary, control them ?

ILLUSTRATION NO. 2

In the early stages of preparing the East Birmingham town planning scheme, it was seen that as soon as Stechford, marked A on plan, is protected from overcrowding by a town planning scheme, it will be necessary to connect it with Bordesley Green Road, marked CC on plan, by means of a 100-ft main artery through back land, marked B on plan. The back land through which this artery will pass had been a drug in the market for many years, owing to the difficulty of developing it without the assistance of a town planning scheme. Those responsible for the East Birmingham scheme recognized that the moment it became known that a main artery was going to be cut through this estate up would go the price of back land, and therefore it was decided to purchase the land at once on behalf of the ratepayers, subject to the approval of the city council and the Local Government Board. The estate comprised eighty-three acres of land, and the sum paid was £11,000, or £133 per acre, a higher price than the owner had been able to obtain from anyone else, and therefore good business for the landowner as well as a very good bargain for the ratepayers. Before the town planning scheme was proposed building land in the vicinity had been selling at £400 to £700 per acre. This purchase had the effect of reducing land values, a very good thing for the community; but even with that reduction, and even under a genuine town planning scheme, which would still further reduce land values, the profit on this purchase will pay for constructing the road, provided cautious methods are adopted, and, in the first instance, only a road for motor-buses is provided. CC is a congested district which badly needs emptying into the open country beyond A provided that that open country has first been protected from overcrowding by a town planning scheme. The question as to which are better and cheaper, motor-buses or trams, is so uncertain at the present time that no cautious municipal administrator will commit the ratepayers to heavy expenditure in laying down tram lines, unless he is absolutely obliged to do so, and especially does this maxim apply to new districts where for one reason or another routes may have to be altered in a few years' time. The 100-ft. main artery, marked B on map, with a motor road down the centre and trees and grass on either side, would provide a handsome radial

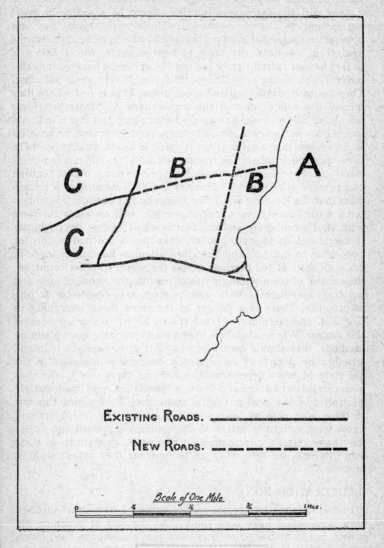

C   B   B   A

C

C

EXISTING ROADS. ──────────

NEW ROADS. ── ── ── ──

Scale of One Mile.

0   ¼   ½   ¾   1 MILE.

T

park, which is very much needed in this district, and the fact that it need cost the ratepayers nothing should be a source of great satisfaction to those responsible. Those who think they are opposed to municipal land purchase, but who in private never vote against it, provided the price is high enough (whose policy is in fact to wait until the price goes up before buying land for the rate-payers) took strong objection to this remarkably good purchase. They called it municipal land speculation. That is just where they missed the whole point of the transaction. A private individual who buys land without knowing what is going to happen to it is a speculator; but when a local authority buys back land because its leaders know that a main artery is going to be cut through it, there is no speculation about the transaction, and it is difficult to under-stand how any man with the slightest pretence to business acumen can pretend that there is. There is a great fear among a certain class that the Housing and Town Planning Act of 1909, if adminis-tered with honesty, care, and discretion, will seriously interfere with land speculation, and this fear is well-founded, but obviously it would not do to state publicly that this is the real reason for opposition to the Act, and therefore attempts have to be made to draw all sorts of red herrings across the scent. In other countries, the control of town planning has fallen into the hands of land and building speculators, with results that are disastrous to the community. There is a danger of the same thing happening in England, and therefore no stone should be left unturned to avert this danger. When ratepayers hear a man criticizing town planning methods, they should ascertain what line of business he is in and whether he is directly or indirectly financially interested in the old style of town development, which, as every one knows, has been carried out by land and building speculators, very inadequately controlled by the local or central authorities. By applying this test to those who pose as town planning experts, the ratepayers will know what weight to attach to the opinions expressed and unless they have reliable information on this point, they must, in their own interests, be very wary as to how far they accept what is said.

ILLUSTRATION NO. 3

In this case the immediate cost of cutting a new street through back land would have been more than the cost of widening old streets, but in the long run, this extra cost would have been much reduced, if indeed it did not disappear altogether, through the increased value of the property acquired by the Corporation, and the improvement effected would have been well worth a great deal more than the immediate extra cost.

The map on page 276 shows both schemes.

1. For continuing Paradise Street, which is a fine wide street through back land, into Broad Street at A, thereby avoiding the very awkward double turn from Paradise Street into Broad Street by way of Easy Row, which turn is all the more dangerous by reason of its being on a hill. By this scheme back land is turned into front land, thereby producing increased assessable value, and a 66-ft. street is provided, of which 42-ft. is roadway with very easy curves and gradients. The distance is forty-five yards shorter than the old route.

2. For widening Broad Street 15 ft. making only a 61-ft. street, of which only 35 ft. 9 in. is roadway, and rounding off the corner of Edmund Street and Easy Row, as shown at B on the plan. Under this scheme, traffic will still have the very dangerous double turn by way of Easy Row to negotiate, or it can go along Edmund Street which is only 42 ft. wide between the building lines and only 25 ft. 6 in. between the kerbs, with high and valuable buildings on either side to a point where traffic is already congested at the corner of Edmund Street and Congreve Street. In the words of the committee, this improvement will be " more apparent than real," as the greater portion of the increased width of street will of necessity be devoted to foot passengers and congestion of traffic will be increased rather than decreased by encouraging it to go along the very narrow Edmund Street to Congreve Street instead of taking it direct to the fine wide Paradise Street.

The finance of the two schemes is:

1. Net cost for sixty years £5,858 per annum, at the end of which period the Corporation would have a property worth, as soon as the street was made, £4,850 per annum, and which may well be worth a great deal more in sixty years' time when the Corporation gets the reversion of the rack rents. There would also be a very large increase in assessable value, for which no credit is taken.

2. Net cost for sixty years rather over £1,616 per annum, at the end of which time the Corporation will have no property to show for their expenditure, only an improvement " more apparent than real." Assessable value may be very considerably reduced by throwing land into the street on which buildings now stand, and on which no rates will be paid when it is thrown into the street; on the other hand, this loss may be partially recouped by the increased value of

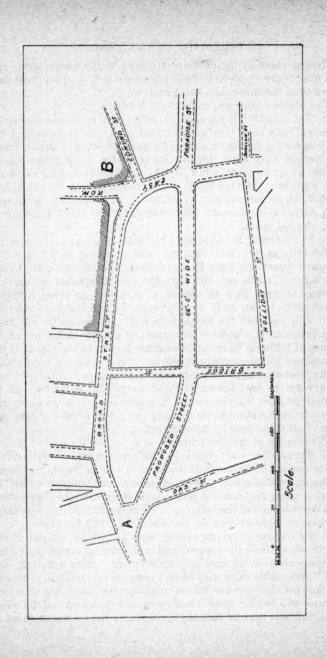

PARADISE ST.

EDMUND ST

WILLOW ST

B

EAST

ROW

BROAD STREET

BRIDGE ST

66'·0" WIDE

HOLLIDAY ST

PROPOSED STREET

GAS ST

A

Scale.

200 YARDS.

the new frontage. If the possible loss in income from rates were added to the cost of this scheme, and if the certain increase in income from rates produced by scheme No. 1 were deducted from the cost of that scheme, the extra annual cost of scheme No. 1 over scheme No. 2 would certainly be very much reduced and probably cancelled out altogether.

One of the principal arguments brought against scheme No. 1 was that some dozen or two shopkeepers in the narrow part of Broad Street might lose part of their custom. This is exactly the same difficulty that the Road Board has met in connexion with its proposed road in London. It will not affect the minds of those who are concerned with the greatest good of the greatest number. They will agree that scheme No. 1 is worth to the general body of ratepayers infinitely more than scheme No. 2, and is a striking example of the economic wisdom of improving communications by cutting new roads or streets through back land wherever it is possible to do so, rather than by widening existing roads or streets.

The Birmingham Corporation method of improving Broad Street is a striking example of how not to do it. It is only fair to say that the landowners reduced their original price by £9,000 because they did not wish to stand in the way of what was considered by the old school of thought at the Council House to be a public improvement, but even this concession cannot compensate the ratepayers for getting no adequate financial benefit from the new and more valuable frontage created by the expenditure of their money, as would have been the case if scheme No. 1 for continuing Paradise Street had been adopted.

The old school are opposed to municipal land purchase and the holding of surplus land by the Corporation. In Sydney it is found that the increased value of surplus lands retained by the Corporation which is due to public improvements is returning sufficient by way of rent to pay interest and sinking fund on the capital cost of the improvements. Birmingham might have benefited very greatly from taking a leaf out of the book of one of our colonies.

It was mentioned during the debate in the council chamber as a justification for paying £35 a yard for land to be thrown into a street that this price compared very favourably with prices paid in similar cases in other parts of the city. Land in Colmore Row has cost the ratepayers £60 a yard, in Easy Row £29, High Street £35, Cherry Street £37, and New Street £50. These figures are a most convincing proof of the economic advantage to the ratepayers

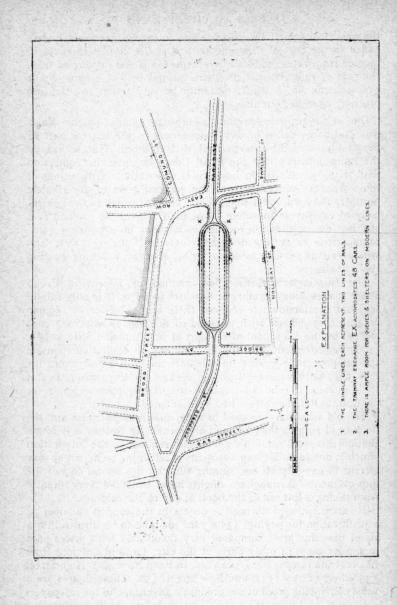

EXPLANATION

1. THE SINGLE LINES EACH REPRESENT TWO LINES OF RAILS.

2. THE TRAMWAY EXCHANGE EX. ACCOMMODATES 48 CARS.

3. THERE IS AMPLE ROOM FOR QUEUES & SHELTERS ON MODERN LINES.

— SCALE —

of cutting new roads through back land rather than widening old ones. Public improvements must of necessity often be costly, but capable administrators can keep down the cost instead of increasing it, as those who are too sympathetic with the shopkeepers invariably do.

It was stated at the Council meeting that the land facing Paradise Street had been taken for other purposes and therefore that scheme could not be revived, but it was not mentioned that during the committee's deliberations in 1912, that is to say, when they were preparing for the City Council debate, a renewed offer of the back land necessary for continuing Paradise Street was made by the Canal company to the Corporation.

To those who believe in trams, or are at any rate satisfied that whatever may be their disadvantages, compared with motor-buses, trams will nevertheless run in our streets for another ten years, this proposal to improve the route to town via Broad Street and Paradise Street, by cutting a new street through back land, instead of by the " shoddy " method of widening the narrow part of Broad Street, has a special and overwhelming attraction in that it provides the one and only practical position for a tramway exchange, which is very badly needed in Birmingham at the present time. Owing to the configuration of the land in the centre of the city, a very steep hill between the existing northern and southern tramway termini, and other local circumstances which need not be detailed here, the solution of this problem is extremely difficult. The location of a tramway exchange on the site of this new street would surmount all difficulties; it would avoid the steep hill, in addition to which this site is by far the most convenient spot on which to link up the various tramway routes which run out north, south, east and west. On this site there would have been room to arrange a tramway exchange on some such plan as that shown on the opposite page, one of the many advantages of which would have been that the general street traffic could have gone down the centre and would not have been interfered with by trams stopping to discharge and pick up passengers. The existing tramway termini are very inconvenient to passengers and most obstructive to other traffic. Some of them are positively dangerous. Sooner or later there will be a bad accident, and then perhaps the authorities will realize what an opportunity they missed by not cutting the new street and not providing a central tramway exchange, but those responsible for this accident are not likely to lose their lives; it will be innocent people who suffer, because in Birmingham municipal elections are mostly fought on party politics.

In spite of the experience of other places, the Birmingham tramway committee have taken no serious steps to provide for the future. Foresight and business acumen have been overruled by narrow-minded huckstering; existing tram termini have been left to develop on haphazard patch-work lines, and the municipal tramway undertaking is left unprovided with a most important weapon * for its coming struggle with motor-buses. The higglers no doubt objected to the temporary loss that would have been incurred in rent and rates by setting the buildings on this new street rather farther back than would have been otherwise necessary in order to provide room for the tramway lines on either side of the street, so as not to interfere with other traffic. This loss would in a very few years have been more than recouped by the increased income due to a complete and much more convenient tramway system than is now possible and the immense saving of public and private time that would ensue from:

1. The improvement of tramway communication.
2. The reduction of obstruction to general traffic.

People travelling across Birmingham by tramway have to change cars two or three times and sometimes walk for considerable distances. This unsatisfactory state of affairs, which has now been perpetuated, must deprive the Birmingham tramway committee of a large number of passengers who would have used the trams to get across Birmingham if there had been reasonable through communication.

ILLUSTRATION NO. 4

This appendix would not be complete without reference to a most attractive proposition brought forward by the Town Council of Birkenhead to purchase the Storeton estate from Sir W. H. Lever. This might have resulted in emptying slums into the country and at the same time protecting that country from being destroyed by land sweating, as happens under our present haphazard by-law methods of town development.

This opportunity of giving an object lesson for the whole country was presented by the proposal of the Birkenhead Town Council to purchase 1,630 acres of land, most of which is purely agricultural,

* L.C.C. trams are most severely handicapped in their struggle with motor-buses by the fact that there is no through communication.

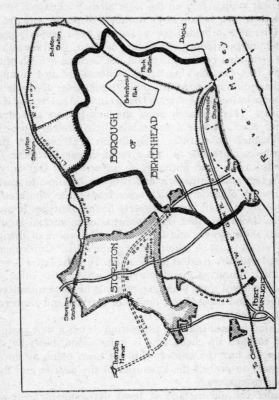

MAP, SHOWING THE BORO OF BIRKENHEAD AND THE STORETON ESTATE

Railways are indicated thus ⊢⊢⊢ Existing roads ⟋⟋ New Road in course of construction ⠿⠿

THE TOWN BOUNDARIES ARE INDICATED BY THE THICK BLACK LINE THUS ▬▬ AND THOSE OF THE ESTATE ARE INDICATED THUS ⫻⫻

TWO SMALL PORTIONS OF THE ESTATE ARE DETACHED FROM THE MAIN PORTION ONE IS CLOSE TO PORT SUNLIGHT AND THE

OTHER WITHIN THE BOROUGH.

but part of which is urban and already has a prospective building value. The average price was £95 per acre or 4¾d. per yard. The land is within easy reach of Rockferry Station, which is only fifteen minutes' ride from the centre of Liverpool and still nearer to the centre of Birkenhead. If this estate had been purchased by the local authority and connected with Rockferry Station by means of a new main artery on the lines already explained, it would not have been long before large numbers of people left the congested districts, and (provided the estate had been properly protected by reasonable restrictions of building density), this new suburb would have remained real country and not become a fresh slum.

The fact that this particular scheme entailed municipal land purchase does not affect the main thesis under discussion, which is the importance of opening up cheap land and protecting it from land sweating. This is exactly what the land-jobbers and slum owners do not want. It would depreciate their wretched property. Is it our business to consider their interests? Have they not shown themselves quite able to look after themselves without any assistance from the local authority or anyone else? Our duty is to the ratepayers and rentpayers, and it is our business to examine very closely any objections which come from those who are financially interested in small house property of the old type. It must not be implied from this that the opponents of municipal land purchase are all slum owners and land-jobbers, but some of them are, and their views must be taken " cum grano salis." Other opponents are imbued with the greatest public spirit. To these latter I would point out that municipal land purchase on careful lines, combined with intelligent town planning, presents in some instances the best, cheapest, and most direct means of carrying out slum reform and slum prevention.

It may be said that the suggestion to cut a new main artery in order to open up cheap land is quite sound, but why should the ratepayers buy the estate? Will not town planning do all that is necessary to protect the amenities of the district and the pockets of the ratepayers?

Under the old method of town development local authorities spent very large sums of the ratepayers' money on road-making, sewer construction and other public necessities, whereas the land-jobbers went off with the profits due to this expenditure of public money. By the new method now being slowly evolved it is possible to ensure a fairer division of capital expenditure and profits between the ratepayers and the landowners, but the 1909

Housing and Town Planning Act and the regulations thereunder are so complicated and so much in favour of property versus the public that a very strenuous and well-informed administration is needed if the negotiations between local authorities and landowners are to result in a fair bargain for the ratepayers. Town planning is very popular in theory, but when it comes to practical details like restriction of building density and reasonable contributions from landowners towards the cost of opening up their land, opposition is very strong, and it is at present very far from clear that really satisfactory results will be attained under the Housing and Town Planning Act, 1909, without the assistance in some cases of municipal land purchase and in all cases of a just system of rating. The Birkenhead proposal was therefore worthy of very careful consideration on the score of efficiency as well as economy. Here is a large supply of cheap land that only needs a continuance of Sir William Lever's Avenue to Rockferry Station, and some expenditure on sewers, in order to throw it into the market for immediate building development. In any case, the local authority will, sooner or later, have to provide the sewers, and if they do not buy this estate, some one else will get the profit due to their expenditure of public money. When a large estate like the Storeton estate is in public ownership the local authority have the whole matter in their own hands; they can open up and develop their own estate, probably spending less money in so doing than would, under the old method, have been spent by them on the same public services, such as roads, sewers, etc., the reason for which is that under the old method there are many private interests to satisfy, whereas if the land belongs to a local authority, they have only themselves to deal with. The position, therefore, is, so far as economy is concerned, that by land purchase such as that proposed by the Birkenhead Town Council, the local authority spends less money on town development than it would have had to spend under the old method, and it secures for the ratepayers the profits due to that expenditure of public money, instead of letting them go to private individuals. It should also ensure better housing at the old or lower rents.

If care is exercised in designing the cross-section of a 100-ft. or 120-ft. main artery, and if in the first instance only sufficient roadway for the immediate needs of traffic is provided, with plenty of grass margin, and other economical amenities, then these wide roads opening up cheap land should not cost more than £6 a yard forward. Under economical town planning methods of estate development, allowing narrow roadways, combined drainage, etc., etc., in purely residential districts, these 100 or 120 ft. main arteries will raise the value of 300 yards of land on either side of them from £95 an acre to the average of £200 an acre. A width of 300 yards on either side of the road gives a total width of 600 yards, that is to say, every 8 yards of main artery constructed at a cost of £6 or less per yard forward opens up an acre of land and increases its value from £95 per acre to £200. The financial position of the local authority, therefore, is:

Cost of land	£95 an acre
Cost of 8 yards of main artery at £6 per yard	£48
Total	£143
Resulting value	£200* per acre

leaving a profit for the ratepayers of £57 on every acre purchased.

Some experts will object that in these figures nothing is allowed for the loss of compound interest during the development of the estate, which they say will take fifty years to complete. They forget that under the old methods of town development public money has been spent on roads, sewers, etc., many years before increased assessable value comes in to pay for it, in addition to which, as we have already seen, some one else gets the profit, whereas under the policy of municipal land purchase the ratepayers get the profit they have created, and this will very soon repay them for any arrears due to loss of compound interest that may accumulate during the first few years. It is most unwise to prophesy that it will take fifty years to develop the Storeton estate. This might have been the case under the old methods, but nowadays the possibilities are very different. A large proportion of the poorer classes are thoroughly dissatisfied with their living conditions, and if only they were given half a chance they would leave the congested districts of Liverpool and Birkenhead and go to live at Storeton. This movement has already taken place to a very marked degree in all our large towns even under the present very imperfect conditions, that is to say, working men are rapidly moving from the centres to the outskirts, even when nothing but a by-law suburb is available, and in garden suburbs there are practically no voids. In the case of Birkenhead and Storeton, this movement outwards could by careful

* £200 is too much for small houses, but richer tenants will pay more.

and energetic town planning methods be greatly speeded up. The Storeton estate might well be fully developed in very much less than fifty years' time, whereas expenditure for development should of course only be incurred as development progresses.

Bad housing is largely due to the monopoly in land that has been created and accentuated by the old method of town development. What this generation has to do is to break this land monopoly by increasing the supply of good cheap land available for housing, and, in this case, the Birkenhead Corporation with the assistance of the Public Works Commissioners who lend two-thirds of the money to co-partnership societies, could by encouraging and assisting such a society have promoted a first-rate housing scheme and at the same time made a profit for the ratepayers instead of a loss. Hereford, working on these lines, has created one of the best garden suburbs in this or any other country, and the results are:

1. No charge on the rates (in the case of Birkenhead there should be a profit for the ratepayers, because Storeton estate was offered to the Birkenhead Town Council at a lower price than Hereford had to pay, and house rents are higher in Birkenhead than in Hereford).

2. Better town development and better housing at reasonable rents.

3. A dividend for the shareholders.

The Hereford scheme is fully described in Chapter V.

It is not wise to say that municipal land purchase is always right. It depends on the price to be paid and many other circumstances. Each case must be dealt with on its merits. The Storeton estate was a clear case for municipal land purchase. There was no speculation about it, and if the Birkenhead and Wirral local authorities could see their way to act in unison in the matter, it would have presented a unique opportunity of a splendid object lesson in efficient and economical town development. The aldermen and councillors who put forward this scheme proved themselves men of insight and caution. They deserved every support and encouragement from the central authority. It is much to be regretted that the Local Government Board rejected their proposal without even troubling to hold a public inquiry.

APPENDIX II

EXTRACT FROM REPORT OF ROYAL COMMISSION ON SEWAGE DISPOSAL (1908) SEPARATE AND COMBINED SYSTEMS OF SEWERS.

296. In recent years there has been a tendency to favour the adoption of separate sewers to carry what is called surface water, and some local authorities have obtained, by means of local acts, special powers enabling them to call upon frontagers in private streets to lay down two sewers instead of one.

In the Public Health Bill of last session (1907) a clause dealing with this subject was originally included, but it was omitted during the passage of the Bill through Parliament.

In our opinion the cases in which the provision of a separate system can properly be justified are rare, and it appears to us that the relative merits of the separate and combined systems have not always been sufficiently considered.

It is obvious that the provision of two systems of sewers and two sets of house drains would very largely increase the initial outlay on drainage works, the exact amount of the increase depending on local circumstances.

It seems generally to have been assumed by advocates of the separate system that the liquid brought down by surface water sewers is sufficiently pure to need no purification, and further, that by excluding this water from the ordinary sewers a much smaller area of land or filters, as the case may be, will suffice for the purification of the sewage.

Neither of these assumptions is altogether justified.

(Note.—Par. 297.—Details of chemical and bacteriological analyses.)

298. The witnesses who have given evidence on this question have agreed that the first flush of water from a surface-water system during a storm is of such a foul nature that it ought to be purified, if practicable, especially if the system brings water from paved open spaces, such as markets, squares, etc.

Messrs G. H. Pickles and Raymond Ross gave the following analysis of a typical sample of surface water from a surface-water drain at Burnley, taken during the early period of a storm :

				Parts per 100,000
Free ammonia	..	..	..	·8
Albuminoid ammonia	..	..	..	·2
Chlorine	..	..	..	4·0
Oxygen absorbed	..	..	..	5·3
Total solids	..	..	..	71·2
Suspended matter	..	..	..	44·0

They stated also that this sample contained about 800,000 bacteria per c.c. as shown by gelatine plate cultivation at 23°C.

Mr Bolton, in his evidence relating to Heywood, gives the following analysis of a sample of road water taken in the principal streets during the first rushes of storm surface water:

			Parts per 100,000
Ammoniacal nitrogen	..	..	1·11
Albuminoid nitrogen	..	..	·49
Oxygen absorbed in three minutes	..		12·5
Oxygen absorbed in four hours	..		19·9
Chlorine	..	..	8·7
Solids in suspension	..	..	84 $\begin{cases} \text{vol. 25} \\ \text{non vol. 59} \end{cases}$
Solids in solution	..	..	73 $\begin{cases} \text{vol. 22} \\ \text{non vol. 51} \end{cases}$
Total solids	..	..	157

299. Experience also shows that with two sets of drains to each house there is danger of the sewage drain being connected with the surface-water sewer, and in densely-populated areas slops and other filthy liquids are often emptied into street gullies, and pass directly into the surface-water sewer.

There can be no doubt, therefore, that the liquid brought down by surface-water sewers is frequently of a polluting nature, and that in many cases it might be necessary to provide for its treatment.

300. As to the other assumption, that by keeping surface water out of the sewers the area of filters or land necessary for purification may be materially reduced, we may refer to the experiments which we carried out at Accrington in regard to the filtration of diluted and undiluted septic tank liquor (see pages 16 and 110 et seq.).

These experiments showed that, within ordinary limits of concentration and volumes treated, the amount and nature of the organic impurity present mainly determine, in practice, the ease or difficulty of purification; in other words, that, within limits, mere dilution does not affect the size of the filtering plant which is necessary. Of course, if the dilution is so great as to cause water-logging of the filters, their purifying power would be seriously diminished, and this statement would not hold good.

We may also observe that the flushing of sewers by rain water, which occurs with the combined system, is in itself useful, and that there is some evidence to show that filters work better when storm sewage, from which the solids have been settled, is occasionally passed through them.

301. As regards the cases in which the adoption of a separate system for surface water may be allowed, we may refer to the evidence of Dr Fowler, Mr Watson and Mr Wilkinson. These gentlemen have had considerable experience, and they expressed the view that in large towns the separate system is impracticable, that in urban districts a combined system is justified on sanitary and economical grounds, and that only in villages, country districts, and suburban areas, where there is little traffic and where the surface water will not be very foul, may the separate system sometimes be adopted with advantage.

With these views we generally concur, and we think it would be unwise to confer on all local authorities power to enforce the adoption of the separate system of sewerage, and the provision of two sets of drains in every house.

In our opinion this power should not be conferred on any local authority until the local circumstances have been carefully considered by some independent tribunal.

RECOMMENDATION

302. We recommend that in any case in which a local authority wishes to adopt the separate system of drainage for the whole or any part of their district, they should be required to apply to the Central Authority, and that the Central Authority should be empowered to confer on the local authority, by order, such powers as may be deemed necessary.

As regards the powers which may be necessary, we may observe that the provisions which are generally contained in local Acts in regard to this matter seem to be defective. If separate sewers are provided, the local authority should have a clear power to enforce the provision of separate drains, but the local Acts to which our attention has been drawn do not modify the powers of the local authority under the general law in regard to by-laws as to the drainage of houses.

Moreover, the powers of the local authority in this connexion should not necessarily be limited to new streets and new houses.

As a general rule, the expense of altering existing drains should fall on the local authority, and there may be some instances in which it would be equitable that they should bear some portion of the additional cost even in the case of drains being constructed for the first time.

The Central Authority should therefore have power to include in their Order such provisions for the allocation of the cost as they consider equitable, having regard to the local circumstances.

APPENDIX III

BIRMINGHAM TAME AND REA DISTRICT DRAINAGE BOARD ENGINEER'S REPORT

TO THE WORKS COMMITTEE ON THE SEPARATE AND COMBINED SYSTEMS OF SEWERAGE IN THE BOARD'S DISTRICT

July 10, 1912.

With the cognizance of the Local Government Board, the Drainage Board has been engaged during the past decade in constructing for the purification of sewage a biological plant of a capacity which corresponds with the recommendations of the Royal Commission on Sewage Disposal.

In regard to such plants, the Local Government Board have adopted the views of the Royal Commission, and now call upon all Local Authorities in constructing new works to provide for the treatment of three times the dry-weather flow on bacteria beds or land, and an additional three times the dry-weather flow in tanks—in all, six times the dry-weather flow—before the sewage-cum-rain is allowed to enter the river untreated.

Notwithstanding the fact that the law has not been altered, and the Board is as much obliged to conform to the requirements of the 17th Section of the Public Health Act as it ever was, there has been created amongst engineers and others whose influence in this regard will be felt when the projected Public Health Bill is brought forward, a conviction that it is absurd to compel Local Authorities to spend money in purifying more than six times the dry-weather flow during time of storm. This conviction has received countenance from the Recommendations of the Royal Commission on Sewage Disposal, dated August 7, 1908, and the regulations which practically embody those recommendations subsequently issued by the Local Government Board.

These facts should be borne in mind in considering the subject of the remit, indeed they are so important that they may be said to justify the Committee in reconsidering the attitude which they should adopt towards Constituent Authorities who are anxious to curtail the expense of sewering new districts.

The Board's chief concern in the question of combined versus separate sewers is almost entirely confined to the effect which either system is likely to have upon the volume of sewage arriving at their works. The relative merits of laying sewers capable of carrying both sewage and rain water (termed the combined system) and sewers to carry sewage only (termed the separate system) embrace considerations other than those in which the Drainage Board are interested. For instance, it may be much more economical for a Local Authority to minimize the size of a main sewer by adopting a separate drain for surface water than by constructing a combined sewer of great length.

Probably the chief advantage of the separate system is the smaller size of pipe or culvert required, which means reduced space for the formation and storage of sewer gas, exclusion of road grit, and less chance of sewers silting up.

The disadvantages of the separate system are:

1. It costs a Local Authority about two-thirds more; there is additional cost for maintenance, and it entails greater expense in the erection of dwellings and other property drained on that system.

2. There is some danger of a foul-water drain being connected to the rain-water drain, and, in densely-populated districts, of slops entering into surface-water gullies.

3. The system tends to engender a false security. For instance, when the system is first started, the surface water may contain nothing more harmful than road grit and sand, but as the population grows imperceptibly, organic matter is added and foulness results.

The merits or demerits of the separate system chiefly concern the Constituent Authority, but the Drainage Board are interested to know that under the separate system there is no guarantee that only sewage will reach the works. For example, the volume which reaches the works from Sutton Coldfield, which is on the separate system, is much greater in time of rain, and in this connexion I may refer to the evidence of the late Mr G. R. Strachan, given before the Royal Commission on Sewage Disposal. He referred to the London suburb of Chiswick, where the system was separate, and where every drop of sewage had to be pumped; there, he stated, as much as twelve times the dry weather flow found its way to the pumps.

There are no storm water overflows on the foul sewers in Sutton Coldfield, and there are only thirteen in Smethwick, but there are eighty on the sewers of Birmingham, and all are set to come into operation when the volume exceeds six times the dry weather flow.

I do not know how the standard of six times the dry weather flow came to be fixed upon by the Local Government Board originally, but it appears to be generally correct. Where a district is exceptionally large, however, it would appear to be somewhat high, and example of this may be readily found in the Board's district, which is 107 square miles in area, with a normal flow of say 30,000,000 gallons per day. If a thunderstorm confined to one square mile produced 107 times the dry weather flow over the 640 acres (and as much as 150 times the dry weather flow has been measured in Birmingham) it is obvious that this volume, which is almost wholly surface water, would not increase the volume arriving at the Outfall Works by more than one dilution, and if that increase of volume had taken place where there was no trunk sewer to receive it, the bulk of it would have been made to flow over a storm water overflow weir into the nearest brook.

The volume arriving at the Saltley Works frequently amounts to ten times—and it occasionally rises to twelve times—the dry weather flow, notwithstanding the existence of the partially separate system in most of the suburban areas, and what is of even more account, the existence of about 100 storm water overflows which come into operation to relieve the trunk sewers when the volume rises to the ten or twelve times the dry weather flow referred to.

The Board must always have a vital interest in the volume of liquid sent to the Sewage Works, and any effort on the part of a Constituent Authority to limit that volume is to be commended, but, in my opinion, it should not be assumed that the Board favours what is called the separate system in order to accomplish that end, as the same end—so far as the Board is concerned—can be accomplished by the adoption of the storm water overflows (when such can be provided) located at suitable places.

The Royal Commission on Sewage Disposal have recently inquired into all the phases of the subject so exhaustively, and their views have been set out so clearly in their Fifth Report, dated August 7, 1908, that I feel it is unnecessary for me to say more than indicate that my views are generally in agreement with those expressed in that Report.

JOHN D. WATSON

APPENDIX IV

EPITOME OF LOCAL GOVERNMENT BOARD REGULATIONS DIVIDED INTO FOUR STAGES

FIRST STAGE

CONSIDERATION AS TO ADVISABILITY OF PREPARING A SCHEME

Committee report to Council suggesting an area for a scheme.
Article II. Council decide to consider the proposal.

SECOND STAGE

APPLICATION FOR PERMISSION TO PREPARE A SCHEME

No. of Article

2. Within 7 days serve notice of decision to consider a scheme on any council interested.

Prepare for deposit and mark " Map No. 1 " (25.344 scale) showing area of scheme; a copy for declaration and a copy for each council interested.

Arrange for place to deposit map and for person to explain it.

Prepare newspaper notice of intention to apply.

Prepare notice to owners, lessees, etc., of intention to apply and as to inspection, etc., of map.

Prepare notice convening meeting of owners, lessees, etc.

Prepare list of owners, lessees and occupiers of land in area and of Councils and Government Departments affected.

1(b). Deposit Map No. 1 and serve 1(d) certified copies on councils affected.

1(a). Insert newspaper notice in some local paper or papers.

1(a). Serve notice of intention to apply on owners, lessees, etc.

3. Serve 14 days' notice of owners' meeting on ditto (preferably at the same time).

1(b). Keep Map No. 1 deposited for one month after serving of last notice.

1(a). After such service wait two months.

3. During this two months hold owners' meeting and open same by an explanation of scheme.

3. Consider written objections or representations and endeavour by conference to secure co-operation.

4(b) 6 and 7. Prepare and mark " Map No. 2 " (25.344 scale).

On this map must be shown:

    1. Land in local authority's area.

2. Land in area of any other local authority.
3. Land already built upon.
4. Land not likely to be used for building purposes.
5. Positions of any buildings erected or in course of erection on the land.
6. Lines and widths of proposed principal roads and their connexion with existing roads.
7. Sewers, gas, water and electric mains.
8. Roads or ways to be diverted or stopped up.
9. Areas for open spaces or special purposes.

The information given upon Map No. 1 may be combined in the copy of Map No. 2, thus saving the cost of one map.

10. Prepare estimate of cost of scheme.
8. Prepare statement describing scheme and land affected, reasons for application, etc., etc.

If any land already built upon is included in the scheme give reasons for including it.

Say how much land values will be increased.

Committee report to the Council.

4(a). Council resolve to apply for leave to make scheme (the resolution must refer to Map No. 2).

Prepare and send to the Local Government Board the following documents:

4(c). Certified copy resolution of Council.
4(c). Statement as to voting.
5(a) and 31. Statutory declaration proving compliance with regulations.
31. List of persons served (exhibited to declaration).
31. Copy of Map No. 1 (exhibited to declaration).
31. Copy of each notice to owners, etc. (exhibited to declaration).
31. Copy of each newspaper.
5(b). Certified copy of Map No. 2 (above-mentioned).
5(c). Map No. 3 (1-in. scale) showing the district.
5(d). Copy of objections.
8. Descriptive statement as to scheme (above-mentioned).
10(a). Estimate (above-mentioned).
10(b). Statement as to rates, etc.
4(c). Covering letter by Clerk to the Council.

11. Advertise notice of application to Board.

Local Government Board inquiry.

Wait for Board's authority to prepare scheme.

On receipt of such authority:

See 12(d). Arrange for place for inspection of and for person to explain Board's order.

12. Prepare and serve notice to owners, lessees, councils, etc., that authority given and that order may be seen, etc. (pending preparation of scheme) at time, etc., to be specified.

12. Prepare and insert newspaper notice to same effect in local paper or papers.

(Both these notices must state that Locality proposes to prepare scheme and that any person interested or affected or any person representing architectural or archæological societies desiring to be HEARD should notify the Clerk to the Council in writing within 21 days from date of notice).

12(b). (If Board exclude any land from proposed scheme Locality must serve exclusion notices.)

THIRD STAGE
PREPARATION OF SCHEME
No. of Article

13. In preparing scheme Locality must consider all written objections and representations including those from architectural or archæological societies and should hear persons who desire to be heard.

After this 21 days, and

14. When Locality have fully considered and developed their proposals and have decided (by further resolution of Council) to prepare a scheme, prepare and print draft scheme and prepare Map No. 4 (or if need be Maps No. 4a, 4b, etc.) (25.344 scale).

This map or these maps must show:

1. Clearly by means of boundary lines sharply defined in colour, the area of land included, distinguishing between that in local authority's area and that outside.

2. All such particulars and details as can conveniently be indicated by the aid of reference numbers or letters, descriptive notes distinguishing colours or otherwise.

3. Existing main roads.

4. Roads repairable by the inhabitants at large.
5. Roads or footways over which the public have a right of way.
6. Roads on which tramways or light railways (a) have been constructed, or (b) are authorized to be constructed.
7. Roads which the local authority propose shall be made as part of the scheme, indicating the widths thereof and any proposals as to the parts thereof to be appropriated or set apart for special purposes, and the connexions of such roads with existing roads.
8. Roads or ways which it is proposed to stop up or divert.
9. Land already built upon.
10. Land not likely to be used for building purposes.
11. Land proposed to be allocated for use as open spaces (a) private, or (b) public.
12. Land to be used for any other purposes including, e.g., buildings for manufacturing purposes or buildings of a special character in reference either to the purposes to which they are to be applied or to their height or otherwise indicating any restrictions— proposals as to the number of buildings which may be erected on any portion of land or each acre in any portion of land.
13. Land to be acquired by the local authority for any purpose.
14. Lines of existing sewers or any existing pipes or mains for the supply of water, gas or electricity.
15. Proposals as to lines of sewers or of pipes or mains for supply of water, gas or electricity.

16(b). Arrange for place for inspection of, and for person to explain printed scheme and Map No. 4.

16(a). Deposit scheme and Map No. 4 accordingly.

16(a). At least one month before Council meet to approve scheme, prepare and serve notice to owners, lessees, councils, etc., that a draft scheme has been prepared and will be submitted to Board—that deposited scheme and map may be inspected, etc., and that Locality will consider written objections or representations received during 21 days.

16(a). At the same time prepare and insert newspaper notice to same effect in local paper or papers.

17. Preferably at same time prepare and serve on owners, lessees, councils, etc., 14 days' notice of owners' meeting.

16(b). (Keep scheme deposited for 21 days).
    Committee report scheme to Council.

18. Council having decided on scheme to submit to Board for approval, make and seal an order making the scheme. They also seal " Map No. 5 " containing same details as " Map No. 4 " and, if identical, Map No. 4 may be used and marked " Map No. 5."

19. Council resolve to apply to Board to approve scheme.

FOURTH STAGE

APPROVAL OF SCHEME

Prepare and send following documents to Board:

No. of Article

19. (a) Certified copy of resolution to apply for approval.

19. (b) Covering letter by Clerk to the Council.

19. (c) Statement as to voting.

20(a) and 31. (d) Statutory declaration and exhibits as required by article 31 (see (w) etc., below).

20(b). (e) A sealed and three other copies of order making scheme.

20(b). (f) Certified copy of every map referred to in order.

20(c). (g) Map No. 6 (6-in. scale) showing the district boundaries and land in scheme. Map No. 6 must also show (by distinctive colouring and reference notes) all recreation grounds or public open spaces and public elementary schools in area shown on Map No. 4, also all buildings then erected and (on land in scheme) which buildings were begun since application to Board for leave to prepare scheme.

20(d). (h) Map No. 7 (25.344 scale or larger) showing separate ownerships of land in scheme with names on them; or numbered with a correspondingly numbered list of owners attached.

20(e). (i) Copies of all outstanding (written) objections.

20(a). (j) A statement giving if altered, or, if not, the particulars required by arts. 8 and 9; i.e., descriptive statement (so far as not in scheme).

21(b) (II). (l) Information as to tramways or light railways constructed or authorized in or near land in scheme.

21(b) (III). (m) Information as to whether lands required by locality itself (or other locality) can probably be acquired by agreement.

21(b) (IV). (n) Particulars of land in scheme belonging to locality or to any other local authority why and under what authority acquired and whether its use is to be altered under scheme.

21(b) (V). (o) Information as to property injuriously affected by scheme and extent of affection.

21(b) (VI). (p) Detailed particulars of works required by scheme to be executed by any person or authority.

21(b) (VII). (q) Explanation of and reason justifying any suspension by scheme of general Act of Parliament, etc.

21(b) (IX). (r) Particulars of common, open space, or allotment land under section 63 of 1909 Act within area of scheme and how it would be affected by scheme.

21(b) (X). (s) Ditto of land near royal parks.

22(a). (t) Estimate of cost of scheme with heads of receipts and expenditure as in art. 22(a).

22(b). (u) Amended statement under art. X if needed; i.e., as to rates, etc.

22(c). (v) List and copy of all local Acts, provisional orders, by-laws, or regulations, in force in any part of any authority's area invading scheme area.

31. The following are to be exhibited to above statutory declaration:
    (w) List of persons served with notice (under art. 12) of proposal to prepare scheme and with notice (under art. 16) of draft scheme having been prepared.
    (x) A copy of the notice served under art. 12.
    (y) Copy of each newspaper containing advertisement under ditto.
    (z) Copy of the notice served under art. 16.
    (aa) Ditto of each newspaper containing advertisement under ditto.
    (bb) Statement showing the several parcels of land in respect of which notice served on each owner, lessee, etc., under art. 16.
    (cc) Copies of the maps deposited for inspection under ditto.

23. Immediately after submitting a scheme to Board for approval advertise fact in local paper or papers and in same notice notify right for a month to inspect copy of scheme submitted and to state objections to Board. Arrange for inspection accordingly.

23. Send copy of papers to Board.

24. Art. 24 deals with procedure in cases where Board approve scheme subject to modifications or conditions. The Board send down a draft order, a copy of which is then to be served on each owner, lessee, etc., with notice that objections may be made to the Board within a month and a newspaper notice is to be given as to deposit and inspection of draft order for a month. Within the month Locality must raise their own objections, and send statutory declaration as to compliance with this article.

   Note. If the Board make any modifications even in the wording of the general provisions various notices must be served on owners and other formalities observed. The first town planning scheme approved by the Board after a three years' struggle with the regulations was delayed a further five months by these safeguards. There are quite enough reasonable difficulties and objections to be dealt with without creating artificial ones.

   Wait for Board's decision.

25(a). When Board transmit to Locality draft order for approving scheme, Locality within 14 days advertise in local paper or papers that Board intend to approve scheme and to publish their intention in " London Gazette " and that objections should be made to the Board within 21 days.

25(b). Send copy paper or papers to Board.

25(c). Deposit draft order of Board approving scheme and keep deposited for inspection for 21 days from " London Gazette " notice. (No notice that such deposit is to be made has to be given.)

27(a). On receipt of order of Board approving scheme publish (under art. 27) notice of approval in local paper and state that for three months inspection may be made of order and any map referred to in it.

27(b). Next serve copy of order on owners, lessees, councils, etc., and notify them that maps may be inspected as above.

27(b). Deposit and arrange for inspection accordingly.

27(c). Within 14 days from receiving order make and send Board statutory declaration as to compliance with art. 27 and exhibit following documents:

31. (a) Copy of order.

31. (b) Copy of notice served.

31. (c) Copy of newspaper containing advertisement.

28 to 36. The remaining regulations deal with general matters, such as service in proper cases of notice on Board of Agriculture, Commissioners of Works, Board of Trade, Light Railway Commissioners, etc., methods of serving notices, provisions as to maps, information to Board, departure from regulations etc.

APPENDIX V. MODEL SET OF GENERAL PROVISIONS

The object of this appendix is to give not precisely an example of the final scheme as mentioned in Chapter III (under the Third Stage, Second Step), but rather a model set of general provisions applicable to any proposed town planning scheme. This must be accomplished by drawings and specifications for road cross-sections and also by the map of the area. The cross-sections given below would not perhaps be generally understood without some explanation of modern road-making. The advent of tramway and motor traffic creates a new problem for surveyors. Again, the success of town planning schemes hinges very largely on the possibilities of economies in town and estate development of which road-making is a very important part.

CROSS-SECTIONS OF ROADS

It is unwise to have more roadway than is sufficient for the traffic, because in that case the road will not be worn evenly all over, which means that the rain will not be carried so readily to the side gutters, and there is nothing worse for a road and more annoying to the public than puddles. There is also the extra cost of construction and upkeep, for the more roadway there is the more it must cost in construction and maintenance. 8 ft. is sufficient width for one line of traffic and 16 ft. allows ample room for two streams of traffic to pass each other at full speed. It is, therefore, advisable to settle the width of roadways in multiples of 8 ft. As regards the material to be used in road-making, it is now slowly but surely coming to be recognized that water-bound roads are out of date. The dust in summer is most obnoxious, and the mud in winter is even more objectionable. What is needed is a material that will be dustless in summer, mudless in winter, and not too slippery for horses. Various means of achieving these ends are now being devised. Different surveyors will choose different methods, and different localities have varying materials at hand, and, therefore, I have in the following cross-sections only shown the WIDTH of roadway, leaving individual surveyors to settle their own construction, in which they will be much assisted by the Road Board specifications. Before leaving this question of road material a word of warning should be given against confining road makers to one or two quarries for their material. It is ridiculous to suggest that suitable material can only be obtained from one or two quarries, and every business man will recognize at once that action like this by public bodies creates a most undesirable monopoly, which must increase the cost of materials, and, therefore, of road-making, for which the ratepayers and rent payers of the district have to pay.

In the first town planning scheme in this country no less than twelve cross-sections are given. This is a relic of the by-law system under which every minutest detail must be laid down and strictly adhered to. It is not only unnecessary, it is most inadvisable, because town planning, to be successful, must be elastic. Our inelastic by-law system is responsible for great evils; it must give way to more elastic common-sense methods.

On the opposite side will be found a cross-section for a 100-ft. main artery when completed, and another section showing all that need be constructed in the first instance in order to open up cheap land for building, so as to keep down expenditure until rate-income is available to pay for it.

In some places, main arteries have been or are being made more than 100 ft. wide. In other places, less than 100 ft. is considered necessary for the traffic and quite sufficiently expensive. I have taken 100 ft. as a fair average width, but of course it can be varied.

SECTION 1

The footpaths should be of some tarry material that will not go soft in summer, and with a rough surface, so that they will not be slippery in winter. Stone flagging is quite unnecessary and very expensive. Near the middle of this section 26 ft. 6 ins. is left for an independent tram track in case trams should be considered necessary. If, as many expect, trams are superseded by motor-buses or some other form of traction, then this part of the road can be appropriated for pedestrians or equestrians and trees planted on either side of it. The building lines should be set back at least 15 ft. but not more, unless so desired by the owner, because front gardens are not nearly so useful as gardens at the back. By setting back the building lines 15 ft. we get 130 ft. between the houses, which, without the demolition of any buildings, gives ample room for adding to the roadways and footpaths, if at any time this artery should become a business street, and no longer

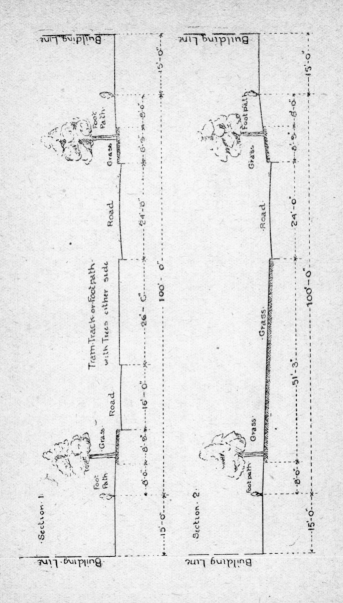

Section · 1.

Building Line

15'-0"

8'-0" × 8'-0" × 16'-0"
Foot Path / Grass / Road

26-0"
Tram Track or foot path.
with Trees either side

24'-0"
Road

6'-0" × 6'-0"
Grass / Foot Path

15'-0"

100'-0"

Building Line

Section · 2.

Building Line

15'-0"

8'-0"
foot path / Grass

51'-3"
Grass.

24'-0"
Road.

6'-0" × 6'-0"
Grass / Foot path

15'-0"

100'-0"

Building Line

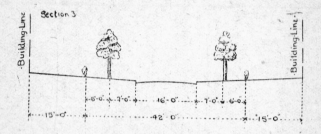

Section 3

Building Line — Building Line

6'-0" · 7'-0" · 16'-0" · 7'-0" · 6'-0"

15'-0" · · · · · 42'-0" · · · · · 15'-0"

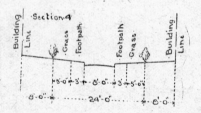

Section 4

Building Line — Grass · Footpath · Footpath · Grass · Building Line

5'-0" · 3' · 8'-0" · 3' · 5'-0"

8'-0" · · · · · 24'-0" · · · · · 8'-0"

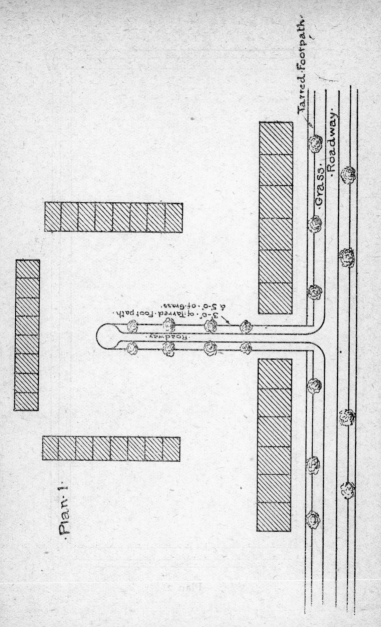

Plan 1.

Tarred Footpath.

Grass.

Roadway.

3'-0" of Tarred Foot path.
& 5'-0" of Grass.

Roadway.

Plan 2.

merely remain a main artery through a residential district. Those who have watched the growth of towns are aware that these changes are continually taking place, and by looking ahead and making provision for such changes town planning will save money for the ratepayers of the future without any extra expense in the present. A 16-ft. roadway will sooner or later be necessary for the convenience of frontagers on the left-hand side of the road.

SECTION 2

In the initial stages, 24 ft. width of roadway will in most cases be ample for the traffic for some years to come. It is unwise as well as extravagant to put more than this width at first. The grass margins should not be cut too often, for this is the best way to protect them from being trampled down in wet weather or scorched by the sun in dry weather.

In cases where a width of less than 100 ft. down to, say, 60 ft. is all that is available these two sections will have to be modified. They give the general idea and general principles on which to work.

No sewers or drains are shown in these cross-sections, but as sewers are, under present conditions, part and parcel of road-making, they must be mentioned here.

For the sake of economy small shallow drains should be laid behind the houses, as on the estate of Harborne Tenants Limited, Birmingham, and not in the roads at all. Disconnecting traps are unnecessary and objectionable (see Appendix VI). Street gullies can be connected to surface-water drains behind the houses.

No manhole covers should be placed in the carriage way; no cover yet designed will stand heavy traffic properly, and these covers with their stone surrounds are a constant source of trouble and annoyance to those who use the road. The road material wears away sooner than the stone surrounds, thereby causing a vexatious bump every time a vehicle is driven over a manhole. Open covers tend to make manholes exceedingly dirty. Sewer manholes should be located in the grass verges. If sewers were put under the grass verges, they would not have to stand heavy traffic. Concrete sewers properly made and protected with tiles or asphalt are quite satisfactory elsewhere, and should be experimented with in England. The methods used for calculating flows are often obsolete. There are many cases where sewers have never been called upon to carry half what they are capable of, and also cases where large sewers have been deliberately laid down to discharge into a smaller one, in spite of the fact that the large sewers had a bigger incline than the smaller one.

SECTION 3

For purely residential districts, this section is adequate and all that the landowner should be called upon to construct when developing his estate for building. The footpaths may be placed next the roadway or next the forecourt. If through traffic demands a greater width of roadway, then it is only fair that the general public should pay for what is done to suit their convenience, the landowner giving free of charge any land that is required. The remarks concerning sewers and drains in roads made to sections 1 and 2 or modifications thereof apply with equal force to this section 3.

SECTION 4

It will be seen from plan 1 that the width of this street is only 24 ft. with 8 ft. of space either side, where it passes between the blocks of houses fronting on to the main 16-ft. roadways, making 40 ft. in all between the houses. But this narrow part is only for the length of road equal to the depth of the houses between which it passes to the quadrangle beyond. There is ample air space round all the houses. By adopting this method of development for the cheaper cottages we supplement the saving in cost of land (see Chapter II), and make cottages at net rents of 4s. 3d. and 3s. 6d. per week a sound business proposition for the builder. There is a crying need for decent, sanitary, and cheerful cottages at these rents. Once make these cheap cottages as good a business proposition as dearer ones and the supply so badly needed will be forthcoming. This 8-ft. roadway is provided with a circle at the end, the radius of which is 12 ft. in order to give vehicles room to turn round. The length of this narrow road should be 500 ft. in order to enable cottages to be built on the main 16-ft. roadway, thereby avoiding a waste of frontage. In this case, it will be noticed that next to the roadway is a 3-ft. footpath, which should be tarred so as to save cost of upkeep. As a rule, the roadway will be used as a footpath, but there must be a narrow footpath to step on to when vehicles drive up to the square. The same section will provide all the access necessary to cottages placed round and fronting on to an open space, such as that shown in plan 2, but in this case it will not be necessary to put a footpath or grass verge on the side of the road next the playing field. It is by means such as these, and because light and air are much cheaper than kerbs and gutters, that we can make decent housing at low rents pay the builder.

GENERAL PROVISIONS

Definitions

1. " The Locality "* means all the members of the local authority and inhabitants of the town, city or district.

" The Board " means the Local Government Board.

" The Act of 1909 " means the Housing, Town Planning, etc., Act of 1909.

" The Map " means the map sealed in connexion with the order of the Locality making the scheme.

The several words or expressions which are not defined or used in Part II of the Act of 1909, but which are defined in the Public Health Act, 1875, shall (subject as hereinafter provided) have the same several meanings when used in this scheme as are specified in the latter Act, and land shall include any interest in land. Provided that for the purpose of clauses 7, 8, 9, 11, 15, 16, 17 and 38 of this scheme " owner " shall have the same meaning as in the Public Health Act, 1875.

The street cross-sections appended to this scheme and numbered 1 to 4 respectively shall operate and have effect as part of this scheme, and are hereinafter referred to as sections 1, 2, 3 and 4.

RESPONSIBLE AUTHORITY

Responsible Authority.

2. The Locality shall be the authority responsible for enforcing the observance of this scheme, and for the execution of any works which under this scheme or Part II of the Act of 1909 are to be executed by a local authority.

AREA

Area.

3. The area to which this scheme shall apply (hereinafter called " the area ") shall be that within the boundary line coloured neutral tint on the map.

* " Locality " is not a good term but it seems to cover best all sorts of town planning authorities.

STREETS

4. Here must come a description of the new streets (which expression shall include widenings of old streets) that are to be constructed by the Locality under and in accordance with the scheme. These streets must be indicated on the map and numbered for identification. Each street must be described under its own number, and in this description should be mentioned well-known landmarks and the numbers of the enclosures on the ordnance map that are crossed by the street. At the end of this descriptive list of new streets should come a proviso that with the consent of the Locality, the new streets above described or any of them or any part thereof may be constructed by any person other than the Locality on such terms as to cost as the Locality may agree.

5. The time must be settled when these new streets or any of them or any part thereof shall be constructed. Any street or streets necessary for providing adequate access to the area must be constructed forthwith in accordance with section 2 or a section similar thereto. Other streets may be commenced at the discretion of the Locality subject to the right of any person aggrieved by the delay of the Locality in completely constructing any such streets to appeal to the Board.

Streets shall be deemed to have been commenced within the meaning of this clause as soon as they are cut or laid out to formation level and the bottom layer of the foundation has been laid thereon.

6. With regard to any one of the new streets above described the Locality shall complete the construction of the carriage way and footways thereof, if and when not less than 75 per cent of the total frontage to the street shall have been built up to or appropriated as curtilages for buildings in existence at the time, and any necessary drains, gas, water or other services in connexion with the buildings in the street have been laid, but otherwise (subject to clause 5 hereof) the streets mentioned in this clause shall (subject to the right of any person aggrieved by the delay of the Locality in constructing the same to appeal to the Board) be constructed by the Locality at such respective times as they shall determine in each case, provided that any street 100 ft. wide to be constructed by the Locality shall be deemed to be constructed within the meaning of this clause when so much of it shall have been completed as appears in street cross-section 2. Provided further that any such street, 100-ft. wide, may be constructed as

appears in street cross-section 1 as and when the Locality shall think fit.

Method of constructing streets; building lines

7. Should give a table as follows:

Number of New Street	Number of Cross-section

(a) The numbers in the first column refer to the numbers of the new streets described above and the numbers in the second column refer to the numbers of street cross-sections, and the respective streets numbered in the said first column shall be constructed in accordance with the respective street cross-sections shown opposite thereto in the said second column. Provided that in the case of any street or part of a street that is to be constructed partly or wholly at the expense of the Locality on the general lines of sections 1 and 2, and which is not 100 ft. wide, the Locality shall determine what width of roadway shall be provided, but the owner of any land deriving benefit shall not be called upon for more than the contribution specified in clause (11) or any other sum that may have been specially agreed upon. Any person deeming himself aggrieved by any delay or requirement by the Locality under this clause may appeal to the Board.

(b) All streets in the area constructed otherwise than by the Locality shall be constructed in conformity with the provisions of this scheme with such turning and crossing places and access ways from the carriage way to the forecourt and of such materials, of such widths (not exceeding 16 ft. width of roadway except by agreement) on such sites and generally in such manner as shall be required by the Locality and shall not be commenced until all necessary notices have been first sent to the Locality and until all plans and sectional drawings shall have been first submitted to and approved by the Locality. The mode of construction of any such street shall conform to such one of the street cross-sections as shows the width required under this clause, or to such other street cross-section submitted by the owner as the Locality may in any particular case approve. Provided that where any street cross-section shall have been determined under this clause the Locality may require that the street in question shall be constructed according to a cross-section involving greater cost in construction, in which case the street shall be constructed in conformity with the last-mentioned cross-section, and the additional cost shall be borne by the Locality. Any person aggrieved by any requirement of the Locality under this clause as to the materials, widths, or sites of any new street may appeal against the same to the Board.

(c) The building lines in respect of the new streets above described shall be those shown on the cross-sections.

Streets giving access to quadrangles.

(d) Where any person intends to erect dwelling-houses round a quadrangle or other open space, such person may construct the roadway giving access to such buildings so that the width thereof shall be not less than 8 ft. if the following conditions are complied with, viz.:

    (i) The total length of such street shall not exceed 500 ft.

    (ii) Such street shall communicate with a street constructed for use as a carriage road with not less than 16-ft. width of roadway.

    (iii) The space within the quadrangle or other open space so far as not occupied by such street shall be laid out as forecourts or gardens.

    (iv) No fence or wall within the quadrangle or other open space shall be erected which shall exceed 3 ft. 6 in. in height.

    (v) The distance between building lines of 40 ft. shown in section 4 shall not extend for a distance of more than 40 ft., see plan 1. Beyond this the distance between building lines for such streets must not be less than 100 ft.

(e) Where the building lines shown on the plans submitted vary from the building lines shown on the sections and applicable to the street in question they shall be subject to the approval of the Locality.

(f) No building or other erection other than a boundary wall or fence shall be constructed nearer to the centre of the street than the building line shown on the street cross-sections aforesaid or approved as aforesaid.

(g) Any consent of the Locality under Section 3 of the Public Health (Building in Streets) Act, 1888, shall not be unreasonably withheld.

(h) The expression " any house or building " where it first occurs in such section shall be deemed to include any hoarding or similar structure used or adapted for use for the purpose of advertising.

8. In the event of the owners representing not less than three-quarters of the total length of frontage to a street requesting the

Locality to pave the footpaths the Locality may, if they deem it desirable to do so, take up the gravel and lay paving in lieu thereof, and declare the cost to be private improvement expenses, in which case such cost shall be dealt with in the same way as private improvement expenses under the Public Health Act, 1875.

Street plans for adjoining estates

9. In addition to any powers now or hereafter conferred upon them by section 17 of the Public Health Amendment Act, 1907, or any Act amending the same, the Locality, whenever any plan for a new street within the area shall be submitted to them for approval, may by notice in writing require any owner or owners of any estate or lands, the development of which will be affected by the construction of such street, to furnish to the Locality at the expense of such owner or owners and within a reasonable time to be specified in such notice, plans and particulars showing generally a scheme for the development or laying out of such estate or lands.

Incidental street works

10. So far as the Locality may deem necessary they may require that any person constructing or laying out streets in the area shall fence the same and plant them with trees and that he shall provide and construct all proper approaches, embankments, bridges, arches, girders, retaining walls, culverts, drains, works and conveniences connected therewith or incident thereto; and for the purpose of commencing or constructing any of the new streets above described the Locality may provide and construct all such works as aforesaid as may be necessary.

Cost of constructing streets

11. The cost of construction of streets shall be defrayed in the following manner: In the case of any street in the area constructed otherwise than by the Locality the whole cost shall be defrayed by the person constructing the street unless the Locality shall agree (and they are hereby empowered to agree) with such person to contribute to the cost. Some of the new streets described and numbered in clause 4 of this scheme shall be constructed by the Locality wholly at their own expense, other streets will be constructed by the Locality partly at their own expense and partly at the expense of the frontagers. It will be necessary to specify which streets are to be constructed wholly at the expense of the Locality and which only partly at their expense. The owner of any land deriving benefit from a new street shall (unless the Locality other-

wise agree with him) if and as soon as any such land shall be brought into rating for other than agricultural purposes repay to the Locality a contribution towards the cost not exceeding £3 10s. per yard of the frontage of his land to the said street or (at the option of the Locality) equal to such sum as may represent the degree of benefit accruing to his land whether fronting to or communicating with the said street from the construction of such street. The amount of such contribution in either case shall be assessed by the surveyor for the time being of the Locality, and approved of by them, and from their decision as to the amount or degree of benefit, any owner may within two calendar months from such decision appeal to the Board or to an arbitrator mutually agreed upon.

Maintenance of streets

12. (a) The Locality shall maintain in a condition suitable for public traffic until constructed, any of the new streets described in clause 4 of this scheme, the construction of which shall have been commenced by them within the meaning of clause (5) of this scheme and which shall have been opened for public traffic.

(b) Any streets constructed by the Locality shall thereafter be maintained by them as public highways.

(c) Streets constructed otherwise than by the Locality, if originally constructed in accordance with this scheme to the satisfaction of the Locality or their duly authorized officer, and subsequently made up and completed to the like satisfaction under any statutory enactment shall when, but unless otherwise agreed not till, they have to the extent of 75 per cent of their total frontage been built up to or appropriated as curtilages for buildings in existence at the time and the necessary services as referred to in clause (6) of this scheme have been laid, be taken over and thereafter maintained by the Locality as public highways.

Grass margins, etc.

13. (a) In the case of any of the new streets described in clause 4 of this scheme, the Locality may plant bushes and shrubs therein and may erect guards or fences for the protection of such bushes and shrubs and of any embankments and grass margins, and may thereafter maintain, alter or renew the same, and may take such steps as seem to them desirable to maintain all trees, bushes, shrubs and grass margins in the streets in good order and condition.

Provided that the powers of the Locality under this clause shall not be exercised nor shall any bushes or shrubs so planted be continued so as to hinder the reasonable use of the street by the public or any person entitled to use the same or so as to become a nuisance injurious to any adjacent owner or occupier.

(b) In the case of any other streets for the time being constructed in the area, the Locality may (subject to the last-mentioned proviso) require the person constructing the same to maintain in good order and condition until the street is taken over by the Locality all trees and grass margins and embankments therein, and to make and so maintain any proper guards and fences to the same.

(c) Every person desirous of forming a communication for horses, cattle or vehicles, across any kerbed or paved footpath or grass margin, so as to afford access from any premises from a street repairable by the inhabitants at large, shall first give notice of such desire to the Locality and shall, if so desired by them, submit to them for their approval a plan of the proposed communication showing where it will cut the footpath or grass margin and what provision (if any) is made for kerbing for gullies and for a paved crossing and the dimensions and gradients of necessary works, and shall execute the works at his own expense under the supervision and to the satisfaction of the surveyor, and, in case such plan shall have been required, then in accordance with the plan so approved and not otherwise, and if any person drives or permits or causes to be driven any horse, cattle or vehicle across any footway unless and until such a communication as aforesaid has been so made, or on or along any part of any such footway other than the part over which such communication has been made, he shall for each such offence be liable to a penalty not exceeding 40s. in addition to the amount of damage (if any) thereby done to such footway. Provided that nothing in this section shall be deemed to apply to the temporary crossing of footways during building operations, if means, satisfactory to the Locality, be taken to protect such footways from injury and for the convenience of foot passengers.

Wilful damages*

14. No person shall wilfully damage any tree, shrub or plant or grass margin in any street or any fence or guard erected thereon, and no person shall ride or drive any horse, cattle, or vehicle over or across any grass margin.

Modification of streets

15. The Board may sanction any modification in detail with reference to the position, construction or widening of any street

* In Scotland this clause is superfluous.

shown on the map which at any time and from time to time may be agreed upon between the Locality and the owner or owners interested.

Provided that no such sanction shall be given until the expiration of 21 days from the date on which notice has been given by advertisement in some newspaper circulating in the town, city or district, to the effect that the Locality have applied under the authority of this clause for the sanction of the Board to a modification to be described in the notice, and that any person objecting to such sanction being given may within such 21 days give written notice of his objection to the Board who shall take any such objection into their consideration before granting any sanction as aforesaid.

Diversion or stopping up of highways

16. The respective public highways described below shall as from but not until the respective dates on which the said proposed new streets set opposite each (or where more than one the last of them to be constructed and opened as herein mentioned) shall respectively have been constructed to an extent rendering them suitable for all traffic and opened for public traffic be deemed to be diverted or stopped up and all public rights thereover shall cease as from such respective dates. The soil up to the middle line of such highways shall thereupon be deemed to vest in the owners of the freehold of the land abutting on such highways, subject always to the rights of the Locality and others being reserved in regard to sewers, gas and water mains, electric wires and other works, but the road materials on highways diverted or stopped up may be removed by the Locality without payment if they so desire within six months of such respective dates.

The highways above referred to are as follows:

Description of highway to be diverted or stopped up	Number of new street

In the construction of any of the new streets referred to in this clause, the Locality shall (if required by the owner and at his expense) do all that may be necessary for transferring to the new street or for abandoning any sewers, gas or water-pipes, electric wires, or other works laying in the highways to be diverted or stopped up, and shall provide proper service pipes from the mains in the new street to connect up with any property now or hereafter being served by any sewers, pipes or works so transferred or abandoned. No such transfer or abandonment shall take place until notice shall have been given to any statutory undertakers affected who may, if they require, do the necessary work themselves and charge the reasonable cost thereof against the Locality, who may recover the same from the owner. Until any such work is completed the Locality or other owner of any such pipes, sewers or works shall have full access to, and the same powers with regard to, the same as they previously had.

BUILDINGS

Number of dwelling-houses and other buildings

17. (a) In this clause " dwelling-houses " shall mean houses designed for occupation by not more than one family, together with such outbuildings as are reasonably required to be used and enjoyed therewith.

(b) In reckoning the number of dwelling-houses to be erected to an acre all roads and private open spaces constructed or to be constructed and set apart or to be set apart by the owner of the lands in question, and half of the width of the highways repairable by the inhabitants at large upon which the said lands abut, shall be included in the measurement of the acre, but no account shall be taken of public open spaces acquired otherwise than by gift, subsequent to the making of this scheme or leased by the Locality and of the sites of the shops and other buildings mentioned in and approved under sub-clause (c) (iii) of this clause and subject to the provisions of this clause, an acre shall be measured so as to include such land as the Locality in each case having regard to all the circumstances determine by the order to be made under sub-clause (c) (iii) of this clause.

(c) The following provisions as to the restrictions on the number of dwelling-houses and other buildings which may be erected in the area shall have effect:

(i) The number of dwelling-houses on any one acre shall not exceed twenty.

(ii) When a plan is submitted for the approval of the Locality in regard to the erection of any building or any land included in the area which has not been previously made or included in a land unit under this clause, then:

If at that time the owner of the land does not own

any other land in the area, which is not included
in a land unit, the land included in the building plan
shall constitute a land unit for the purposes of this
clause. If at that time the owner of the land owns
other land in the area which is not included in a
land unit there shall be submitted to the Locality by
the owner an estate plan in duplicate, showing
the whole of the land of such owner in the area, but
not included in a land unit; and the Locality shall
thereupon determine whether the land included in
the building plan shall constitute by itself a land
unit, or whether all or any part of the remaining
land of such owner shall at that time, having regard
to the effect of the development of the land included
in the building plan, be added to the last-mentioned
land to form a land unit, and shall show on each
copy of the estate plan, the land they determine shall
form a land unit and return one copy of the plan to
the owner. Provided always that no land unit shall
be less than ten acres in extent and, where separate
ownerships are less than ten acres in extent, the
Locality shall upon the application of such owner
or owners determine to which land unit or land
units his or their land shall be added.

(iii) The owner before commencing to erect any dwelling-house
or other buildings on the land unit shall deposit with the
Locality a statement of the number and description of the
dwelling-houses or other buildings which he desires to
erect on the land unit, and subject to sub-clause (c) (vi)
and (d) of this clause, the Locality shall, as soon as
practicable, by order sanction the maximum number
of dwelling-houses which may be erected on the land
unit, or on each acre or other portion of the land unit,
and sanction the number and define the character or
purposes of the other buildings to be erected thereon,
but in no case shall the Locality approve the erection of
a greater or require the erection of a less number of
dwelling-houses on the land unit than will give an average
over the land unit of ten to the acre. The Locality shall
also include in the order such further provision as may
be necessary in pursuance of sub-clause (b) of this
clause in regard to the measurement of the acre. Any such

order shall be forthwith communicated to the owner, and shall, subject to any appeal as hereinafter provided, be binding on the owner and every successive owner of the land unit or any part thereof until revoked or altered, and no dwelling-houses or other buildings shall be erected on any land in the area in the absence or in contravention of any order made under this clause, or when erected, be used or adapted for purposes other than those sanctioned; and the Locality shall keep a register of such orders and a map showing all land units, which register and map shall be open to inspection by any person interested.

(iv) If, after any order as aforesaid has been made, part of the land unit to which the order relates is sold or let on building lease, and the order only specifies the number of dwelling-houses which may be erected on the part of the land unit so sold or let, together with the remainder of the land unit or some part thereof, the number of dwelling-houses to be erected on the part so sold or let and the part not so sold or let respectively, shall, subject to the maximum number sanctioned by the order of the Locality not being exceeded, and subject also to sub-clause (c) (i) of this clause, be a matter for agreement between the owners of the respective parts or be determined by the Locality in default of such agreement. The Locality may at any time on the application of any owner review any such order and by further order revoke, alter or amend the same, provided that the number of dwelling-houses on the land unit shall never be greater than will give an average over the unit of ten to the acre, and any revocation, alteration or amendment of the order shall be registered, and be binding in like manner as aforesaid.

(v) The restriction of building density to an average of ten dwelling-houses per gross acre shall apply in all cases where no guarantee is given as to the maximum weekly rent that will be charged per house, but notwithstanding any clause or sub-clause of these general provisions when an owner guarantees that the weekly rent per dwelling-house shall not exceed 4s. 3d. exclusive of rates, he shall be allowed to put twelve houses per gross acre and where the weekly rent is guaranteed not to exceed 3s. 6d. per week exclusive of rates an average of fifteen houses per gross acre shall be allowed. The observance of this condition must be ensured by an agreement between the Locality and the owner, which agreement shall form part of the scheme and be binding on all future owners of the land in question.

(vi) By the consent of the Locality, but not otherwise, such consent to be expressed by sanction as aforesaid in the orders to be made under sub-clause (c) (iii) of this clause there may be erected in the area such shops or buildings other than dwelling-houses as the Locality may think fit. Provided always that shops or buildings other than dwelling-houses shall conform in all respects to the Acts and by-laws in force for the time being in the area and applicable thereto.

(d) Any person aggrieved by any determination of the Locality under this clause whether with regard to the ascertainment of a land unit or to any order of the Locality or by any proposal to give or to any withholding of consent to the erection of shops or buildings other than dwelling-houses may appeal to the Board within one calendar month after such determination has been come to whereupon the Board shall take the matter of such appeal into their consideration and make such order as they may think just and such order shall be final and binding upon all parties concerned.

(Note.—This provision is very long and complicated. Those who believe in simplicity will probably consider that the following alternative provision covers all points.)

ALTERNATIVE

Number of dwelling-houses and other buildings

17. (a) On any owner submitting for the approval of the Corporation building plans with respect to any land for the time being owned by him, the Corporation may ascertain from such owner the total acreage of the estate at the time owned by him and may, by resolution, fix the maximum number of houses which may at any time be built on such estate always provided that the average number shall not exceed ten per gross acre and that there shall not be more than twenty houses on any one acre, and in coming to their determination they shall have regard to the open spaces reserved or agreed to be reserved, and to the number of

houses built or sanctioned in the vicinity and to any provision for streets or open spaces or reduced number of houses or to any other contribution to the amenities of the area which any owner affected by the resolution has made or has agreed to make. " Houses " shall mean dwelling-houses designed for occupation by not more than one family, and such outbuildings as are reasonably required to be used or enjoyed therewith.

By the consent of the Corporation, but not otherwise, there may be erected in the area such shops or buildings other than houses as the Corporation may think fit. Provided always that shops or other buildings shall conform in all respects to the Acts and by-laws in force for the time being in the area, and that in the event of any such approved shops or other buildings being erected the above maximum number of houses shall be reduced in such manner as the Corporation may think just.

No buildings or erections except those above sanctioned shall at any time be built in the area, and in reckoning the limit of buildings prescribed to an acre, all roads and private open spaces constructed or to be constructed and set apart or to be set apart by the owner of the lands in question, and one-half of the width of highways repairable by the inhabitants at large upon which the said lands abut shall be included in the measurement of the area, but no account shall be taken of public open spaces acquired or leased by the Corporation.

(b) The restriction of building density to an average of ten dwelling-houses per gross acre shall apply in all cases where no guarantee is given as to the maximum weekly rent that will be charged per house, but notwithstanding any clause or sub-clause of these general provisions when an owner guarantees that the weekly rent per dwelling-house shall not exceed 4s. 3d. exclusive of rates, he shall be allowed to put 12 houses per gross acre, and where the weekly rent is guaranteed not to exceed 3s. 6d. per week exclusive of rates an average of 15 houses per gross acre shall be allowed. The observance of this condition must be ensured by an agreement between the Locality and the owner, which agreement shall form part of the scheme and be binding on all future owners of the land in question.

(c) Any person aggrieved by any determination of the Locality under this clause whether with regard to the ascertainment of a land unit or to any order of the Locality or by any proposal to give or to any withholding of consent to the erection of shops or buildings other than dwelling-houses may appeal to the Board within one calendar month after such determination has been come to, whereupon the Board shall take the matter of such appeal into their consideration and make such order as they may think just and such order shall be final and binding upon all parties concerned.

Breaks in building

18. Not more than eight dwelling-houses shall in any place be built under one continuous roof or without a break in building down to ground level and no such break shall be of less width than 5 ft.

Air space and height of buildings

19. No building wall or erection of any kind shall be built or erected and no addition shall be made to any building wall or erection which (if built, erected or made) would be so situate that by reason of its proximity to or contact with any other buildings it would:

(a) Stop or impede ventilation or would otherwise make or conduce to make such other buildings in a condition unfit for human habitation or dangerous or injurious to health; or

(b) Prevent proper measures from being carried into effect for remedying any nuisance injurious to health or other evils complained of in respect to such other buildings.

Measurement of height

(c) No buildings shall be erected at a greater height measured from the level of the street in front thereof to the eaves or parapet or to half the height of the gable, whichever is the highest, than the distance from the main front wall of such building to the centre of the street in front.

Corner buildings

(d) In the case of a building on a corner site, the opposite boundary of the street shall be substituted for the centre of the street mentioned in the preceding clause for the purpose of measuring the height of the flank wall of such building.

Storeys in domestic buildings

(e) No domestic building (other than shops or flats or sets of chambers) erected in areas in which the limit of buildings to the acre exceeds eight shall contain more than two storeys exclusive of any storey constructed wholly or partly in the roof.

LANDS

Lands set apart for purpose of scheme

20. The following lands shall be deemed to be set apart for the purpose of this scheme, viz.:

(a) For the purpose of parks, open spaces, playgrounds and playing fields. The Locality shall have the like powers in regard to the said lands or any of them when acquired by the Locality, as if the same were acquired for the purposes of public walks and pleasure grounds under the Public Health Acts.

(b) For the purpose of allotments and small holdings.

(c) Any other lands which are shown on the map as set apart for sites, for public buildings, or any other purposes of this scheme, including the sites of the new streets above described and of any necessary slopes or accessory works in connexion therewith.

AMENITIES

Preservation of trees

21. No tree, the trunk of which already has or hereafter shall have attained a girth exceeding 36 ins. measured at a height of 4 ft. above the ground, shall, unless actually interfering with the erection, convenience or maintenance of any building other than fences, be destroyed without the consent of the Locality, unless it can be shown to stop or impede ventilation to dwelling-houses that are going to be erected.

Streams blocked

22. Any river, stream or watercourse or any part or parts thereof respectively so choked or silted up as to obstruct or impede the proper flow of water along the same and thereby to cause or render probable an overflow of such river, stream or watercourse on to or into the land and property adjacent thereto shall be deemed to be a nuisance within Section 91 (Definition of Nuisances) of the Public Health Act, 1875, and all the provisions of that Act relating to nuisances shall apply to every such river, stream or watercourse, notwithstanding that the same may not be injurious to health.

Culverting streams

23. (a) Before the owner of any land shall culvert or cover over any watercourse thereon forming part of the natural drainage of the area involved, he shall submit for the approval of the Locality plans, sections and specifications of such watercourse and the

method of culverting or covering over the same and the Locality may, subject as herein provided, require such owner to so construct any such culvert or so to cover over any such watercourse as to secure the free and uninterrupted passage of the water flowing in any such watercourse.

(b) Provided always that wherever it is possible to do so the Locality may insist upon watercourses being left open.

MISCELLANEOUS

24. No factory of any kind shall be erected and no manufacturing business carried on except with the consent of the Locality and in areas set aside for the purpose. But this provision shall not extend to making and burning of bricks and tiles on land already used or appropriated for the purpose or to any building now used as a factory or workshop or to any manufacture now carried on therein.

25. All private gardens, private open spaces or private allotments shall be kept in such a state as not to be a nuisance or annoyance to neighbours or to persons using the highways. The Locality may, on the report of their surveyor, serve notice on any person or persons, whether individually or jointly owning, occupying, or using any such lands as aforesaid, requiring that the nuisance or annoyance shall be abated within a reasonable time to be specified in such notice and in default of compliance with such notice, the Locality may do what is necessary to abate the nuisance or annoyance and may recover the cost from the person or persons served with the notice or from any one or more of them.

Railway sidings

26. For the purpose of facilitating the adaptation, use, or development of factory areas for business purposes, it shall be lawful for the Locality (a) to make, lay down and maintain railway sidings, sheds and other works; (b) to acquire any land necessary or convenient for any such purpose; (c) by arrangement with any railway company to connect such sidings with any railway; (d) to make terms with any person or firm for the use of any such buildings, sheds or works; and (e) to provide terminal facilities for canals.

Prohibition of advertisements

27. No person shall in the area erect, fix, place or use or permit to be used any building, hoarding, framework, structure or device

for the purpose wholly or in part of advertising without first obtaining the written consent of the Locality and then subject only to such conditions as the Locality may prescribe, but this prohibition shall not apply to the exhibition of traders' names on shops or factories or to any notices exhibited on churches, chapels or mission rooms. It shall be lawful for the Locality to remove or pull down any advertisements displayed in contravention of this clause and to enter on any land or premises for the purpose. Any person aggrieved by the Locality withholding consent under this clause may appeal to a Petty Sessional Court.

Adjustment of boundaries

28. (a) It shall be lawful for the Locality for the purposes of securing the proper laying out or development of any estate or lands within the area in respect of or in connexion with which any of the new streets described in this scheme are to be constructed, or any plans for any other new street to be constructed in the area have been submitted to the Locality for approval, to require that provision shall be made for adjusting and altering the boundaries of any such estate or lands or any lands adjacent or near thereto and for effecting such exchanges of land as may be necessary or convenient for such purposes and the provision to be so made and the terms and conditions upon which such provision is to be made shall, failing agreement between the Locality and the respective persons interested in such estates or lands on the application of the Locality or any such person, be determined by an arbitrator to be appointed by the Board.

(b) Any award made under the provisions of this clause shall operate to effect any adjustment or alteration of boundaries or exchange of lands which may be provided for by such award, or be necessary for giving effect thereto, and shall be duly stamped accordingly, and the costs, charges and expenses of any such arbitration shall, unless and except in so far as the award shall otherwise provide, be borne and paid by the Locality.

(c) Any lands or moneys received by any person in or in respect of an adjustment or alteration of boundaries or exchange of lands under the provisions of this clause shall be held by such person, subject to the same trusts (if any) and any lands so received shall also be held subject to the same covenants restrictions and conditions (if any) as the lands exchanged therefor.

(d) For the purpose of the adjustment or alteration of the boundaries of any such estate or lands as aforesaid the Locality may themselves purchase, subject to the provisions of the Act of 1909, any land, and may sell or lease the same in whole or in part at such time or times, at such price or prices, and on such conditions as they may think fit, or may appropriate the same for any public purpose approved by the Board and until such sale or appropriation, may occupy, manage or let the same or any part thereof in such manner as the Locality may think reasonable.

Claims for compensation or betterment

29. (a) Claims under Section 58 of the Act of 1909 for compensation or in respect of any increase in value of property shall, failing agreement between the parties concerned, be submitted to an arbitrator mutually agreed upon or, failing such agreement, to an arbitrator appointed by the Board. Such claims can be made at any time during the carrying out of this scheme unless there be a mutual agreement properly registered cancelling all claims of this nature, provided always that any claims under this clause must be made within a fixed period (say six months) after the damage complained of or betterment has taken place.

Demolition or alteration of buildings

(b) The Locality may demolish or alter any buildings in the area so far as may be necessary for carrying this scheme into effect, but where buildings have been erected before the inauguration of this scheme compensation must be paid in accordance with sub-clause (a) of this clause 29.

Entry for inspection

30. (a) The Locality or any of their officers or servants on production of the written authority of the Locality, shall be admitted into or upon any property in the area for the purpose of any inspection necessitated by the provisions of this scheme or for the purpose of enforcing any of such provisions at any time between the hours of 9 in the forenoon and 6 in the afternoon.

(b) If admission for any of the purposes of this clause is refused, any Justice on complaint thereof on oath by any officer of the Locality (made after reasonable notice in writing of the intention to make the same has been given to the person having custody of the property) may by order under his hand require such person to admit the Locality and their officers and servants into or upon such property during the hours aforesaid, and if no person having such custody can be found, the Justice shall on oath made before him of that fact, authorize the Locality and their officers and servants to enter such premises during the hours aforesaid.

(c) Any such order made by a Justice shall continue in force until the purposes for which such admittance was required shall have been fulfilled or executed.

Enforcement of scheme

31. In addition to and notwithstanding any other procedure or remedy any person committing or knowingly permitting any breach or non-observance of any of the conditions of this scheme shall be guilty of an offence, and shall be liable on conviction in any court of summary jurisdiction to a penalty not exceeding 40s. for each offence, and to a further penalty not exceeding 20s. for each day upon which any offence is continued after conviction or after notice in writing of the offence has been served by the Locality or by any party interested on the party charged. Furthermore, the High Court of Justice may on the application of the Locality or any party interested grant any injunction (mandatory or otherwise) which such Court may consider necessary in order to enforce the due and continued observance of this scheme and may make such order as to costs and as to enforcing any such injunction as to such Court may seem expedient.

Works contravening scheme

32. Where it appears to the Locality that any building or other work in the area is at any time such as to contravene this scheme or that in the erection or carrying out of such building or other work, any provision of this scheme has not been complied with, or that any person has failed to execute any work which it is the duty of such person to execute under this scheme and it appears to the Locality that delay in the execution of the work would prejudice the efficient operation of this scheme, the person by whom, at whose order, or on whose behalf such building shall have been erected or such work shall have been begun or done, or the person who has failed to execute any work as aforesaid, shall (by a notice in writing signed by the Clerk to the Council and served upon such person and containing a copy of Section 57 of the Act of 1909 and of this clause) be required on or before such day as shall be specified in such notice (not being less than one calendar month from the date of service of such notice) by a statement in writing under his hand or under the hand of an agent duly authorized in that behalf and served upon the Locality to show

sufficient cause why such building or other work should not be removed, pulled down or altered, or be executed by the Locality.

If at the expiration of the notice such person shall have failed to show sufficient cause why such building or other work should not be removed, pulled down or altered or (as the case may be) be executed by the Locality and it shall not have been notified to the Locality by such person or by the Board that such person has referred any question to the Board under Sub-section (3) of Section 57 of the Act of 1909 the Locality after giving such person notice that, at the expiration of a further period specified in the notice (not being less than 14 days from the date of service of such notice) they intend to exercise their powers under Section 57 of the Act of 1909, may proceed to remove, pull down or alter, or execute such building or work (as the case may be). Provided that a power proposed to be so exercised shall not be exercised pending the determination of any question referred to the Board under Sub-section (3) of the said section in relation to the building or other work in respect of which that power is proposed to be exercised and of which reference the Locality shall have received written notice within the last-mentioned period.

When on any question referred to the Board under sub-section 3 of the said section, it is determined that any building or work contravenes this scheme or that any provision of this scheme is not complied with in the erection or carrying out of any such building or work the Locality, after giving such person as aforesaid notice that, at the expiration of a period specified in the notice (not being less than one calendar month from the date of service of such notice) they intend to exercise their powers under the said section, may proceed to remove pull down or alter any such building or works.*

Notices

33. Notices under this scheme must be in writing and may be served on the Locality by being delivered addressed to the Clerk to the Council at his office or on owners or occupiers by being sent by post addressed to them respectively or to their respective agents at the last known place of abode or business of such owners or agents.

Agreements

34. The Locality may, subject to the approval of the Board, make any agreements they think fit with any person or persons

* This lengthy procedure is considered necessary by English lawyers. Mr J. L. Jack, Town Clerk of Dunfermline, prefers a simpler method.

for the purpose of carrying out this scheme or any part thereof or any adjustment in connexion therewith. Any provision in any such agreement shall be void if inconsistent with this scheme, but otherwise all such agreements shall have full force and effect and shall be deemed to apply to and bind all persons, parties to such agreements and all successors in title to such persons.

Suspension and application of Acts and by-laws

35. (a) So far as necessary for the proper carrying out of this scheme: (1) The following enactments contained in public general Acts shall be suspended in the area, namely, the Highway Act, 1835, in regard to the stopping up and diversion of highways, so far as regards the highways referred to in clause 16 of this scheme; and Section 41 of the Public Health Amendment Act, 1890, if and so far as the same is in force in the area. (2) All other statutory enactments not being contained in a public general Act and all by-laws, regulations or other provisions under whatever authority made, which are in operation in the area shall be suspended.

(b) Except as aforesaid all such statutory enactments, by-laws, regulations or other provisions shall be deemed to be in full force in the area, and nothing in this scheme shall prevent the adopting or putting in force at any time in the area of any adoptive Act or any part thereof or the making of new by-laws to apply therein. Provided that the adoption or putting in force of such Act and the making of such by-laws shall have been confirmed and sanctioned as required by law.

36. (a) For the purposes of this scheme the Council may from time to time appoint committees of their members and may delegate to each such committee such of their powers and duties under this Act as they think fit.

(b) The Council may from time to time make such regulations as they think fit for the guidance of a committee and may from time to time remove any members of a committee and appoint in the stead of them or any of them other members of the Council.

(c) The proceedings of a committee shall not unless so ordered by the Council or required by this scheme require the approval of the Council.

(d) A committee may appoint a sub-committee of its members to execute and discharge any of the powers and duties of the committee, but the acts of such sub-committee shall, unless the Council on the appointment of the committee otherwise direct, be submitted for approval to the committee by which such sub-committee was appointed.

(e) In no case shall a committee be authorized to borrow any money or to make any rate and no expenditure or payment or contract to expend or pay any sum of money made by a committee and exceeding £100 shall be lawful or valid unless the committee shall have been authorized either generally or specially by the Council to make such expenditure, payment or contract or unless if not so authorized such expenditure, payment, or contract shall be approved by the Council.

(f) Subject to the foregoing provisions Section 22 of the Municipal Corporations Act, 1882, applies to committees and sub-committees under this scheme.

(g) A committee appointed under this scheme may (subject to regulations of the Council) meet from time to time and adjourn as they think fit; but no business shall be transacted at any meeting of such committee unless the number of members (if any) fixed by the Council and if no number be fixed three members be present.

(h) At the first meeting of every committee or sub-committee one of its members shall be appointed chairman of the committee or sub-committee and all questions shall be determined by a majority of the votes of the members present and in case of an equal division of votes the chairman shall have a casting vote in addition to his vote as a member of the committee or sub-committee.

(i) Where in any legal proceedings taken by or on behalf of the Locality or the Council, whether under any general or local Act of Parliament and whether passed before or after the passing of this Act, it becomes necessary to prove the appointment or authority of any officer, servant, solicitor or agent of the Locality or of any committee of the Council or to prove any resolution of the Council or of any committee of the Council, a certificate of such appointment, authority, or resolution purporting to be authenticated by the signature of the chairman of the Council or the Clerk to the Council shall be prima facie evidence of such appointment, authority, or resolution, and of the performance of all conditions, precedent or necessary, to the validity thereof without further proof of the holding of any meeting or the production of any minute book or other record or document.

Disposal of lands, appropriation, etc.

37. (a) Whenever it can be shown that during the preparation

of this scheme, it was in the interests of the ratepayers to acquire land before the intentions of the Locality were publicly known the Board shall approve such purchase provided the price paid is fair to the ratepayers and the Locality shall not be called upon to specify exactly what purpose the land is to be used for.

(b) The Locality shall be empowered to hold such land until it is required making the best possible income out of it meanwhile and further shall have power to lease it, but not sell it, for any purpose consistent with the objects of the scheme.

(c) The Locality may make special regulations in regard to any matter affecting the user of any land acquired by them under this scheme for the purpose of parks or open spaces and particularly may limit the right to use the same or any part thereof and may receive rent and may make other charges for the use of the land or any part thereof.

Recovery of expenses by Locality from the owners.

38. (a) Where the Locality have incurred expenses for repayment whereof the owner of the premises deriving benefit therefrom or for or in respect of which the same shall have been incurred is made liable under this scheme or the Act of 1909 or by any agreement with the Locality such expenditure may be recovered in a Court of Summary Jurisdiction, together with interest at a rate not exceeding £5 per centum per annum from the date of service of a demand for the same until payment thereof from any person who is the owner of such premises when the works are completed for which such expenses have been incurred, and until recovery of such expenses and interest, the same shall be a charge on the premises deriving benefit therefrom, or for or in respect of which they were incurred. In all summary proceedings by the Locality for the recovery of any such expenses the time within which such proceedings may be taken shall be reckoned from the date of the service of notice of demand.

(b) The Locality may by order declare any such expenses to be payable by annual instalments within a period of not exceeding thirty years with interest at a rate not exceeding £5 per centum per annum from the date of the service of notice of demand until the whole amount is paid, and any such instalments and interest or any part thereof may be recovered in a summary manner from the owner for the time being of such premises, and may be deducted from the ent of such premises in the same proportions as are allowed in the case of private improvement rates under the Public Health Act, 1875.

(c) The Locality, if they think fit, from time to time (in addition and without prejudice to any other remedy) may recover in a Court of Summary Jurisdiction, or as a simple contract debt by action in any court of Competent Jurisdiction, from the owner for the time being of any such premises the whole or any portion of any such expenses and interest.

(d) Any expenses incurred by the Locality under Section 57 of the Act of 1909 which are not expenses recoverable as hereinbefore provided, may be recovered by the Locality in any Court of Summary Jurisdiction or as a simple contract debt by action in any Court of Competent Jurisdiction from the person by whom, at whose order or on whose behalf, any building or other work contravening this scheme shall have been erected or done, or whose duty it was to execute the work executed by the Locality.

Recovery of betterment

(e) Where the value of any land is increased by the operation of this scheme, the sum lawfully required to be paid in respect of that increase shall, until payment, be a charge on the inheritance of such land and such sum may, if required to be paid otherwise than by instalments, be dealt with and recovered in the same way that expenses may be dealt with and recovered under this clause, or if required to be paid by instalments any arrears of such instalments may be dealt with and recovered in the same way as instalments of expenses in arrear may be dealt with and recovered under this clause.

Appeal to Quarter Sessions

39. Any person deeming himself aggrieved by any conviction or order made by a Petty Sessional Court under or pursuant to the provisions of this scheme may, if no other mode of appeal is provided by this scheme or any Act of Parliament, appeal to the next practicable Court of Quarter Sessions under and according to the provisions of the Summary Jurisdiction Acts and in regard to any such order made by a Petty Sessional Court the Locality may in like manner appeal and the Court of Quarter Sessions shall accordingly be and are hereby empowered to deal with any such appeal as if it were an ordinary appeal under those Acts.

Accounts

40. All amounts recovered by the Locality under Section 58 of the Act of 1909, in respect of the increase in value of property

or received from owners as contributions towards the cost of street construction, shall be applied in repayment of moneys borrowed under the Act of 1909 for purposes of this scheme or to such other purposes as may be approved by the Board.

Inquiries by Local Government Board

41. Section 85 of the Housing of the Working Classes Act, 1890, as amended by the Act of 1909 shall apply for any purposes of this scheme as it applies for the purpose of the execution of the powers and duties of the Board under the former Act.

42. In all cases where the consent of the Locality is required to be given under this scheme such consent shall be in writing and shall either be under the hand of the Clerk to the Council or the seal of the Locality.

Duration of scheme and short title

43. This scheme shall commence on the day on which it is approved by the Board and shall continue in operation until varied by any subsequent scheme and may be cited as ''
."

APPENDIX VI

EXTRACTS FROM LOCAL GOVERNMENT BOARD REPORT ON INTERCEPTING TRAPS
1912

This Report is too long to reprint in full. These extracts give the salient points. Those who want further information can obtain the full report from Wyman & Sons, Fetter Lane, London, E.C.

Part of para. 10. With few exceptions the evidence before us was unanimous that the air inlet is an objectionable feature of the house drainage system. When it is level with the ground, not only may nuisance arise from its action as an outlet for smell, but it is frequently itself responsible for blockage of the intercepting trap, for in this position it serves as a surface gully and admits of the passage of earth and other detritus from the surface into the trap.

Part of para. 15. The results of experiments show how uniform was the tendency of all the traps used to retain a large proportion of the solids at any given flush. A noticeable feature also of many of the experiments was that solids accumulated in the trap during two or three successive flushes until a certain amount of obstruction had been reached and that then a flush effected a considerable clearance.

Part of para. 17. Both series of experiments support the contention that the trap is an important impediment to the passage of solid matter in sewage from the house drain to the sewer and that it tends to promote decomposition of sewage before it can reach the sewer.

It is reasonable to expect and the Islington experiments bear this out, that the liability of an intercepting trap to contain decomposing sewage at any given time is less in a house containing a bath in daily use, than in one without a bath. It is possible, however, that, in actual practice, a bath may not be so useful in this respect as the experiments seem to indicate, for in many dwellings the bath discharges commonly take place before those from closets. It would appear however that in the absence of a bath the intercepting trap is unlikely to be free at any time from solid fæcal matter. It is a fair inference, therefore, that when conditions favour active decomposition the contents of numerous intercepting traps may become very offensive before they reach the sewer.

Para. 18. Perhaps the most important disadvantage alleged against the intercepting trap is that besides its liability to be a passive impediment to the passage of sewage solids to the sewer, it may be the active cause of more or less complete obstruction of the house drain, with consequent accumulation of sewage in the drain.

Opponents of the trap contend that this blocking of the trap is a very serious matter; that the resulting accumulation of sewage may leak, through the joints of the drain and the brickwork of inspection chambers, into the basements and foundations of houses, and that to deal with this accumulation of sewage and to remove the obstruction is a difficult and offensive proceeding.

Para. 22. We had an opportunity of seeing some of the traps thus ascertained to be blocked and they were in a remarkable condition. They had evidently been blocked for a long time, the inspection chambers each containing an accumulation of sewage covered with a dense scum, similar to that which forms in the septic tanks of sewage disposal works, but nevertheless the house drains were acting as though a block did not exist. In one case in which the scum on the sewage in the inspection chamber was especially dense and old, and the level of accumulated sewage was high, even the discharge from a fixed bath, filled with water to the brim, failed to reveal the fact that the drain was blocked. All the bath water passed freely through the gully trap into which the bath waste discharged, as if the drain was free from any obstruction. In the inspection chamber, the level of sewage rose slowly, and when the discharge ceased, slowly fell again.

Para. 39. On the other hand it is urged that if the intercepting trap may be omitted with safety there could be material simplification of house drainage. The proper setting of an intercepting trap appears in itself to be by no means a simple proceeding. For instance, it may be fixed so that it is tilted in one direction or another, in which event the water seal is either so great that the chances of obstruction are much increased or so small as to be almost non-existent.

Moreover, when the available fall between house and sewer is limited, the introduction of the intercepting trap may prove a serious difficulty and render necessary still further limitation of the gradient of the house drain.

Part of Para. 52. The problem really resolves itself, therefore, into the question whether there is any essential difference between the escape of sewer air plus drain air and drain air only; that is, whether the two together are more objectionable or more likely to cause ill health than drain air alone.

Part of para. 76. This accumulated bacteriological evidence which exhibits very few discrepancies establishes the essential fact that the number of micro-organisms in sewer air is extremely small. This is established not only in the case of good sewers and those which are well ventilated, but also in the case of bad sewers, even those containing more or less stagnant sewage with much deposit and those in which ventilation is small or absent. Indeed, it is in the latter kind of sewer that the number of sewer air microbes would appear to be at a minimum.

Part of para. 90. The practical importance of this essential bacterial difference between sewer air and drain air is very great.

One of the dangers feared from the omission of the intercepting trap is that pathogenic microbes, given off from sewage, may be wafted from the air of the sewer into the house drain, and thence into the dwelling itself. It is obvious, however, that, if as appears usually to be the case, micro-organisms of sewage origin are not present in sewer air, there can be no wafting of pathogenic microbes from sewer to drain as has been apprehended. It is likewise obvious that if sewer air contains, as apparently it does contain sometimes, such microbes of sewage origin, but so few in number that their presence can be demonstrated only with difficulty, the chance that they can be wafted into a house drain is very small, while the chance that any of them can pass further and enter the dwelling itself must be smaller still. Consequently, even if, in any particular instance, sewage microbes can gain admission into a house from the air of the drain belonging to it, the possibility that such microbes can include any derived from sewer air, if the intercepting trap is absent, must be very remote.

Para. 97. The results of these experiments emphasize the point to which we have already referred, namely, that the bacteriological evidence indicates that, if any bacterial danger exists at all in house drainage, it is to be found in the drain air that may escape from the outlets of ventilating shafts of house drains. But even this danger requires to be regarded in its true perspective.

Part of para. 99. Thus Dr Haldane expressed the opinion in his evidence that the theory of sewer air infection was based on " worthless evidence " and that as a general rule " illness was put down to sewer air if the cause was unknown," particularly so " at the time when the influence of water and of milk and of personal infection was not really understood." He was even " very suspicious of the theory " that sewer air, apart from its smell, can be a predisposing cause of disease.

Para. 113. There is a considerable amount of evidence also which indicates in a more general way that the passage of sewer air into house drains, owing to the absence of intercepting trap is not productive of harm to communities.

We have already referred to Leeds. It may be mentioned that notwithstanding the general absence of intercepting traps in this city (both on house drains and at street gullies) its health, as judged by its rate of mortality and by its incidence of such a disease as typhoid fever, compares very favourably with that of other large towns.

In Bristol, both the average general death rate and the death rate from typhoid fever, are exceptionally low for so large a city. Here, in addition to the entire absence of designed sewer ventilation a large proportion of the houses occupied by the working classes are not provided with intercepting traps. Nevertheless, Dr Davies, the Medical Officer of Health, informed us that he had been unable to establish any relationship between ill health or any definite disease and drainage defects in any part of Bristol. The following statistics for Bristol may be quoted. During the decennia 1881-1890 and 1891-1900 and the quinquennia 1901-1905 and 1906-1910, the average annual " all causes " death rate in Bristol was 19·3, 18·3, 15·6 and 13·1 per 1,000 respectively, as compared with 21·6, 20·2, 17·0 and 14·8 per 1,000 respectively in the principal towns of England and Wales. During the same periods, the death rate from enteric fever in Bristol was 17, 11, 9 and 3 per 100,000 respectively, as compared with 26, 20, 12 and 7 in all large towns.

In Leicester again, the drains of most of the houses are not intercepted from the sewer, and here also, the rates of mortality are low. For the same periods as given above for Bristol, the annual average death rate from all causes in Leicester was 20·6, 18·3, 14·5 and 12·8 per 1,000 respectively, that from enteric fever was 21, 18, 6 and 3 per 100,000.

In Sheffield, many houses are without intercepting traps; Dr Scurfield, the Medical Officer of Health, being of opinion that the danger of admitting sewer air into the house drain has been exaggerated. In Stockport, also, the majority of houses are without intercepting traps, and in this town many such traps have been removed. The Medical Officer of Health, Dr Corbin, has been unable to find evidence that harm has resulted. Similar experience is to be found in other large towns, but of these we have no exact particulars.

Para. 118. So far we have dealt with the question of the inter-

z

cepting trap without reference to the ventilation of sewers. We have done so intentionally, because, as we pointed out at the outset, the objection adduced by opponents of the trap that it prevents the ventilation of the sewer by the house drain, is regarded by those who favour the trap as the main reason for retaining it. But now that we have investigated the advantages and disadvantages of the trap apart from their bearing on sewer ventilation, we may briefly consider the latter point of view. The opposing contentions are, on the one hand, that the intercepting trap makes the ventilation of sewers difficult and costly, and that without the trap the ventilation of sewers may be effected through the soil pipes of house drains, safely and without nuisance; on the other hand, that it is the business of the responsible public authority to make independent provision for the ventilation of public sewers, and that it is improper to make use of house drains for this purpose, not only because they are private property, but also because, even if such a proceeding is unlikely to cause illness, it may be offensive from the escape of sewer air near windows and chimneys.

As to the latter objection, we have already pointed out that the experience of East Grinstead and other places shows that the result of using private house drains for ventilating sewers is usually not to increase but to lessen the nuisance that may arise from the escape of sewer air. There can be no doubt, too, for it has been repeatedly proved that so far as nuisance is concerned, the escape of sewer air at a height is much to be preferred to its escape at the ground level.

Para. 125. In the foregoing pages, we have shown that the disadvantages involved by the use of the intercepting trap are substantial and of serious practical importance, and that as the most important of the effects of these disadvantages are concealed from view, they may remain in existence quite unknown to the householder. On the other hand, the construction of house drainage may be simplified by the omission of the intercepting trap.

The tendency of the intercepting trap to retain a considerable proportion (averaging according to our experiments from 42 to 79 per cent) of the solid matters of the sewage passing through it at any given time, and thus to favour blocking of the trap as well as putrefaction of the sewage before it reaches the sewer may be diminished to a great extent by using a trap of smaller diameter than is customary at present.

The liability of the trap to become blocked appears however to be insuperable, and it is this liability which constitutes its most serious disadvantage. The accumulation of sewage in the drain produced by the block and from which many undesirable consequences may follow, is not usually evident with ordinary use of the drain and, therefore, may long remain undiscovered. This unsuspected blocking of the trap and accumulation of sewage appears to be very common, evidence of it having been found in more than 23 per cent of 5,600 traps which were specially examined.

Para. 134. It is also confirmed by the general and epidemiological evidence which is to the effect that human beings deliberately exposed to the effects of sewer air do not appear to be affected in health; that the association of the incidence of certain specific diseases, such as enteric fever and diphtheria, with drain effects which allow of the entry of sewer air as well as of drain air into houses is almost identically the same as the association of similar defects with the absence of disease, and that the experience of districts without intercepting traps does not show that their absence has been harmful.

APPENDIX VII

PUBLIC HEALTH (SEWERS AND DRAINS) (No. 2) BILL
INTRODUCED BY MR HENRY VIVIAN

MEMORANDUM

This measure is intended to remedy a defect in the draftsmanship of the Public Health Acts which has frequently been made the subject of judicial comment.

Lord Russell of Killowen, C.J., in 1896, concluding a long judgment on the meaning of " single private drain," said: " I cannot avoid pointing out the highly unsatisfactory state of the existing legislation relating to the question of public health, and to cognate questions of local authority under the Acts dealing with that subject. It is entirely unsystematic and most confused, and, in the public interest, steps ought to be speedily taken to reduce the existing chaos into system and order." 1906, 2 Q.B., p. 213, Bradford v. Mayor, etc., of Eastbourne.

In 1904, Lord Alverstone, C.J., dealing with the subject matter of this Act, said: " Speaking for myself I may say that I hope that the Court of Appeal or the House of Lords may be able by sweeping away some of the conflicting decisions upon this subject, to reduce the law to a logical system, or else that the Act of 1890 may be amended by the insertion of a definition of the expression ' single private drain.' " 1904, 2 K.B., p. 5, Thompson v. Eccles Corporation.

In a later case in that year, Lord Alverstone, C.J., commenced his judgment by saying: "I hope that the day will arrive when no question can arise as to what is a sewer and what is a drain, and that something may some day be done in the way of a declaratory or an amending Act to put these questions beyond the range of discussion." 1904, 2 K.B., p. 263, Jackson v. Wimbledon Urban Council.

Mr Justice Channell, in the same year, in delivering judgment used the following words: " I have commented on the extraordinary result of this legislation, that the same structure must be repaired by the local authority if it serves the houses of one person only, but that if it serves different owners, those different owners may be required to repay the expense of making it good. It is, however, right to point out that the thing which is extraordinary is not the enactment as to several owners, but the omission to enact the same thing when there is only one owner. This omission appears clearly accidental. The draftsman of the section must have thought, and the legislature which adopted his language must have thought, that this had been already provided and, consequently, by a misapprehension, omitted to provide for it." 1904, 2 K.B., p. 281, Haedicke v. Friern Barnet Urban Council.

In the case of Wood Green Urban Council v. Joseph, in 1907, 1 K.B., 187, Lord Alverstone, C.J., again dealing with the subject-matter of this Bill, said: " It seems to me, as I have before pointed out, to be essential that there should be some amendment of the law upon this subject. The state of the authorities is such that it appears to be impossible either to reconcile the various decisions or to deduce from them any logical rule. It seems to be ridiculous that, if a pipe which receives the drainage of two or more houses belonging to the same owner is a sewer, it should cease to be a sewer if it also receives the drainage from another house belonging to another owner; and as Wills, J., pointed out in Bradford v. Mayor, etc., of Eastbourne, there is no reason either in justice or policy which can be urged in support of such a distinction."

A BILL TO

A.D. 1908

Amend the Public Health Acts with respect to the combined drainage of two or more houses belonging to the same owner.

Be it enacted by the King's Most Excellent Majesty, by and with the advice and consent of the Lords Spiritual and Temporal, and Commons, in the present Parliament assembled, and by the authority of the same, as follows:

1. Where any person desires newly to erect or to rebuild or redrain any pair or group or block of houses and to provide for the effectual drainage thereof by a combined drain or drains and shall before commencing to erect, rebuild, or redrain the same, give notice to the local authority of his intention to provide one or more single private drain or drains for the purpose of draining such pair or group or block of houses into a sewer vested in the local authority, every such single private drain when constructed shall be a drain and not a sewer within the meaning of Section 4 of the Public Health Act, 1875:

Provided that nothing in this section shall be deemed to exempt such person from complying with any enactment, by-law, rule, or regulation with which he would otherwise have to comply.

2. In any urban district the provisions of Section 25 of the Public

Health Act, 1875, shall be satisfied as regards such pair or group or block of houses as aforesaid by the construction of such private single drain or drains as aforesaid as may appear to the urban authority to be necessary for the effectual drainage of such pair or group or block of houses, provided that the single private drain or drains so constructed shall empty into any sewer which the urban authority is entitled to use, and which is within 100 ft. of some part of the site of such pair or group or block of houses.

3. (1) This Act shall be construed as one with the Public Health Acts.

(2) This Act may be cited as the Public Health Acts Amendment Act, 1908, and this Act and the Public Health Acts may be cited together as the Public Health Acts.

APPENDIX VIII

HOUSING, TOWN PLANNING, ETC. ACT, 1909. [9 Edw. 7 Ch. 44.]

ARRANGEMENT OF SECTIONS

Part I. Housing of the Working Classes

FACILITIES FOR ACQUISITION OF LANDS AND OTHER PURPOSES OF THE HOUSING ACTS

POWERS OF ENFORCING EXECUTION OF HOUSING ACTS

CONTRACTS BY LANDLORD

AMENDMENT OF PROCEDURE FOR CLOSING ORDERS AND DEMOLITION ORDERS

AMENDMENTS WITH RESPECT TO IMPROVEMENT AND RECONSTRUCTION SCHEMES

AMENDMENTS WITH RESPECT TO FINANCIAL MATTERS

An Act to amend the Law relating to the Housing of The Working Classes, to provide for the making of Town Planning schemes, and to make further provision with respect to the appointment and duties of County Medical Officers of Health, and to provide for the establishment of Public Health and Housing Committees of County Councils. [December 3, 1909]

BE it enacted by the King's Most Excellent Majesty, by and with the advice and consent of the Lords Spiritual and Temporal, and Commons, in this present Parliament assembled, and by the authority of the same, as follows:

PART I

HOUSING OF THE WORKING CLASSES

FACILITIES FOR ACQUISITION OF LANDS AND OTHER PURPOSES OF THE HOUSING ACTS

1. Part III of the Housing of the Working Classes Act, 1890 (in this Part of this Act referred to as the principal Act), shall, after the commencement of this Act, extend to and take effect in every urban or rural district, or other place for which it has not been adopted, as if it had been so adopted.

Provisions as to acquisition of land under Part III of the principal Act

2. (1) A local authority may be authorized to purchase land compulsorily for the purposes of Part III of the principal Act, by means of an order submitted to the Local Government Board and confirmed by the Board in accordance with the First Schedule to this Act.

(2) The procedure under this section for the compulsory purchase of land shall be substituted for the procedure for the same purpose under Section 176 of the Public Health Act, 1875, as applied by Sub-section (1) of Section 57 of the principal Act.

38 and 39 Vict. c. 55

(3) A local authority may, with the consent of and subject to any conditions imposed by the Local Government Board, acquire land by agreement for the purposes of Part III of the principal Act, notwithstanding that the land is not immediately required for those purposes.

3. Where a loan is made by the Public Works Loan Commissioners to a local authority for any purposes of the Housing Acts:

(a) The loan shall be made at the minimum rate allowed for the time being for loans out of the Local Loans Fund; and

(b) If the Local Government Board make a recommendation to that effect, the period for which the loan is made by the Public Works Loan Commissioners may exceed the period allowed under the principal Act or under any other Act limiting the period for which the loan may be made, but the period shall not exceed the period recommended by the Local Government Board, nor in any case 80 years ; and

(c) As between loans for different periods, the longer duration of the loan shall not be taken as a reason for fixing a higher rate of interest.

4. (1) Where a loan is made by the Public Works Loan Commissioners under Section 67, Sub-section (2) (d), of the principal Act, to a public utility society, the words " two thirds " shall be substituted for the words " one moiety."

(2) For the purposes of this section a public utility society means a society registered under the Industrial and Provident Societies Act, 1893, or any amendment thereof, the rules whereof prohibit the payment of any interest or dividend at a rate exceeding £5 per centum per annum.

5. (1) Any purchase money or compensation payable in pursuance of the Housing Acts by a local authority in respect of any lands, estate, or interest of another local authority which would, but for this section, be paid into court in manner provided by the Lands Clauses Acts or by para. (20) of the Second Schedule to the principal Act may, if the Local Government Board consent, instead of being paid into court, be paid and applied as the Board determine.

(2) Any such decision of the Board as to the payment and application of any such purchase money or compensation shall be final and conclusive.

6. Any local authority in connexion with the exercise by them of their powers under Part III of the principal Act may lay out and construct public streets or roads on any land acquired or appropriated by them for the purpose of that part of that Act, or contribute towards the cost of the laying out and construction of any streets or roads on any such land by other persons on the condition that those streets or roads are to be dedicated to the public.

7. (1) The following paragraph shall be substituted for paragraph (b) of Sub-section (1) of Section 74 of the principal Act:

(b) The improvements on which capital money arising under the Settled Land Act, 1882, may be expended, enumerated in Section 25 of the said Act and referred to in Section 30 of the said Act, shall, in addition to cottages for labourers, farm servants, and artisans, whether employed on the settled land or not, include the provision of dwellings available for the working classes, either by means of building new buildings or by means of the reconstruction, enlargement, or improvement of existing buildings, so as to make them available for the purpose, if that provision of dwellings is, in the opinion of the court, not injurious to the estate or is agreed to by the tenant for life and the trustees of the settlement.

(2) The provision by a tenant for life, at his own expense, of dwellings available for the working classes on any settled land shall not be deemed to be an injury to any interest in reversion or remainder in that land; provided that the powers conferred upon a tenant for life by this sub-section shall not be exercised by him without the previous approval in writing of the trustees of the settlement.

8. A local authority may accept a donation of land or money or other property for any of the purposes of the Housing Acts, and it shall not be necessary to enrol any assurance with respect to any such property under the Mortmain and Charitable Uses Act, 1888.

51 and 52 Vict. c. 42

9. (1) If in any case it appears to the Local Government Board that the institution of legal proceedings is requisite or desirable with respect to any property required to be applied under any trusts for the provision of dwellings available for the working classes, or that the expediting of any such legal proceedings is requisite or desirable, the Board may certify the case to the Attorney-General, and the Attorney-General, if he thinks fit, shall institute any legal proceedings or intervene in any legal proceedings already instituted in such manner as he thinks proper under the circumstances.

(2) Before preparing any scheme with reference to property required to be applied under any trusts for the provision of dwellings available for the working classes, the court or body who are responsible for making the scheme shall communicate with the Local Government Board and receive and consider any recommendations made by the Board with reference to the proposed scheme.

POWERS OF ENFORCING EXECUTION OF HOUSING ACTS

10. (1) Where a complaint is made to the Local Government Board:

(a) As respects any rural district by the council of the county in which the district is situate, or by the parish council

or parish meeting of any parish comprised in the district,
or by any four inhabitant householders of the district; or

(b) As respects any county district, not being a rural district,
by the council of the county in which the district is
situated, or by four inhabitant householders of the
district; or

(c) As respects the area of any other local authority by four
inhabitant householders of the area;

that the local authority have failed to exercise their powers under
Part II or Part III of the principal Act in cases where those
powers ought to have been exercised, the Board may cause a
public local inquiry to be held, and if, after holding such an
inquiry, the Board are satisfied that there has been such a failure
on the part of the local authority, the Board may declare the
authority to be in default, and may make an order directing
that authority, within a time limited by the order, to carry out
such works and do such other things as may be mentioned in
the order for the purpose of remedying the default.

(2) Before deciding that a local authority have failed to exercise
their powers under Part III of the principal Act, the Board shall
take into consideration the necessity for further accommodation
for the housing of the working classes in such district, the probability that the required accommodation will not be otherwise
provided, and the other circumstances of the case, and whether,
having regard to the liability which will be incurred by the rates,
it is prudent for the local authority to undertake the provision of
such accommodation.

(3) Where an order originally made under this section on the
council of a county district is not complied with by that council,
the Local Government Board may, if they think fit, with the
consent of the county council, instead of enforcing that order
against the council of the county district, make an order directing
the county council to carry out any works or do any other things
which are mentioned in the original order for the purpose of
remedying the default of the district council.

(4) Where the Board make an order under this section directing
a county council to carry out any works or do any other thing, the
order may, for the purpose of enabling the county council to give
effect to the order, apply any of the provisions of the Housing
Acts or of Section 63 of the Local Government Act, 1894, with such
modifications or adaptations (if any) as appear necessary or
expedient.

56 and 57 Vict. c. 73

(5) An order made by the Local Government Board under this section shall be laid before both Houses of Parliament as soon as may be after it is made.

(6) Any order made by the Local Government Board under this section may be enforced by mandamus.

11. (1) Where it appears to the Local Government Board that a local authority have failed to perform their duty under the Housing Acts of carrying out an improvement scheme under Part I of the principal Act, or have failed to give effect to any order as respects an obstructive building, or to a reconstruction scheme, under Part II of that Act, or have failed to cause to be made the inspection of their district required by this Act, the Board may make an order requiring the local authority to remedy the default and to carry out any works or do any other things which are necessary for the purpose under the Housing Acts within a time fixed by the order.

(2) Any order made by the Local Government Board under this section may be enforced by mandamus.

12. Where a complaint is made to the council of a county by the parish council or parish meeting of any parish comprised in any rural district in the county, or by any four inhabitant householders of that district, the county council may cause a public local inquiry to be held, and if, after holding such an inquiry, the county council are satisfied that the rural district council have failed to exercise their powers under Part III of the principal Act in cases where those powers ought to have been exercised, the county council may resolve that the powers of the district council for the purposes of that Part be transferred to the county council with respect either to the whole district or to any parish in the district, and those powers shall be transferred accordingly, and, subject to the provisions of this Act, Section 63 of the Local Government Act, 1894, shall apply as if the powers had been transferred under that Act.

13. (1) Where the council of a county are of opinion that for any reason it is expedient that the council should exercise, as respects any rural district in the county, any of the powers of a local authority under Part III of the principal Act, the council, after giving notice to the council of the district of their intention to do so, may apply to the Local Government Board for an order conferring such powers on them.

(2) Upon such an application being made, the Board may make

an order conferring on the county council as respects the rural district all or any of the powers of a local authority under Part III of the principal Act, and thereupon the provisions of the Housing Acts relating to those powers (including those enabling the Public Works Loan Commissioners to lend, and fixing the terms for which money may be lent and borrowed) shall apply as if the council were a local authority under Part III of the principal Act. Provided that the expenses incurred by the county council under any such order shall be defrayed as expenses for general county purposes.

(3) Where, under any such order, the county council have executed any works in a rural district they may transfer the works to the council of that district on such terms and subject to such conditions as may be agreed between them.

CONTRACTS BY LANDLORD

14. In any contract made after the passing of this Act for letting for habitation a house or part of a house at a rent not exceeding:

- (a) in the case of a house situate in the administrative county of London, £40;
- (b) in the case of a house situate in a borough or urban district with a population according to the last census for the time being of 50,000 or upwards, £26;
- (c) in the case of a house situate elsewhere, £16;

there shall be implied a condition that the house is at the commencement of the holding in all respects reasonably fit for human habitation, but the condition aforesaid shall not be implied when a house or part of a house is let for a term of not less than three years upon the terms that it be put by the lessee into a condition reasonably fit for occupation, and the lease is not determinable at the option of either party before the expiration of that term.

15. (1) The last foregoing section shall, as respects contracts to which that section applies, take effect as if the condition implied by that section included an undertaking that the house shall, during the holding, be kept by the landlord in all respects reasonably fit for human habitation.

(2) The landlord or the local authority, or any person authorized by him or them in writing, may at reasonable times of the day, on giving 24 hours' notice in writing to the tenant or occupier, enter any house, premises, or building to which this section applies for the purpose of viewing the state and condition thereof.

(3) If it appears to the local authority within the meaning of Part II of the principal Act that the undertaking implied by virtue of this section is not complied with in the case of any house to which it applies, the authority shall, if a closing order is not made with respect to the house, by written notice require the landlord, within a reasonable time, not being less than 21 days, specified in the notice, to execute such works as the authority shall specify in the notice as being necessary to make the house in all respects reasonably fit for human habitation.

(4) Within 21 days after the receipt of such notice the landlord may by written notice to the local authority declare his intention of closing the house for human habitation, and thereupon a closing order shall be deemed to have become operative in respect of such house.

(5) If the notice given by the local authority is not complied with, and if the landlord has not given the notice mentioned in the immediately preceding sub-section, the authority may, at the expiration of the time specified in the notice given by them to the landlord, do the work required to be done and recover the expenses incurred by them in so doing from the landlord as a civil debt in manner provided by the Summary Jurisdiction Acts, or, if they think fit, the authority may by order declare any such expenses to be payable by annual instalments within a period not exceeding that of the interest of the landlord in the house, nor in any case five years, with interest at a rate not exceeding £5 per cent per annum, until the whole amount is paid, and any such instalments or interest or any part thereof may be recovered from the landlord as a civil debt in manner provided by the Summary Jurisdiction Acts.

(6) A landlord may appeal to the Local Government Board against any notice requiring him to execute works under this section, and against any demand for the recovery of expenses from him under this section or order made with respect to those expenses under this section by the authority, by giving notice of appeal to the Board within 21 days after the notice is received, or the demand or order is made, as the case may be, and no proceedings shall be taken in respect of such notice requiring works, order, or demand, whilst the appeal is pending.

(7) In this section the expression '' landlord '' means any person who lets to a tenant for habitation the house under any contract referred to in this section, and includes his successors in title; and the expression '' house '' includes part of a house.

(8) Sections 49 and 50 of the principal Act as amended by Section 13 of the Housing of the Working Classes Act, 1903 (which relate to the service of notices and the description of owner in proceedings) shall apply for the purposes of this section, with the substitution, where required, of the landlord for the owner of a dwelling-house.

(9) Any remedy given by this section for non-compliance with the undertaking implied by virtue of this section shall be in addition to and not in derogation of any other remedy available to the tenant against the landlord, either at common law or otherwise.

16. (1) The power of making and enforcing by-laws under Section 90 of the Public Health Act, 1875, and Section 94 of the Public Health (London) Act, 1891, with respect to houses or parts of houses which are let in lodgings or occupied by members of more than one family, shall, in the case of houses intended for the working classes, extend to the making and enforcing of by-laws imposing any duty (being a duty which may be imposed by the by-laws and which involves the execution of work) upon the owner within the meaning of the said Acts, in addition to or in substitution for any other person having an interest in the premises, and prescribing the circumstances and conditions in and subject to which any such duty is to be discharged.

(2) For the purpose of discharging any duty so imposed, the owner or other person may at all reasonable times enter upon any part of the premises, and Section 51 of the principal Act shall apply as if for the reference to the provisions of Part II of that Act there were substituted a reference to the provisions of such by-laws, and as if the person on whom such duty is imposed were the owner and any inmate of the premises were the occupier of a dwelling-house.

(3) Where an owner or other person has failed to execute any work which he has been required to execute under the by-laws, the local authority or sanitary authority, as the case may be, may, after giving to him not less than 21 days' notice in writing, themselves execute the works and recover the costs and expenses, and for that purpose the provisions of Sub-section 5 of the last foregoing section, with respect to the execution of works and the recovery of expenses by local authorities, shall apply as if the owner or other person were the landlord, and with such other adaptations as may be necessary.

AMENDMENT OF PROCEDURE FOR CLOSING ORDERS AND DEMOLITION ORDERS

17. (1) It shall be the duty of every local authority within the meaning of Part II of the principal Act to cause to be made from time to time inspection of their district, with a view to ascertain whether any dwelling-house therein is in a state so dangerous or injurious to health as to be unfit for human habitation and for that purpose it shall be the duty of the local authority, and of every officer of the local authority, to comply with such regulations and to keep such records as may be prescribed by the Board.

(2) If, on the representation of the medical officer of health, or of any other officer of the authority, or other information given, any dwelling-house appears to them to be in such a state, it shall be their duty to make an order prohibiting the use of the dwelling-house for human habitation (in this Act referred to as a closing order) until in the judgment of the local authority the dwelling-house is rendered fit for that purpose.

(3) Notice of a closing order shall be forthwith served on every owner of the dwelling-house in respect of which it is made, and any owner aggrieved by the order may appeal to the Local Government Board by giving notice of appeal to the Board within 14 days after the order is served upon him.

(4) Where a closing order has become operative, the local authority shall serve notice of the order on every occupying tenant of the dwelling-house in respect of which the order is made, and, within such period as is specified in the notice, not being less than 14 days after the service of the notice, the order shall be obeyed by him, and he and his family shall cease to inhabit the dwelling-house, and in default he shall be liable on summary conviction to be ordered to quit the dwelling-house within such time as may be specified in the order.

(5) Unless the dwelling-house has been made unfit for habitation by the wilful act or default of the tenant or of any person for whom as between himself and the owner or landlord he is responsible, the local authority may make to every such tenant such reasonable allowance on account of his expense in removing as may be determined by the local authority with the consent of the owner of the dwelling-house, or, if the owner of the dwelling-house fails to consent to the sum determined by the local authority, as may be fixed by a court of summary jurisdiction, and the amount of the said allowance shall be recoverable by the local authority from

the owner of the dwelling-house as a civil debt in manner provided by the Summary Jurisdiction Acts.

(6) The local authority shall determine any closing order made by them if they are satisfied that the dwelling-house, in respect of which the order has been made, has been rendered fit for human habitation.

If, on the application of any owner of a dwelling-house, the local authority refuse to determine a closing order, the owner may appeal to the Local Government Board by giving notice of appeal to the Board within 14 days after the application is refused.

(7) A room habitually used as a sleeping place, the surface of the floor of which is more than 3 ft. below the surface of the part of the street adjoining or nearest to the room, shall for the purposes of this section be deemed to be a dwelling-house so dangerous or injurious to health as to be unfit for human habitation, if the room either:

(a) is not on an average at least 7 ft. in height from floor to ceiling; or

(b) does not comply with such regulations as the local authority with the consent of the Local Government Board may prescribe for securing the proper ventilation and lighting of such rooms, and the protection thereof against dampness, effluvia, or exhalation: Provided that if the local authority, after being required to do so by the Local Government Board, fail to make such regulations, or such regulations as the Board approve, the Board may themselves make them, and the regulations so made shall have effect as if they had been made by the local authority with the consent of the Board:

Provided that a closing order made in respect of a room to which this sub-section applies shall not prevent the room being used for purposes other than those of a sleeping place; and that, if the occupier of the room after notice of an order has been served upon him fails to comply with the order, an order to comply therewith may, on summary conviction, be made against him.

This sub-section shall not come into operation until the first day of July, 1910, and a closing order made in respect of any room to which this sub-section applies shall not be treated as a closing order in respect of a dwelling-house for the purposes of the next succeeding section.

18. (1) Where a closing order in respect of any dwelling-house has remained operative for a period of three months, the local

authority shall take into consideration the question of the demolition of the dwelling-house, and shall give every owner of the dwelling-house notice of the time (being some time not less than one month after the service of the notice) and place at which the question will be considered, and any owner of the dwelling-house shall be entitled to be heard when the question is so taken into consideration.

(2) If upon any such consideration the local authority are of opinion that the dwelling-house has not been rendered fit for human habitation, and that the necessary steps are not being taken with all due diligence to render it so fit, or that the continuance of any building, being or being part of the dwelling-house, is a nuisance or dangerous or injurious to the health of the public or of the inhabitants of the neighbouring dwelling-houses, they shall order the demolition of the building.

(3) If any owner undertakes to execute forthwith the works necessary to render the dwelling-house fit for human habitation, and the local authority consider that it can be so rendered fit for human habitation, the local authority may, if they think fit, postpone the operation of the order for such time, not exceeding six months, as they think sufficient for the purpose of giving the owner an opportunity of executing the necessary works.

(4) Notice of an order for the demolition of a building shall be forthwith served on every owner of the building in respect of which it is made, and any owner aggrieved by the order may appeal to the Local Government Board by giving notice of appeal to the Board within 21 days after the order is served upon him.

19. Any owner of or other person interested in a dwelling-house on which an annuity has been charged by a charging order made under Section 36 of the principal Act (which relates to the grant of charges) shall at any time be at liberty to redeem the annuity on payment to the person entitled to the annuity of such sum as may be agreed upon, or in default of agreement determined by the Local Government Board.

20. The charges excepted in Sub-section (1) of Section 37 of the principal Act (which relates to the incidence of charges) shall include charges on the dwelling-house created or arising under any provision of the Public Health Acts, or under any provision in any local Act authorizing a charge for recovery of expenses incurred by a local authority.

21. Sub-section (3) of Section 47 of the principal Act (which gives power to a court of summary jurisdiction to enlarge the time for

certain matters) shall cease to have effect as respects the time allowed for the execution of any works or the demolition of a building under a closing order or under an order for the demolition of a building.

AMENDMENTS WITH RESPECT TO IMPROVEMENT AND RECONSTRUCTION SCHEMES

22. In Section 4 of the principal Act (which relates to an official representation), the words " that the most satisfactory method of dealing with the evils connected with such houses, courts, or alleys, and the sanitary defects in such area is an improvement scheme " shall be substituted for the words " that the evils connected with such houses, courts, or alleys, and the sanitary defects in such area cannot be effectually remedied otherwise than by means of an improvement scheme."

23. (1) Section 6 of the principal Act (which relates to the contents of an improvement scheme) shall be read as if in Sub-section (1) the words " for sanitary purposes " were omitted in paragraph (a); and as if the following paragraph was inserted at the end of that sub-section:

" and

(e) may provide for any other matter (including the closing and diversion of highways) for which it seems expedient to make provision with a view to the improvement of the area or the general efficiency of the scheme."

(2) Provision may be made in a reconstruction scheme under Part II of the principal Act for any matters for which provision may be made in an improvement scheme made under Part I of that Act.

24. (1) Paragraphs (a) and (b) of Sub-section (2) of Section 5 of the Housing of the Working Classes Act, 1903 (which limit the cases under which an order confirming an improvement scheme takes effect without confirmation by Parliament), shall cease to have effect.

(2) An order of the Local Government Board sanctioning a reconstruction scheme, and authorizing the compulsory purchase of land for the purpose shall, notwithstanding anything in Section 39 of the principal Act, take effect without confirmation.

25. The Local Government Board may, in the exercise of their power under Section 15 or Sub-section (9) of Section 39 of the principal Act, permit the local authority to modify their scheme, not only by the abandonment of any part of the scheme which it

may appear inexpedient to carry into execution, but also by amending or adding to the scheme in matters of detail in such manner as appears expedient to the Board.

26. Any inspector or officer of the Local Government Board, or any person employed by the Board, may be directed to make any inspection or inquiry which is required for the purposes of Section 16 of the principal Act (which relates to inquiries made on the default of a medical officer), and Section 85 of that Act (which relates to inquiries by the Local Government Board), as amended by this Act, shall apply as respects any inspection or inquiry so held as it applies to local inquiries held under that section.

27. An improvement scheme under Part I of the principal Act may, with the consent of the person or body of persons entitled to any right or easement which would be extinguished by virtue of Section 22 of the principal Act, provide for any exceptions, restrictions, or modifications in the application to that right or easement of that section, and that section shall take effect subject to any such exceptions, restrictions, or modifications.

28. (1) The amount of any compensation payable under Section 38 of the principal Act (which relates to obstructive buildings) shall, when settled by arbitration in manner provided by that section, be apportioned by the arbitrator between any persons having an interest in the compensation in such manner as the arbitrator determines.

(2) The power of the arbitrator to apportion compensation under the foregoing provision and to apportion any part of the compensation to be paid for the demolition of an obstructive building amongst other buildings under Sub-section (8) of the said Section 38 may be exercised in cases where the amount to be paid for compensation has been settled, otherwise than by arbitration under the principal Act, by an arbitrator appointed for the special purpose, on the application of the local authority, by the Local Government Board, and the provisions of that Act shall apply as if the arbitrator so appointed had been appointed as arbitrator to settle the amount to be paid for compensation.

29. For removing doubts it is hereby declared that a local authority may tender evidence before an arbitrator to prove the facts under the headings (first) (secondly) (thirdly) mentioned in Sub-section (2) of Section 21 and Sub-section (3) of Section 41 of the principal Act, notwithstanding that the local authority have not taken any steps with a view to remedying the defects or evils disclosed by the evidence.

AMENDMENTS WITH RESPECT TO FINANCIAL MATTERS

30. No deficiency in the Dwelling-house Improvement Fund shall be supplied under Sub-section (2) of Section 24 of the principal Act out of borrowed money unless the deficiency arises in respect of money required for purposes to which borrowed money is, in the opinion of the Local Government Board, properly applicable.

31. (1) The expenses incurred by a rural district council after the passing of this Act in the execution of Part III of the principal Act shall be defrayed as general expenses of the council in the execution of the Public Health Acts, except so far as the Local Government Board on the application of the council declare that any such expenses are to be levied as special expenses charged on specified contributory places, or as general expenses charged on specified contributory places, in the district, in such proportions as the district council may determine, to the exclusion of other parts of the district, and a rural district council may borrow for the purposes of Part III of the principal Act in like manner and subject to the like conditions as for the purpose of defraying the above-mentioned general or special expenses.

(2) The district council shall give notice to the overseers of any contributory place proposed to be charged of any apportionment made by them under this section, and the overseers, if aggrieved by the apportionment, may appeal to the Local Government Board by giving notice of appeal to the Board within 21 days after notice has been so given of the apportionment.

32. Where any land vested in a local authority for the purposes of Part III of the principal Act is sold under Section 60 of that Act (which relates to the sale and exchange of lands), the proceeds may be applied not only as provided by that section, but also for any purpose, including repayment of borrowed money, for which capital money may be applied, and which is approved by the Local Government Board.

33. Any payment or contribution agreed or ordered to be made under Sub-section (6) or (7) of Section 46 of the principal Act, as amended by Section 14 of the Housing of the Working Classes Act, 1903 (which relate to payments or contributions by borough councils towards the expenses of the county council or by the county council towards the expenses of borough councils in London, may be made either by means of the payment of a lump sum or by means of an annual payment of such amount and for such number of years as may be agreed upon or ordered.

34. Section 133 of the Lands Clauses Consolidation Act, 1845 (relating to Land Tax and Poor Rate), shall not apply in the case of any lands of which a local authority becomes possessed by virtue of the Housing Acts.

35. (1) The assessment to Inhabited House Duty of any house occupied for the sole purpose of letting lodgings to persons of the working classes, at a charge of not exceeding sixpence a night for each person, shall be discharged by the Commissioners acting in the execution of the Acts relating to the Inhabited House Duties, upon the production of a certificate to the effect that the house is solely constructed and used to afford suitable accommodation for the lodgers, and that due provision is made for their sanitary requirements.

53 and 54 Vict. c. 8

(2) The provisions of Sub-section (2) of Section 26 of the Customs and Inland Revenue Act, 1890, in relation to the certificate mentioned therein, shall, so far as applicable, apply to the certificate to be produced under this section.

GENERAL AMENDMENTS

36. Any person authorized in writing stating the particular purpose or purposes for which the entry is authorized, by the local authority or the Local Government Board, may at all reasonable times, on giving 24 hours' notice to the occupier and to the owner, if the owner is known, of his intention, enter any house, premises, or buildings:

(a) for the purpose of survey or valuation, in the case of houses, premises, or buildings which the local authority are authorized to purchase compulsorily under the Housing Acts; and

(b) for the purpose of survey and examination, in the case of any dwelling-house in respect of which a closing order or an order for demolition has been made; or

(c) for the purpose of survey and examination, where it appears to the authority or Board that survey or examination is necessary in order to determine whether any powers under the Housing Acts should be exercised in respect of any house, premises, or building.

Notice may be given to the occupier for the purposes of this section by leaving a notice addressed to the occupier, without name or further description, at the house, buildings, or premises.

37. If it appears to the Local Government Board that owing to density of population or any other reason, it is expedient to inquire into the circumstances of any area with a view to determining whether any powers under the Housiug Acts should be put into force in that area or not, the Local Government Board may require the local authority to make a report to them containing such particulars as to the population of the district and other matters as they direct, and the local authority shall comply with the requirement of the Local Government Board, and any expenses incurred by them in so doing shall be paid as expenses incurred in the execution of such Part of the principal Act as the Local Government Board determine.

38. Where, upon an application made by one of the local authorities concerned, the Local Government Board are satisfied that it is expedient that any local authorities should act jointly for any purposes of the Housing Acts, either generally or in any special case, the Board may by order make provision for the purpose, and any provisions so made shall have the same effect as if they were contained in a provisional order made under Section 279 of the Public Health Act, 1875, for the formation of a united district.

39. (1) The procedure on any appeal under this Part of this Act, including costs, to the Local Government Board shall be such as the Board may by rules determine, and on any such appeal the Board may make such order in the matter as they think equitable, and any order so made shall be binding and conclusive on all parties, and, where the appeal is against any notice, order, or apportionment given or made by the local authority, the notice, order, or apportionment may be confirmed, varied, or quashed, as the Board think just.

Provided that:

(a) the Local Government Board may at any stage of the proceedings on appeal, and shall, if so directed by the High Court, state in the form of a special case for the opinion of the court any question of law arising in the course of the appeal; and

(b) the rules shall provide that the Local Government Board shall not dismiss any appeal without having first held a public local inquiry.

(2) Any notice, order, or apportionment as respects which an appeal to the Local Government Board is given under this

Part of this Act shall not become operative, until either the time within which an appeal can be made under this Part of this Act has elapsed without an appeal being made, or, in case an appeal is made, the appeal is determined or abandoned, and no work shall be done or proceedings taken under any such notice, order, or apportionment, until it becomes operative.

(3) The Local Government Board may, before considering any appeal which may be made to them under this Part of this Act, require the appellant to deposit such sum to cover the costs of the appeal as may be fixed by the rules made by them with reference to appeals.

40. Notwithstanding anything contained in the principal Act it shall not be obligatory upon a local authority to sell and dispose of any lands or dwellings acquired or constructed by them for any of the purposes of the Housing Acts.

41. (1) The Local Government Board may by order prescribe the form of any notice, advertisement, or other document, to be used in connexion with the powers and duties of a local authority or of the Board under the Housing Acts, and the forms so prescribed or forms as near thereto as circumstances admit, shall be used in all cases to which those forms are applicable.

(2) The Local Government Board may dispense with the publication of advertisements or the service of notices required to be published or served by a local authority under the Housing Acts, if they are satisfied that there is reasonable cause for dispensing with the publication or service.

(3) Any such dispensation may be given by the Local Government Board either before or after the time at which the advertisement is required to be published or the notice is required to be served, and either unconditionally or upon such conditions as to the publication of other advertisements or the service of other notices or otherwise as the Board think fit, due care being taken by the Board to prevent the interests of any person being prejudiced by the dispensation.

42. Where under the Housing Acts, any scheme or order or any draft scheme or order is to be published in the "London Gazette," or notice of any such scheme or order or draft scheme or order is to be given in the "London Gazette," it shall be sufficient in lieu of such publication or notice to insert a notice giving short particulars of the scheme, order, or draft, and stating where copies thereof can be inspected or obtained in two local newspapers circulating in the area affected by the scheme, order, or draft,

or to give notice thereof in such other manner as the Local Government Board determine.

43. Notwithstanding anything in any local Act or by-law in force in any borough or district, it shall not be lawful to erect any back-to-back houses intended to be used as dwellings for the working classes, and any such house commenced to be erected after the passing of this Act shall be deemed to be unfit for human habitation for the purposes of the provisions of the Housing Acts.

Provided that nothing in this section:

(a) shall prevent the erection or use of a house containing several tenements in which the tenements are placed back to back, if the medical officer of health for the district certifies that the several tenements are so constructed and arranged as to secure effective ventilation of all habitable rooms in every tenement; or

(b) shall apply to houses abutting on any streets the plans whereof have been approved by the local authority before the first day of May, 1909, in any borough or district in which, at the passing of this Act, any local Act or by-laws are in force permitting the erection of back-to-back houses.

44. If the Local Government Board are satisfied, by local inquiry or otherwise, that the erection of dwellings for the working classes within any borough, or urban or rural district, is unreasonably impeded in consequence of any by-laws with respect to new streets or buildings in force therein, the Board may require the local authority to revoke such by-laws or to make such new by-laws as the Board may consider necessary for the removal of the impediment. If the local authority do not within three months after such requisition comply therewith, the Board may themselves revoke such by-laws, and make such new by-laws as they may consider necessary for the removal of the impediment, and such new by-laws shall have effect as if they had been duly made by the local authority and confirmed by the Board.

45. Nothing in the Housing Acts shall authorize the acquisition for the purposes of those Acts of any land which is the site of an ancient monument or other object of archæological interest, or the compulsory acquisition for the purposes of Part III of the Housing of the Working Classes Act, 1890, of any land which is the property of any local authority or has been acquired by any corporation or company for the purposes of a railway, dock, canal,

water, or other public undertaking, or which at the date of the order forms part of any park, garden, or pleasure ground, or is otherwise required for the amenity or convenience of any dwelling-house.

46. The amendments specified in the second column of the Second Schedule to this Act, which relate to minor details, shall be made in the provisions of the Housing Acts specified in the first column of that Schedule, and Section 63 of the principal Act (which relates to the disqualification of tenants of lodging-houses on receiving poor relief) shall be repealed.

DEFINITIONS

47. (1) Any provisions of this Act which supersede or amend any provisions of the principal Act shall be deemed to be part of that Part of the principal Act in which the provisions superseded or amended are contained.

(2) Any reference in the Housing Acts to a closing order or to an order for the demolition of a building shall be construed as a reference to a closing order or an order of demolition under this Act.

48. The expression " street " shall, unless the context otherwise requires, have the same meaning in Part I of the principal Act as it has in Part II of that Act, and shall include any court, alley, street, square, or row of houses.

49. (1) The words " means any inhabited building and " shall be omitted from the definition of " dwelling-house " in Section 29 of the principal Act.

(2) For the definition of owner in the same section the following definition shall be substituted:

" The expression ' owner,' in addition to the definition given by the Lands Clauses Acts, includes all lessees or mortgagees of any premises required to be dealt with under this Part of this Act, except persons holding or entitled to the rents and profits of such premises under a lease, the original term whereof is less than 21 years."

50. For the definition of cottage in Section 53 of the principal Act the following definition shall be substituted:

The expression " cottage " in this Part of this Act may include a garden of not more than one acre.

51. In this Part of this Act the expression " Housing Acts " means the principal Act, and any Act amending that Act, including this Act.

APPLICATION OF PART I TO SCOTLAND

52. Subject as hereinafter provided, the Housing of the Working Classes Act, 1900, and the Housing of the Working Classes Act, 1903, shall as amended by this Act apply to Scotland.

53. In addition to the provisions of the principal Act respecting the application of that Act to Scotland, the following provisions shall have effect in the application of the Housing Acts to Scotland:

(1) The Local Government Board for Scotland (hereinafter in this section referred to as the Board) shall, except as otherwise provided, be substituted for the Local Government Board, and shall also in Part III of the principal Act as amended and in Section 5 of the Housing of the Working Classes Act, 1900, be substituted for the county council:

(2) The Lord Advocate shall be substituted for the Attorney-General:

60 and 61 Vict. c. 38

(3) The expression " Public Health Acts " means the Public Health (Scotland) Act, 1897, and any Act amending the same. References to the Public Health Act, 1875, shall, unless the context otherwise requires, be construed as references to the Public Health (Scotland) Act, 1897, a reference to an order under Section 83 of the Public Health (Scotland) Act, 1897, shall be substituted for a reference to a provisional order under Section 279 of the Public Health Act, 1875, and a reference to Section 72 of the Public Health (Scotland) Act, 1897, shall be substituted for a reference to Section 90 of the Public Health Act, 1875:

(4) The reference in Section 57 of the principal Act to sections of the Public Health Act, 1875, relating to the purchase of lands, shall be construed as a reference to the corresponding sections of the Public Health (Scotland) Act, 1897: Provided that for the purposes of Part III of the principal Act the procedure under Section 2 of this Act for the compulsory purchase of land shall be substituted for the procedure for the compulsory purchase of land under Section 145 of the Public Health (Scotland) Act, 1897:

(5) The district and the local authority for the purposes of the Public Health (Scotland) Act, 1897, shall respectively be the district and the local authority, and the public

health general assessment shall be the local rate, for the purposes of the Housing Acts; provided that such local rate shall not be reckoned in any calculation as to the statutory limit of the public health general assessment; and provided further that a local authority not being a town council may, where so authorized by the Board in terms of the Housing Acts, assess and levy such local rate upon all lands and heritages within one or more of the parishes or special districts comprised in their district, to the exclusion of other parishes or special districts within the district:

(6) A local authority may, with the consent of the Board, borrow money for the purposes authorized in the Housing Acts on the security of the local rate in the same manner, and subject to the same conditions as nearly as may be, as they may borrow for the provision of permanent hospitals under the Public Health (Scotland) Act, 1897; provided that all money so borrowed shall, notwithstanding the terms of Section 141 of the said Act, be wholly repaid together with the accruing interest within such period not exceeding 80 years from the date of the loan as the Board may determine in each case:

(7) The expressions "urban sanitary authority" and "rural sanitary authority" or "rural district council" mean respectively the local authority (for the purposes of the Public Health (Scotland) Act, 1897) of a burgh and of a district not being a burgh, and the expressions "urban district" and "rural district" shall be construed accordingly:

60 and 61 Vict. c. 38. 52 and 53 Vict. c. 50

(8) The Acts relating to nuisances mean as respects any place the Public Health (Scotland) Act, 1897, and the Local Government (Scotland) Act, 1889, and any Act amending the same or either of them, and any local Act which contains any provisions with respect to nuisances in that place:

(9) Except so far as inconsistent with the provisions of Sub-section (1) of Section 85 of the principal Act, Sections 7, 8, 9, and 10 of the Public Health (Scotland) Act, 1897, shall apply for the purpose of local inquiries ordered by the Board under the Housing Acts:

(10) Section 1, Sub-section (1) of Section 4, and Section 10 of the Housing of the Working Classes Act, 1903, shall not apply. In the last-mentioned Act, Sections 3 and 12 shall apply with the substitution of the date of the passing of this Act, for the date of the passing of that Act, and the Schedule shall apply with the modifications specified in the Third Schedule to this Act:

(11) Where a complaint is made to the Board:

    (a) as respects the district of a local authority not being a town council, by the county council, or by the parish council or landward committee of any parish comprised in the district, or by any four inhabitant householders of the district; or

    (b) as respects any other district by any four inhabitant householders of the district;

that the local authority have failed to exercise their powers under Part II or Part III of the principal Act in cases where those powers ought to have been exercised, the Board may cause a public local inquiry to be held, and if, after holding such an inquiry, the Board are satisfied that there has been such a failure on the part of the local authority, it shall be lawful for the Board, with the approval of the Lord Advocate, to apply by summary petition to either Division of the Court of Session, or during vacation or recess to the Lord Ordinary on the Bills, which Division or Lord Ordinary are hereby authorized and directed to do therein and to dispose of the expenses of the proceedings as to the said Division or Lord Ordinary shall appear to be just. Section 10 of this Act shall not apply:

(12) Where it appears to the Board that a local authority have failed to perform their duty under the Housing Acts of carrying out an improvement scheme under Part I of the principal Act, or have failed to make, or, if made, to give effect to, any order as respects an obstructing building, or any reconstruction scheme, under Part II of that Act, or have failed to cause to be made the inspection of their district required by this Act, it shall be lawful for the Board to apply by summary petition to either Division of the Court of Session, or during vacation or recess to the Lord Ordinary on the Bills, which Division or Lord Ordinary are hereby author-

ized and directed as in the immediately preceding sub-section. Section 11 of this Act shall not apply:

(13) Section 12 and Section 13 of this Act shall not apply:

(14) Sections 15, 17, 18 and 39 of this Act shall apply with the substitution (except as regards the making of or consenting to regulations) of the sheriff for the Local Government Board and of the Court of Session for the High Court; provided that the reference to a public local inquiry shall not apply, and provided further that where an appeal is competent under any of these sections, an appeal shall not be competent under Section 35 of the principal Act, and provided also that the power to make rules under Section 39 of this Act shall be exercised by the Court of Session by act of sederunt. Section 146 of

60 and 61 Vict. c. 38

the Public Health (Scotland) Act, 1897 prescribing the procedure if a local authority neglect its duty), shall have effect as if the duties imposed upon a local authority by Sections 17 and 18 of this Act were duties imposed by that Act:

(15) In the application to Scotland of Section 14 of this Act, the limit of rent shall be £16:

(16) References to special expenses shall not apply:

(17) " Overseers " means parish council, " paid into court " means " paid into bank," " as a civil debt in manner provided by the Summary Jurisdiction Acts " means in a summary manner.

PART II

TOWN PLANNING

54. (1) A town planning scheme may be made in accordance with the provisions of this Part of this Act as respects any land which is in course of development or appears likely to be used for building purposes, with the general object of securing proper sanitary conditions, amenity, and convenience in connexion with the laying out and use of the land, and of any neighbouring lands.

(2) The Local Government Board may authorize a local authority within the meaning of this Part of this Act to prepare such a town planning scheme with reference to any land within or in the neighbourhood of their area, if the authority satisfy the Board that there is a prima facie case for making such a scheme

or may authorize a local authority to adopt, with or without any modifications, any such scheme proposed by all or any of the owners of any land with respect to which the local authority might themselves have been authorized to prepare a scheme.

(3) Where it is made to appear to the Local Government Board that a piece of land already built upon, or a piece of land not likely to be used for building purposes, is so situated with respect to any land likely to be used for building purposes that it ought to be included in any town planning scheme made with respect to the last-mentioned land, the Board may authorize the preparation or adoption of a scheme including such piece of land as aforesaid, and providing for the demolition or alteration of any buildings thereon so far as may be necessary for carrying the scheme into effect.

(4) A town planning scheme prepared or adopted by a local authority shall not have effect, unless it is approved by order of the Local Government Board, and the Board may refuse to approve any scheme except with such modifications and subject to such conditions as they think fit to impose:

Provided that, before a town planning scheme is approved by the Local Government Board, notice of their intention to do so shall be published in the " London or Edinburgh Gazette," as the case may be, and, if within 21 days from the date of such publication any person or authority interested objects in the prescribed manner, the draft of the order shall be laid before each House of Parliament for a period of not less than 30 days during the session of Parliament, and, if either of those Houses before the expiration of those 30 days presents an address to His Majesty against the draft, or any part thereof, no further proceedings shall be taken thereon, without prejudice to the making of any new draft scheme.

(5) A town planning scheme, when approved by the Local Government Board, shall have effect as if it were enacted in this Act.

(6) A town planning scheme may be varied or revoked by a subsequent scheme prepared or adopted and approved in accordance with this Part of this Act, and the Local Government Board, on the application of the responsible authority, or of any other person appearing to them to be interested, may by order revoke a town planning scheme if they think that under the special circumstances of the case the scheme should be so revoked.

(7) The expression " land likely to be used for building pur-

poses " shall include any land likely to be used as, or for the purpose of providing open spaces, roads, streets, parks, pleasure or recreation grounds, or for the purpose of executing any work upon or under the land incidental to a town planning scheme, whether in the nature of a building work or not, and the decision of the Local Government Board, whether land is likely to be used for building purposes or not, shall be final.

55. (1) The Local Government Board may prescribe a set of general provisions (or separate sets of general provisions adapted for areas of any special character) for carrying out the general objects of town planning schemes, and in particular for dealing with the matters set out in the Fourth Schedule to this Act, and the general provisions, or set of general provisions appropriate to the area for which a town planning scheme is made, shall take effect as part of every scheme, except so far as provision is made by the scheme as approved by the Board for the variation or exclusion of any of those provisions.

(2) Special provisions shall in addition be inserted in every town planning scheme defining in such manner as may be prescribed by regulations under this Part of this Act the area to which the scheme is to apply, and the authority who are to be responsible for enforcing the observance of the scheme, and for the execution of any works which under the scheme or this Part of this Act are to executed by a local authority (in this Part of this Act referred to as the responsible authority), and providing for any matters which may be dealt with by general provisions, and otherwise supplementing, excluding, or varying the general provisions, and also for dealing with any special circumstances or contingencies for which adequate provision is not made by the general provisions, and for suspending, so far as necessary for the proper carrying out of the scheme, any statutory enactments, by-laws, regulations, or other provisions, under whatever authority made, which are in operation in the area included in the scheme:

Provided that, where the scheme contains provisions suspending any enactment contained in a public general Act, the scheme shall not come into force unless a draft thereof has been laid before each House of Parliament for a period of not less than 40 days during the session of Parliament, and, if either of those Houses before the expiration of those 40 days presents an Address to His Majesty against the proposed suspension no further proceedings shall be taken on the draft, without prejudice to the making of any new scheme.

BB2

(3) Where land included in a town planning scheme is in the area of more than one local authority, or is in the area of a local authority by whom the scheme was not prepared, the responsible authority may be one of those local authorities, or for certain purposes of the scheme one local authority and for certain purposes another local authority, or a joint body constituted specially for the purpose by the scheme, and all necessary provisions may be made by the scheme for constituting the joint body and giving them the necessary powers and duties:

Provided that, except with the consent of the London County Council, no other local authority shall, as respects any land in the county of London, prepare or be responsible for enforcing the observance of a town planning scheme under this Part of this Act, or for the execution of any works which under the scheme or this Part of this Act are to be executed by a local authority.

56. (1) The Local Government Board may make regulations for regulating generally the procedure to be adopted with respect to applications for authority to prepare or adopt a town planning scheme, the preparation of the scheme, obtaining the approval of the Board to a scheme so prepared or adopted, and any inquiries, reports, notices, or other matters required in connexion with the preparation or adoption or the approval of the scheme or preliminary thereto, or in relation to the carrying out of the scheme or enforcing the observance of the provisions thereof.

(2) Provision shall be made by those regulations:

    (a) for securing co-operation on the part of the local authority with the owners and other persons interested in the land proposed to be included in the scheme at every stage of the proceedings, by means of conferences and such other means as may be provided by the regulations;

    (b) for securing that notice of the proposal to prepare or adopt the scheme should be given at the earliest stage possible to any council interested in the land; and

    (c) for dealing with the other matters mentioned in the Fifth Schedule to this Act.

57. (1) The responsible authority may at any time, after giving such notice as may be provided by a town planning scheme and in accordance with the provisions of the scheme:

    (a) remove, pull down, or alter any building or other work in the area included in the scheme which is such as to contravene the scheme, or in the erection or carrying out of which any provision of the scheme has not been complied with; or

(b) execute any work which it is the duty of any person to execute under the scheme in any case where it appears to the authority that delay in the execution of the work would prejudice the efficient operation of the scheme.

(2) Any expenses incurred by a responsible authority under this section may be recovered from the persons in default in such manner and subject to such conditions as may be provided by the scheme.

(3) If any question arises whether any building or work contravenes a town planning scheme, or whether any provision of a town planning scheme is not complied with in the erection or carrying out of any such building or work, that question shall be referred to the Local Government Board, and shall, unless the parties otherwise agree, be determined by the Board as arbitrators, and the decision of the Board shall be final and conclusive and binding on all persons.

58. (1) Any person whose property is injuriously affected by the making of a town planning scheme shall, if he makes a claim for the purpose within the time (if any) limited by the scheme, not being less that three months after the date when notice of the approval of the scheme is published in the manner prescribed by regulations made by the Local Government Board, be entitled to obtain compensation in respect thereof from the responsible authority.

(2) A person shall not be entitled to obtain compensation under this section on account of any building erected on, or contract made or other thing done with respect to, land included in a scheme, after the time at which the application for authority to prepare the scheme was made, or after such other time as the Local Government Board may fix for the purpose:

Provided that this provision shall not apply as respects any work done before the date of the approval of the scheme for the purpose of finishing a building begun or of carrying out a contract entered into before the application was made.

(3) Where, by the making of any town planning scheme, any property is increased in value, the responsible authority, if they make a claim for the purpose within the time (if any) limited by the scheme (not being less than three months after the date when notice of the approval of the scheme is first published in the manner prescribed by regulations made by the Local Govern-

ment Board), shall be entitled to recover from any person whose property is so increased in value one-half of the amount of that increase.

(4) Any question as to whether any property is injuriously affected or increased in value within the meaning of this section, and as to the amount and manner of payment (whether by instalments or otherwise) of the sum which is to be paid as compensation under this section or which the responsible authority are entitled to recover from a person whose property is increased in value, shall be determined by the arbitration of a single arbitrator appointed by the Local Government Board, unless the parties agree on some other method of determination.

(5) Any amount due under this section as compensation to a person aggrieved from a responsible authority, or to a responsible authority from a person whose property is increased in value, may be recovered summarily as a civil debt.

(6) Where a town planning scheme is revoked by an order of the Local Government Board under this Act, any person who has incurred expenditure for the purpose of complying with the scheme shall be entitled to compensation in accordance with this section in so far as any such expenditure is rendered abortive by reason of the revocation of the scheme.

59 (1) Where property is alleged to be injuriously affected by reason of any provisions contained in a town planning scheme, no compensation shall be paid in respect thereof if or so far as the provisions are such as would have been enforceable if they had been contained in by-laws made by the local authority.

(2) Property shall not be deemed to be injuriously affected by reason of the making of any provisions inserted in a town planning scheme, which, with a view to securing the amenity of the area included in the scheme or any part thereof, prescribe the space about buildings or limit the number of buildings to be erected, or prescribe the height or character of buildings, and which the Local Government Board, having regard to the nature and situation of the land affected by the provisions, consider reasonable for the purpose.

(3) Where a person is entitled to compensation under this Part of this Act in respect of any matter or thing, and he would be entitled to compensation in respect of the same matter or thing under any other enactment, he shall not be entitled to compensation in respect of that matter or thing both under this Act and under that other enactment, and shall not be entitled to any greater

compensation under this Act than he would be entitled to under the other enactment.

60. (1) The responsible authority may, for the purpose of a town planning scheme, purchase any land comprised in such scheme by agreement, or be authorized to purchase any such land compulsorily in the same manner and subject to the same provisions (including any provision authorizing the Local Government Board to give directions as to the payment and application of any purchase money or compensation) as a local authority may purchase or be authorized to purchase land situate in an urban district for the purposes of Part III of the Housing of the Working Classes Act, 1890, as amended by Sections 2 and 45 of this Act.

(2) Where land included within the area of a local authority is comprised in a town planning scheme, and the local authority are not the responsible authority, the local authority may purchase or be authorized to purchase that land in the same manner as the responsible authority.

61. (1) If the Local Government Board are satisfied on any representation, after holding a public local inquiry, that a local authority:

- (a) have failed to take the requisite steps for having a satisfactory town planning scheme prepared and approved in a case where a town planning scheme ought to be made; or
- (b) have failed to adopt any scheme proposed by owners of any land in a case where the scheme ought to be adopted; or
- (c) have unreasonably refused to consent to any modifications or conditions imposed by the Board;

the Board may, as the case requires, order the local authority to prepare and submit for the approval of the Board such a town planning scheme, or to adopt the scheme, or to consent to the modifications or conditions so inserted:

Provided that, where the representation is that a local authority have failed to adopt a scheme, the Local Government Board, in lieu of making such an order as aforesaid, may approve the proposed scheme, subject to such modifications or conditions, if any, as the Board think fit, and thereupon the scheme shall have effect as if it had been adopted by the local authority and approved by the Board.

(2) If the Local Government Board are satisfied on any representation, after holding a local inquiry, that a responsible

authority have failed to enforce effectively the observance of a scheme which has been confirmed, or any provisions thereof, or to execute any works which under the scheme or this Part of this Act the authority is required to execute, the Board may order that authority to do all things necessary for enforcing the observance of the scheme or any provisions thereof effectively, or for executing any works which under the scheme or this Part of this Act the authority is required to execute.

(3) Any order under this section may be enforced by mandamus.

31 and 32 Vict. c. 119

62. Where the Local Government Board are authorized by this Part of this Act or any scheme made thereunder to determine any matter, it shall, except as otherwise expressly provided by this Part of this Act, be at their option to determine the matter as arbitrators or otherwise, and, if they elect or are required to determine the matter as arbitrators, the provisions of the Regulation of Railways Act, 1868, respecting arbitrations by the Board of Trade, and the enactments amending those provisions shall apply as if they were herein re-enacted and in terms made applicable to the Local Government Board and the determination of the matters aforesaid.

63. Section 85 of the Housing of the Working Classes Act, 1890 (which relates to inquiries by the Local Government Board), as amended by this Act, shall apply for any purposes of this Part of this Act as it applies for the purpose of the execution of the powers and duties of the Local Government Board under that Act. Laying general provisions before Parliament. 56 and 57 Vict. c. 66

64. All general provisions made under this Part of this Act shall be laid as soon as may be before Parliament, and the Rules Publication Act, 1893, shall apply to such provisions as if they were statutory rules within the meaning of Section 1 of that Act.

65. (1) For the purposes of this Part of this Act the expression " local authority " means the council of any borough or urban or rural district.

(2) Any expenses incurred by a local authority under this Part of this Act, or any scheme made thereunder, shall be defrayed as expenses of the authority under the Public Health Acts, and the authority may borrow, for the purposes of this Part of this Act, or any scheme made thereunder, in the same manner and subject

to the same provisions as they may borrow for the purposes of the Public Health Acts.

(3) Money borrowed for the purposes of this Part of this Act, or any scheme made thereunder, shall not be reckoned as part of the debt of a borough or urban district for the purposes of the limitation on borrowing under Sub-sections (2) and (3) of Section 234 of the Public Health Act, 1875.

66. (1) This Part of this Act shall apply to the administrative county of London, and, as respects that county, the London County Council shall be the local authority.

(2) Any expenses incurred by the London County Council shall be defrayed out of the general county rate and any money may be borrowed by the Council in the same manner as money may be borrowed for general county purposes.

67. This Part of this Act shall apply to Scotland subject to the following modifications:

(1) The Local Government Board for Scotland (hereinafter referred to as the Board) shall be substituted for the Local Government Board, and shall for the purposes of this Part of this Act have the same powers of local inquiry as for the purposes of the Housing Acts as defined in Part I of this Act.

(2) Sub-section (1) and Sub-section (3) of the section of this Part of this Act which relates to the definition of local authority and expenses shall not apply.

(3) The local authority and the area of such authority for the purposes of this Part of this Act shall respectively be the local authority for the purposes of the Housing Acts as defined in Part I of this Act, and the district of that authority.

(4) References to the Public Health Acts shall be construed as references to the Housing Acts as defined in Part I of this Act.

(5) Any local rate for the purposes of this Part of this Act (including the purposes of any loan) shall not be reckoned in any calculation as to the statutory limit of the public health general assessment.

(6) The Board shall not themselves make an order under Section 61 of this Act on any authority, but in lieu thereof it shall be lawful for the Board, after holding a local inquiry at which the authority shall have had an opportunity of being heard, and with the approval of the Lord

Advocate, to apply for such an order by summary petition to either Division of the Court of Session, or during vacation or recess to the Lord Ordinary on the Bills, which Division or Lord Ordinary are hereby authorized and directed to do therein and to dispose of the expenses of the proceedings as to the said Division or Lord Ordinary shall appear to be just.

(7) In any proceedings under this Part of this Act the Board shall have regard to the powers and jurisdiction of the dean of guild court in burghs.

(8) The provision respecting the Rules Publication Act, 1893, shall have effect as if Section 1 of that Act applied to Scotland, with the substitution of the " Edinburgh Gazette " for the " London Gazette."

PART III

COUNTY MEDICAL OFFICERS, COUNTY PUBLIC HEALTH AND HOUSING COMMITTEE, Etc.

68. (1) Every county council shall appoint a medical officer of health under Section 17 of the Local Government Act, 1888.

(2) The duties of a medical officer of health of a county shall be such duties as may be prescribed by general order of the Local Government Board and such other duties as may be assigned to him by the county council.

(3) The power of county councils and district councils under the said section to make arrangements with respect to medical officers of health shall cease, without prejudice to any arrangement made previously to the date of the passing of this Act.

(4) The medical officer of health of a county shall, for the purposes of his duties, have the same powers of entry on premises as are conferred on a medical officer of health of a district by or under any enactment.

(5) A medical officer of health of a county shall be removable by the county council with the consent of the Local Government Board and not otherwise.

(6) A medical officer of health of a county shall not be appointed for a limited period only:

Provided that the county council may with the sanction of the Local Government Board make any temporary arrangement for the performance of all or any of the duties of the medical officer of health of the county, and any person appointed by virtue of any such arrangement to perform those duties or any of them shall, subject to the terms of his appointment, have all the powers, duties, and liabilities of the medical officer of health of the county.

(7) A medical officer of health appointed after the passing of this Act under the said section as amended by this section shall not engage in private practice, and shall not hold any other public appointment without the express written consent of the Local Government Board.

(8) An order under this section prescribing the duties of medical officers of health of a county shall be communicated to the county council and shall be laid before Parliament as soon as may be after it is made, and, if an address is presented to His Majesty by either House of Parliament within the next subsequent 21 days on which that House has sat next after the order is laid before it praying that the order may be annulled, His Majesty in Council may annul the order and it shall thenceforward be void, but without prejudice to the validity of anything previously done thereunder.

69. (1) The clerk of a rural district council shall forward to the medical officer of health of the county a copy of any representation, complaint, or information, a copy of which it is the duty of the district council to forward to the county council under Section 45 of the Housing of the Working Classes Act, 1890 (which relates to the powers of county councils).

(2) The medical officer of health of a district shall give to the medical officer of health of the county any information which it is in his power to give, and which the medical officer of health of the county may reasonably require from him for the purpose of his duties prescribed by the Local Government Board.

(3) If any dispute or difference shall arise between the clerk or the medical officer of health of a district council and the medical officer of health of a county council under this section, the same shall be referred to the Local Government Board, whose decision shall be final and binding.

(4) If the clerk or medical officer of health of a district council fails to comply with the provisions of this section, he shall on information being laid by the county council, but not otherwise, be liable on summary conviction in respect of each offence to a fine not exceeding £10.

70. The foregoing provisions of this Part of this Act shall not apply to Scotland or, except Sub-section (4) of Section 68, to the administrative county of London, and, in the application of the said sub-section to London, the reference to a medical

officer of health of a district shall be construed as a reference to the medical officer of health of a metropolitan borough.

71. (1) Every county council shall establish a public health and housing committee, and all matters relating to the exercise and performance by the council of their powers and duties as respects public health and the housing of the working classes (except the power of raising a rate or borrowing money) shall stand referred to the public health and housing committee, and the council, before exercising any such powers, shall, unless in their opinion the matter is urgent, receive and consider the report of the public health and housing committee with respect to the matter in question, and the council may also delegate to the public health and housing committee, with or without restrictions or conditions as they think fit, any of their powers as respects public health and the housing of the working classes, except the power of raising a rate or borrowing money and except any power of resolving that the powers of a district council in default should be transferred to the council.

(2) This section shall not apply to Scotland or the London County Council.

72. (1) The county council may promote the formation or extension of and may, subject to the provisions of this section, assist societies on a co-operative basis, having for their object or one of their objects the erection or improvement of dwellings for the working classes.

(2) The county council, with the consent of and subject to the regulations made by the Local Government Board, may for the purpose of assisting a society make grants or advances to the society, or guarantee advances made to the society, upon such terms and conditions as to rate of interest and repayment, or otherwise, and on such security, as the council think fit, and the making of such grants or advances shall be a purpose for which a council may borrow:

Provided that the regulations of the Board shall provide that any such advance made on the security of any property shall not exceed two-thirds of the value of that property.

PART IV
SUPPLEMENTAL

73. (1) Where any scheme or order under the Housing Acts or Part II of this Act authorizes the acquisition or appropriation to

any other purpose of any land forming part of any common, open space, or allotment, the scheme or order, so far as it relates to the acquisition or appropriation of such land, shall be provisional only, and shall not have effect unless and until it is confirmed by Parliament, except where the scheme or order provides for giving in exchange for such land other land, not being less in area, certified by the Local Government Board after consultation with the Board of Agriculture and Fisheries to be equally advantageous to the persons, if any, entitled to commonable or other rights and to the public.

(2) Before giving any such certificate the Board shall give public notice of the proposed exchange, and shall afford opportunities to all persons interested to make representations and objections in relation thereto, and shall, if necessary, hold a local inquiry on the subject.

(3) Where any such scheme or order authorizes such an exchange, the scheme or order shall provide for vesting the land given in exchange in the persons in whom the common or open space was vested, subject to the same rights, trusts, and incidents as attached to the common or open space, and for discharging the part of the common, open space, or allotment acquired or appropriated from all rights, trusts, and incidents to which it was previously subject.

(4) For the purposes of this Act the expression " common " shall include any land subject to be enclosed under the Inclosure Acts, 1845 to 1882, and any town or village green; the expression " open space " means any land laid out as a public garden or used for the purposes of public recreation, and any disused burial ground; and the expression " allotment " means any allotment set out as a fuel allotment or a field garden allotment under an Inclosure Act.

74. (1) Where any land proposed to be included in any scheme or order to be made under the Housing Acts or Part II of this Act, or any land proposed to be acquired under the Housing Acts or Part II of this Act, is situate within the prescribed distance from any of the royal palaces or parks, the local authority shall, before preparing the scheme or order or acquiring the land, communicate with the Commissioners of Works, and the Local Government Board shall, before confirming the scheme or order or authorizing the acquisition of the land or the raising of any loan for the purpose, take into consideration any recommendations they may have received from the Commissioners of Works with reference to the proposal.

(2) For the purposes of this section '' prescribed '' means prescribed by regulations made by the Local Government Board after consultation with the Commissioners of Works.

75. The enactments mentioned in the Sixth Schedule to this Act are hereby repealed to the extent specified in the third column of that schedule.

76. (1) This Act may be cited as the Housing, Town Planning, etc., Act, 1909, and Part I of this Act shall be construed as one with the Housing of the Working Classes Acts, 1890 to 1903, and that Part of this Act and those Acts may be cited together as the Housing of the Working Classes Acts, 1890 to 1909.

(2) This Act shall not extend to Ireland.

SCHEDULES

FIRST SCHEDULE

A.D. 1909

Section 2

PROVISIONS AS TO THE COMPULSORY ACQUISITION OF LAND BY A LOCAL AUTHORITY FOR THE PURPOSES OF PART III OF THE HOUSING OF THE WORKING CLASSES ACT, 1890

1. Where a local authority propose to purchase land compulsorily under this Act, the local authority may submit to the Board an order putting in force as respects the land specified in the order the provisions of the Lands Clauses Acts with respect to the purchase and taking of land otherwise than by agreement.

2. An order under this schedule shall be of no force unless and until it is confirmed by the Board, and the Board may confirm the order either without modification or subject to such modifications as they think fit, and an order when so confirmed shall, save as otherwise expressly provided by this schedule, become final and have effect as if enacted in this Act; and the confirmation by the Board shall be conclusive evidence that the requirements of this Act have been complied with, and that the order has been duly made and is within the powers of this Act.

3. In determining the amount of any disputed compensation under any such order, no additional allowance shall be made on account of the purchase being compulsory.

8 and 9 Vict. c. 18; 8 and 9 Vict. c. 20

4. The order shall be in the prescribed form, and shall contain such provisions as the Board may prescribe for the purpose of carrying the order into effect, and of protecting the local authority and the persons interested in the land, and shall incorporate, subject to the necessary adaptations, the Lands Clauses Acts (except Section 127 of the Lands Clauses Consolidation Act, 1845) and Sections 77 to 85 of the Railways Clauses Consolidation Act, 1845, but subject to this modification, that any question of disputed compensation shall be determined by a single arbitrator appointed by the Board, who shall be deemed to be an arbitrator within the meaning of the Lands Clauses Acts, and the provisions of those Acts with respect to arbitration shall, subject to the provisions of this schedule, apply accordingly.

5. The order shall be published by the local authority in the prescribed manner, and such notice shall be given both in the locality in which the land is proposed to be acquired, and to the owners, lessees, and occupiers of that land as may be prescribed.

6. If within the prescribed period no objection to the order has been presented to the Board by a person interested in the land, or if every such objection has been withdrawn, the Board shall, without further inquiry, confirm the order, but, if such an objection has been presented and has not been withdrawn, the Board shall forthwith cause a public inquiry to be held in the locality in which the land is proposed to be acquired, and the local authority and all persons interested in the land and such other persons as the person holding the inquiry in his discretion thinks fit to allow shall be permitted to appear and be heard at the inquiry.

7. Where the land proposed to be acquired under the order consists of or comprises land situate in London, or a borough, or urban district, the Board shall appoint an impartial person, not in the employment of any Government Department, to hold the inquiry as to whether the land proposed to be acquired is suitable for the purposes for which it is sought to be acquired, and whether, having regard to the extent or situation of the land and the purposes for which it is used, the land can be acquired without undue detriment to the persons interested therein or the owners of adjoining land, and such person shall in England have for the purpose of the inquiry all the powers of an inspector of the Local Government Board, and, if he reports that the land, or any part thereof, is not suitable for the purposes for which it is sought to be acquired, or that owing to its extent or situation or the purpose for

which it is used it cannot be acquired without such detriment as aforesaid, or that it ought not to be acquired except subject to the conditions specified in his report, then, if the Local Government Board confirm the order in respect of that land, or part thereof, or, as the case may require, confirm it otherwise than subject to such modifications as are required to give effect to the specified conditions the order shall be provisional only, and shall not have effect unless confirmed by Parliament.

Where no part of the land is so situated as aforesaid, before confirming the order, the Board shall consider the report of the person who held the inquiry, and all objections made thereat.

8. The arbitrator shall, so far as practicable, in assessing compensation act on his own knowledge and experience, but, subject as aforesaid, at any inquiry or arbitration held under this schedule the person holding the inquiry or arbitration shall hear, by themselves or their agents, any authorities or parties authorized to appear, and shall hear witnesses, but shall not, except in such cases as the Board otherwise direct, hear council or expert witnesses.

9. The Board may, with the concurrence of the Lord Chancellor, make rules fixing a scale of costs to be applicable on an arbitration under this schedule, and an arbitrator under this schedule may, notwithstanding anything in the Lands Clauses Acts, determine the amount of costs, and shall have power to disallow as costs in the arbitration the costs of any witness whom he considers to have been called unnecessarily and any other costs which he considers to have been caused or incurred unnecessarily.

10. The remuneration of an arbitrator appointed under this schedule shall be fixed by the Board.

11. In construing for the purposes of this schedule or any order made thereunder, any enactment incorporated with the order, this Act together with the order shall be deemed to be the special Act, and the local authority shall be deemed to be the promoters of the undertaking.

12. Where the land is glebe land or other land belonging to an ecclesiastical benefice, the order shall provide that sums agreed upon or awarded for the purchase of the land, or to be paid by way of compensation for the damage to be sustained by the owner by reason of severance or other injury affecting the land, shall not be paid as directed by the Lands Clauses Acts, but shall be paid to the Ecclesiastical Commissioners to be applied by them as money paid to them upon a sale, under the provisions of the Ecclesiastical Leasing Acts, of land belonging to a benefice,

13. In this schedule the expression " Board " means the Local Government Board, and the expression " prescribed " means prescribed by the Board.

14. The provisions of this schedule, except those relating to land belonging to an ecclesiastical benefice, shall apply to Scotland, subject to the following modifications:

(a) for the reference to Section 127 of the Lands Clauses Consolidation Act, 1845, there shall be substituted a reference to Section 120 of the Lands Clauses Consolidation (Scotland) Act, 1845, and for the reference to Sections 77 to 85 of the Railways Clauses Consolidation Act, 1845, there shall be substituted a reference to Sections 70 to 78 of the Railways Clauses Consolidation (Scotland) Act, 1845;

8 and 9 Vict. c. 19; 8 and 9 Vict. c. 33

(b) for references to an arbitrator there shall be substituted references to an arbiter;

(c) for the references to the Lord Chancellor there shall be substituted a reference to the Lord Advocate;

(d) for the reference to the Local Government Board there shall be substituted a reference to the Local Government Board for Scotland, and for the reference to a borough or urban district there shall be substituted a reference to a burgh.

SECOND SCHEDULE

Section 46

MINOR AMENDMENTS OF HOUSING ACTS

Enactment to be amended	Nature of Amendment
Housing of the Working Classes Act, 1890 (53 and 54 Vict. c. 70)	
Section 23 - -	After the word " displaced " the words " in consequence of " shall be substituted for the word " by."
Section 34 - -	The words " the order becomes operative " shall be substituted for the words " service of the order."

Enactment to be amended	Nature of Amendment
Housing of the Working Classes Act, 1890 (53 and 54 Vict. c. 70)	
Section 35 - -	The words " if he is not entitled to appeal to the Local Government Board against the order " shall be inserted after the word " may " where it first occurs.
Section 38 (1) (a)	The words " or impedes " shall be inserted after the word " stops."
Section 38 (7) -	The words " house or other building or manufactory " shall be substituted for the words " house or manufactory " wherever they occur in that sub-section.
Section 39 (8) -	The words " as amended by any subsequent Act " shall be inserted after the word " Act " where it first occurs, and the words " to the power of the Local Government Board to enforce that duty " shall be inserted after the word " execution."
Section 40 - -	After the word " displaced " the words " in consequence of " shall be substituted for the word " by."
Section 85 - -	The words " powers and " shall be inserted before the word " duties."
Section 88 - -	The words " or Part III " shall be inserted after the words " Part II."
Section 89 - -	After the word " Act " where it first occurs the words " or any person authorized to enter dwelling-houses, premises, or buildings in pursuance of this Act " shall be inserted; the words " authority or person " shall be substituted for the words " or authority," and the word " he " shall be substituted for the words " such person."

Section 53

MODIFICATIONS OF THE SCHEDULE TO THE HOUSING OF THE WORKING CLASSES ACT, 1903, IN ITS APPLICATION TO SCOTLAND

In the above-mentioned schedule, as applying to Scotland, the expression " district within the meaning of the Public Health (Scotland) Act, 1897," shall be substituted for the expressions " borough," " urban district," and " parish " respectively; " Local Government Board for Scotland " shall be substituted for " Local Government Board "; " every such appropriation of lands shall be recorded as a real burden affecting such lands in the appropriate register of sasines " shall be substituted for " every conveyance, demise, or lease of any such lands shall be endorsed with notice of this provision "; " Sub-sections 1 and 3 (with the substitution of the Local Government Board for Scotland for the Secretary for Scotland) of Section 93 of the Local Government (Scotland) Act, 1889 " shall be substituted for " Sub-sections 1 and 5 of Section 87 of the Local Government Act, 1888 "; " Court of Session " shall be substituted for " High Court "; " order of the Court of Session on the application of the Board " shall be substituted for " mandamus "; and " local authority for the purposes of the Public Health (Scotland) Act, 1897, in whose district " shall be substituted for " council of any administrative county and the district council of any county district; or in London the council of any metropolitan borough, in which."

FOURTH SCHEDULE

Section 55

MATTERS TO BE DEALT WITH BY GENERAL PROVISIONS PRESCRIBED BY THE LOCAL GOVERNMENT BOARD

1. Streets, roads, and other ways, and stopping up, or diversion of existing highways.

2. Buildings, structures, and erections.

3. Open spaces, private and public.

4. The preservation of objects of historical interest or natural beauty.

5. Sewerage, drainage, and sewage disposal.

6. Lighting.

7. Water supply.

8. Ancillary or consequential works.

9. Extinction or variation of private rights of way and other easements.

10. Dealing with or disposal of land acquired by the responsible authority or by a local authority.

11. Power of entry and inspection.

12. Power of the responsible authority to remove, alter, or demolish any obstructive work.

13. Power of the responsible authority to make agreements with owners, and of owners to make agreements with one another.

14. Power of the responsible authority or a local authority to accept any money or property for the furtherance of the objects of any town planning scheme, and provision for regulating the administration of any such money or property and for the exemption of any assurance with respect to money or property so accepted from enrolment under the Mortmain and Charitable Uses Act, 1888.

51 and 52 Vict. c. 42

15. Application with the necessary modifications and adaptations of statutory enactments.

16. Carrying out and supplementing the provisions of this Act for enforcing schemes.

17. Limitation of time for operation of scheme.

18. Co-operation of the responsible authority with the owners of land included in the scheme or other persons interested by means of conferences, etc.

19. Charging on the inheritance of any land the value of which is increased by the operation of a town planning scheme the sum required to be paid in respect of that increase, and for that purpose applying, with the necessary adaptations, the provisions of any enactments dealing with charges for improvements of land.

FIFTH SCHEDULE

Section 56

1. Procedure anterior to and for the purpose of an application for authority to prepare or adopt a scheme:
   (a) Submission of plans and estimates.
   (b) Publication of notices.

2. Procedure during, on, and after the preparation or adoption and before the approval of the scheme:
   (a) Submission to the Local Government Board of the proposed scheme, with plans and estimates.

    (b) Notice of submission of proposed scheme to the Local Government Board.

    (c) Hearing of objections and representations by persons affected, including persons representing architectural or archæological societies or otherwise interested in the amenity of the proposed scheme.

    (d) Publication of notice of intention to approve scheme and the lodging of objections thereto.

  3. Procedure after the approval of the scheme:

    (a) Notice to be given of approval of scheme.

    (b) Inquiries and reports as to the beginning and the progress and completion of works, and other action under the scheme.

  4. Duty, at any stage, of the local authority to publish or deposit for inspection any scheme or proposed scheme, and the plans relating thereto, and to give information to persons affected with reference to any such scheme or proposed scheme.

  5. The details to be specified in plans, including, wherever the circumstances so require, the restrictions on the number of buildings which may be erected on each acre, and the height and character of those buildings.

SIXTH SCHEDULE

Section 75

ENACTMENTS REPEALED

Session and Chapter	Short Title	Extent of Repeal
51 and 52 Vict. c. 41	The Local Government Act, 1888	Section 17, from " who shall not hold " to end of the section
53 and 54 Vict. c. 70	The Housing of the Working Classes Act, 1890	The words " for sanitary purposes " in paragraph (a) of Sub-section (1) of Section 6 Sub-section (6) of Section 8, and Section 9 Sub-section (5) of Section 12 Sub-section (2) of Section 15, including the proviso thereto Sections 17, 18 and 19

Session and Chapter	Short Title	Extent of Repeal
53 and 54 Vict. c. 70	The Housing of the Working Classes Act, 1890—cont.	In Section 25, the words at the end of the section " such loan shall be repaid within such period, not exceeding 50 years, as may be recommended by the confirming authority " Sections 27 and 28 In Section 29, the words " means any inhabited building and " in the definition of " dwelling-house " Sections 32 and 33 In Section 39, the words " by agreement " in Sub-section (4) where those words first occur, and all after the word " sanctioned " to the end of that sub-section; Sub-sections (5) and (6); the words " to costs to be awarded in certain cases by a Committee of either House of Parliament " in Sub-section (8); and Sub-section (9) from " Provided that " to the end. In Sub-section (3) of Section 47, the words " the time allowed under any order for the execution of any works or the demolition of a building, or " In Section 53, Sub-section (2) Section 54, so far as unrepealed Section 55, so far as it applies to Scotland Section 63 Section 65, from " and (iii) " to the end of the section In Section 66, the words " or special "

Session and Chapter	Short Title	Extent of Repeal
53 and 54 Vict. c. 70	The Housing of the Working Classes Act, 1890—cont.	Section 77 Section 83 In Section 85, the words " not exceeding three guineas a day " Section 92, from " but in " to the end of the section Sub-section (3) except paragraph (c), and Sub-section (4) of Section 94 Sub-sections (1), (2), (7), (8), and (14) of Section 96 In Sub-section (3) of Section 97 the words " the time allowed under any order for the execution of any works or the demolition of a building, or " The First Schedule, so far as it applies to Scotland The Third, Fourth, and Fifth Schedules
59 and 60 Vict. c. 31	The Housing of the Working Classes Act, 1890, Amendment (Scotland) Act, 1896	Section 3
63 and 64 Vict. c. 59	The Housing of the Working Classes Act, 1900	Sections 2, 6 and 7 In Section 8 the words " Scotland or "
3 Edw. 7, c. 39	The Housing of the Working Classes Act, 1903	Paragraphs (a) and (b) of Sub-section (2) of Section 5, Sections 6 and 8, in Section 10 the words " in the manner provided by Sub-section 3 of Section 32 of the principal Act," and Section 16 In Section 17 the words " Scotland or "

APPENDIX IX

CIRCULAR—LONDON COUNTY COUNCIL; TOWN COUNCILS. AND URBAN AND DISTRICT COUNCILS.

Order No. 55373.

HOUSING, TOWN PLANNING, Etc., ACT, 1909

Local Government Board,
Whitehall, S.W.,
3rd May, 1910.

Sir,

I am directed by the Local Government Board to forward to you the enclosed copies of the Regulations which they have issued for regulating generally the procedure to be adopted with respect to the preparation or adoption of town planning schemes, and for making provision in regard to certain other matters in accordance with Section 56 of the Housing, Town Planning, etc., Act, 1909. A provision is also included prescribing under and for the purposes of sub-section (4) of Section 54 of the Act the manner in which any objection should be made to the approval of the Board being given to a scheme.

The regulations are drawn so as to be of general application. They will extend on the one hand to schemes which relate to small areas or contain only proposals of a simple character and affecting few interests, and on the other hand to schemes which may deal with extensive areas and affect numerous ownerships and other interests and involve serious considerations of expense. It is probable that the circumstances of particular cases will be such as to require or justify some relaxation or alteration of the Regulations in their application to the case, and the board have, with a view to meeting any such case, included in Article 34 provisions which will enable them, subject to the proviso to that Article, to dispense with or vary any requirement of the regulations where reasonable cause is shown.

In the absence of authority for departure from any provisions of the regulations, great care should be taken to comply strictly with them, as any failure in this respect might involve considerable delay and expense.

In the Circular Letter which they addressed to town councils and urban and rural district councils on the 31st December, 1909, the Board drew attention to the importance of co-operation on the part of the local authority with the owners and other persons interested in the land proposed to be included in a town planning scheme. The Board desire again to emphasize this point. Sub-section (2) of Section 56 of the Act enacts that provision shall be made by the regulations "for securing co-operation on the part of the local authority with the owners and other persons interested in the land proposed to be included in the scheme at every stage of the proceedings, by means of conferences and such other means as may be provided by the regulations." The Board have included provisions on this subject in the regulations, which also contain provisions requiring notices to be given at various stages of the procedure to owners and other persons, including local authorities or companies, interested or affected, and facilities to be afforded to all such persons to place their views or objections before the local authority, or, at the later stage, the Board.

In a case in which the owners of land propose a scheme for the adoption of the local authority, the Board consider it very desirable that the local authority should, before applying to the Board for authority to adopt the scheme, obtain from the owners definite information or undertakings on the question of any compensation which might become payable in respect of property injuriously affected by the scheme in the event of its becoming operative, whether in respect of property of the owners proposing the scheme, or of the property of any other person. Under Section 58 (1) of the Act any compensation payable in accordance with the provisions of that Section and Section 59 would be payable by "the responsible authority" referred to in Section 55 (2), that is to say, the authority who are to be responsible for enforcing the observance of the scheme and for the execution of any works which under the scheme or Part II of the Act are to be executed by a local authority. In regard also to a scheme proposed to be prepared by a local authority, it appears to be a matter of the greatest importance that these provisions as to compensation should be carefully borne in mind from the earliest stage of the proceedings, and that, as in the case of the proposed adoption of a scheme, the local authority should endeavour to secure definite agreements with any person who may be affected by the proposals.

In regard to the provisions of Section 58 above-mentioned the Board are aware that questions have arisen as to the meaning to be attached to the words "by the making of any (or a) town planning scheme" in sub-section (1) and (3) of the Section. The Board have no authority to determine the interpretation to be placed upon provisions in the Act, but they are advised that, in giving effect to the section, no loss in value or gain in value of the property affected which is not due solely to the making of the scheme can be taken into account. There will no doubt be exceptional cases, but as a general rule the loss or gain in value would seem to depend upon a comparison of the full value of the property immediately prior to and irrespective of the making of the scheme with the full value of the property immediately after the making of the scheme, regard being had to the provisions of Section 59 of the Act.

In preparing the regulations the Board have been desirous of limiting as far as possible the specific requirements to be complied with for the purpose of an application to the Board for authority to prepare or adopt a town planning scheme, and it does not appear to them that as a general rule it should be necessary for a local authority to incur much expense at this stage of the proceedings.

The full development of the details of a scheme might, the Board consider, be reserved until after the preliminary stage is passed, at all events in the case of a scheme which is being prepared by the local authority. In ordinary circumstances the Board would probably find it necessary or desirable to direct a local inquiry before giving the necessary authority to prepare or adopt a scheme, and the Board may here repeat what was stated in their Circular Letter of the 31st December, 1909, viz., that if it is thought that at any stage prior to the submission of a scheme for their approval the assistance or advice of any of the Board's experts might tend to facilitate agreements with owners concerned or to save labour or expense, the Board will be quite ready to arrange for such assistance or advice being given.

It will be observed that the regulations require the preparation of maps at various stages of the proceedings in connexion with a scheme. In Article 18 of the regulations express provision is made under which the maps prepared in accordance with Article 14 or Article 15 may be used for the purposes of Article 18 and be marked as required by that Article, but such user would only be permissible if the maps required under the later Article would be identical in every respect with those previously prepared for the purposes of Article 14 or Article 15. This provision has been inserted with the view of saving the expense of preparing further maps, and the Board would not offer any objection to a similar course being followed, subject to similar conditions, as regards the use of Map No. 1 (required by Article 1 of the Regulations) in lieu of preparing a further map (Map No. 2) for the purpose of Article 4. It should be clearly understood, however, that a map which has been prepared and deposited to meet specific requirements of an Article of the Regulations should not be subsequently altered to meet the requirements of a subsequent Article.

It was suggested to the Board that provision should be made in the regulations for definite schemes of colouring being adopted in the preparation of the maps required by the regulations, so as to provide for uniformity of practice in regard to the colouring of all maps relating to town planning schemes under the Act. The Board have not regarded it as practicable to carry out this suggestion, but they think it would be desirable that, in preparing the maps required at the several stages of a scheme, the local authority should as far as possible follow the same scheme of colouring throughout all the maps so that, e.g., if a particular colour is used to indicate some special feature on Map No. 1, the same colour should be used to indicate the same feature on any map at a later stage of the proceedings.

Suggestions have been made that contour models of the areas proposed to be included in town planning schemes should be prepared. The Board have not considered it desirable to include any provision on this matter in the regulations, and they are disposed to think that it would not as a general rule be expedient to incur the expense of preparing such models, and that it would be found in practice that plans with contour lines drawn or coloured thereon so as to show the variations in the levels of the land would meet adequately the necessities of the case.

Under Section 54 (1) of the Act, read with Section 55 of the Fourth Schedule and Section 59 (2), it would be practicable to include in a town planning scheme provisions restricting the use of certain areas of land to specified purposes, and it will be seen that the regulations recognize the possibility of provisions of this character. To what extent the power should be used will be a matter for very careful consideration in each case, and the provisions of Sections 58 and 59 of the Act in regard to compensation should be borne in mind in connexion with the matter. The Board refer to this point at the present time as they understand that some doubt has been expressed whether the Act authorizes the inclusion in a scheme of provisions such as are here referred to.

It will be observed that the present regulations do not include provisions " in relation to the carrying out of the scheme or enforcing the observance of the provisions thereof " (Section 56 (1) of the Act), or as to " inquiries and reports as to the beginning and the progress and completion of works, and other action under the scheme " (Fifth Schedule, 3 (b)). The Board propose to defer the making of any regulations under these heads until they are in a better position for determining the precise regulations which may be desirable.

The Board think it desirable that local authorities and others concerned in the making of a town planning scheme should realize at the outset that a considerable period must of necessity elapse between the time of the inception of a scheme and its final approval. The necessity of giving effect to the clearly expressed intention of the Act in regard to affording persons interested or affected full opportunity of considering the proposals at all stages involves considerable delay, but the Board in settling the regulations have made the periods for notices as short as possible, having due regard to the objects to be attained. So far as administrative action upon the part of the Board is concerned they will endeavour to expedite as much as is practicable the dealing with applications to them in regard to town planning schemes, but the careful consideration of a case in all its aspects and the arrangements for the holding of the necessary local inquiries must necessarily take a substantial amount of time.

The regulations and this circular will be placed on sale, so that copies can shortly be purchased from Messrs Wyman and Sons, Limited, Fetter Lane, London, E.C.

I am, Sir,

Your obedient Servant,

H. C. MONRO,

Secretary.

To

    The Clerk to the London County Council

or

    The Town Clerk

or

    The Clerk to the Urban or Rural District Council.

No. 436.

TOWN PLANNING, ENGLAND.

THE TOWN PLANNING PROCEDURE REGULATIONS (ENGLAND AND WALES) 1910. DATED MAY 3, 1910.

(55373.)

To the several Local Authorities in England and Wales for the purposes of Part II of the Housing, Town Planning, etc., Act, 1909:

And to all others whom it may concern.

Whereas by Sections 54, 55 and 56 of the Housing, Town Planning, etc., Act, 1909 (hereinafter referred to as "the Act of 1909"), which Sections are included in Part II of the Act of 1909, it is enacted as follows :

"54. (1) A town planning scheme may be made in accordance with the provisions of this Part of this Act as respects any land which is in course of development or appears likely to be used for building purposes, with the general object of securing proper sanitary conditions, amenity, and convenience in connexion with the laying out and use of the land, and of any neighbouring lands.

"(2) The Local Government Board may authorize a local authority within the meaning of this Part of this Act to prepare such a town planning scheme with reference to any land within or in the neighbourhood of their area, if the authority satisfy the Board that there is a prima facie case for making such a scheme, or may authorize a local authority to adopt, with or without any modifications, any such scheme proposed by all or any of the owners of any land with respect to which the local authority might themselves have been authorized to prepare a scheme.

"(3) Where it is made to appear to the Local Government Board that a piece of land already built upon, or a piece of land not likely to be used for building purposes, is so situated with respect to any land likely to be used for building purposes that it ought to be included in any town planning scheme made with respect to the last-mentioned land, the Board may authorize the preparation or adoption of a scheme including such piece of land as aforesaid, and providing for the demolition or alteration of any buildings thereon so far as may be necessary for carrying the scheme into effect.

" (4) A town planning scheme prepared or adopted by a local authority shall not have effect, unless it is approved by order of the Local Government Board, and the Board may refuse to approve any scheme except with such modifications and subject to such conditions as they think fit to impose :

" Provided that, before a town planning scheme is approved by the Local Government Board, notice of their intention to do so shall be published in the London or Edinburgh Gazette, as the case may be, and, if within 21 days from the date of such publication any person or authority interested objects in the prescribed manner, the draft of the order shall be laid before each House of Parliament for a period of not less than 30 days during the session of Parliament, and, if either of those Houses before the expiration of those 30 days presents an address to His Majesty against the draft, or any part thereof, no further proceedings shall be taken thereon, without prejudice to the making of any new draft scheme.

" (5) A town planning scheme, when approved by the Local Government Board, shall have effect as if it were enacted in this Act.

" (6) A town planning scheme may be varied or revoked by a subsequent scheme prepared or adopted and approved in accordance with this Part of this Act, and the Local Government Board, on the application of the responsible authority, or of any other person appearing to them to be interested, may by order revoke a town planning scheme if they think that under the special circumstances of the case the scheme should be so revoked.

" (7) The expression ' land likely to be used for building purposes ' shall include any land likely to be used as, or for the purpose of providing, open spaces, roads, streets, parks, pleasure or recreation grounds, or for the purpose of executing any work upon or under the land incidental to a town planning scheme, whether in the nature of a building work or not, and the decision of the Local Government Board, whether land is likely to be used for building purposes or not, shall be final.

" 55. (1) The Local Government Board may prescribe a set of general provisions (or separate sets of general provisions adapted for areas of any special character) for carrying out the general objects of town planning schemes, and in particular for dealing with the matters set out in the Fourth Schedule to this Act, and the general provisions, or set of general provisions appropriate to the area for which a town planning scheme is made, shall take effect as part of every scheme, except so far as provision is made by the scheme as approved by the Board for the variation or exclusion of any of those provisions.

" (2) Special provisions shall in addition be inserted in every town planning scheme defining in such manner as may be prescribed by regulations under this Part of this Act the area to which the scheme is to apply, and the authority who are to be responsible for enforcing the observance of the scheme, and for the execution of any works which under the scheme or this Part of this Act are to be executed by a local authority (in this Part of this Act referred to as the responsible authority), and providing for any matters which may be dealt with by general provisions, and otherwise supplementing, excluding, or varying the general provisions, and also for dealing with any special circumstances or contingencies for which adequate provision is not made by the general provisions, and for suspending, so far as necessary for the proper carrying out of the scheme, any statutory enactments, by-laws, regulations, or other provisions, under whatever authority made, which are in operation in the area included in the scheme:

" Provided that, where the scheme contains provisions suspending any enactment contained in a public general Act, the scheme shall not come into force unless a draft thereof has been laid before each House of Parliament for a period of not less than 40 days during the session of Parliament, and, if either of those Houses before the expiration of those 40 days presents an Address to His Majesty against the proposed suspension no further proceedings shall be taken on the draft, without prejudice to the making of any new scheme.

* * * * * * *

" 56. (1) The Local Government Board may make regulations for regulating generally the procedure to be adopted with respect to applications for authority to prepare or adopt a town planning scheme, the preparation of the scheme, obtaining the approval of the Board to a scheme so prepared or adopted, and any inquiries, reports, notices, or other matters required in connexion with the preparation or adoption or the approval of the scheme or preliminary thereto, or in relation to the carrying out of the scheme or enforcing the observance of the provisions thereof.

" (2) Provisions shall be made by those regulations :

" (a) for securing co-operation on the part of the local authority with the owners and other persons interested in the land proposed to be included in the scheme at every stage of the proceedings, by means of conferences and such other means as may be provided by the regulations;

" (b) for securing that notice of the proposal to prepare or adopt the scheme should be given at the earliest stage possible to any council interested in the land; and

" (c) for dealing with the other matters mentioned in the Fifth Schedule to this Act."

And whereas by Sub-section (1) of Section 65 of the Act of 1909, it is provided that for the purposes of Part II of the Act of 1909 the expression " local authority " means the Council of any Borough or Urban or Rural District:

And whereas by Sub-section (1) of Section 66 of the Act of 1909 it is provided that Part II of the Act of 1909 shall apply to the Administrative County of London, and that, as respects that County, the London County Council shall be the local authority:

And whereas the following are the matters mentioned in the Fifth Schedule to the Act of 1909, namely:

1. Procedure anterior to and for the purpose of an application for authority to prepare or adopt a scheme:

(a) Submission of plans and estimates.

(b) Publication of notices.

2. Procedure during, on, and after the preparation or adoption and before the approval of the scheme:

(a) Submission to the Local Government Board of the proposed scheme, with plans and estimates.

(b) Notice of submission of proposed scheme to the Local Government Board.

(c) Hearing of objections and representations by persons affected, including persons representing architectural or archæological societies or otherwise interested in the amenity of the proposed scheme.

(d) Publication of notice of intention to approve scheme and the lodging of objections thereto.

3. Procedure after the approval of scheme:

(a) Notice to be given of approval of scheme.

(b) Inquiries and reports as to the beginning and the progress and completion of works, and other action under the scheme.

4. Duty, at any stage, of the local authority to publish or deposit for inspection any scheme or proposed scheme, and the plans relating thereto, and to give information to persons affected with reference to any such scheme or proposed scheme.

5. The details to be specified in plans, including, wherever the circumstances so require, the restrictions on the number of buildings which may be erected on each acre, and the height and character of those buildings.

Now therefore, We, the Local Government Board, in pursuance of the powers given to Us in that behalf, by this Order, make the following Regulations; that is to say:

Notices of intention to apply for authority to prepare or adopt a scheme: Deposit of Map No. 1 showing land proposed to be included.

PROCEDURE ANTERIOR TO AND FOR THE PURPOSE OF AN APPLICATION FOR AUTHORITY TO PREPARE OR ADOPT A SCHEME

Article I (a) At least two months before making an application to the Local Government Board (hereinafter referred to as " the Board ") for authority to prepare a town planning scheme, or for authority to adopt a town planning scheme proposed by all or any of the owners of any land with respect to which the local authority might themselves have been authorized to prepare a scheme, the local authority shall serve upon the owners or reputed owners, lessees or reputed lessees, and occupiers of the land proposed to be included in the scheme, and upon the council of any borough or of any urban or rural district within which any part of that land is comprised, and also, if any main road is or may be affected by the proposed scheme, upon the County Council, a notice of their intention to make such application. The local authority shall also give notice of their intention to make such application by advertisement in some newspaper or newspapers circulating in the area of the local authority, and the advertisement shall be published at least two months before making the application.

(b) The local authority shall, not later than the date on which the first of the said notices is given, deposit at a place convenient for the purposes of inspection and shall keep deposited thereat for a period not being less than one month from the date on which the latest of the said notices is given, a map of the land proposed to be included in the scheme. The said map (to be marked and known as " Map No. 1 ") shall be on the scale of 25.344 inches to the mile, and shall be open for inspection by any person interested, without payment of any fee, at all reasonable hours on any week-day during the said period. The local authority shall also make suitable provision for affording to any person inspecting the map any necessary explanation in regard thereto.

(c) The said notices shall describe the land proposed to be included in the scheme and shall state the place at which a map of the land is deposited, and the period and times during which the same will be open for inspection by any person interested.

(d) A certified copy of Map No. 1 shall be furnished by the local authority to the council of any borough or of any urban or rural district within which any part of the land proposed to be included in the scheme is comprised.

Special notice to councils interested (Section 56 (2) (b) of Act of 1909)

Article II. With the view of securing that notice of the proposal to apply for authority to prepare or adopt a scheme in respect of any land shall be given at the earliest stage possible to any council interested in the land, the local authority, independently of the notices required to be given as aforesaid, shall, within seven days after they have decided to consider a proposal for authority to prepare or adopt a scheme in reference to any area of land, serve notice of their decision upon any council interested in the land.

Consideration by local authority of objections, etc., Conferences: Meeting of parties interested

Article III. The local authority before making an application to the Board for authority to prepare or adopt a scheme shall consider any objections or representations made to them in writing in reference to the proposed scheme whether by owners or other persons interested in the land proposed to be included in the scheme, or by owners or other persons interested in any lands in the neighbourhood of the land proposed to be included in the scheme which may be affected by the scheme, or by the council of any borough or of any urban or rural district within which any part of the land proposed to be included in the scheme is comprised, or by any other council who may be interested in or affected by the scheme; and shall endeavour, by conferences between the local authority or their officers and such owners, persons, or councils and by any other means available, to secure the co-operation of such owners, persons, or councils in promoting the scheme.

The local authority shall arrange for at least one meeting being held, at which all such owners, persons, or councils as aforesaid shall be entitled to attend or be represented, for the purpose of considering the proposed scheme. Notice of the time and place fixed for such meeting shall be served by the local authority upon all such owners, persons, or councils so far as they can ascertain the same, not less than 14 days before the time fixed for the meeting.

The Mayor (if the local authority are the Town Council of a borough) or the chairman of the council (if the local authority are the London County Council or an Urban or Rural District Council) shall be the president of the said meeting, or, in the event of the Mayor or chairman being unable or unwilling to act, any person appointed for the purpose by the local authority shall be the president, or, in default of such appointment, the meeting shall choose some person present at the meeting to be president thereof. On opening the meeting the president, or a member or officer of the local authority, shall give such explanation of the proposed scheme as he thinks expedient.

Application to the Board to be by resolution: Map No. 2 to be prepared in connexion with resolution

Article IV. (a) An application to the Board by a local authority for authority to prepare or adopt a scheme shall be made by a resolution of the local authority.

(b) The resolution shall define, by reference to a map prepared on a scale of not less than 25.344 inches to the mile (to be marked and known as " Map No. 2 "), the land in reference to which it is desired to prepare or adopt the scheme, and shall state whether the land is entirely within the area of the local authority or wholly or partly within a neighbouring area. In addition to any other particulars required by these regulations to be shown thereon the said map shall show clearly by means of boundary lines sharply defined in colour the area of the land included in the proposed scheme, distinguishing between the parts of the land included within the area of the local authority and within the area of any other local authority. If the area of the land includes any piece of land already built upon or any piece of land not likely to be used for building purposes, any such lands shall be indicated on the map by distinctive colours and any necessary reference notes, and there shall also be shown on the map in like manner the positions of any buildings which have been erected on the land or of any buildings which are in course of erection.

(c) A copy of the resolution certified by the Clerk of the local authority shall be transmitted without delay to the Board by the Clerk, with a covering letter, and accompanied by a statement as to the total number of members of the local authority, the number who voted for the resolution, the number who voted against the resolution, the number who were present at the meeting but did not vote, and the number absent from the meeting.

Documents, etc., to accompany application : Map No. 3 to be prepared

Article V. The application to the Board shall be accompanied by:

(a) The statutory declaration and exhibits required by Article XXXI of these Regulations in proof of compliance with the requirements of Article I.

(b) Map No. 2 or a copy thereof duly certified by the Clerk to the local authority.

(c) A map on the scale of 1 inch to the mile (to be marked and known as " Map No. 3 "), showing, by distinguishing colours or boundary lines in colour, the district of the local authority, the land included in the proposed scheme, and the area within a distance of five miles from any part of the district of the local authority:

Provided that, if the scheme is proposed to be made or adopted by the council of a rural district, it shall not be obligatory that the map shall extend to the whole of the rural district, but it shall extend to the contributory place or places therein in which any part of the land included in the scheme is comprised, and to the area within a distance of five miles from such place or places:

Provided also that, if in any case the land included in a scheme is wholly outside the district of the local authority, the map shall show at least the area within a distance of five miles from any part of such land.

(d) A copy of all objections made in writing in reference to the proposed scheme so far as the objections have not been withdrawn or removed.

(e) If the application relates to the adoption of a scheme

proposed by owners, a copy of the scheme so proposed and a statement of any modifications which the local authority are of opinion should be made in the scheme.

Additional particulars to be shown on Map No. 2 in a case of preparation of scheme by local authority

Article VI. If the application relates to the preparation of a scheme by the local authority there shall be shown on Map No. 2 the lines and widths of the principal roads which the local authority propose shall be made as part of the scheme, the connexions of the proposed roads with existing roads, and the lines of any existing sewers or any existing pipes or mains for the supply of water, gas, or electricity. Any existing roads or ways which it would be necessary to stop up or divert shall also be indicated on the said map, and if the local authority contemplate that the scheme to be prepared shall provide for certain areas being used for the purpose of open spaces or for other special purposes those areas shall as far as possible be indicated on the said map.

Additional particulars to be shown on Map No. 2 in a case of adoption of scheme by local authority

Article VII. If the application relates to the adoption of a scheme proposed by owners of land there shall be shown on Map No. 2 the lines and widths of all roads proposed as part of the scheme, the connexions of the proposed roads with existing roads, and the lines of any existing sewers or any existing pipes or mains for the supply of water, gas, or electricity. Any existing roads or ways which it is proposed to stop up or divert shall be indicated on the said map, which shall also indicate the areas proposed by the scheme to be allocated for the purpose of open spaces, private or public, or to be used for any other special purposes. The said map shall also show all such further particulars in relation to the scheme proposed to be adopted as are suitable for indication thereon, e.g., any proposals as to lines of sewers, or of pipes or mains for the supply of water, gas, or electricity.

Information to be furnished to the Board in connexion with all applications

Article VIII. In connexion with an application for authority to prepare or adopt a scheme, the local authority shall furnish the Board with a statement or statements giving the particulars and information hereinafter indicated:

(a) A general description of the scheme including information as to the general character of the land proposed to be included in the scheme, the extent to which the scheme applies to land in course of development, the extent to which it applies to land likely to be used for building purposes, and, as regards the last-mentioned land, the grounds for considering that the land is likely to be so used.

(b) The reasons on which the local authority rely in support of their application.

(c) If the scheme includes land already built upon or land not likely to be used for building purposes, the reasons which in the opinion of the local authority, render it necessary or desirable to include such lands in the scheme; particulars of the buildings on the lands; such information as the local authority may be in a position to give in regard to the extent to which it would be necessary to provide for the demolition or alteration of the buildings for the purpose of carrying the scheme into effect; and, as regards any land not likely to be used for building purposes, the grounds on which it is considered that such land would not be so used.

(d) Information as to the arrangements in operation in the area of the local authority in regard to sewerage, drainage and sewage disposal, water supply and lighting, and the like information in regard to the area of any other local authority in which any part of the land included in the scheme is comprised, and also information to show to what extent the arrangements as to sewerage, drainage, and sewage disposal would be available or would require alteration or modification for the purposes of the area included in the scheme. If any company, whether statutory or otherwise, is supplying or has power to supply water, gas, or electricity in the area included in the scheme, it should be so stated and particulars given in regard thereto.

(e) If the area of the land included in the scheme is not wholly within the area of the local authority making the application, information shall be supplied as to the proposals in regard to the authority who are to be responsible for enforcing the observance of the scheme and for the execution of any works which under such scheme, or under Part II of the Act of 1909, may have to be executed by a local authority.

(f) Information as to any monuments or ancient monuments, within the meaning of the Ancient Monuments Protection Acts, 1882 to 1900, situate within the area included in the scheme, and as to the manner in which they would be affected.

(g) If any land or property of any Government Department would be affected by the scheme, particulars in regard to any such property and as to the Government Departments concerned.

Additional information to be furnished to the Board in a case of adoption of scheme by local authority

Article IX. In connexion with an application for authority to adopt a scheme, the local authority shall furnish the Board with a statement or statements giving the additional particulars and information hereinafter indicated:

(a) The names and addresses of the owners, lessees, and occupiers of each parcel of the land included in the scheme, and the approximate extent of each such parcel.

(b) Information showing in what respects the proposals in the scheme would involve the suspension of any statutory enactments, by-laws, regulations or other provisions which are in operation in the area included in the scheme.

(c) Information as to the extent to which it may be contemplated or necessary under the scheme that land included in the scheme shall be acquired (1) by the local authority making the application or (2) by any other local authority.

(d) Definite information as to whether any of the owners by whom the scheme is proposed will, in the event of the scheme being adopted by the local authority and approved by the Board, claim compensation on the ground that his property would be injuriously affected by the making of the scheme; and particulars of any information in the possession of the local authority in regard to the probability of any other person making a claim for compensation on that ground.

(e) If, in the opinion of the local authority, any property will be increased in value by the making of the proposed scheme, information as to such property and as to the estimated increase in value.

Estimate as to cost of scheme: Information as to area, population, rates, debt, etc.

Article X. (a) In connexion with an application for authority to prepare or adopt a scheme the local authority shall state as nearly as may be practicable the estimated cost of carrying out the scheme, so far as the cost is expected to be borne by (1) the local authority making the application, and (2) any other local authority. The local authority shall also furnish the Board with such information as they may require as to the manner in which the estimated cost is arrived at.

(b) Subject to the proviso hereinafter contained, the local authority shall also furnish a statement showing the following particulars with respect to the district of the local authority, that is to say :

(i) the acreage;

(ii) the population according to the last census;

(iii) the rateable value for the purposes of the poor rate;

(iv) the amount in the £ of every rate levied during the three last preceding financial years;

(v) the amount of the balances of the outstanding loans contracted by the local authority and the sum included in such amount in respect of loans for sanitary purposes; and

(vi) the amount of the loans sanctioned but not raised though proposed to be raised, and the sum included in such amount in respect of loans for sanitary purposes:

Provided that if it is proposed that the cost of the scheme to be borne by the local authority shall be charged upon any contributory place or places in their district the particulars required under heads i, ii, iii, and iv hereof shall be given with respect to such place or places only.

(c) If any part of the cost of the scheme is expected to be borne by a local authority other than the local authority making the application, the first-mentioned local authority shall make a statement showing in regard to their district the several particulars indicated in paragraph (b) of this Article, and shall supply the same to the last-mentioned local authority, who shall transmit it to the Board with the said application.

Notice by advertisement of application having been made to the Board

Article XI. When the local authority have transmitted to the Board an application for the approval of the Board to the preparation or adoption of a scheme, the local authority shall forthwith give notice of such application and of the date of the resolution making the application by advertisement in some newspaper or newspapers circulating in the area of the local authority.

PROCEDURE DURING, ON, AND AFTER THE PREPARATION
OR ADOPTION AND BEFORE THE APPROVAL OF THE
SCHEME

Notices of authority having been given to prepare or adopt a scheme,
and of intention to prepare or adopt a scheme: Persons desiring
to be heard to give notice to local authority

Article XII. (a) When authority has been given by the Board
to the preparation by a local authority of a scheme with reference
to any land or to the adoption by a local authority, with or without modifications, of a scheme proposed by owners of land, the
local authority shall forthwith serve upon the owners or reputed
owners, lessees or reputed lessees, and occupiers of the land in
reference to which authority to prepare or adopt a scheme has
been so given, and upon the council of any borough or of any
urban or rural district within which any part of that land is
comprised, and also, if any main road is or may be affected by
the scheme, upon the County Council, a notice that such authority has been given and that a copy of the Order or instrument
giving such authority may be inspected, and any necessary explanation or information in regard thereto may be obtained, without
payment of any fee, at a place which shall be specified in the
notice, at all reasonable hours (specifying the same) on any week-
day pending the preparation or adoption of the scheme. They shall
also give notice to the same effect by advertisement in some newspaper or newspapers circulating in the area of the local authority.

(b) If the land in reference to which authority to prepare or
adopt a scheme has been given as aforesaid excludes any land in
regard to which an application under Article IV of these Regulations was made to the Board, the local authority shall serve
notice of the exclusion of such land upon the owners or reputed
owners, lessees or reputed lessees, and occupiers of such excluded
land and upon the council of any borough or of any urban or
rural district within which any part of the excluded land is comprised, and also, if any main road would or might have been affected
by the inclusion of the excluded land, upon the County Council.

(c) The notices to be served on owners or other persons or to
be given by advertisement under paragraph (a) of this Article
shall also state that the local authority propose to prepare a
scheme or, as the case may be, to adopt with or without modifications the scheme proposed by owners, and that any person
interested or affected desiring to be heard in reference to such

proposal, including any persons representing architectural or archæological societies or otherwise interested in the amenity of the proposed scheme, should give notice in writing to the Clerk to the local authority within 21 days from the date of the notice.

(d) The local authority shall make suitable provision for affording to any person interested or affected inspecting the Order or instrument of the Board giving authority to prepare or adopt a scheme any necessary explanation or information in regard thereto.

Consideration by local authority of objections, etc.

Article XIII. In connexion with the preparation or adoption of a scheme the local authority shall carefully consider all objections and representations made to them in writing by any persons or councils interested or affected, including persons representing architectural or archæological societies or otherwise interested in the amenity of the proposed scheme.

Preparation of scheme by local authority: Draft scheme to be printed and Map No. 4 to be prepared showing details of proposals

Article XIV. When the local authority have fully considered and developed their proposals and have decided to prepare a scheme in regard to an area of land in respect of which they have been authorized to prepare a scheme, they shall cause to be printed a draft scheme embodying their proposals and shall cause a map or, if the case so require, maps (to be marked and known as " Map No. 4 " or " Map No. 4 (A)," " Map No. 4 (B)," etc.) to be prepared on a scale of not less than 25.344 inches to the mile, showing clearly by means of boundary lines sharply defined in colour the area of the land included in the proposed scheme distinguishing between the parts of the land included within the area of the local authority and within the area of any other local authority, and also showing thereon all such particulars and details in relation to the proposed scheme as can conveniently be indicated thereon by the aid of reference letters or numbers, descriptive notes, distinguishing colours, or otherwise; and especially there shall be indicated and distinguished on the said map or maps:

Existing main roads;
Roads repairable by the inhabitants at large;
Roads or footways over which the public have a right of way;

Roads on which tramways or light railways (a) have been constructed or (b) are authorized to be constructed:

Roads which the local authority propose shall be made as part of the scheme, indicating the widths thereof and any proposals as to the parts thereof to be appropriated or set apart for special purposes, and the connexions of such roads with existing roads;

Roads or ways which it is proposed to stop up or divert;

Land already built upon;

Land not likely to be used for building purposes;

Land proposed to be allocated for use as open spaces (a) private or (b) public;

Land to be used for any other purposes, including, e.g., buildings for manufacturing purposes or buildings of a special character in reference either to the purposes to which they are to be applied or to their height or otherwise, indicating any restrictions proposed as to the number of buildings which may be erected on any portion of land or each acre in any portion of land;

Land to be acquired by the local authority for any purpose;

Lines of any existing sewers or any existing pipes or mains for the supply of water, gas or electricity.

Proposals as to lines of sewers or of pipes or mains for supply of water, gas, or electricity.

Adoption of scheme by local authority: Scheme of owners to be printed and also memorandum of any modifications proposed and Map No. 4 to be prepared showing details of proposals

Article XV. When the local authority have fully considered the scheme proposed by owners in respect of an area of land in regard to which the local authority have been authorized to adopt a scheme with or without modifications and have decided to adopt the same with or without modifications, they shall cause to be printed a copy of the scheme proposed by owners, and shall prepare and cause to be printed a memorandum of all modifications which they propose should be made in such scheme and shall obtain from the owners or shall themselves provide a map or maps (to be marked and known as " Map No. 4 " or " Map No. 4 (A)," " Map No. 4 (B) " etc.) on a scale of not less than 25.344 inches to the mile, showing thereon all such particulars and details as are required to be shown on the map or maps referred to in Article XIV of these Regulations.

Notices of scheme prepared or of scheme intended to be adopted
by local authority : Deposit of draft scheme, etc., and of Map
No. 4 for inspection

Article XVI. (a) At least one month before deciding upon the
scheme to be submitted to the Board for approval, whether in regard to a scheme prepared by the local authority or a scheme proposed by owners and proposed to be adopted by the local authority
the local authority shall serve upon the owners or reputed owners,
lessees or reputed lessees, and occupiers of the land included in the
scheme, and upon the council of any borough or of any urban or
rural district within which any part of the said land is comprised,
and also, if any main road is or may be affected by the scheme,
upon the County Council, a notice that a draft scheme has been
prepared by the local authority or (as the case may be) that the
local authority intend to adopt a scheme proposed by owners, and
that it is proposed to submit the same, with or without modifications, to the Board for approval; and shall also give notice of such
proposal by advertisement in some newspaper or newspapers circulating in the area of the local authority, and the advertisement
shall be published at least one month before deciding upon the
scheme to be submitted to the Board.

(b) The local authority shall, not later than the date on which
the first of the said notices is given, deposit at a place convenient
for the purposes of inspection and shall keep deposited thereat, for
a period not being less than 21 days from the date on
which the latest of the said notices is given, the draft scheme and
the map or maps referred to in Article XIV of these Regulations
or (as the case may be) the scheme and memorandum and the map
or maps referred to in Article XV of these Regulations, and the
same shall be open for inspection by any persons interested or
affected, without payment of any fee, at all reasonable hours on
any week-day during the said period. The local authority shall
also make suitable provision for affording to any such person inspecting the said documents and maps any necessary explanation
or information in regard thereto.

(c) The said notices shall describe the land proposed to be included in the scheme, and shall state the place at which the
documents and maps referred to in paragraph (b) of this Article
are deposited and the period and times during which the same will
be open for inspection by any person interested or affected. The
notices shall state that the local authority will be prepared to
consider any objections or representations which may be made to

them in writing during the said period, and the notice to be given by advertisement shall also state that the local authority will be prepared to consider any objections or representations made in writing by any persons affected, including any persons representing any architectural or archæological society or otherwise interested in the amenity of the proposed scheme.

Application of Article III of Regulations

Article XVII. Article III of these Regulations shall apply also in regard to procedure before the local authority decided upon the scheme to be submitted to the Board for approval, whether in regard to a scheme prepared by the local authority or a scheme proposed by owners and proposed to be adopted by the local authority.

Making or adoption of scheme to be by Order of local authority and Map No. 5 to be sealed in connexion with the Order

Article XVIII. When the local authority have decided upon the scheme to be submitted to the Board for their approval, whether in regard to a scheme prepared by the local authority or a scheme proposed by owners and proposed to be adopted by the local authority, they shall make an Order under their seal, authenticated by the signature of their Clerk or deputy Clerk, making the scheme or (as the case may be) adopting the scheme proposed by owners with such modifications as may have been decided upon by the local authority.

A map or, if the case so require, maps prepared in the manner and containing the particulars and details required by Article XIV of these Regulations, but to be marked and known as " Map No. 5 " or " Map No. 5 (A)," " Map No. 5 (B)," etc., shall be sealed with the seal of the local authority in connexion with the Order:

Provided that if the map or maps required by this Article to be prepared and sealed in connexion with the Order would be identical in all respects with the map or maps prepared in accordance with Article XIV or (as the case may be) Article XV of these Regulations, the last-mentioned map or maps may, if the local authority think fit, be used for the purposes of this Article, but if so used they shall also be marked as indicated in this Article as well as in the manner required by Article XIV or Article XV.

Application to the Board to approve scheme to be by resolution

Article XIX. An application to the Board to approve the scheme as made or adopted by the local authority by an Order in pursuance of Article XVIII of these Regulations shall be made by a resolution of the local authority; and a copy of the resolution, certified by the clerk to the local authority, shall be transmitted without delay to the Board by the clerk, with a covering letter, and accompanied by a statement as to the total number of members of the local authority, the number who voted for the resolution, the number who voted against the resolution, the number who were present at the meeting but did not vote, and the number absent from the meeting.

Documents, etc., to accompany applications for approval of a scheme: Map No. 6 and Map No. 7 to be prepared

Article XX. When the local authority transmit to the Board the resolution of the local authority requesting the approval of the Board to the scheme as made or adopted by the local authority, they shall transmit to the Board:

(a) The statutory declarations and exhibits required by Article XXXI of these Regulations in proof of compliance with the requirements of Articles XII and XVI.

(b) A sealed copy and three other copies of the Order of the local authority containing the scheme as made or adopted by them, and a certified copy of every map referred to in the Order.

(c) A map on the scale of 6 inches to the mile to be marked and known as " Map No. 6," showing, by distinguishing colours or boundary lines in colour, the district of the local authority and the land included in the scheme:

Provided that, if the scheme is made or adopted by the council of a rural district, it shall not be obligatory that the map shall extend to the whole of the rural district, but it shall extend to the contributory place or places therein in which any part of the land included in the scheme is comprised:

Provided also that, if in any case the land included in a scheme is wholly outside the district of the local authority, the map shall show all the area intervening between that land and the district of the local authority.

There shall also be shown on the map by some distinctive

colours and any necessary reference notes all recreation grounds or public open spaces and public elementary schools in the area required to be shown on the map, and also the buildings which have been erected, in that area up to the time when the map is sent to the Board, distinguishing so far as regards the land included in the scheme the buildings begun to be erected after the application was made to the Board for their approval to prepare or adopt the scheme.

(d) A map on a scale of not less than 25.344 inches to the mile, or a plan drawn to some larger scale (to be marked and known as "Map No. 7") showing the area of the land included in the scheme so divided as to indicate as nearly as may be the portions of such land belonging to different owners. The map or plan shall show as regards each portion of the land the name of the owner, or shall bear numbers having reference to a statement, to be annexed to the map or plan, showing the names of the owners.

(e) A copy of all objections made in writing in reference to the scheme so far as the objections have not been withdrawn or removed in the scheme as finally prepared or adopted by the local authority.

Information to be furnished to the Board in connexion with an application for approval of a scheme

Article XXI. (a) The local authority shall furnish the Board with a statement or statements giving in regard to the scheme prepared or adopted by the local authority the particulars and information indicated in Articles VIII and IX of these Regulations so far as such particulars and information are not contained in the scheme.

The said particulars and information shall be given in regard to every scheme whether prepared by the local authority or adopted by them:

Provided that where the particulars and information furnished to the Board in accordance with Article VIII or Article IX or any division of either of those Articles represent fully and accurately the particulars and information required by this Article in regard to the scheme as prepared or adopted by the local authority it shall be sufficient if a reference be made to the particulars and information previously furnished under Article VIII or Article IX or any division thereof.

(b) The local authority shall also furnish the Board with a statement or statements giving the particulars and information indicated below so far as they are not contained in the scheme:

(i) Information to show whether the scheme admits of satisfactory provision being made in regard to the supply of water, gas, or electricity within the area included in the scheme.

(ii) Information in regard to any tramways or light railways constructed or authorized to be constructed in the area included in the scheme or in the immediate neighbourhood thereof.

(iii) In regard to any lands proposed to be acquired by (a) the local authority submitting the scheme or (b) any other local authority, any information available as to the probability of the lands being acquired by agreement.

(iv) Particulars in regard to any land included in the scheme which belongs to (a) the local authority submitting the scheme or (b) any other local authority; the purposes for which and the authority under which such land was acquired or is held; and also information as to any proposal in regard to its use for any other purposes under the scheme.

(v) If the local authority are of opinion that any property will be injuriously affected by the making of the scheme, within the meaning of the Act of 1909, information, so far as it is practicable to give the same, in regard to such property and as to the extent to which the local authority consider that it may be injuriously affected.

(vi) Detailed particulars of any works which are to be executed under the scheme by any person or local authority, so far as any such particulars are available.

(vii) If the scheme contains provisions suspending any enactment contained in a public general Act, a full explanation of any such provisions and the reasons which are considered to justify their insertion.

(viii) If the scheme contains provisions suspending any other statutory enactments, by-laws, regulations or other provisions which are in operation in the area included in the scheme, a full explanation of any such provisions and the reasons which are considered to justify their insertion.

(ix) Particulars of any land forming part of any common, open space, or allotment, within the meaning of Section 73 of the Act of 1909, which is within the area included in the scheme, and of any part of that land which under the scheme is authorized to be acquired or appropriated to any other purpose, and particulars in regard to any land proposed to be given in exchange for the land so to be acquired or appropriated.

(x) Particulars of any land included in the scheme which is situate within the distance prescribed by Regulations made by the Board under Section 74 of the Act of 1909 from any of the royal palaces or parks.

Estimate and particulars as to cost of scheme : Information as to area, population, rates, debt, local Acts, orders, by-laws, etc.

Article XXII. (a) In connexion with an application to the Board for their approval of the scheme prepared or adopted by the local authority, information shall be furnished in regard to the estimated cost of carrying out the scheme, so far as the cost is to be borne by (1) the local authority making the application and (2) any other local authority. Separate particulars shall be given under the following heads:

Expenditure.
> Purchase of land for open spaces.
> Purchase of land for other purposes, specifying them.
> Purchase of buildings.
> Demolition or alteration of buildings.
> Compensation in respect of property injuriously affected by the scheme.
> Making or alteration of roads or ways.
> Sewerage or drainage.
> Cost of preparing the scheme.
> Other purposes, specifying them.

Receipts.
> In respect of property increased in value.
> From other sources, specifying them.

(b) If the statement or statements of particulars furnished under Article X (b) or (c) of these Regulations has or have owing to lapse of time or other circumstances become inaccurate in any material respect, an amended statement or amended statements of such particulars shall be supplied.

(c) There shall also be supplied a list and a copy of all local

EE

Acts, Provisional Orders, by-laws, or regulations in force in the area of any local authority any part of whose district is included in the scheme; and in the case of any part of a district other than that of the local authority making the application to the Board being so included, such list and copy shall be supplied by the local authority of that district to the local authority making the application, who shall transmit them to the Board.

Notice by advertisement of submission of scheme to the Board: Objections, etc., may be made to the Board

Article XXIII. When the local authority have submitted to the Board for their approval the scheme prepared or adopted by the local authority they shall forthwith give notice of such submission by advertisement in some newspaper or newspapers circulating in the area of the local authority. The notice shall also state that a copy of the scheme submitted to the Board may be inspected by persons affected, including persons representing architectural or archæological societies or otherwise interested in the amenity of the scheme, at a place to be specified in the notice, without payment of any fee, at all reasonable hours (specifying the same) on any week-day within a period of one month from the date of the notice, and that any objections and representations by any such persons should be made in writing and addressed to the Board, at their Office, within the said period. A copy of the newspaper or newspapers containing such advertisement shall be forwarded to the Board by the Clerk to the local authority.

Notices of modifications or conditions proposed by the Board: Objections, etc., may be made to the Board

Article XXIV. (a) If the Board propose to make any modifications in, or to attach any conditions to, the scheme submitted for their approval and transmit to the local authority a draft order for approving the scheme with such modifications and conditions, the local authority shall within 14 days after the receipt of the draft Order serve a copy of the draft order upon the owners or reputed owners, lessees or reputed lessees, and occupiers of the land included in the scheme, and upon the council of any borough or of any urban or rural district within which any part of the said land is comprised, and also, if any main road is affected, upon the County Council, together with a notice that any objections or representations in regard to such modifications and conditions should be made in writing and addressed to the Board at their office within a period of one month from the date of the serving of such draft order and notice.

(b) The local authority shall also within 14 days after the receipt of the draft order give notice by advertisement in some newspaper or newspapers circulating in the area of the local authority that the Board have caused a draft order to be prepared for approving the scheme subject to modifications or conditions, that a copy of the draft order may be inspected and any information in regard thereto may be obtained, without payment of any fee, at a place which shall be specified in the notice, at all reasonable hours (specifying the same) on any week-day during the period of one month from the date of the notice, and that any objections or representations in regard to such modifications and conditions should be made in writing and addressed to the Board at their office within a period of one month from the date of the notice.

(c) The local authority shall furnish the Board within a period of one month from the receipt of the draft order for approving the scheme with modifications or subject to conditions any objections or representations which they may desire to make in regard to the proposed modifications and conditions, and shall also within the same period transmit to the Board the statutory declaration and exhibits required by Article XXXI of these Regulations in proof of compliance with the requirements of this Article.

Notice by advertisement of intention of the Board to approve scheme and to publish notice of such intention in " London Gazette "

Article XXV. (a) When the Board have decided to approve the scheme submitted for their approval, with or without modifications, and notify the local authority of the decision and transmit to the local authority a draft order for approving the scheme, the local authority shall within 14 days after the receipt of such notification give notice by advertisement in some newspaper or newspapers circulating in the area of the local authority that the Board intend to approve the scheme and propose, after the receipt by the Board of a copy of the newspaper or newspapers containing the advertisement, to publish forthwith in the " London

Gazette," in accordance with sub-section (4) of Section 54 of the Act of 1909, a notice of such their intention, and that any person or authority interested and deciding to object to the scheme being approved should make his or their objection in the manner prescribed by Article XXVI of these Regulations within 21 days from the date of such publication in the "London Gazette."

(b) A copy of the newspaper or newspapers containing the advertisement shall be forwarded to the Board by the Clerk to the local authority immediately on the publication thereof.

(c) The local authority shall deposit at a place convenient for the purposes of inspection and shall keep deposited thereat the draft order forwarded to them under this Article, for the full period of 21 days from the date of the said publication in the "London Gazette," and the draft order shall be open for inspection by any person interested, without payment of any fee at all reasonable hours on any week-day during the said period.

Prescribing manner of objection to approval of scheme under and for the purposes of Section 54 (4) of the Act of 1909

Article XXVI. When the notice of the intention of the Board to approve a scheme has been published in pursuance of Sub-section (4) of Section 54 of the Act of 1909, any person or authority interested and deciding to object to the scheme being approved shall make his or their objection in the following manner, that is to say:

The objection shall be made to and be brought before the Board by means of a letter, or other representation in writing, which shall be addressed and posted, or shall be otherwise given, sent, or delivered to the Board at their office. The letter or representation shall indicate clearly the scheme to which the objection is taken, and shall state fully in what respects the person or authority objecting claims or claim to be interested in the scheme and the grounds on which the objection is made.

PROCEDURE AFTER THE APPROVAL OF THE SCHEME

Notices of approval of scheme by the Board

Article XXVII. (a) The local authority, on receipt of a copy of the order of the Board approving a scheme, shall without delay first publish notice of the approval of the scheme by advertisement in some newspaper circulating in the area of the local authority. The notice shall state that the scheme has been approved, with or without modifications or conditions as the case may be, and that the order of the Board giving the approval and a copy of any map or plan referred to in the order or scheme may be inspected and any necessary explanation or information in regard thereto may be obtained without payment of any fee at a place which shall be specified in the notice at all reasonable hours (specifying the same) on any week-day during the period of three months after the date of the order. They shall also, not earlier than the second day after the first publication in a newspaper as aforesaid, serve upon the owners or reputed owners, lessees or reputed lessees, and occupiers of the land included in the scheme, and upon the council of any borough or of any urban or rural district within which any part of the said land is comprised, and also, if any main road is or may be affected by the scheme, upon the County Council, a copy of the order approving the scheme and a notice that a copy of any map or plan referred to in the order or scheme may be inspected, and any necessary explanation or information in regard thereto may be obtained as above-mentioned.

(b) The local authority shall make suitable provision for affording any person inspecting the order or scheme or any map or plan referred to therein within the said period any necessary explanation or information in regard thereto.

(c) The local authority shall within fourteen days after the receipt of the said order transmit to the Board the statutory declaration and exhibits required by Article XXXI of these Regulations in proof of compliance with the requirements of paragraph (a) of this Article.

Notices, etc., to Board of Agriculture and Fisheries and to Commissioners of Works in certain cases

GENERAL

Article XXVIII. Wherever in these Regulations any notice or order or scheme or draft order or scheme is required to be served by the local authority upon any owner of land, the local authority shall send a like notice or order or scheme or draft order or scheme to the Board of Agriculture and Fisheries at their office if in the scheme or proposed scheme there is any provision for the acquisition or appropriation to any other purpose of any land forming part of any common, open space, or allotment within the meaning of Section 73 of the Act of 1909, and to the Commissioners of Works if any land included in the scheme or proposed scheme is situated within the distance prescribed by Regulations made by the Board under Section 74 of the Act of 1909 from any of the royal palaces or parks.

Notices, etc., to Board of Trade and to Light Railway Commissioners in certain cases

Article XXIX. Where in a scheme proposed to be prepared or adopted by a local authority any land is proposed to be included on which tramways or light railways are constructed or are authorized to be constructed, the local authority shall, when they give the notices required to be given under Article I of these Regulations, also give notice to the Board of Trade and, as regards light railways, to the Light Railway Commissioners, of the intention of the local authority to apply for authority to prepare or (as the case may be) to adopt a scheme in regard to the said land, and shall from time to time thereafter furnish all such information as the Board of Trade or the Light Railway Commissioners may require in regard to the proposals so far as any tramways or light railways or an authorized route of any tramways or light railways may be affected.

Service of Notices

Article XXX. A notice required to be served in pursuance of these Regulations shall be served:

(a) by delivery of the same personally to the person required to be served, or, if such person is absent abroad or cannot be found, to his agent; or

(b) by leaving the same at the usual or last known place of abode of such person as aforesaid; or

(c) by post addressed to the usual or last known place of abode of such person; or

(d) in the case of a notice required to be served on a local authority or corporate body or company, by delivering the same to their clerk or secretary or leaving the same at his office with some person employed there, or by post addressed to such clerk or secretary at his office:

Provided that if the owner of any land is not known to and after diligent inquiry cannot be found by the local authority then the notice may be served by leaving it, addressed to the owner, with some occupier of the land, or, if there be not an occupier, then by causing it to be put up on some conspicuous part of the land:

Provided also that a notice required to be given to an occupier may be addressed by the description of the " occupier " of the land or premises (describing it or them) in respect of which the notice is given, without further name or description.

Proofs of compliance with certain Regulations to be furnished by statutory declarations

Article XXXI. Proofs of compliance with the requirements of Articles I, XII, XVI, XXIV, and XXVII of these Regulations as extended by Articles XXVIII and XXIX shall to the extent herein mentioned be furnished to the Board by statutory declarations made by the Clerk to the local authority or other person competent to make the same. The declarations shall in each case specify the manner in which the notices required by those Articles to be served upon owners, lessees, and occupiers, and upon any other local authority or council, were served, and the names of the persons so served, and shall also show that the other requirements of those Articles as to notices required to be given and as to the deposit of maps or plans or any documents required to be deposited have been duly complied with. There shall also be annexed to the declarations as exhibits:

In regard to Article I,

(1) a copy of the form of notice served, (2) a copy of the map deposited for inspection, and (3) a copy of each newspaper containing the advertisement.

In regard to Article XII,

(1) copies of the forms of notices served, and (2) a copy of each newspaper containing the advertisement.

In regard to Article XVI,

(1) a copy of the form of notice served, (2) a copy of each newspaper containing the advertisement, (3) a statement showing the several parcels of land in respect of which notice was served upon each owner, lessee and occupier, (4) a copy of the draft scheme prepared by the local authority and deposited for inspection, or (4a) a copy of the scheme proposed by owners and deposited for inspection, together with a copy of any memorandum prepared by the local authority of modifications in such scheme and deposited with the scheme

for inspection, and (5) copies of the maps deposited for inspection.

In regard to Article XXIV,

(1) a copy of the form of notice served, and (2) a copy of each newspaper containing the advertisement.

In regard to Article XXVII,

(1) a copy of the order, (2) a copy of the form of notice served, and (3) a copy of the newspaper containing the advertisement.

Provisions as to maps

Article XXXII. (a) The maps required in pursuance of these Regulations shall be Ordnance Maps wherever such maps are published in respect of the district or area in relation to which the maps are required, shall be on a scale not less than that specified in each case, shall be mounted on linen and folded in book form, and shall have a scale properly drawn thereon.

(b) Any person interested in or affected by any scheme or proposed scheme shall be entitled to a copy of or extract from any map or plan required in pursuance of these Regulations, on payment of a reasonable fee to be determined by the local authority, and shall be entitled to inspect at all reasonable times any map or plan referred to in Article XXVII of these Regulations. Any fees received by the local authority shall be carried to the credit of the fund liable to be charged with the expenses of the local authority in connexion with the scheme.

Local authority to furnish all information, etc., required by the Board

Article XXXIII. The local authority shall prepare and furnish to the Board all such maps, plans, sections, elevations and specifications, and all such particulars or information as the Board shall require to be prepared and furnished in connexion with any scheme or proposed scheme at any stage of the proceedings in relation thereto.

Board may consent to departures from Regulations

Article XXXIV. Where the Board are satisfied that there is reasonable cause for dispensing, either conditionally or unconditionally, with compliance with any requirement of these Regulations, or for varying any such requirement, the Board may, by order or otherwise as they may think fit, give the necessary dispensation, or may make and give effect to the necessary variation and to any incidents or consequences of that variation; and, in the case of any such dispensation when given subject to any condition, or in the case of any such variation, the local authority or other authorities or persons, as the case may be, shall comply in all respects with the condition or variation and with any requirement of the order or other writing or direction of the Board giving the dispensation or making the variation as if the condition, variation or requirement formed part of these Regulations:

Provided that the Board shall not exercise their powers under this Article in such a manner as to dispense with any provisions of these Regulations which are necessary to give effect to the requirements of the Act of 1909 or as so to vary any such provisions that they would cease to give effect to those requirements.

Interpretation

Article XXXV. In these Regulations " the Act of 1909 " means the Housing, Town Planning, etc., Act, 1909.

Short Title

Article XXXVI. These Regulations may be cited as the Town Planning Procedure Regulations (England and Wales), 1910.

Given under the Seal of Office of the Local Government Board, this Third day of May, in the year One thousand nine hundred and ten.

(L.S.)

JOHN BURNS,
President.

H. C. MONRO,
Secretary.

APPENDIX X

SPEECH MADE BY THE CHAIRMAN OF THE HOUSING COMMITTEE TO THE BIRMINGHAM CITY COUNCIL. ON PRESENTATION OF THE HOUSING COMMITTEE'S REPORT. 3 JULY, 1906.

I have to move: " That the Council hereby approve of the Housing Reform policy as set out in the present report of the Housing Committee, and expresses itself in favour of such legislation as is necessary to enable the same to be carried out."

My Lord Mayor.—It is often said that he is a bold man who prophesies, and yet I venture to predict that if this resolution is passed to-day, the vote given will in years to come be recognized as epoch-making in the progress of the City which we all love.

In barbaric times the greatest warriors were the greatest men; nowadays our greatest men devote their energies to saving life, improving health, and increasing the happiness of their fellow-citizens. That is the object to which we are going to devote to-day what abilities we may happen to possess. We are the first City Council to discuss in a practical, definite manner those ideas which all Housing reformers have in their minds. The Garden City idea, the Garden Suburb idea, have taken hold of the minds of Englishmen. We cannot hope to make Birmingham into a Garden City, although something can be done towards that end, but we can, if we will, create Garden Suburbs around Birmingham.

The report before us is voluminous, and therefore, will require a somewhat lengthy exposition. I pray for your indulgence whilst I get through that task as quickly as possible. For five long weary years the Housing Committee have been struggling with a difficult and complicated problem in face of the most strenuous and skilful opposition. They have had to fight a curious combination. More than once municipal socialists joined hands with property owners and their representatives in order to vote down those who dared to work at the solution of the Housing problem as well as talk about it. But pioneers must not complain. The Housing Committee did not complain: they stuck to their work, they stuck to their guns, and now to-day their work is generally applauded as well as approved by the vast majority of the citizens of Birmingham, as also by Housing reformers who come from all over the country to see what is being done in Birmingham.

In view of the cry for economy that has been raised, and let me say properly raised, it is perhaps not out of place to remind this Council and the public of Birmingham that whilst others have been talking economy, the Housing Committee have been practising it. They have dealt with nearly 1,600 insanitary houses at the small charge of two guineas per house, plus a reasonable but not excessive compensation for obstructive buildings that have been removed. In addition to that, something like twelve acres have been added to the open spaces of the City, without the cost of a penny piece to the ratepayers. St Lawrence area, dealt with under Part I of the 1890 Act, would have cost the ratepayers of Birmingham at least £150,000. Other properties if dealt with under Part I, instead of Part II of the Housing of the Working Classes Act, 1890, as they have been in Birmingham, would also have cost the ratepayers large sums of money, but here the property-owners have been persuaded to put their houses right at their own expense, and it has been done with such reasonableness, and with such willingness, looking at the matter from the property-owner's point of view as well as from the point of view of the sanitary authority, that we may say the great majority of the property owners are working hand in hand with the Housing Committee. The result is that far more has been done than would otherwise have been possible. (Hear, hear.) There are, of course, a few unreasonable people, there always are, and those people have spent far more money than they need have done if they had been willing to accept the Housing Committee's help in doing what was necessary at the least possible expenditure of money. Courts have been converted into terraces at a very low cost, in addition to which, the rates have been relieved by means of a lower death rate and less fever, whilst the police will tell you that the change has also resulted in better supervision at a less cost.

Slum reform is now well in hand in Birmingham. There is a great deal still to be done, but the work is well started. To-day it is hoped a new departure will be made, a new era inaugurated. (Hear, hear.) To-day proposals are laid before you for preventing the creation of new evils as bad as, or nearly as bad as those with which we have to deal at present. The poorer classes are no longer condemned to sudden death without a fair trial, but they are still condemned to a slow death, and, moreover, to dreary unhealthy lives by the haphazard growth of our big cities. Some of the newer parts of the City and suburbs are almost as bad as the old courts in the centre. It is often said that housing conditions are due to the habits of the tenants. That is partly true, but it is not entirely true. Environment has a great effect on human nature. Do you think that we should lead blameless lives (as, of course, we all do now)—(laughter)—if we were transplanted to the hovels in which so many working men in Birmingham exist to-day? It may be heresy to say so, but I do say that in my opinion even the Spartan virtue of this City Council would give way under the trials and temptations to which so many of the people who live in our slums are subjected. We cannot entirely undo the past, but we may control the future, and there is no work more important to the City, the nation, and the empire. The home of the individual is the most important factor in the prosperity of the nation, and the strength of the Empire. We can, if we will, arrange for healthy, wholesome surroundings for every Birmingham adult, and, even more important, give every Birmingham child the " light and air " that are so essential to its healthy development.

The Housing Committee, whilst attending to the reform of the slums that exist, have been continuously considering how best to prevent the creation of future evils. They very soon came to the conclusion that patch-work was no good; that a few nice cheap houses here and there were no good. They saw the necessity of going further and deeper : the necessity of finding some means whereby it is possible to provide nice cheap houses for every one. Having learnt the results of English efforts at housing reform there was nothing left for them to do but to find out what was being done in other countries, and with that desire they last summer sent a deputation to Germany.

It is now my duty to summarize the report of the Deputation.

In Berlin, we learnt the general principles on which town planning is worked, more especially the provision of open spaces and playgrounds before the land has become too expensive. We also saw a great mistake being made. Roads were being constructed wider and more expensively than was necessary, thereby forcing up the price of adjacent building areas, and causing the erection of huge blocks of tenements which would not, I am glad to say, be approved in Birmingham.

At Ulm, we found the opposite policy adopted—wide, well-made streets wherever necessary, but narrow, inexpensive streets in purely residential quarters, front gardens being provided in order to preserve a proper distance between the houses on either side of the street. Here we also learned how the corporation assist working men to acquire the houses they live in, thereby ensuring that the houses are well kept, as well as wellbuilt. Another interesting feature was their far-sighted policy of encouraging manufacturers to build works in the town by letting them have land on favourable terms, and giving them every convenience. But most important of all is Ulm's municipal land purchase policy. A few years ago they owned three-fifths of the land within their boundaries; to-day they own four-fifths, an increase of $33\frac{1}{3}$ per cent. Whilst others have been explaining what every one knows—that the land question is largely at the root of the housing question—Ulm has been acting, and has been buying land with most satisfactory results. It is to be hoped that it will not be long before Birmingham is able and willing to carry out vigorously and judiciously a similar policy. (Hear, hear.)

In Stuttgart we saw more of the artistic side of town planning. We also learned about a most successful method of dealing with the tenant's side of the question. In that City, there are 120 voluntary inspectors who visit systematically all the houses, and who explain to the tenants in a friendly way the advantage it is to them to take care and be proud of the houses they live in. These inspectors, when necessary, report any repairs that are required to the Central Housing Office. Unfortunately, in Birmingham, there are too many cases where houses that have been repaired by property owners have, through neglect, or mis-usage, become almost as bad as they were before repair. I will not pretend that the landlords are not partly to blame for this, but there is a great deal to be said on their side, and I, at any rate, have long been of opinion that the corporation ought to show the way how to deal with that most important branch of housing reform, the maintenance of improvements that have been effected. We cannot suddenly introduce 120 housing inspectors, but we can make a start in the right direction, and Miss Octavia Hill has shown us how to do it.

Mannheim gave us another object lesson in the prevention of land speculation by a bold and judicious Municipal land purchase policy. Here also they give facilities to manufacturers, at the same time preventing annoyance to citizens and interference with the amenities of the City. Further, we saw here a most inspiring example of the application of town planning to existing cities. A few years ago they took in what was really a town in itself, but what they call a suburb. It was in a most unsatisfactory sanitary condition. They set to work and planned out how they would have liked it built, and they have gradually brought up this unsatisfactory suburb to their standard, with results which were most encouraging and inspiring, as showing what can be done even in Birmingham itself with town planning.

Frankfort was perhaps the most successful of all in encouraging and assisting Public Utility Building Societies willing to provide healthy houses at the lowest possible rents. Here we also had a most impressive object lesson in the cutting of fine broad new streets through the older parts of the town. Birmingham has one Corporation Street, she could do with a few more, and with our experience of Corporation Street, and the experience of other cities, I have not the slightest hesitation in saying that the next Corporation Street need not cost so much as the last. (Hear, hear.) But, perhaps, the most distinctive lesson in Frankfort was the masterly method they have of dealing with the development of land where several different property owners are concerned. They plan it out as if it all belonged to one owner. After they have ascertained what land is available for building, and after providing for streets and open spaces, they give back to each original owner the same percentage of his original holding as the land available for building is in percentage to the total land laid out. The position of the new site is governed as far as possible by the position of the old site and by other considerations. There are, of course, in Frankfort, as in other places, a few quarrelsome and grasping people, but the methods of the corporation have been found to be so fair and reasonable that they have succeeded in getting special powers that enable them to bring into line the few people who used to make these redistribution schemes extremely difficult. Another most useful lesson in Frankfort was what we should call their Town Dwellings Improvement Trust. They buy up old insanitary slums and repair them in accordance with the requirements of the Local Authority.

If some one who has money to spare were to take up that idea in Birmingham it would not only assist housing reform very much, but it would be a sensible relief to those people who unfortunately, through no fault of the Housing Committee, now have to suffer in some cases more than is necessary from the present condition of their property. Some of these people have no money to spend on repairs. It is extremely difficult and trying to the Housing Committee to insist on the work being done, but having been told to carry out Part II it is their duty to do it. They do everything they can to make the burden as light as possible for these unfortunate owners, but there are cases where even they cannot do all that is required, and some such Town Dwellings

Improvement Trust as that which they have in Frankfort would be a great relief to some of the poorer property owners of Birmingham, and expedite slum reform.

In Cologne we saw the mistake of thinking that people will live in suburbs without cheap and efficient tramway communication. It is quite evident that Housing reformers to be successful must be in close touch with the tramway development of their district. If a Municipal land purchase policy is to be carried out it would be the duty of Housing reformers to buy the land first and put the tramways down afterwards. At the present time, the local authorities are forced into the position of putting the cart before the horse. The tramway is put down and the value of the land is sent up against any people who wish to buy for housing purposes.

We also learned something about the system of levying a tax on the increased value of land over the price at which it was last sold.

In Cologne they guarantee large sums lent by Public Trusts to Public Utility Building Societies which, as already explained, have to undertake to provide good housing accommodation at the lowest possible price.

Dusseldorf, the last town we visited, was a striking example of how an intelligent system of town planning will make a city attractive. Although it is on the borders of the Black Country of Germany, rich men go to live at Dusseldorf because it is a pleasant city to live in. I never heard of any rich Englishmen going near our Black Country because it was pleasant to live in. Factories are encouraged and assisted, but they are not allowed to injure the town. The corporation is also extremely active in Municipal Land Purchase, and in assisting and encouraging the erection of houses in every possible manner.

These are the principal lessons learnt last summer, encouragingly corroborative of the general line of policy so often indicated by your Housing Committee. The policy of Town Planning and Municipal Land Purchase is delineated in a masterly manner by Mr W. H. Lever, on pages 119 to 127 in the report we have before us. Mr Lever is no hot-headed youth; he is a Housing reformer who has done something real and substantial towards the solution of the Housing reform problem. He is a life-long trade-unionist, and a most successful business man.

The policy advocated to-day is neither idealistic nor untried. It has already been successfully carried out at Bournville by a private individual. Is this City Council going to say it will fail where Mr Cadbury has succeeded? Is this City Council going to declare itself inferior to City Councils in Germany?

The other day Alderman Clayton seemed to be afraid that the Housing Committee wanted to spend a lot of money. There is no need for that if corporations had the power, subject to proper safeguards, to pay for land with corporation stock secured on the land bought, and bringing in the same income as the land was earning when it was bought. The landowner would not be justified in complaining, because he would get the same income as before, with the added security of the City rates, and the ratepayers would not suffer even in the initial stages from land purchased by this method, because the interest from land purchased would pay the interest on the stock issued. This patent like all good patents, is quite simple; but, no doubt, Alderman Clayton will be able to improve upon it. The Council will no doubt forgive me for making a further quotation from the same eminent authority. Alderman Clayton, commenting on a proposal to reduce the Housing Committee's Estimates, said: "If there is one member of the Council whom we can trust not to spend money unnecessarily it is Councillor Nettlefold." Such a testimonial as that from the most energetic critic on the Council should, I think, inspire some confidence in the financial methods of the Chairman of the Housing Committee.

With the rising rates already on us, and others threatened, the policy of Town Planning and Municipal Land Purchase is worthy of the most careful consideration. In Baden there are 121 Local Authorities which have no rates whatever, owing to their income from land. In Bavaria, there are no fewer than 526 in a similar position. One local authority in Germany not only has no ratepayers at all, but it actually pays a dividend of £15 a year to those who in other cities would be ratepayers. (Laughter.) It will be a long time before Birmingham gets to that happy state, but in this, as in many other ways, we can make a start in the right direction.

In case any member of the Council is still unpersuaded as to the wisdom of the Housing Reform Policy advocated in the report I would remind him that voting for the resolution commits him not one jot or tittle further than to the general approval of the proposed scheme that Birmingham should have statutory powers to plan undeveloped districts; to plan the existing city as it ought to be, and to buy land without specifying the exact purpose for which it is purchased. It is impossible to settle details to-day;

we cannot do more than settle on the general principle as to whether or not Birmingham should have these powers. Beyond that no one is committed. When the powers are obtained, and only then, will the question arise as to how to use them, if at all. Surely, there can be no objection to having powers that have been successfully exercised elsewhere. You are not even asked to spend so much as one penny of the ratepayers' money on a Local Act. The Housing Committee are too economical, too business-like, for that. Their method is to put the cost of legislation on to other shoulders. But you are asked to remember the deplorable way in which the suburbs of Birmingham and other large cities are being developed to-day. The lack of public control over this development is laying up serious trouble in the very near future for those responsible for the public health and happiness.

The Public Works Committee's cartoon which hangs on the wall over my head, and which Sir James Smith has kindly allowed me to use this afternoon, gives an interesting example of this very thing. Here (pointing to the cartoon) you have a main street, wider than it was, but yet not as wide as it ought to be, and side streets wider and far more expensive than is necessary. You and I know the sort of houses that are likely to go up there. In addition to all that, a vote was passed at the last Council meeting putting a charge of nearly £12,000 on the ratepayers, which ought to have gone on to the adjacent building areas. This was no doubt the very best possible arrangement the Public Works Committee could make under the powers the Corporation now possess, but we see from this example how inadequate our present powers are to prevent the creation of possible slums.

Only this morning I made a little tour of inspection. First I came to a typical modern suburb. True, the houses were in accordance with modern by-laws, but they were almost one on the top of the other. Fine trees had been cut down which could not be replaced in fifty years, no playgrounds or open spaces had been provided, and the building materials were already beginning to show signs of decay, in fact, " they had done all those things which they ought not to have done, and they had left undone those things which they ought to have done." Near by was Bournville, laid out as you all know, with trees and open spaces, and cheap as well as good cheerful houses. They can be made cheaper still if we can get power to allow narrower streets where the present minimum width of street is not required.

My Lord Mayor, in considering a matter of this sort, it is

necessary to avoid being emotional, but it is nothing less than heartrending to look at the suburbs now being created under the present by-laws, especially when one knows how it could be done well and cheaply with cheaper house-rent, if only we had the power they possess in other places. Careful investigation shows that on the lines advocated to-day houses can not only be built better, with more cheerful surroundings than at present, but actually cheaper. On Municipal land wisely bought and leased to Public Utility Building Societies, houses can be provided at about 5s. per week, without any charge on the rates. On the contrary, the rates can be relieved. There is no reason why we should not have Bournvilles all around Birmingham instead of the dismal distressing working-men's quarters that now exist, and are being daily increased in numbers and extent.

That, My Lord Mayor, brings me near to the end of my task, the result of much careful study and hard thinking. Details must be considered later on; to-day I have not attempted more than to outline the general policy.

It may be suggested that Town Planning and Municipal Land Purchase are no use unless the City boundaries are extended. (Hear, hear.) No doubt that would be helpful, but it is not essential. There are 10,000 acres of land in Birmingham, of which 3,000 are still uncovered. We might at least see that that 3,000 are properly developed. For myself, I would like to see the City boundaries extended, but, as a sensible man, I suggest that we should not try to do too much at once and risk making a total failure; and it must not be forgotten that there is an alternative to the extension of the City boundaries, and that is, the creation of scientific areas for dealing with housing and similar problems.

The Municipal house builders will probably object to the corporation leasing land that has been bought instead of itself building the houses. There are many objections to "Municipal" House Building, the chief one is, that £1 spent in land goes at least seven times as far as £1 spent in house-building towards the solution of the Housing problem, and we want all the money we can get for land purchase alone. At the same time, the report clearly and intentionally leaves it open for the Council to add Municipal House Building to Municipal Land Purchase if it ever so decides. The Housing Committee's views on this subject remain what they always were, as does their promise to build as soon as they are instructed to do so.

I would respectfully suggest, nay, I would invite those who

believe in Municipal House Building to bring up their scheme
at some time most convenient to themselves, but I do ask them
not to vote against Town Planning and Municipal Land Purchase
(that is, if they agree with it), merely because Municipal House
Building does not happen to be included. The principles of Town
Planning and Municipal Land Purchase are already being considered and discussed, and sooner or later they will be adopted
by the whole country. I am very proud to belong to the City
Council which is the first to discuss in a practical definite manner
this important proposal; I shall be prouder than ever to belong
to Birmingham if she decides to take the lead in this, as she has
done in so many other Municipal reforms. (Applause.)

The resolution was carried by thirty votes to sixteen.

· APPENDIX XI

HOUSING OF THE WORKING CLASSES BILL PRESENTED BY SIR ARTHUR GRIFFITHS BOSCAWEN AND COMMENTS THEREON

MEMORANDUM TO THE BILL

" This Bill amends and adds to the powers of the Local Government Board, and those of local authorities under the Housing Acts. These Acts are already very complicated, and until a consolidating enactment is passed, an amending Bill, drafted as it must be with reference to the existing Acts, cannot avoid adding to the complication.

" The Bill adopts the principle of the existing Acts, especially those of the principal Act of 1890, and apart from some minor alterations, aims only at the better enforcement of those principles in the view that, subject to minor alterations, existing legislation would be sufficient, if it were properly enforced.

" The main alterations proposed with a view to enforcing the Acts are:

" (a) A special department of the Local Government Board is to be formed which will be employed exclusively in the supervision of the operations of local authorities under the Housing Acts. This department will co-ordinate the work of the various officers of the Board already employed in the work. It will assist local authorities by advice and information, and will annually make a special report to Parliament on housing matters.

" Where a local authority is culpably neglecting its housing duties the Local Government Board will be empowered, after application to the court, to deal with slums and to provide housing accommodation itself in place, and at the cost of the local authority.

" (b) In some areas the failure to deal with the slum evil and to carry out housing schemes under Part III of the principal Act arises not from any unwillingness on the part of the local authority but from financial difficulties. It is, therefore, proposed by the Bill to provide a parliamentary grant in aid of housing operations upon the analogy of the funds administered by the Road Board in aid of road improvements."

Various other alterations of the existing Acts are proposed by the Bill with a view to lessening the cost of, and of facilitating in other ways the exercise by local authorities of their housing functions. In particular, an amendment is proposed of the compensation sections of the Act of 1890, which aims at carrying the principles of these sections—at present often nugatory—into effect.

HOUSING OF THE WORKING CLASSES BILL

Arrangement of Clauses

Clause

A.D. 1912

A BILL TO

" Provide for the better application and enforcement of the Housing of the Working Classes Acts, and to amend the Small Dwellings Acquisition Act, 1899.

" BE it enacted by the King's most Excellent Majesty by and with the advice and consent of the Lords Spiritual and Temporal and Commons in this present Parliament assembled, and by the authority of the same as follows:

Housing Commissioners

1. (1) " With a view to the more effectual application and enforcement of the Housing of the Working Classes Acts, 1890 to 1909, as amended by this Act it shall be the duty of the Local Government Board to exercise the powers vested in them by the said Acts, and this Act and for that purpose within three months after the passing of this Act to appoint three officers to be called

Housing Commissioners, who shall be employed by the Board exclusively for the said purpose.

(2) " One of the Housing Commissioners shall possess the qualifications of a medical officer of health and another shall have had large experience in urban areas of the practical development and administration of working class dwellings, and another shall have had similar experience in rural areas.

(3) " The Local Government Board, acting through the Housing Commissioners, shall from time to time ascertain whether and to what extent there is or is likely to arise in the district of any local authority any need:

(a) " for any improvement schemes under Part I of the Housing of the Working Classes Act, 1890 (in this Act referred to as the principal Act):

(b) " for the closing or demolition of houses or for the removal of obstructive buildings or for reconstruction schemes under Part II of the principal Act.

(c) " for the provision of housing accommodation under Part III of the principal Act:

" and the extent to which it is or will be reasonably practical to satisfy such need and shall report the information acquired by them to the local authority (being the authority under the principal Act for the purposes to which the need relates) stating what, if any, steps in their opinion should be taken to satisfy the need.

Enforcement of Powers

2. (1) " A Housing Commissioner in default of an official representation by a medical officer of health, under Sections 4 and 5 of the principal Act, may at any time if he thinks fit, himself make a representation to a local authority and any such representation of a Commissioner shall be treated as an official representation for the purpose of the principal Act.

(2) " Wherever under the Housing of the Working Classes Acts, 1890 to 1909, the Local Government Board have power to take any action with a view to enforcing any of the provisions of the said Acts on the representation, appeal or complaint of any body or person, the said action may be taken on a report of a Housing Commissioner advising that it should be taken.

Power of Local Government Board to take Action

3. (1) " Wherever under the Housing of the Working Classes Acts, 1890 to 1909, any order of the Local Government Board is

enforceable against a local authority by mandamus, the Local Government Board, may, upon any application for a mandamus, apply for an order of the court authorizing the Board to take action under this section to carry out the order of the Board in place of the local authority and to take such other steps as may be necessary to make good the default of the local authority, and the court in lieu of or in addition to the issue of a mandamus may make an order accordingly, subject to such terms and conditions, including any amendment of the original order of the Board as may seem to the court desirable.

(2) '' An order of the court under this section may vest in the Local Government Board any of the powers of the local authority (including the power of making and levying rates and of requiring overseers to raise contributions and all powers incidental thereto), which in the opinion of the court ought to be exercised by the Board in order to make good the default of the local authority, and may authorize the Board to appoint persons to exercise locally any powers so vested in the Board, at such salaries as the court may determine, and to do such other acts as may be necessary to enable the board to carry out the order and make good the default of the local authority.

(3) '' Any expenses incurred by or on behalf of the Local Government Board under an order of the court made under this section, including the salaries of any persons appointed locally to exercise the powers of the local authority, shall be a debt due to the Crown from the local authority, and without prejudice to any other remedy may be recovered by means of rates raised by or on the authority of the Local Government Board in the exercise of the powers of the local authority vested in the Board by the order of the court.

(4) '' Any order of the court under this section shall have effect as if enacted in this Act, but may be revoked or varied by a subsequent order.

(5) '' The Local Government Board, if at any time they are satisfied that the local authority are willing to exercise the powers and fulfil the duties in respect of which the order of the court was made, may by order transfer to the local authority any property acquired by them under the order of the court, and revest in the local authority any powers vested in them thereunder.

Use of Land Acquired under Part III of Principal Act

4. (1) '' If a local authority propose to acquire any estate or

area of land exceeding in extent ten acres for the purpose of exercising their powers under Part III of the principal Act, and are of opinion that in order to exercise those powers most economically and suitably it is desirable to acquire more land than is needed to be used for the actual purposes of those powers, the Local Government Board may, if they think fit, make an order authorizing the local authority to acquire under Part III of the principal Act such an extent of land as may be specified in the order.

(2) " Any part of the land so acquired which is not used for the actual purpose aforesaid shall be dealt with and developed in accordance with a town planning scheme made under Part II of the Housing, Town Planning, etc., Act, 1909, or may with the consent of the Local Government Board, be appropriated by the local authority for the purposes of any other of their powers:

" Provided that the part of any such land to be used for purposes other than those authorized under Part III of the principal Act shall in no case exceed one-third of the whole area acquired in pursuance of the order of the Local Government Board, and shall be developed as ancillary to and for the purpose of facilitating the provision of housing accommodation.

(3) " The Local Government Board may, if they think fit, make an order authorizing a local authority to deal with any land acquired by the authority under Part III of the principal Act before the passing of this Act as though it had been acquired in pursuance of an order made under this section, and every such order shall have effect accordingly.

Power to Acquire Land in Advance of Requirements

5. " The power of a local authority under Sub-section 3 of Section 2 of the Housing, Town Planning, etc., Act, 1909 to acquire land in advance of requirements shall apply to the purposes of Parts I and II of the principal Act as well as to the purposes of Part III thereof.

Relaxation of By-laws.

6. (1) " For the purpose of carrying out any particular improvement scheme under Part I or reconstruction scheme under Part II, or of providing housing accommodation under Part III of the principal Act, a local authority may, with the consent of the Local Government Board, relax or modify to such extent as they deem expedient any by-laws with respect to streets and buildings.

(2) " The consent of the Local Government Board under this section shall not be given unless the Board are satisfied that notwithstanding any such relaxation or modification of by-laws sufficient provision is made for the proper circulation of air and for ventilation and for other sanitary requirements.

Amendments as Regards Housing

7. (1) " Notwithstanding anything in Section 11 or in Section 40 of the principal Act or in Section 3 of the Housing of the Working Classes Act, 1903, and the schedule thereto, wherever facilities for cheap travel enable persons of the working class to live at some distance from their place of employment, and the local authority or the undertakers, as the case may be are prepared to provide the new accommodation required to replace that destroyed by the operation of an improvement scheme or a reconstruction scheme or an undertaking under those enactments in outlying and suburban districts to which such facilities for cheap travel give access, the Local Government Board shall regard the requirements of the said enactments with respect to the replacing of the accommodation so destroyed as having been complied with to the extent to which accommodation is so provided.

(2) " The words ' be less than ' shall be substituted for the word ' exceed ' in paragraph two of the schedule to the Housing of the Working Classes Act, 1903.

Compensation for Demolition

8. " The powers of the local authority under Part II of the principal Act shall include:

(1) a power to pay compensation to the owner of any building upon its demolition under that Part of that Act on the ground of its being or forming part of a dwelling-house unfit for human habitation, where the owner agrees that no buildings shall be erected upon the cleared site except with the consent of the local authority:

(2) " a power at the cost of the owner at any time to abate any building erected without that consent, on a site in respect of which such an agreement has been made.

Compensation

9. " For the purpose of enforcing more effectually the principle of assessing compensation laid down in Sub-section 2 of Section 21

and in Section 41 of the principal Act, in cases where compensation is based on rental, an arbitrator shall act in accordance with the following regulations:

(1) " If the house or premises fall under the description of property which may be constituted an unhealthy area under the said Act, evidence shall be receivable by the arbitrator to show that the said house or premises by reason of their character or the general character of the locality or the poverty or habits of the inhabitants thereof, or for any other reason, are likely to be so overcrowded as to be dangerous or injurious to the health of the inmates:

(2) " Where the arbitrator is satisfied by such evidence the burden of proof shall lie upon the persons claiming compensation to show that the house or premises are not so overcrowded and that the rental is not so enhanced:

(3) " Evidence shall be receivable by the arbitrator to show the amount of the rental of other premises in the neighbourhood which are not overcrowded, in order to ascertain the rental which would have been obtainable if the house or premises were occupied only by the number of persons whom they are under all circumstances fitted to accommodate without such overcrowding as is dangerous or injurious to the health of the inmates.

Local Inquiries

10. Any local inquiry held by the Local Government Board for the purpose of confirming an improvement scheme under Part I, or a reconstruction scheme under Part II of the principal Act at which inquiry is made as to the expediency of sanctioning the exercise by the local authority of their power to borrow for the purpose of the scheme may be treated as a sufficient inquiry for the purpose of sanctioning such borrowing, and no further inquiry shall be necessary unless the sum proposed to be borrowed exceeds the estimate of the cost of the scheme given by the local authority at the inquiry held for the purpose of confirming the scheme, and appears to the Local Government Board to be unreasonable.

Salaries and Expenses

11. " The salaries of the Housing Commissioners and all expenses incurred by them or by the Local Government Board

in pursuance of this Act (other than expenses recoverable from a local authority under an order of the court under this Act) shall be defrayed out of moneys provided by Parliament.

Treasury Grants

12. (1) " There shall be annually charged on and paid out of the Consolidated Fund or the growing produce thereof, a sum (to be called the housing grant) of five hundred thousand pounds.

(2) " The housing grant shall be carried to a separate account to be established under regulations to be made by the Treasury for the purpose, and shall be subject to such regulations as the Treasury may make with respect to accounts and accumulation of moneys standing to the account.

(3) " The Treasury may grant out of the housing grant to a local authority undertaking an improvement scheme under Part I or a reconstruction scheme under Part II of the principal Act, such an amount not exceeding one-half of the net cost of the scheme as the Local Government Board may determine.

(4) " If a local authority engaged in providing housing accommodation under Part III of the principal Act satisfy the Local Government Board in any particular case that to charge rents in respect of the accommodation provided such as persons of the working classes in the district could reasonably be expected to pay, would cause an annual deficiency upon the cost of the provision of the accommodation the Treasury may make a grant to the local authority out of the housing grant of an amount to be determined by the Local Government Board not exceeding one-half of the capital amount of the deficiency as estimated by the Treasury.

Existing Powers not Diminished

13. " The powers conferred by this Act shall be in addition to and not in derogation of the powers conferred by the Housing of the Working Classes Acts, 1890 to 1909.

Annual Report

14. " The Housing Commissioners, in addition to any reports made by them under the foregoing provisions of this Act shall make an annual report to the Local Government Board of their proceedings, and of the proceedings of the Board under this Act, and of the results of the inquiries made by the Commissioners and the Local Government Board shall lay the report before Parliament.

Amendment of Small Dwellings Acquisition Act, 1899.

15. (1) " For the purpose of enabling local authorities more effectually to carry out the objects of the Small Dwellings Acquisition Act, 1899, the following amendments of the said Act shall have effect:

(a) " In paragraph (a) of Sub-section 1 of Section 1 of the said Act, *ninety per centum* instead of *four-fifths of the value of the ownership* shall be the limit of any advance made by a local authority, and in paragraph (b) thereof *three hundred pounds* and *three hundred and sixty pounds* shall be the limits of any such advance in place, respectively, of *two hundred and forty pounds* and *three hundred pounds*.

" Provided that the term ' house ' in the said Act shall include premises consisting of a shop and dwelling-house combined, and in respect of such premises the limit shall be four hundred pounds, or in the case of a fee simple or leasehold of not less than ninety-nine years unexpired at the date of the purchase four hundred and sixty pounds, and an advance may be made if the market value of the premises does not in the opinion of the local authorities exceed five hundred pounds.

(b) " Sub-section 2 of Section 1 of the said Act shall be repealed, and the following provision shall be substituted for it:

" ' Interest and repayment of every such advance shall be provided by weekly, monthly, quarterly or half-yearly payments, exceeding by not more than twenty per centum, the net rental value of the house for the period in respect of which each such payment is made.'

(c) " Sub-section 4 of Section 1 of the said Act shall be repealed, and the following provision shall be substituted for it:

" ' The balance of each periodical payment made as aforesaid which remains after satisfying the charge for interest shall be applied to the redemption of the capital sum borrowed on the basis of a sinking fund accumulating at the rate of three per centum per annum.'

(d) " All the words in Sub-section 5 of Section 1 of the said Act, after the second ten pounds shall be repealed.

(e) " Notwithstanding anything in Section 2 of the Small Dwellings Acquisition Act, 1899, a local authority may make an advance under that Act, to a person who is already the proprietor of the house in respect of which the advance so made for the purpose of enabling him to repay any sum borrowed by him from any other person in order to acquire the house, or may take a transfer of a mortgage previously effected for that purpose, and any sum paid by the local authority to the mortgagee in consideration of such a transfer shall be treated as an advance to the mortgagor under the said Act.

(2) " A local authority having powers under the Small Dwellings Acquisition Act, 1899, may at any time exercise those powers in respect of any lodging house provided by the authority under Part III of the Housing of the Working Classes Act, 1890, notwithstanding anything in Section 64 of the last mentioned Act.

Short Title and Construction

16. " This Act may be cited as the Housing of the Working Classes Act, 1912, and shall be construed as one with the Housing of the Working Classes Acts, 1890 to 1909; and this Act and those Acts, may be cited together as the Housing of the Working Classes Acts, 1890 to 1912.

Application

17. " This Act shall not apply to Scotland or Ireland."

COMMENTS

This Bill proposes Parliamentary grants in aid of housing operations.

Charity is always to be avoided when justice and good management can achieve the same end and, therefore, State loans for decent housing (see Chapter VII) are much to be preferred to grants in aid. Another objection to this Bill is that the money is to be administered by local authorities. Several reasons have already been given why municipal house building has not succeeded in solving the housing problem, and why it is never likely to do so. Another reason may be added here. Decent housing at reasonable rents will not be a financial success without careful management. Public bodies are not fitted for careful business management. When politics come in at the door careful business methods fly out of the window, and it is extremely difficult to eliminate political predilections from local council elections. The first object of most public men—and a very natural one too—is to be popular. Popularity and careful business management often clash, whereas public utility building societies whose members have a definite personal financial stake in the concern have every chance of being managed on sound lines. This point is of first rate importance. It is not enough to settle a policy, success will not be achieved unless precautions are taken to ensure careful day by day business management, and the only way to ensure this is to arrange that those responsible shall have a personal stake in the undertaking. This Bill was objected to in Parliament on the ground that farm rents would be increased by building cottages convenient to them. A profit to the landlord; a loss to the public. Decent cottages cannot be provided without benefiting the farms, but if better housing is encouraged by State loans on careful lines (see Chapter VII) there will be no valid objection to benefiting the farms, because the landowner will have done his share towards providing the cottages. It was also feared that this Bill would result in tied cottages; that objection would be surmounted by the co-partnership system. A fatal objection to this Bill is that it contemplates the impossibility of ever enabling agricultural labourers to pay an economic rent. There is no natural law that makes it impossible for an agricultural labourer to get enough to live upon. Experience shows that when he is treated fairly he can produce from the land a sufficient livelihood and, therefore, no policy (such as building down to starvation wages) should be adopted that would tend to perpetuate the present artificial conditions. What ought to be done is to take steps that will increase wages to a living standard. On the other hand the question is urgent, and wages do not jump up. It has been suggested that a temporary subsidy of some kind might be made, diminishing in amount, until wages can be raised to a living minimum, and some reformers think the State should support uneconomic rents for a short time where there is a binding guarantee from responsible persons that these rents shall be raised to an economic standard within a short period of years. The object of this suggestion is to give a little time for the inevitable rise in wages that is bound to follow from the decent housing of the workers, because, their health and general physique being improved, they will be worth more money to their employers; but it is very doubtful whether even such a severely restricted eleemosynary method as this would not do more harm than good, and would not in the long run delay the higher wages and better housing that are desired.

Justice, not charity is the only safe method to employ in the solution of our land and housing problem.

The proposal in this Bill to obtain information as to the need in any locality for the mending or ending of old property and the provision of up-to-date housing accommodation is very sound but housing commissioners under the Local Government Board would, for reasons given in the body of this book, be unable to effect anything useful. The proposal to widen the land purchase powers of local authorities and to enable them to acquire land in advance of requirements for town planning purposes is all in the right direction.

Clause 6 with regard to the relaxation of by-laws is a great improvement on Clause 44 of the 1909 Act, but even this does not go far enough. Progressive landowners are constantly obstructed by local by-law authorities and the only way to get over this difficulty is to give landowners a simple, cheap and direct right of appeal to an independent and up-to-date central authority.

Clause 8 would have been of very great value to London. Under present conditions slum reform under Part I of the 1890 Act which rewards owners for neglecting their property, is administered by the London County Council, whereas Part II calling on owners to repair their insanitary property or demolish it at their own expense is administered by the borough councils. The question as to which is the wiser method is, therefore, confused in London by the side issues as to which authority shall pay the bill. Borough councils have been known to refuse to administer Part II so as to save themselves any expenditure, and have thereby forced the County Council into an immensely expensive improvement scheme under Part I. This result gives the borough council the appearance of being very economical because they personally have spent no money, but in reality they have been very extravagant by forcing on the big scheme, and it is the same ratepayers who support both bodies. It does not matter to the ratepayers who spends their money, but it does matter very much when large sums are wasted through careless legislation and thoughtless administration. Clause 8 gets over this difficulty by empowering the London County Council to make agreements with borough councils on the question as to whether Part I or Part II shall be enforced, and which public body shall pay the bill.

Another good point in this Bill is the power given to the central authority to act in default of a local authority, and to charge the cost to them instead of having to proceed by mandamus " a rusty old instrument." This power would be very useful in cases where local authorities neglect their duties under Part II of the 1890 Act and Clauses 15, 17 and 18 of the 1909 Act, to call upon owners of insanitary property to make it fit for human habitation or demolish it. It would also be very useful in the hands of a competent central authority in cases where town planning schemes are urgently needed in order to increase the supply of good cheap housing accommodation, but where local influence prevents anything useful being done. At present the only remedy in such cases is for the central authority to proceed by way of mandamus, an extremely clumsy method which in practice is quite ineffective.

It is well known to housing reformers that scattered all over the country there is a considerable number of landowners who have at their own expense built cottages, and let them at a loss in order that the labourers on their estates should be decently housed; but, as Lady Gwendolen Cecil pointed out some years ago at Letchworth, eleemosynary housing schemes whether carried out by private individuals or by public bodies seriously injure the permanent and general solution of the housing problem. They are not in themselves nearly sufficient to meet the needs of the case, and they discourage others who are willing to meet the demand on a sound economic basis.

THE ONLY WAY TO SOLVE AN ECONOMIC PROBLEM IS TO MEET IT WITH ECONOMIC REMEDIES, AND NOT MERELY WITH CHARITY RENTS, WHICH ARE REALLY ONLY PALLIATIVES, NOT REMEDIES, AND THEREFORE IN THE LONG RUN WILL DO MORE HARM THAN GOOD.

APPENDIX XII

"THE INCIDENCE OF LOCAL TAXATION WITH SOME SUGGESTIONS AS TO POLICY."
SEE MARSHALL'S "PRINCIPLES OF ECONOMICS" APPENDIX G, PAGE 794, SIXTH EDITION—1910.

The incidence of all local taxes is influenced by the migration of the population, and by the manner in which the rates are expended

1. "We have noted that the incidence of a new local tax on printing would differ from that of a national tax mainly by causing such parts of the local printing industry as could conveniently migrate beyond the boundaries of the local tax to do so. Those customers who needed their printing to be done in the locality would pay rather higher for it. Compositors would migrate till only enough remained to find employment locally at about the same wages as before; and some printing offices would be transferred to other industries. The incidence of general local rates on immovable property follows different lines in some respects. The power of migration beyond the boundaries of the rates is a very important factor here, as in the case of a local tax on printing. But of perhaps even greater importance is the fact that a large part of the local rates is spent in ways that conduce directly to the comfort of those very residents and workers in the locality who might otherwise be driven away. Here two technical terms are needed."

Onerous rates

"Onerous rates are those which yield no compensating benefit to the persons who pay them. An extreme case is that of rates devoted to paying interest on a loan incurred by a municipality for an enterprise which failed and has been abandoned. A more representative case is that of a poor rate levied mainly from the well-to-do. Onerous rates tend, of course, to drive away those persons on whom they would fall.

Beneficial or remunerative rates

"On the other hand beneficial or remunerative rates are those spent on lighting, draining, and other purposes; so as to supply the people who pay the rates with certain necessaries, comforts and luxuries of life, which can be provided by the local authority more cheaply than in any other way. Such rates ably and honestly administered, may confer a net benefit on those who pay them, and an increase in them may attract population and industry instead of repelling it. Of course, a rate may be onerous to one class of the population and beneficial to another. A high rate spent on providing good primary and secondary schools may attract artisan residents, while repelling the well-to-do. ' Services which are preponderantly national in character ' are ' generally onerous,' while those which are preponderantly local in character generally confer upon ratepayers a direct and peculiar benefit more or less commensurate with the burden.*

Extent to which it may be assumed that the occupier is mobile

" The occupier generally regards the rates which are collected from him as forming a single aggregate with his rent; but he makes his reckoning also for the amenities of life which are secured by remunerative local expenditure of rates; that is he tends, other things equal, to select districts in which the aggregate of rents, and onerous rates is low. But there is great difficulty in estimating the extent to which migration is actually governed by this consideration. It is probably hindered less than is commonly supposed by ignorance and indifference. But it is much hindered by the special requirements of each individual. Low rates in Devonshire will not draw there people who prefer London life; and certain classes of manufactures have practically little choice as to the place in which they settle. To say nothing of personal and business ties, the tenant is further hindered by the expense and trouble of moving; and if that were the equivalent of two years' rent, he would lose by moving unless the advantage which he secured in rates amounted to two shillings in the pound for thirty years. When, however, a person is changing his abode for any reason, he is likely to allow their full weight to all considerations as to the present and prospective rates in different localities which may be suitable for his purpose.

" The mobility of the working classes is, in some respects, greater than that of the well-to-do; but when rates are compounded friction sometimes acts on the side of the tenant, and delays the transference to him of his share of new burdens. The manufacturer is often affected as much by the rates on his workmen's dwellings as by those on his own premises: and though high rates may be among the causes which have driven some

* Final Report of Royal Commission on Local Taxation, 1901.

manufacturers out of large towns, it is doubtful whether, when economically administered, they have had much net effect in this direction. For most new expenditure from the rates, when under able and upright management, materially increases local comforts or lessens local discomforts from the point of view of the workpeople if not of the manufacturer himself. Further, although the balance of evidence goes to show that lessees consider carefully the present and probable immediate future of local rates, yet they cannot see far ahead, and they seldom even try to do so.

Difficulties of prediction when changes are rapid and adjustments are slow

" Any analysis that is offered of the incidence of rates must be taken to refer to general tendencies rather than actual facts. The causes which prevent these tendencies from being applied in prediction resemble those which prevent mathematical reasonings from being applied to the course of a ball on the deck of a ship that is rolling and pitching in cross seas. If the ship would but stay at one inclination the movement of the ball could be calculated. But before any one tendency has had time to produce much result it will have ceased to exist, and its successor cannot be predicted. Just so, though economists settled once for all nearly a century ago, the general tendencies of the shifting of taxation; yet the relative weight of onerous rates in different places often changes so rapidly that a tendency may make but little headway before it is stopped off, or even reversed by changes which cannot be predicted.

The term building value

2. " We have already seen that the ground rent which a builder is willing to pay for any site is governed by his estimate of the additional value which that site will give to the buildings erected on it. Before taking the lease his capital, and that which he will borrow for the purpose, is ' free ' and expressed in terms of money. The anticipated income from his investment is expressed also in money. He sets on the one side his outlay for building and on the other side the excess of the rental value of the building, with its site over the ground rent to which he is about to commit himself. He works out—perhaps roughly and by instinct rather than definite arithmetical calculations—the present (discounted) value of this excess for the (say) ninety-nine years of his lease.

Finally he takes the lease if he sees his way to a good margin of profit ; and no better opening for his enterprise is at hand.*

" He contrives to the best of his ability that the site and the house (or other building) which he puts upon it shall be permanently appropriate the one to the other. In so far as he succeeds the rent of the property at any future time is the sum of its annual site value, and the annual value of the building; and this he expects to yield him full profits on his outlay, allowing for insurance against the risks of a rather hazardous industry. This second part of the rent is commonly, though perhaps not with strict propriety, called the (annual) building value, or the building rent of the house.

If a Building has become inappropriate to its site, the whole value may be only that of the site

" As time goes on the purchasing power of money may change; the class of house for which that site is suitable is likely to change; and the technique of building is certain to be improved. Consequently the total annual value of the property at a later date consists of its annual site value, together with profits on the cost of building a house giving accommodation equally desirable at that date with the existing house. But all this is subject to the dominant condition that the general character of the house has remained appropriate to its site; if it has not no precise statement as to the relation between total value, site value and building value can be made. If, for instance, a warehouse or a dwelling-house of quite a different character is needed to develop the full resources of the site, the total value of the property as it stands may be less than its site value alone. For the site value cannot be developed without pulling down those buildings and erecting new. And the value of the old material in those buildings may be less than the cost of pulling them down, allowance being made for the obstruction and loss of time incident thereto.

Onerous taxes on site values in so far as foreseen are deducted from ground rents in new leases

3. " As between two buildings equally eligible in other respects

---

* The builder generally looks to sell his lease before much of it has run out, but the price which he expects to get is the (discounted) excess of the rental value of the property over the ground rent for the remaining years, and, therefore, the substance of his calculations is nearly the same as it would be if he intended to keep the property in his own hands.

the occupier will pay for that which has the better situation, an annual sum equivalent to its special advantages: but he does not care what part of this sum goes as rent and what as taxes. Therefore, onerous taxes on site values tend to be deducted from the rental, which the owner or lessee received; and they are accordingly deducted, in so far as they can be foreseen from the ground rent which a builder or anyone else is willing to pay for a building lease. Such local rates as are remunerative are in the long run paid by the occupier, but are no real burden to him. The condition ' in the long run ' is essential; for interest rates levied on account of interest and sinking fund on a town improvement, which will for several years to come disturb the public thoroughfares, and yield none of its good fruit, will be onerous to the occupier if he pays it. In strict justice it should be deducted from his rent, because when the improvement is in full working order, and especially when the debt has been paid off, so that the rate in question lapses, the owner of the property will reap the benefit of the onerous rates levied on account of it from the first.*

Taxes on building values, if uniform all over the country cannot be evaded by the occupier except in so far as he selects a less expensive building

4. " Taxes on building values are on a different footing. If uniform all over the country, they do not alter the differential advantages of favoured sites and, therefore, do not—directly at least—make the builder or anyone else less willing to pay a high ground rent for a good site. If they are so heavy as materially to narrow the area of ground built upon, they will indeed lower the value of all building ground; and special site values will fall with the rest. But their effect in this direction is so small that no great error is made by saying that uniform taxes on building values do not fall on the ground owner. The builder in so far as he anticipates such taxes adjusts his plans to them, he aims at putting up buildings of only such expense as can be let to tenants at rents that will yield him normal profits; while the tenant pays the rates. He may,

---

* This assumes that the land is assessed to the tax at the same amount, whatever the use to which it is put. If agricultural land were exempt from the tax then the tenant of a house or factory in the country would escape that part of the site tax which is assessed on the excess of the value of the land for building uses over its value for agriculture. This might slightly increase concentration in towns and thus take a little from the burden on site owners in them, but it would not materially affect the values of sites in the centres of towns.

of course, miscalculate. But in the long run builders as a class, like all other able business men, are nearly right in their calculations. And in the long run, uniform taxes on building values fall upon the occupier; or at the last on his customers if he uses the building for trade purposes, and his competitors are subject to similar rates.

Remunerative rates are, of course, no net burden

" But the case is quite different in regard to special high onerous local rates on building values; and here comes in the chief difference between the incidence of national taxes on immovable property and local rates on it. Remunerative expenditure from the rates, which adds more to the conveniences of life than the equivalent of its cost, do not, of course, repel the occupier; that part of them which is assessed on building values is paid by him, but is no real burden on him as we have seen in the case of remunerative rates on site values.

Exceptionally onerous rates on building values tend to be shifted on to owners in the same way as if assessed on site values

" But that part of the rates on building values which is onerous and in excess of corresponding charges in other localities, does not fall mainly on the occupiers. Any exceptional pressure will cause them to migrate beyond its reach in sufficient numbers to reduce the demand for houses and other buildings in the locality, till the burden of these exceptional rates falls upon the lessees or owners. Builders, therefore, in so far as they can foresee the future, deduct the equivalent of these exceptional onerous rates on building values, together with all rates and taxes on site values from the ground rents which they are willing to pay.

Grave inequalities of onerous rates seldom last long

" But the cases in which great deductions of this kind are made are not numerous and important. For permanent inequalities of onerous rates, though considerable, are less than is commonly thought: and many of them are due to accidents which cannot easily be foreseen, such as mismanagement by a particular group of local administrators. There is indeed one broad and perhaps permanent cause, which throws its shadow before, namely the tendency of the well-to-do to move away from crowded districts to roomy and fashionable suburbs: thus leaving the working classes to bear an undue share of the national duties towards the very poor. But no sooner does this evil become conspicuous, than legislation is evoked to remedy it, by widening the areas of rating for some purposes so as to include poor and rich districts under the same budget; and in other ways.

Specially onerous rates in one district are a bounty to ground landlords in others

" It is of greater importance to remember that exceptional onerous rates on building values, while tending to lower site rents, and to lower the ground rents on new leases in the districts to which they apply are not as great a burden on the whole body of owners of land as seems at first sight. For much of the building enterprise, which is checked by such rates, is not destroyed but directed to other districts, and raises the competition for new building leases there.

Old rates and taxes established before the sale of a property are no burden to the purchaser

5. " The incidence of a long-established rate is little affected by its being collected from the tenant, and not from the owners; though it is vitally affected by the proportions in which the rate is assessed on site and building values respectively. On the other hand, the incidence for the first few years of an increase in onerous rates is much affected by the mode of collection. The occupier bears more of the new burden than he would if part of the rates were collected from the owners or he were allowed to deduct a part of them from his rent. This applies only to neighbourhoods that are making progress. Where the population is receding and building has ceased, onerous rates tend to press upon owners. But in such places friction is generally strong.

The evils of sudden great changes in rates

" It seems probable that the total pressure of onerous rates on the enterprise of building speculators and other interim owners is not very great; and that many rates, of which they have complained have really enriched them. But vicissitudes of the rates increase slightly the great risks of the building trade, and inevitably the community pays for such risks more than their actuarial equivalent. All this points to the grievous evils which arise from great and sudden increases in the rates, especially in regard to premises the rateable value of which is high relatively to the net income of the occupier.

The case of the shopkeeper

" The trader, especially if a shopkeeper, is often able to throw some part of the burden of his rates on his customers, at all events if he deals in things which cannot be easily got from a distance. But the shopkeeper's rates are very large relatively to his income; and some of that expenditure from the rates which is remunerative from the point of view of well-to-do residents, appears onerous to him. His work belongs to that group in which economic progress is raising supply relatively to demand. A little while ago his remuneration was artificially high, at the expense of society; but now it is falling to a lower and perhaps more equitable level, and he is slow to recognize the new conditions. His mind fastens on the real injustice which he suffers when rates are suddenly raised much; and he attributes to that some of the pressure on him which is really due to deeper causes. His sense of injustice is sharpened by the fact that he does not always bargain on quite even terms with his landlord; for to say nothing of the cost of fixtures and general expense of a change, he might lose a great part of his custom by moving to equally good premises even a little way off. It must, however, be remembered that the shopkeeper does migrate sometimes, that his mind is alert and he takes full account of the rates; and thus after a few years he shifts the burden of onerous rates on to the owners and customers more fully than a man of almost any other class does. (The hotel and lodging-house keeper may rank here with the shopkeeper.)

The assessment of vacant building land on its capital value

6. " Land near to a growing town which is still used for agriculture may yield very little net rent; and yet be a valuable property. For its future ground rents are anticipated in its capital value; and further its ownership is likely to yield an income of satisfaction outside of the money rent received for it. In this case it is apt to be under-assessed even when rated at its full rental value; and the question arises whether it should not be assessed at a percentage on its capital value instead of at a percentage on its rent.

" Such a plan would hasten on building and thus tend to glut the market for buildings. Therefore, rents would tend to fall and builders would be unable to take building leases on high ground rents. The change would, therefore, transfer to the people at large some part of ' the public value ' of land which now goes to owners of land, that is built upon or is likely to be built upon. BUT UNLESS ACCOMPANIED BY ENERGETIC ACTION ON THE PART OF URBAN AUTHORITIES IN PLANNING OUT THE LINES ON WHICH TOWNS SHOULD GROW IT WOULD RESULT IN HASTY AND INAPPROPRIATE BUILDING; A MISTAKE FOR WHICH COMING GENERATIONS WOULD PAY A HIGH PRICE IN THE LOSS OF BEAUTY AND PERHAPS OF HEALTH.*

And a partial transference of assessments generally from building values to site value

" The principle which lies at the base of this scheme is capable of larger application and something may be said as to one suggestion of an extreme character, which has recently attracted some attention, to the effect that in future rates should be assessed mainly or even wholly on site values, with little or no reference to the value of the buildings. Its immediate effect would be an addition to the value of some properties at the expense of others. In particular it would raise the value of high and expensive buildings in districts in which the rates were heavy, even more than those in which they were low; because it would afford relief from a greater burden. But it would lower the value of low obsolete buildings on large sites in heavily rated districts. After a time the amount of building put upon a site would vary generally, subject to the by-laws, with its advantages of situation; instead of as now partly in proportion to these advantages and partly inversely as the rates. This would increase concentration and tend to raise gross site values in advantageous districts; but it would also increase the aggregate expenditure from the rates; and as this would fall on site values the net site values might be very low; WHETHER ON THE WHOLE THE CONCENTRATION OF POPULATION WOULD BE INCREASED IT IS DIFFICULT TO SAY : FOR THE MOST ACTIVE BUILDING WOULD PROBABLY BE IN THE SUBURBS WHERE VACANT LAND NO LONGER

* See Chapters II and VI.

ESCAPED HEAVY RATING. MUCH WOULD DEPEND ON THE BUILDING BY-LAWS; THE CONCENTRATION MIGHT BE MUCH LESSENED BY A RIGOROUS RULE THAT THERE SHOULD BE A LARGE FREE SPACE AT THE BACK AS WELL AS IN FRONT OF ALL HIGH BUILDINGS.*

Rural rates

7. " Reference has already been made to the latent partnership between tenant and landlord in British agriculture generally. Competition is less effective in rural than in urban districts. But on the other hand the contributions which the landlord makes to the effective capital of the farm are elastic, and liable to variation according to the stress of circumstances, and these adjustments obscure the incidence of agricultural rates, as the eddies of wind rushing past a house will often carry snow-flakes upwards, over-bearing, but not destroying, the tendency of gravitation.

" However rural populations probably bear less onerous rates than is commonly supposed. They have gained by improved police service, and the abolition of turnpikes, and they have increasing access to advantages purchased by rates in the neighbouring towns, to which they do not contribute and which are generally much higher than their own rates. In so far as the rates are remunerative in the immediate present, they are no net burden to the occupier though he pays them. But rates are a considerable percentage on the farmer's net income; and the burden on him is apt to be heavy in those very rare cases in which onerous rural rates are increased greatly. As already indicated an onerous rate confined to one district is likely to press more heavily on the local landlords and farmers than if general throughout the country.

* See Chapters II and VI.

* For instance, suppose an area of a million square feet to be covered with rows of parallel buildings, 40 ft. high and 40 ft. deep; a by-law that the sky must subtend half a right angle at the ground looking straight back as well as front, will cause the distance between each row and the next to be 40 ft. and the aggregate volume of building will be 40 ft. multiplied into half the total area, i.e., 20,000,000 cubic feet. Now suppose the height of the buildings to be trebled. Under the by-law the distances between the rows must be 120 ft.; and on the supposition that it is not convenient to increase the depth of the houses beyond 40 ft., the aggregate volume of building will be 120 ft. multiplied into a quarter of the total area, that is 30,000,000 cubic feet. Thus the total accommodation will be increased by only one-half instead of being trebled as would have been the case if the old distances of 40 ft between the rows had been maintained.

Reasons for departing from the general plan of the volume and applying these considerations to some practical issues.

8. " This volume is mainly occupied with scientific inquiries; but yet not without some glances at the practical issues, which supply a motive to economic studies. But some consideration of policy seems desirable in regard to rates. For all economists are agreed that land in an old country resembles other forms of wealth in many respects, and that it differs in others; and in some recent controversial writings there has appeared a tendency to relegate the points of difference to a secondary place, and to give almost exclusive prominence to those of similarity. A moderate tendency in that direction might be judicious if the points of similarity alone were of high importance in urgent practical issues. But the contrary is the fact. And, therefore, it may be well to consider some great issues of administrative finance, in which a leading part is played by those attributes of land which are not largely shared by other forms of wealth. But first a little must be said as to equity.

Particular remunerative rates to be judged separately; enormous taxation to be judged as a whole

" When a special tax is levied for a particular purpose, and the case is not one for any interference by public authority with existing rights of ownership—as, for instance, when an arterial system of land drainage is created—THE OWNERS OF THE PROPERTIES TO BE BENEFITED MAY FITLY BE ASSESSED ON THE ' JOINT STOCK PRINCIPLE ' * according to which calls are made from shareholders in proportion to their stake in the common venture. The equity of every such charge must be judged separately. But on the other hand all onerous taxes and rates must be judged in equity as a whole. Almost every onerous tax taken by itself presses with undue weight on some class or other, but this is of no moment if the inequalities of each are compensated by those of others, and variations in the several parts synchronize. If that difficult condition is satisfied, the system may be equitable though any one part of it regarded alone would be inequitable.

Taxes on houses are roughly proportionate to expenditure and equitable in themselves

" Secondly there is a general agreement that a system of taxa-.

* See Chapters II and VI.

tion should be adjusted in more or less steep graduation to people's incomes; or better still to their expenditure. For that part of a man's income, which he saves, contributes again to the Exchequer until it is consumed by expenditure. Consequently when considering the fact that our present system of taxation, general and local, bears heavily on houses, it should be remembered that large expenditure generally requires large house room; and that while taxes and especially graduated taxes on expenditure in general present great technical difficulties to the tax collector and cost much more to the consumer directly and indirectly than they bring into the revenue, taxes on houses are technically simple, cheap in collection, not liable to evasion and easy of graduation.*

But heavy taxes on trade premises are equitable only in so far as they are shifted, and new taxes cannot be shifted quickly

"But thirdly this argument does not apply to buildings other than houses. And for that reason it may be equitable to tax shops, warehouses, factories, etc., on a lower scale than houses, at all events as far as new rates are concerned; the burden of old rates is already shifted from the occupiers of business premises partly on to their landlords and partly on to their customers. This process of shifting is constantly going on; and therefore no great hardship would be inflicted on the trading classes in urban districts if they were charged at once with a farthing for every penny of new rates; while a part or the whole, of the remaining three farthings were left to be added to their burden gradually by small annual percentages. It may be that some such plan will be necessary, if the expenses of urban local government continue to increase fast.

The statesman has heavy and many-sided responsibilities in relation to land

"These considerations lead us to repeat that whether in an

---

* In old times the windows of a house were taken as representative of the house, and were taxed heavily; but the tax did not strike and was not intended to strike, persons as owners and users of windows only; it was intended to strike them, and did strike them as owners and users of houses. And, just as the window is a more or less good representative of the house, so the house is a representative, perhaps a better representative, of a certain scale and style of household expenditure in general, and when houses are taxed, the tax is, and is intended to be a tax upon the ownership and use of the means of living in certain general conditions of comfort and social position. If part of the tax assessed on houses were removed, and the deficit made up by taxes assessed on furniture and indoor servants, the true incidence of the taxes would be nearly the same as now.

old or a new country a far-seeing statesman will feel a greater responsibility to future generations when legislating as to land than as to other forms of wealth; and that from the economic and from the ethical point of view, land must everywhere and always be classed as a thing by itself. If from the first the State had retained true rents in its own hands, the vigour of industry and accumulation need not have been impaired, though in a very few cases the settlement of new countries might have been delayed a little. Nothing at all like this can be said of the incomes derived from property made by man. But the very greatness of the public interests concerned makes it specially necessary to bear in mind, when discussing the equities of the public value of land, that a sudden appropriation by the State of any incomes from property, the private ownership of which had once been recognized by it, would destroy security and shake the foundations of society. Sudden and extreme measures would be inequitable; and partly, but not solely for that reason, they would be unbusinesslike and even foolish.

" Caution is necessary. But the cause of high site values is that concentration of population, which is threatening a scarcity of fresh air and light and play-room so grievous as to lower the vigour and the joyousness of the rising generation. Thus rich private gains accrue not merely through causes which are public rather than private in their character, but also at the expense of one of the chief forms of public wealth. Large expenditure is needed to secure air and light and play-room. And the most appropriate source from which that expense can be defrayed seems to be those extreme rights of private property in land, which have grown up almost imperceptibly from the time when the king, representing the State, was the sole landowner. Private persons were but landholders subject to the obligation to work for the public well-being; they have no equitable right to mar it by congested building.

Sudden disturbances of old rates are to be avoided

9. " Accordingly the following suggestions seem to emerge: As regards old rates a sudden change in the person from whom they are collected seems unadvisable; but additional rates should, as far as may be convenient, be collected from the person on whom they are ultimately to fall; unless like the income tax under Schedule A they are collected from the tenant with the instruction that they are to be deducted from his rent.

New rates should be imposed as far as may be on those by whom they are ultimately to be paid.

" The reasons for this are that nearly the whole of that part of old rates, which is assessed on public or site value of land, is already borne by owners (including lessees, so far as those rates go, which, though old, were not anticipated when their leases were taken); and nearly all the remainder of it is borne by tenants or their customers. This result would not be very greatly disturbed by allowing the tenant to deduct half or even the whole of his rates from his rent; though such a law would run some risk of handing over some of the property of the owners to lessees, who had reckoned for paying those old rates when taking their leases. On the other hand, a provision for the division of new, that is additional, rates would have great advantages, the occupier whether of a farm, of business premises or a house would deduct one-half of the new rates from his rent; his immediate landlord would deduct in proportion from his payments to the superior holder next to him, and so on. And in addition new local taxes on business premises of all kinds might be assessed, as has just been suggested at less than full rates in the first instance and gradually increased. By these provisions farmers, shopkeepers, and other traders would be relieved from the occasional injustice and the constant fear of injustice, which are now associated with sudden, disproportionate additions to the public burdens thrown upon particular classes.

Urban land might be charged with a general site rate and a special fresh air rate

" In regard to site values, it would seem well to rule that all land, whether technically urban or not should be regarded as having a special site value if, when cleared of buildings, it could be sold at even a moderately high price, say £200 an acre. It might then be subjected to a general rate assessed on its capital value, and in addition to a ' fresh air rate ' to be spent by local authority under full central control for the purposes indicated above. This fresh air rate would not be a very heavy burden on owners for a good deal of it would be returned to them in the form of higher values for those building sites which remained. AS IT IS THE EXPENDITURE OF SUCH PRIVATE SOCIETIES AS THE METROPOLITAN PUBLIC GARDENS ASSOCIATION AND MUCH OF THE RATES RAISED ON BUILDING VALUES FOR

PUBLIC IMPROVEMENTS IS REALLY A FREE GIFT OF
WEALTH TO OWNERS WHO ARE ALREADY FORTUNATE.*

Rates should be graduated but no one wholly excepted.

" For rural and urban districts alike after reckoning for the
initial rates on land the remainder of the necessary funds would
perhaps best be obtained by rates on immovable property, supplemented by some minor local taxes at the discretion of the local
authorities. The Inhabited House Duty might be suppressed unless
it was needed for any great new expenditure such as old age pensions; and the main rates might be graduated as the present
Inhabited House Duty is, but more gently for houses of moderate
size, and more severely for very large houses. But no one should be
exempted altogether; for so long as a person retains the right of
voting on the levying and expenditure of rates it is not safe that he
should wholly escape their pressure. It may, however, be safe and
reasonable to return to him or his children the equivalent of his
payments in such benefits as will increase physical and mental
health and vigour and will not tend towards political corruption.†

" The recent Commission on Local Taxation was much occupied with the difficulty of assessing site values and with the even
greater difficulty of making ad interim arrangements by which an
equitable share (whether more or less) of the rates which were
designed in the long run to be paid by the ultimate landowners,
might be transferred from the occupiers to lessees. THE DIFFI-
CULTY OF ASSESSMENT, THOUGH UNDOUBTEDLY VERY
GREAT, IS OF A KIND TO BE DIMINISHED RAPIDLY BY
EXPERIENCE. THE FIRST THOUSAND SUCH ASSESSMENTS
MIGHT PROBABLY GIVE MORE TROUBLE AND YET BE
LESS ACCURATELY MADE THAN THE NEXT TWENTY
THOUSAND." ‡

* See Chapter III.   † See Chapter V.   ‡ See Chapter VII.

APPENDIX XIII

THE ELIMINATION OF THE SLUMS, BY MISS ANNIE HANKINSON, REPRINTED FROM THE "MANCHESTER COURIER," JULY 12 and 19.

" How are we to get rid of the slums?" This question, which has recently been occupying your columns has so long been the problem (and despair) of housing reformers that it seems hardly possible to advance anything new on the subject. The best that can be done is to bring forward and compare the experiences of different workers, as you have been doing, with a view to informing and forming public opinion—at present sadly indifferent to the question.

In the first place, it should be clearly recognized that there is no one plain, unmistakable path out of the dense jungle of slumdom which has been allowed to grow up in our midst unchecked through the ignorance, neglect and greed of past generations, and which, in too many instances, is still perpetuated through the same faults and mistakes to-day, combined with a colossal indifference to the miseries and discomforts of others, so long as they do not manifestly affect ourselves.

Broadly speaking, however, there are two great lines—main roads, as it were—which reformers follow in dealing with the slums, according to their point of view, namely, the " root and branch " policy of wholesale demolition and rebuilding and the policy of preserving property where structurally worth it, and, by a process of thorough repair, making it sanitary and habitable for people needing that class of accommodation at low rentals and near to their work. The one policy is embodied in Part I of the Housing of the Working Classes Act, 1890, the other in Part II of the same Act.

For full and clear details as to the working out of these respective methods, may I refer readers not yet acquainted with them to Mr J. S. Nettlefold's excellent book " Practical Housing " (Letchworth Garden City Press, Ltd.: price 1s.).

Both systems are necessary; both have their place in all great schemes of housing reform; and if, in the course of this article, the second (Part II) seems brought into prominence, it is because its value seems somewhat in danger of being obscured by the larger more arresting movement for drastic clearance and rebuilding.

You have recently published a most interesting account of this " root and branch " policy (Part I) in a series of articles by

Colonel G. Kyffin-Taylor, M.P., Chairman of the Liverpool Corporation Housing Committee. In dealing with insanitary property, he strongly advocates the methods therein embodied, viz., to buy up, pull down, and rebuild on the same sites—with the additional proviso that the new houses shall be reserved for the same tenants—(the dispossessed) at practically the same rents as those charged on the old houses, the deficiency in returns on capital outlay to be met out of the rates. He gives an account of an area where this was done with good results. The district in question was overcrowded, the people very poor, and their weekly earnings averaging not more than 15s. per family, and the goods of each household valued at less than £1. He claims for the system that when once these poor people are re-housed in decent, sanitary dwellings, they mostly rise to the occasion, and improve physically and morally.

These results, if they could always be relied upon to follow on this line of reform, would go far to commend it—at any rate as a temporary expedient—to meet urgent cases, for though it works out that the community makes up the deficit, money returns are not the only returns to be aimed at in removing abuses which concern the whole community, and for which that community is responsible. But its drawbacks must not be lost sight of. In the first place, the process is too costly for any but great Corporations with great powers or very wealthy individuals willing to work at a loss. Then, too, the charging of a non-commercial rent places private enterprise in building at a disadvantage, and so tends to check it. Would it not be better to aim at raising the very inadequate standard of wages of these poor people rather than at subsidizing their rents? A living wage and an economic rent are two indispensable factors in any lasting housing reform; without these there can be no solid building up of a healthy independence and self-respect among the people housed and no solid security for the community that a sound financial basis will ultimately be attained.

And how sorely this " living wage " is needed only those with close and intimate knowledge of the poor can testify. Besides the very poorest type of casual or " sweated " worker there are hundreds of decent families of the unskilled labouring class living—or rather, quietly, slowly, starving—on wages inadequate to keep them in efficient health. They do not know it themselves: they take the death of this child, the illness of that bread-winner, the hard, patient struggle of the weak and overburdened mother,

HH

as " all in the nature of things "—part of a great machine which grinds on and cannot be altered or stopped—and they die without ever knowing what full, joyous life really is. The process is slow, but it is sure. When I see in the papers sometimes wonderful little housekeeping lists, showing how Mr and Mrs X and their three young children live on 18s. a week, and no debts. I know only too well all the pathetic pinching and weary contriving and " going short " which lie behind the clever little budget.

Then, too, the contention of Colonel Kyffin-Taylor that better housing will of itself improve the slum-tenant is not always so satisfactorily borne out by results as in the cases he instances. Undoubtedly, it has a beneficial influence, as all right things have, but do we get the full value out of it unless the tenant is also dealt with? Many housing reformers working on these lines have encountered the very different experience well described by the writer of your third article and summed up in his statement that " dirty and disreputable tenants will create slums in whatever district they infest, and whatever may be the type of house they occupy." Or, as Mr Horsfall puts it: "It is not enough to provide decent houses for the people; you must also teach them how to live decently in them." And this brings me to the point which this little article is designed specially to emphasize.

Only through some system of personal dealing with house and tenant together, such as Miss Octavia Hill originated and successfully carried out for nearly 50 years in London, does the road for thorough reform of the slums lie. It is not easy to say exactly how her great principles can be best applied to new and changing conditions, but there can be no question that a humanizing of the relationship between landlord and tenant is sadly needed in these poor districts, and that it behoves us, who live in ease and comfort to-day, to strive—in the light of our fuller knowledge—to atone for the ignorance, carelessness, and greed which created this state of things in the past, by a wise, ungrudging outlay of time, thought, money, and laborious personal effort to undo what has been done amiss and set right what is so plainly wrong.

This does not mean, however, that the duties lie all on the one side. These poor people have obligations also, and it is no real kindness to do their duties and shoulder their responsibilities for them. The utter breakdown of the old " Lord and Lady Bountiful " systems of charity testify to this. What it does mean is that tenants should be taught and encouraged to fulfil their own obligations while the landlord fulfils his. " Mutual duties mutually done " is one of Miss Hill's great underlying principles. By all means, let us see to it that these poor folk have decent houses, and then show them how to live decently in them; by all means give them a real living wage, and then charge an adequate rent and expect them to pay it.

"But," the objector will say, "the ordinary agent has neither the time nor the knowledge to do this." True, but, nevertheless, means should be found whereby it may be done. Sanitary inspectors, health visitors, district nurses and others are all steps in the right direction; but for this particular work demanding as it does many of the qualities and much of the knowledge possessed by these trained officials, one other thing is needed, namely the power to dismiss a tenant who refuses to conform to reasonable requirements. And the combination of all these qualifications, Miss Hill contended, best embodied on the trained woman, property manager and rent collector.

Then too, Miss Hill distinctly favoured the preservation of old cottages where structurally worth it, as very many are. Writing to her fellow workers in 1896, she says:

"Old cottages are of immense value to the poor, and the longer they can be preserved the better. They are quite irreplaceable. No one now can under present conditions and cost of building, give to the poor anything like the amount of home peace, comfort and accommodation at so small a cost. The old cottages look shabby and those who do not know the life of the people object to owning them, and they are looked upon without favour; but well managed, and essentials secured, they are an inestimable boon to those who live there, and every one that can be preserved, with security for health, should be jealously guarded."

And again:

"In old houses, moreover, unsatisfactory tenants can be tested much more easily; there is no risk of their destroying expensive appliances; they can be encouraged by the gradual improvement in proportion to their own care of the places they are in. In new houses nothing is to be gained by tenants by their care, for nothing is to be added, while much may be lost by their carelessness. In old houses the reverse is the case: the fresh distemper, the mended grate, the new cupboard can be offered as a reward for care, while one or two more banisters broken or burnt are not a very serious loss to the landlord."

"She realized," writes one of her ladies, "as so few reformers even now seem to be able to realize, that the progress of mankind depends far more on the improvement of the individual than on the variation of institutions. How true this doctrine is as applied to the housing problem all persons who have practical experience in the housing of the poor are fully aware."

Areas there are, no doubt, such as some of those described by Colonel Kyffin-Taylor, where clearance is the only policy; but in all large towns there is much old property—neglected and run down, it is true, but structurally worth keeping—where all that is needed is to follow out the lines of " thorough repair " laid down in Part II of the Housing of the Working Classes Act, 1890, so well described by Mr J. S. Nettlefold, and then apply Miss Hill's system of using the houses as a means of educating the tenants in habits of good conduct, cleanliness, and common honesty as exemplified in the punctual payment of rent.

Repairs promptly executed, references carefully taken up, arrears not allowed to accumulate, dirt and disorder firmly dealt with, above all, a word of encouragement or praise when deserved— all these are among the potent factors employed by Miss Hill to raise the general standard; and the " atmosphere " in which her work is carried on constantly suggests to the tenant that this strict management is enforced not so much in the interest of the landlord as in that of the tenant himself.

The results are highly rewarding as all who have studied and worked on Miss Hill's lines can testify, and, given a little time, a sound financial position is secured. For though the outlay on management and repairs is larger than that of the ordinary agent so are the receipts larger. To give an instance of this: On what was, three years ago, one of our worst properties, consisting of small four-roomed houses at 4s. 3d. and 4s. 6d. weekly, and paying badly when taken over, the gross quarterly rental is £83 17s. Of this, £82 9s. 7d. was taken in rents on the quarter just closed. The standard of health, too, is wonderfully raised, so that one cannot avoid the conclusion that if more money could be spent in buying up, renovating and managing poorer class property on these lines, there would be less need for the vast and increasing hospital accommodation, which, for some strange reason, seems to be a cause for pride rather than for heart-searching in our great cities. As one of our leading medical authorities has said, the time will come when we shall feel ashamed that these great institutions were ever considered a necessity.

And, with the raising of the standard of health, comes greater happiness, greater intelligence and capacity for work, so that the whole community benefits a hundredfold for what has been expended on this problem, in time, money, thought and labour.

The slums are with us now, but they are not "come to stay." The many causes which have created and are conserving them all need to be tackled courageously, as well as the slum dwellings themselves, and great wisdom is called for; but once the public conscience is fully aroused the work will be carried forward. The wealthy "slum landlord" to whom (as has been well said) "his slums are gilt-edged securities"; the poor owner, too poor and often too ignorant to fulfil his duties towards his property rightly, however willing; the far too frequent drinking facilities in poor neighbourhoods (the poorer the district the more public-houses there seem to be); and last, but not least, the slum tenant himself, and our very slow and faulty eviction laws for dealing with incorrigibles—laws which the bad tenant thoroughly understands, and is not slow to take advantage of—all these hindrances and impediments must be dealt with before this great social blot of slumdom can be removed from the pages of our national civilization.

APPENDIX XIV

A PAPER READ AT A CONFERENCE WITH DELEGATES FROM LOCAL AUTHORITIES, HELD BY THE INSTITUTION OF MUNICIPAL AND COUNTY ENGINEERS, AT GREAT YARMOUTH, JULY 16 and 17, 1913.

LEGAL ASPECTS OF TOWN PLANNING (By John L. Jack, Town Clerk of the City and Royal Burgh of Dunfermline)

Since the passing of the Housing, Town Planning, etc., Act, 1909, much has been written and many have been the writers on what the author might call the "technical side" of town planning. On the other hand, the legal aspect of the Act with regard to town planning has been dealt with by a very few, and those who have dealt with it have confined themselves chiefly to the legal procedure involved in the preparation of a town planning scheme. This doubtless arises from the fact that, until a few town planning schemes are actually in operation, occasion for testing the effect of the provisions of the Act of 1909, in the Law Courts, cannot very well arise. As is well known, a legal treatise unsupported by the authority of the Courts is, after all, of very little more value than the considered opinion of any solicitor who has carefully studied the Act himself. What has just been said must necessarily apply to this paper. Not only so, but one other disadvantage must be added by the fact that the Act of 1909 can only be dealt with from the point of view of a Scots lawyer. Owing to the difference in the legal systems on either side of the border, it must necessarily follow that the actual effect of the Act on these systems will not be identical, nor is the author's knowledge of English law sufficient to enable him to point out wherein differences may occur. The author will do his best, however, to put before you some legal aspects of the Act as it appears to him, both from a careful study and from the practical administration thereof in connexion with the largest town planning scheme yet undertaken in Scotland, and one of the largest town planning schemes undertaken in the United Kingdom.

To begin with, therefore, let us first consider to what extent the town planning part of the Act of 1909 extended or amended the existing law. First, and most important of all, it conferred upon local authorities the right to town plan lands not only in their own area, but also in the area of other local authorities, provided always, of course, that these lands were likely to be used for building purposes.

THE RIGHT TO TOWN PLAN

The right to town plan is one of the most valuable powers that have yet been entrusted to local authorities, and, conversely, it is one of the greatest restrictions which have been imposed upon landowners in dealing with their properties. Consequently, in the administration of the Act, its provisions must be subject to the very strictest interpretation, and any deviation therefrom, however small, in dealing with a town planning scheme might prove disastrous thereto. The author might make his meaning clearer by suggesting this to you, that if, for any reason, after a town planning scheme has been completed, it were to be found, as the result of an appeal to the Courts, that the provisions of the Act had been neglected or exceeded in any way, the whole scheme might be declared to be ineffectual. The time involved in the rectification, by the promotion of another scheme, or otherwise, during which a large area of land might be sterilized for building purposes, might entail a considerable financial loss on the local authority and landowners interested. In addition, such a situation would undoubtedly give rise to the question whether landowners are entitled to compensation by such a delay. In the author's view, they would be entitled to compensation where the delay is occasioned by the fault or neglect of the local authority. One other point with regard to the right to town plan that should be borne in mind is that that right is not quite an absolute one, in respect that local author-ities promoting schemes are directed to endeavour, by means of conferences or otherwise, to secure the co-operation of owners, parties interested, and local authorities interested in the lands affected by any scheme. That obviously means that where a landowner has views with regard to the laying out of his own lands, a local authority is bound to give these every consideration. It is the author's opinion that, if in a town planning scheme a landowner has already initiated a scheme of development and partly carried out same, local authorities would be well advised to accept that development, if the objects of the scheme were not interfered with thereby, in preference to entering upon a lengthy controversy with the view of forcing a scheme of development differing from that proposed by the landowner in unimportant engineering details.

LANDS OUTWITH THE AREA OF LOCAL AUTHORITY PROMOTING SCHEME

With regard to the right of a local authority to town plan the lands which are outwith their own jurisdiction, it may interest you to know that in connexion with the Dunfermline town planning scheme the Corporation have included in that scheme an area of land immediately adjoining the city, which lies within the jurisdiction of the Dunfermline District Committee of the County Council of Fife. One peculiarity about the inclusion of this land is, that in the year 1911, the Corporation of Dunfermline promoted in Parliament a Bill for the extension of the city boundaries which, inter alia, included this area, now included in their town planning scheme. The Bill was passed without alteration by the House of Commons, but the House of Lords Committee struck out from the area proposed to be annexed to the city the area to which the author is now referring. It is an area presently unbuilt upon, and the buildings in the city are built close up to the boundary thereof. The Corporation felt that the development of this area must be made to harmonize with the lay-out of the existing city immediately adjoining, and accordingly, in promoting their town planning scheme, they asked the Local Government Board to include it therein. The proposal was opposed by the County Council of Fife, who appeared before the Local Government Board Commissioner and stated that, while they agreed that the area in question, if it were developed, should be planned in conformity with the city development, they were of opinion that it was rural in character. The Local Government Board, however, took the view of the Corporation that it was land likely to be used for building purposes, and allowed its inclusion in the city scheme. Perhaps their decision was influenced to some extent by the Corporation stating at the inquiry that they had no objection to constituting the county authority the responsible authority for the administration of the scheme so far as within their jurisdiction after it had been completed. Be that as it may, the author is convinced that the case he has put to you is just such a one as the Legislature had in contemplation when they gave local authorities power to include in a town planning scheme lands in the area of another authority.

Before a local authority can successfully include in a town planning scheme land in the area of another authority, they must be in a position to show that it is necessary in the interests of the amenity and convenience of a scheme being prepared by them, or of their existing town, that they should have control of the development therein. The author has heard the view expressed by members of some burghal authorities that it would be well for a burgh, in anticipation of a future extension of boundaries, to ask for authority to town plan county areas in the immediate neighbourhood of the burgh, and he is of opinion that any application for a town planning scheme of that nature would be foredoomed to failure. There can be no doubt that the Local Government Board would be inclined to resent rather than encourage anything which might look like putting them in the position of supporting one local authority against another. At the same time, the author does not believe that the fact that a county authority has initiated and carried through a town planning scheme for land in the immediate neighbourhood of a burgh will prevent any burghal authority from obtaining an extension of boundaries, although it may entail payment of a larger amount of compensation. The preparation of a town planning scheme does not in the slightest impair the powers of burghal authorities to apply for extension by any of the recognized methods.

LAND LIKELY TO BE USED FOR BUILDING PURPOSES

There is another point which was discussed at the Local Government Board inquiry into the Dunfermline scheme, viz. that land proposed to be included in a scheme is likely to be used for building purposes, or is so situated with respect to land likely to be used for building purposes, that it ought to be included in a scheme.

At the Dunfermline inquiry an agent for one of the landowners appeared and objected to the inclusion of certain lands within the city on the extreme eastern boundary thereof. It was urged on behalf of the landowner that this was land which would not in all likelihood be built upon for the next 20 or 30 years, or perhaps 50 years. The answer on behalf of the Local Authority was, that the words " likely to be used for building purposes " did not necessarily mean that it was likely to be so used within the next year or two, and further, that these very lands had, only a few months previously, been included by Parliament within the city, thus showing that Parliament had considered the land to be burghal in character; that if lands were burghal in character, it must necessarily follow that they were liable at any moment to be feued or leased for building purposes; and that while it might be quite true that no feuing or leasing for building purposes might take place for even 50 years, the Local Authority could not very well run the risk of leaving these lands out, because they would undoubtedly form a danger zone to any town planning scheme for the remainder of the city area, in respect that they would be absolutely free of all the restrictions of the town planning scheme designed for the preservation of the amenity and health of the district, and would become an attraction for the speculative builder. In this case also, the Local Government Board took the view of the Corporation, and included the lands objected to. That decision is eminently reasonable and does not confer any hardship on the landowner. If his lands are not likely to be built upon in the near future, the mere fact of their being planned does not necessarily entail upon him any disadvantage.

Suppose that lands are presently in use for agricultural or any other purposes, there is nothing, in the author's view, to prevent the Local Government Board making provision in a town planning scheme that additional buildings necessary for the proper working of the farm, and which will be occupied by persons employed in connexion therewith, shall be put up, even if these do not harmonize with the proposals of the scheme. Such a condition is eminently reasonable. In fact, it is only fair to landowners that until actual development takes place, they should be in a position to continue to erect such buildings as are necessary for the proper working of their estates. The author thinks that if, as the result of a town planning scheme, landowners were prevented from erecting such necessary buildings as those referred to, they would undoubtedly have a good claim for compensation in respect of any loss incurred by them thereby. If, however, the landowner desires to erect new buildings for purposes other than those to which his lands are put at the time a town planning scheme is initiated, that goes to show that his lands are likely to be used for building purposes, and he is not worse off than his neighbours who are nearer the heart of the city, in being compelled to have these buildings erected in conformity with the town planning scheme.

The conclusion to be drawn from the above is that local authorities are not compelled to take too narrow a view of what is land likely to be used for building purposes, but are entitled to take a broad view thereof, even to the extent of including lands which may not be built upon for generations, so long as the interests of the landowner and his tenants are properly safeguarded. It is not sufficient for a landowner to show that to the best of his knowledge it is unlikely that his land shall be built upon in the near future. If, owing to its proximity to a populous centre, it is doubtful when any particular area of land might be built upon, the author thinks local authorities should have no hesitation in including such an area in a town planning scheme.

COMPENSATION

The author would now like to deal with another point which arose in connexion with the Dunfermline scheme. Under Section 58 (2) of the Act of 1909, it is provided that no compensation shall be payable on account of any building erected on or contract made or other thing done with respect to land included in a town planning scheme after the time at which the application for authority to prepare the scheme is made, or after such other time as the Local Government Board may fix for the purpose.

Some time before the Dunfermline Corporation resolved to make application for permission to prepare a town planning scheme, a building syndicate acquired an area of ground in the vicinity of Rosyth naval base practically in the heart of the area proposed to be included in the town planning scheme. They lodged plans in the Dean of Guild Court for the erection of a number of three-story tenements on that area, having a density of about 60 houses per acre. This was considered by the Corporation to be objectionable but owing to the period of two months which requires to elapse between the date of notice of intention to make an application, and the actual making of the application, there was abundance of time to enable the syndicate to complete their contracts for the erection of the houses, and in fact to have the actual erection begun to some extent before the time at which the application for authority to prepare the scheme could be made. The author advised the Corporation that, according to his reading of the Act, although they had not actually made their application to the Local Government Board, there was nothing to prevent the Board from fixing a date anterior to the date of making application. They accordingly authorized him to make application to the Local Government Board to fix the date of their first advertisement of intention to apply for authority to prepare a scheme, as the date after which no compensation should be payable on account of any building erected on, or contract made, or other thing done with respect to the land proposed to be included in the Corporation's town planning scheme. The author was heard by the Board in support of the application. From what passed he gathered that the Board were in some dubiety as to whether they were justified in fixing a date anterior to an application being made to them, and he was asked what guarantee the Board had that there should be any town planning scheme put forward at all. His answer was that as a guarantee of the Corporation's good faith, they had already advertised their intention to apply, and that if they failed to apply within a reasonable time, the Board had ample power, under Section 61 of the Act of 1909, to compel the Corporation to proceed with their scheme. It was suggested that perhaps the proper course was to wait until such time as the application had been actually made to the Board, who might then issue an order making the date after which no compensation would be payable retrospective as far back as the date of the first advertisement. Against that view the author contended that such a course would be a distinct hardship, and was one which would be unlikely to be upheld in a Court of Law, in respect that any persons erecting buildings within the town planning area up till the date of the application to the Board, were quite within their legal rights even if the buildings being erected did not harmonize with the proposed scheme, and that the author held the view that the Board had not the power to make an order retrospective in such circumstances, the effect of which might ultimately be to confiscate property which was quite legally brought into existence. As a result of the application and discussion, the Board issued an order fixing the date of publication of the first notice of the Corporation's intention to apply for authority to prepare a scheme as the date after which a person should not be entitled to compensation under Section 58, on account of any building erected on or contract made or other things done with respect to land included in the Corporation's town planning scheme conditionally upon the Corporation making application to the Board within a period of two months and three days after the date of publication of the notice referred to. This all goes to show that once a local authority has resolved to proceed with a town planning scheme they are in a position to effectually protect the amenity of the area proposed to be included therein pending the decision of the Local Government Board on their application.

It is true that there is no direct prohibition against the erection of buildings in the prescribed area, and any one who cares to take the risk can build in that area, if they choose, but the author fancies there are few who are willing to take that risk if the local authority indicate that there is a likelihood of the building being disconform to the proposals of the town planning scheme then in preparation.

In Scotland, the erection of new buildings and the demolition of old buildings is regulated by a Court known as the Dean of Guild Court, and so long as the buildings proposed to be erected are in conformity with the provisions of the Police Acts, the Dean of Guild Court cannot do otherwise than grant warrant for the erection of such buildings.

In Dunfermline, houses have been erected within the town planning area since the Town Council made application to the Local Government Board, but in granting warrant for their erection, the Dean of Guild Court have invariably inserted therein a notice to the effect that the proposed buildings are within the town planning area, and at the hearing in Court applicants have invariably been informed of the risk which they incur if the buildings referred to should eventually turn out to be disconform to the town planning scheme.

BETTERMENT

There is, perhaps, no provision in the Act which will give rise to greater difficulties than that which entitles the local authority to claim betterment from landowners. In Dunfermline, the Corporation have pursued a policy of '' give and take '' in this matter. There can be little doubt that where a town planning scheme makes provision for the construction of some special feature, such as a park or a main thoroughfare of some considerable width, it must naturally follow that the ground abutting thereon will become specially valuable for building purposes. Consequently, the landowner can obtain a very much greater rent or feu-duty than he would have done if this special feature were not constructed on his estate. If the local authority were themselves to undertake the construction or provision of this special feature, as has been done in some of the large cities in England, obviously they would be entitled to lodge a claim for betterment against the landowner. Against that, however, the landowner would be entitled to set off his claim for land taken for the construction of the roadway, if not to the whole extent, at least to the extent to which the roadway exceeds the width of road which must be provided under existing by-laws or statutes. In Dunfermline, the corporation have been successful in arranging with landowners, through whose estates specially wide thoroughfares are to be constructed, that, in consideration of the landowners giving off the land necessary for the construction of the roadways and contributing towards the cost thereof the expense of the construction of an ordinary statutory road, they should not lodge a claim for betterment, and that the landowner should not lodge any claim for compensation. That is a policy which will doubtless be pursued successfully in connexion with most town planning schemes. But it is conceivable that cases may arise where local authorities will be compelled to make claims for betterment, and the point which the author wishes to make with regard thereto is one which was recently put to him, viz., that as a result of the Finance Act of 1910, the Government valuators are in course of making valuations of all estates; that with respect to land in the immediate vicinity of large centres these are treated as lands which are immediately available for building purposes, and the valuations are consequently fixed at a very full price, the result of which will be that there is very little room, if any, for any claim for betterment. The author personally knows of lands at present included in a town planning scheme which are let for agricultural purposes at a rate of from £2 to £3 per acre. These very same lands have quite recently been valued by the Government valuators at £20 and upwards per acre. It will, therefore, be seen that if a local authority were to construct any special feature through lands of this description the betterment which they could recover would be bound to be of small amount and the onus of proving same would be entirely on them. On the other hand, you have the landowner in a strong position, he being armed with no less authority than that of the Government as to the present value of his land. The author mentions this point in order to put before you the necessity of making inquiry as to the valuations which have recently been put upon lands, so that if any of you are anticipating substantial claims for betterment in connexion with town planning schemes, you may be led to inquire more carefully into same before incurring expenditure which you would hesitate to incur were it not for the expectation of being recouped to some extent by means of a claim for betterment.

WIDTH OF ROADS

There is one other small matter which the author must mention before closing this paper, and that is as to the powers of local authorities with regard to roads. It is undoubted, that a local authority may plan roads of a much greater width than those which are authorized by statute, but the cost of doing so, in so far as the road exceeds the present statutory requirements, must be borne by the local authority. Under the General Police Acts in Scotland, local authorities cannot demand a road of greater width than 60 ft. between building lines, 40 ft. of which is devoted to carriage-way and footpaths. This makes it necessary that buildings must at least be 10 ft. back from the inner line of the footways. If, however, a local authority desires that the buildings shall be further apart than the width prescribed by the General Acts, the author is of opinion that they can secure this under the Act of 1909 without incurring any claim for compensation. In this way, under the Act of 1909, Section 59, no compensation will be payable on account of any provisions in a town planning scheme which prescribe the space about buildings or limit the number of buildings to be erected. The author's view of that provision is that local authorities can, in Scotland at least, insist on a much wider space than 10 ft. being left between the inner line of the footway of an ordinary statutory road and the building line, and by this means they can secure wider streets without compensation so long as they do not demand a carriage-way and footpaths of greater width than 40 ft. In what the author has written above, he has endeavoured to confine himself to a few points which are likely to crop up in most town planning schemes, and he hopes that the views expressed by him will give rise to some discussion, as he thinks every one will agree that the valuable part of any conference is the discussion which usually follows the various papers submitted.

APPENDIX XV

NOTES ON STATE-AIDED HOUSING IN IRELAND AND RURAL HOUSING IN ENGLAND.

The report on experimental State-aided housing in Ireland recently issued by a few convinced municipal house-builders does not give sufficient attention to the economic aspect of the question. They ascertained that " a marked improvement in all respects had been effected in the habits of the people." All reformers know that better environment improves the habits of the people, but that fact does not prove that charity rents are good in the long run for either the tenants or the taxpayers. They found that " in no case did rents bear any calculated relation to the cost of providing the cottage. . . . It did not appear that the authorities ever anticipate being able to exact an economic rent for the cottages." That is to say, taxes will be levied on the whole country in order that Irish employers shall be able to obtain the labour they require for less than its economic value. It was also ascertained that in some cases the tenants pay more for rent than they used to do and " IN SOME CASES LESS " that is to say, this housing policy is in some cases actually tending to lower wages which must be detrimental to the nation as well as harmful to the individuals concerned.

Irish working men who have not got State-aided housing are asking why they should pay 5s. a week rent when their neighbours are only paying 1s. 6d. for houses that cost as much as theirs. They are also saying that those in authority are giving doles to their friends.

The health of the tenants has been improved by the erection of these cottages, which have been used for re-housing people dispossessed from unfit houses, and it has been made possible for local authorities to " take a strong line in closing unfit dwellings." These results are quite satisfactory but would have been of far greater permanent value if they had been achieved on a sound economic basis instead of by eleemosynary means.

The average cost per cottage including roads and land varies from " £176 in Munster to £211 in Connaught." This is much too high, and only what was to be expected from State-aided or eleemosynary work. There are cottages at Harborne, Birmingham, which only cost £143 each for building, management charges, land, roads and sewers. The land for this scheme cost £300 per acre and development where these cheap cottages are built cost £120 per acre.

The Irish report tells us that for most of the cottages inspected land cost "from £25 to £60 per acre, though in some cases up to £100 per acre." Detailed costs of development in Ireland were not given, but it is not reasonable to suppose that in rural or semi-rural areas in Ireland, estate development has cost as much as in the city of Birmingham. Private enterprise at Harborne had no financial advantage over municipal house-building in Ireland with regard to the cost of land and development and yet the very popular cheap cottages at Harborne only cost for land, development and building, £143 per cottage as against costs varying from £176 to £211 per cottage* in the Irish municipal house-building schemes supported by State grants. In spite of this fact, the report advocates the application of this eleemosynary policy to rural housing in other parts of Great Britain. "Doles" should always be avoided if it is in any way possible to do so, and in the matter of housing the British agricultural labourer it should be possible to do so. At present he is denied a fair opportunity of earning an honest living for himself and his family, and in place thereof is offered doles which must tend to sap his spirit of independence and perpetuate the low wages in rural districts which every student of economics knows are thoroughly bad for the family and the nation.

The Rural Housing Association consider that a State grant would be "merely tampering with the symptoms. State-aided housing will not raise wages, worse—it would lower them." They want "the cash wage raised to a level that would enable the agricultural labourer to pay an economic rent for his cottage. The policy of supplementing the low wages of one industry by levying a tax upon other industries does not commend itself to the Association as being a sound one. A State subsidy would tend to stop building by unsubsidized agencies. At present building is being done by private individuals who give personal care and attention to detail, which are essential to successful cottage building. Voluntary effort would probably be entirely checked by a State subsidy. State aid in this connexion would be a direct subsidy to wages. If the strictest economy were practised rent might be kept reasonably low; and if gardens were given with the cottages they would enable the labourer to meet an increased rent."

A minimum wage enabling labourers to pay a rent of 3s. 9d. per week is much to be desired, but it is very doubtful if this can be brought about by a stroke of the pen or an Act of Parliament.

* The Irish cottages are built in small quantities on scattered sites, but this only partially accounts for the extra cost.

The sounder and more permanent method is to increase opportunities of employment (allot one-eighth of an acre to each new cottage built) and by improving the living conditions of the working classes increase their stamina. When there is more opportunity or demand for labour and when the labour is of a better quality employers will pay more for it. There is an example of highly paid agricultural labourers imported into a low wage district. They were found to be well worth the extra money and the effect was very soon to raise the wages of all labourers in the district. The native labourers were by the increase of wages enabled to feed themselves better, with the result that they were worth more to their employers. More profit was earned on the dearer, but more efficient, labour than had previously been earned on the cheap, underfed labour.

State-aided municipal house building seems an easy way of solving the problem, and herein lies its danger. It is so showy and it sounds so nice, that well meaning but unthoughtful enthusiasts are misled into thinking that something useful has been done, while all the time its tendency is to lower wages instead of raising them. Its effect is the same as that of the old Poor Law which had to be abolished, because it was found to be nothing but a subsidy in aid of wages. It is in fact adding a new wrong to the old one and thereby perpetuating it. Reforms to be sound must right wrongs, not perpetuate them.

APPENDIX XVI

UNIONIST LAND POLICY

The Unionist land policy as enunciated by Lord Lansdowne at Matlock Bath, on June 21, 1913, is to encourage occupying ownerships in rural districts by the State lending to private individuals the whole of the purchase money instead of only four-fifths as at present. This is, in principle, to apply to England what has worked so unjustly in Ireland. The taxpayers of Great Britain have been saddled with the cost of expropriation of Irish landlords at fancy prices, and whenever this public extravagance comes before the House of Commons men of all parties complain bitterly of the enormous expenditure that has been incurred. Economists and business men are not surprised at what has happened. The Wyndham Act was bound to produce this result. A sudden large demand for any commodity the supply of which cannot be increased, is bound to put up prices, and in the purchase of rural land another force is set at work in the same direction. That is our ridiculous land system under which, when a man by the sweat of his brow gets more out of any land than it previously produced, or when a proposal is made that is likely to produce such a result, the landlord exacts a heavy toll by increasing the rent or raising his selling price. Lord Lansdowne at Matlock Bath, on June 21, 1913, complained of the high rents charged by county councils for small holdings. When I was on the management committee of the Rural Labourers' League, we always found that the price for ordinary farm land was immediately increased the moment the owner become aware that it was wanted for allotments or small holdings, and exactly the same thing is happening to-day. Lord Lansdowne may well grumble at the excessive rent charged to tenants, and it is to be hoped that he will use his great influence to ensure for tenants fairer treatment in the future than they have received in the past.

He announced at Matlock Bath that the Unionist party " favour a policy of small holdings "; it is, therefore, to be hoped that the county councils which are largely composed of Unionists, will in future attend more diligently to this part of their work than they have done in the past. He also said:

" 1. More ought to be got out of the land than at present.

" 2. History shows . . . that the decay of agriculture has been the presage of national decay.

" 3. Agriculture is the only antidote to that disease . . . the tendency of the people to desert the land and congregate in the great cities."

The only sure way of getting more out of the land, encouraging agriculture and stopping migration to the towns, is to take steps to ensure that those who work on the land shall be fully and fairly rewarded for their pains. Judicious public land purchase and land leasing might help in this direction, but experience shows that unless it is accompanied by a just rating system there is grave danger that it will once more be the landlords who reap the chief profits of other men's industry.

It is said that our land system has worked very well in the past, and so it has for the landlords, but the condition of the rural labourer (the man who does the work) is so abject that all political parties are now constrained to consider how best to give him a fair chance of getting what he earns. If and when this eminently reasonable object is achieved there will be no further need to advocate State-aided land purchase or State grants to rural housing schemes. Dangerous palliatives of this nature will be no longer necessary, because a genuine remedy will have been discovered and applied.

The policy of occupying ownerships is very attractive to well meaning but short-sighted landowners. They see the profit to themselves that comes from wholesale public land purchase, and most of them honestly believe that what is good for them must be good for the nation. The poor men whom we are told will be helped by the Unionist land policy do not view this proposal in quite the same light. A recent report to Parliament by Mr Cheney (Small Holdings Commissioner) states that in 1912 out of 4,070 small holdings inaugurated in that year only 70 were for purchase and the remaining 4,000 tenants preferred to lease. This confirms my experience when I was on the committee of the Rural Labourers' League; a poor man has no money to spare for land purchase even by instalments. In the words of Lord Lansdowne, " He wants the whole of his capital to improve his holding."

The advantage of occupying ownership is that there is no liability to disturbance SO LONG AS THE OWNER IS ABLE TO PAY HIS WAY, whereas under a lease from a private individual a farmer, small holder, or allotment worker may have his land sold over his head. " He knows the land and can probably treat it better than anyone else, but the new owner may want the land for himself and the farmer has to go." (Lord Lansdowne at Matlock Bath.)

This liability to disturbance could be overcome by a policy of public land purchase and leasing; with this additional advantage, that the working man who needs all the small capital he possesses for the improvement of his holding, would not be called upon at inconvenient times for instalments of the purchase money for his land. Fixity of tenure would, therefore, be safer under a policy of public land purchase and leasing than under a policy of occupying ownership, but it must not be forgotten that up till now public bodies have always paid considerably more for land bought by them than would have been paid by private individuals, and until " price not purpose " is made the governing factor in the approval of proposals for public land purchase, it will be a few private individuals and not the general public who will reap the chief benefit from the public acquisition of land.

Occupying ownership has in practice proved most disastrous in other countries for farmers and small holders. It has thrown them into the hands of moneylenders, who exact an even heavier toll on industry in the form of interest than landowners do in the form of rent. It is, therefore, necessary to find an alternative policy and the only one that seems at all likely to meet the immediate needs of the case is public land purchase and leasing. This policy provided it is properly safeguarded could be made quite useful, but there must be at least three safeguards:

1. Public bodies should not be in too great a hurry to purchase land.

2. Price not purpose should be the governing factor in public land purchase.

3. Land values should be rated in the same proportion as other property and assessments fixed at the price demanded by the owners when the land is needed for small holdings, allotments or building. The present system of encouraging landowners and their agents to hold up land for purely artificial prices is most unjust to the workers, and, therefore, thoroughly bad for the nation. It would be only common justice if landowners had to pay rates and taxes on the market value of their property in the same proportion as other people.

INDEX